Substitute
Parents

Studies of the Biosocial Society

General Editor: **Catherine Panter-Brick,** Professor of Anthropology, University of Durham, UK

The Biosocial Society is an international academic society engaged in fostering understanding of human biological and social diversity. It draws its membership from a wide range of academic disciplines, particularly those engaged in "boundary disciplines" at the intersection between the natural and social sciences, such as biocultural anthropology, medical sociology, demography, social medicine, the history of science and bioethics. The aim of this series is to promote interdisciplinary research on how biology and society interact to shape human experience and to serve as advanced texts for undergraduate and postgraduate students.

Substitute Parents

Biological and Social Perspectives on Alloparenting in Human Societies

● ● ●

Edited by Gillian Bentley & Ruth Mace

Berghahn Books

New York • Oxford

First published in 2009 by

Berghahn Books

www.berghahnbooks.com

©2009, 2012 Gillian Bentley and Ruth Mace
First paperback edition published in 2012

Library of Congress Cataloging-in-Publication Data

Substitute parents : biological and social perspectives on alloparenting in human
societies / edited by Gillian Bentley and Ruth Mace.
    p. cm. — (Studies of the biosocial society ; v. 3)
    Includes bibliographical references and index.
    ISBN 978-1-84545-106-6 (hbk.) -- ISBN 978-0-85745-641-0 (pbk.)
    1. Foster parents.   2. Child care.   I. Bentley, Gillian R., 1957–   II. Mace,
Ruth.

HQ759.7.S83 2009
306.874—dc22

                                                           2009015808

British Library Cataloguing in Publication Data
A catalogue record for this book is available from the British Library

Printed in the United States on acid-free paper.

ISBN: 978-0-85745-641-0 (paperback)   ISBN: 978-0-85745-642-7 (ebook)

Contents

● ● ●

PART II: The Effect of Alloparenting on Children

List of Tables

● ● ●

List of Figures

● ● ●

PROLOGUE

● ● ●

Allomothers across Species, across Cultures, and through Time

Sarah B. Hrdy

A New Paradigm Emerges

Mother mammals are guaranteed to be on hand at birth, and after months of gestating, are hormonally primed to respond to infantile signals. Maternal commitment to young is the best single predictor of their survival. No wonder mothers have played a key role in evolution. For two hundred million years, till the very recent discovery of pasteurized milk and baby bottles, breast milk was, so far as baby mammals were concerned, the only brand in town and mothers the only source of safety (Bowlby 1969). It would be hard to overstate the importance of the emotional bonds between baby mammals and their mothers (Carter et al. 2005). That said, Western cultural traditions have gone beyond these facts.

Moralists and psychologists alike focus on the presumed 'naturalness' of parental – and especially maternal – care, to the exclusion of considering care by others. Matricentric thinking has long been deeply entrenched in scientific as well as popular world views. It was in order to highlight the naturalness of maternal care that in 1735 taxonomist Carolus Linnaeus identified all members of the class *Mammalia* with milk-secreting glands, a trait possessed only by females. Linnaeus' reasons for selecting *mammae* had more to do with his personal convictions about women's roles than with the usefulness of teats as taxonomic tools, since other traits would have worked better (Schiebinger 1995). But Linnaeus lived at a time when many European women resorted to the use of wet nurses, and as an ardent promoter of maternal breastfeeding, Linnaeus was making a point about women's 'natural' role. In this volume, Helen Penn and Alma Gottlieb each discuss how such moralistic presumptions have spilled over into supposedly dispassionate and objective assumptions underlying psychological theories of child development.

Large literatures in developmental psychology have been built upon the presumption that throughout hominid evolution, mothers were *exclusively* responsible for nurturing offspring, and that, like chimps, baboons and macaques, early human mothers remained in nearly continuous skin-to-skin contact with their babies (Bowlby 1969; see update and overview in Konner 2005). In the process, we grossly underestimated the sustained effort it requires to rear healthy human children. Anthropologists calculate that in a hunter-gatherer setting it may take around thirteen million calories, along with incalculable hours and opportunity costs, to nurture a child from birth to nutritional independence around age eighteen or older (Kaplan 1994). Since this is far more than a gathering woman by herself, particularly one with other children, can provide, it was assumed that shortfalls in the material needs of woman the nurturer and her children were made up by man the hunter (Lovejoy 1981). In spite of recent criticisms of the feasibility of this Pleistocene scenario (Hawkes 2001), it remains widely assumed that anything less than exclusive maternal care is out of step with Nature, a modern deviation from what Bowlby deemed humankind's 'Environment of Evolutionary Adaptedness'. Yet matricentric models are far from the whole story. As Nancy Solomon will explain in this volume, some mammals, including humans, are cooperative breeders, where group members other than genetic parents help to rear young. Ancestral human populations almost certainly fell among those species with shared care.

To explore the role of care by others, Gillian Bentley and Ruth Mace convened a conference on 'Alloparenting in Human Societies' that was held in London, 7–8 May 2003. Its aim was to bring together for the first time researchers from biology, sociology, anthropology, economics and psychology to examine what alloparents meant in the evolutionary past, and more importantly, to begin to explore what they mean across societies, including modern industrial ones at the present time.

Theory and Terminology

Prodded by sociobiological studies of other species with cooperative rearing of young, by the end of the twentieth century evolutionary anthropologists were expanding hypothetical models of family life during the Pleistocene to include contributions by group members other than parents (Hawkes et al. 1998; Hrdy 1999, 2005; Hewlett and Lamb 2005; Voland et al. 2005, especially chapter by Mace and Sear in that volume). At a theoretical level, early interest in caregivers other than parents derived from asking how genetically 'selfish' individuals could evolve so as to care for offspring other than their own? In 1964 British geneticist William D. Hamilton proposed that individuals should help others when the cost of caring is less than the benefit to the infant calibrated by the caretaker's degree of genetic relatedness. Today, Hamilton's formulation for explaining the evolution of alloparental care is referred to either as 'kin selection' or as 'Hamilton's rule'. The term Hamilton's rule is often preferable because even though altruistic care originally evolved in contexts involving close kin, not all such care is directed towards relatives. The term highlights the cost and benefit components of Hamilton's initial equation. The individual helped is *typically* a close relative, but not necessarily. If for example, inexperienced young females gain valuable practice from caring for another's infant (as is true in some species of monkeys), or if help is proffered in exchange for some other benefit (such as group membership), benefits may outweigh the cost no matter how closely the infant is related. Furthermore, some helpers only volunteer when they can afford to do so at little risk or cost to themselves. Once alloparents have evolved to be sensitive to signals of need from immatures, care of non-kin may persist even without fitness benefits, which is why adoption of unrelated infants tends to be so successful among primates generally, including humans. Nevertheless, as David Howe (this volume) points out, the probability of success tends to be higher with very young infants, possibly because this more nearly simulates genetic relatedness in the social environments in which our species evolved.

The term 'alloparents' derives from sociobiology but has seeped into other disciplines. It was coined in 1975 by the evolutionary biologist Edward O. Wilson who decided that different forms of caretaking referred to variously as 'aunting behaviour' (in primatology), 'helping at the nest' (in ornithology), and so forth, needed a more uniform and dignified terminology. Wilson paired 'allo-', a learned borrowing from the Greek meaning 'other than', with parent to designate any group member other than the mother or the genetic father who helps care for young. Under many circumstances the term 'allomother' is more precise simply because in the absence of a DNA lab it is difficult to know for certain which male is the father. Although it takes getting used to, 'allomothers' can refer to male as well as female caretakers.

Alloparents as a Social Good

Long before biologists started talking about 'alloparents' or discussing the possibility that humans evolved as 'cooperative breeders', historians of the family, social workers, and sociologists were aware of the advantages to human children from living in extended families. Helen Penn's descriptions of South African family life (this volume) and Alma Gottlieb's descriptions of childcare in a West African village emphasize the importance of communities in traditional child-rearing. Humans everywhere are predisposed to tolerate and nurture youngsters in their vicinity, and human immatures seek out such attention, and thrive on receiving it. Noting the benefits, social scientists took kindness towards immatures for granted. It simply did not occur to anyone to ask why on encountering a child an omnivore would seek to comfort her, carry her, help her learn to walk or feed her, rather than eating her up. Yet it is worth keeping in mind that not all creatures would behave so. Our benevolence towards children is not just because we are 'civilized' acculturated creatures, but also because primates generally, and especially humans, descend from a long line of intensely social creatures, innately predisposed to help vulnerable immatures whether they be foundlings or kin born into their group.

Family support takes many forms and affects child well-being in myriad ways ranging from cognitive and emotional functioning, to survival (Sear and co-authors this volume). As demonstrated by the pioneering work of Mark Flinn (this volume) alloparental support also affects a child's response to stress, and through stress, immune functioning. For children potentially at risk (as is sometimes the case for children living with stepfathers), the role of alloparents can be especially significant. Alloparental support also impacts on maternal commitment and the quality of mothering, especially in the pre- and immediately post-partum period. For example, mothers with allomaternal support are less likely to abandon newborn infants. In this way allomaternal support can have an almost immediate effect on infant survival (Hrdy 1999). Allomaternal interventions, be it from a grandmother, an older sibling, an uncle, or a schoolteacher, can be critical for children considered 'at risk' from poverty, paternal defection or maternal neglect (e.g., see Werner 1984). Intervention from real or 'fictive' kin, be they godparents, adoptive parents, teachers, or fellow 'soccer parents', can have lasting effects. Long-term controlled studies summarized in Olds et al. (2002) reveal that even intermittent visits to new mothers by trained nurses who provide advice, and perhaps most importantly, social support, affect maternal care sufficiently so as to correlate with improved outcomes (measured in terms of the child's cognitive development, school success and life choices) many years later.

Such findings raise important but little asked questions about the shift from kin-based to institutional care in schools and daycare centres (see chapter by Berry Mayall in this volume), as well as vexing questions about how such programmes are to be paid for. As Gillian Paul pointed out at the conference, the 'economics' of alloparenting makes for a type of 'good' quite different from 'inclusive fitness benefits'. Although human alloparental psychologies originally evolved in a context where individuals strove to maximize inclusive fitness, today people may be 'maximizing' elaborately different utilities, and use of communal funds to finance childcare may be recouped in various ways, such as freeing mothers to seek paid employment or helping children grow up to become more productive citizens.

Human behaviour not only evolves, it develops in specific ecological, economic, cultural and historical contexts. In her chapter describing the Toba people of Northern Argentina, Claudia Valeggia provides the first detailed study of the transformation of childcare from more traditional kin-based care with a great deal of assistance provided by maternal grandmothers (as was typical of nomadic foraging peoples, Hewlett and Lamb 2005), to more matricentric caretaking in settled, wage-earning communities. Babies in settled communities come at a much faster pace, and grandmothers with still-nursing infants of their own may be unavailable to caretake. Thus the diminished proximity of committed alloparents is a common concomitant of modernization. Causes range from increased maternal fertility and shorter birth intervals, to the demands of wage economies, greater mobility, and increasingly compartmentalized families, rendering children especially vulnerable to other disruptions, including divorce (see chapter by Margaret Robinson, Lesley Scanlan and Ian Butler in this volume). Lorraine Young's chapter focuses on a rapidly spreading new source of family attrition that is decimating parents and alloparents alike, HIV/AIDS. Young's chapter focuses on the current acute crisis in South Africa, but a more general crisis prompted Jay Belsky to point out in his conference presentation that 'More and more children at younger and younger ages are spending more and more time in childcare in societies that lack adequate infrastructures for child-rearing'. Ours is a world where proportionally more children survive but with fewer individuals positioned to care for them, and less time devoted to social interactions.

Alloparents and Child Survival

Children are growing up in increasingly compartmentalized worlds, yet as novelist (and also anthropologist) Kurt Vonnegut (2006) recently put it, 'we can do without an extended family about as easily as we can do without vitamins or essential minerals'. Why children need such families is becoming increasingly clear as fieldworkers have begun to examine the impact of *alloparental* as well as parental assistance in societies where infant mortality rates are high enough for the full range of their impact to be detected. Data from such societies are critical for reconstructing the developmental context for early human populations where child survival was similarly tenuous. Compared to child-rearing, theoretical attentions of evolutionists have been primarily directed towards mating competition and mate choice, even though so far as Darwinian natural selection is concerned, the outcomes of reproductive struggles count for little unless offspring thus conceived survive, an imbalance only now being corrected (Hrdy 1999).

In their chapter, Rebecca Sear and Ruth Mace analyse data on maternal and child well-being that were collected in the middle of the last century from a West African population in the Gambia. Their analysis reveals how significant alloparental care is in promoting child survival (and with it, maternal reproductive success) under conditions with high rates of child mortality. This unusually extensive and detailed data set derived from a population in which 50 per cent of children died before the age of five, permitting the first quantitative estimates of the statistically significant impact grandmothers, fathers, siblings and others have on child survival in a traditional, horticultural African society. Not surprisingly, mothers in this Gambian population were critical for child survival during the first two years of life, but thereafter, other kin mattered more. For children under five but past the age of weaning, those with older sisters or maternal grandmothers on hand grew larger, grew faster, and, remarkably, were almost twice as likely to survive. By contrast, the presence of fathers had no significant impact on growth or survival, unless a father died and the mother remarried, in which case, stepfathers could prove detrimental. The Sear and Mace study is also noteworthy for illuminating the different impact of matrilineal versus patrilineal kin on Gambian mothers and their children. Whereas the presence of patrilineal grandmothers and other patrilineal kin are correlated with increased maternal fertility, it is the availability of matrilineal kin that is correlated with enhanced growth and survival of children (see also recent overviews in Voland et al. 2005).

Several chapters, including the one by Sear and Mace and the one by Karen Kramer on caretaking patterns among the Yucatec Maya, stress the importance of the local ecological and customary context, and caution against extrapolating from kin effects in one society to societies with very different local ecologies. As Karen Kramer points out, the Mayan mothers in her study received the most help from their older children, their mothers and their siblings, but fathers also made important contributions to the well-being of their children. The more universal truth to emerge here has less to do with just who cared than with how long it takes human juveniles to become independent and the massive amount of help mothers require to rear successive offspring. Where that help comes from varies with local circumstances, and such circumstances may change through time, sometimes quite rapidly, as is happening in the Maya case, among the Toba people studied by Claudia Valeggia, as well as in AIDS-stricken South Africa.

Mothers, Allomothers, and the Needs of Developing Children

The chapters in this book illustrate the extraordinary flexibility of the human species regarding who provides care. However, contributors are also informed by an understanding of the fundamental and relatively nonnegotiable need of vulnerable and slow-maturing children for responsive care. At a theoretical level, I would hope that this volume will mark a shift in paradigms of human development as psychologists move beyond matricentric assumptions to recognize that human infants evolved to elicit help from multiple caretakers. As Alma Gottlieb makes clear for the West African Beng community that she studied, children can feel secure and prosper in a world populated by many different alloparents. But the key phrase here has to do with feeling 'secure'. For Beng children are never far away from familiar kin, and need only exhibit a bit of initiative to be back in touch with their mothers or another family member. The theme of control surfaces again in the innovative research being done by Joachim Bensel and his team on children's peek-a-boo games: it is the child who controls when someone appears and disappears. In terms of the stress experienced by the child, this is quite different from some run-of-the-mill daycare centre where a parent drops off a protesting child early in the morning, leaving him there with a chronically fluctuating staff till a late afternoon pick-up. There is a critical difference between the daycare settings that Jay Belsky (this volume) rightly criticizes, and a stable world of familiar and responsive alloparents among whom a child feels secure – the kind of daycare so many working mothers wish that they could find, or, could afford.

In line with questions about how daycare can be improved and better suited to infant needs, Joachim Bensel and colleagues introduce two key concepts related to an infant or toddler's experience of stress versus security. These involve familiarity of the available caretakers and the child's sense of how much control he or she has. If humans evolved in social environments where infants were cared for by responsive allomothers as well as mothers either right from birth, or probably more commonly from the beginning of weaning onward, there is no reason to presume that mother-only rearing is essential for healthy development. However there is every reason to suppose that responsive care and felt security is.

References

Bowlby, J., 1969. *Attachment*. New York: Basic Books.

Carter, C.S., Ahnert, M., Grossmann, K.E., et al., eds., 2005. *Attachment and Bonding: A New Synthesis*. Cambridge, MA: M.I.T. Press.

Hamilton, W.D., 1964. The genetical evolution of social behaviour, Part 1. *Journal of Theoretical Biology* 7, 1–16.

Hawkes, K., 2001. Hunting and nuclear families: some lessons from the Hadza about men's work. *Current Anthropology* 42(5), 691–709.

Hawkes, K., O'Connell, J.F., Blurton Jones, et al., 1998. Grandmothering, menopause and the evolution of human life histories. *Proceedings of the National Academy of Sciences* 95, 1336–39.

Hewlett, B., and Lamb, M., eds., 2005. *Hunter-Gatherer Childhoods*. New Brunswick: Aldine/Transactions.

Hrdy, S.B., 1999. *Mother Nature: A History of Mothers, Infants and Natural Selection*. New York: Pantheon.

———— 2005. Evolutionary context of human development: the cooperative breeding model. In. S. Carter et al., eds., *Attachment and Bonding: A New Synthesis*. Cambridge, MA: M.I.T. Press, 9–32.

Kaplan, H., 1994. Evolutionary and wealth flows theories of fertility: empirical tests and new models. *Population and Development Review* 20, 753–91.

Konner, M., 2005. Hunter-gatherer infancy and childhood: the !Kung and others. In B. Hewlett and M. Lamb, eds., *Hunter-Gatherer Childhoods*. New Brunswick: Aldine/Transactions, 19–64.

Lovejoy, O., 1981. The origin of man. *Science* 211, 341–50

Olds, D., Robinson, J., and O'Brien, R., 2002. Home visiting by paraprofessionals and nurses: a randomized controlled trial. *Pediatrics* 110, 486–96.

Schiebinger, L., 1995. *Nature Body: Gender in the Making of Modern Science*. Boston: Beacon Press.

Vonnegut, K., 2006. Interview. National Public Radio, U.S., 24 January 2006.

Voland, E., Hasiotis, A., and Schiefenhovel, W., eds., 2005. *Grandmotherhood: The Evolutionary Significance of the Second Half of Female Life.* New Brunswick: Rutgers University Press.

Werner, E., 1984. *Child Care: Kith, Kin and Hired Hands.* Baltimore: University Park Press.

Wilson, E.O., 1975. *Sociobiology: The New Synthesis.* Cambridge: Harvard University Press.

• 1 •

The Pros and Cons of Substitute Parenting

An Overview

Gillian R. Bentley and Ruth Mace

Alloparenting as a Trade-off

Providing adequate care to dependent children in the face of competing time constraints is a problem faced by all human societies from foragers to modern industrialized nations. Alloparenting – or alternative caregiving to dependent offspring – is also a common phenomenon among many mammalian and avian species, as detailed by Nancy Solomon and Loren Hayes in Chapter 2 (Sarah Hrdy also provides an historical summary of the origin of this term in the Prologue). Although scholarly books have been published on alloparenting among birds (e.g., Woolfenden and Fitzpatrick 1984; Stacey and Koenig 1990) and mammals (Lee 1989; Solomon and French 1997) and while works exist on the topic of children lacking parental care, such as street children (e.g., Panter-Brick and Smith 1990), there are so far no published volumes exclusively addressing alloparenting in human societies. This edited volume is designed to fill this gap.

Childcare is a topic that strikes a chord among many (Hrdy 1999, this volume). Most working parents in industrialized countries face the challenge of finding reliable and caring childminders for their offspring, and spend hours agonizing about the wisdom of their choice and the repercussions for their children. And there is little doubt that this is not a new phenomenon: historically mothers must always have faced trade-offs between work, food gathering or production, and childcare.

Recent changes in the structure of some families as a result of advances in reproductive technologies also raise novel issues in the realm of alloparenting. For example, the phenomena of surrogate mothers and mixed biological–social relationships among offspring create new difficulties in defining what it means to be a parent or alloparent, as well as constructing new dimensions for children. The general appeal of the topic of alloparenting (although many may not know it by this name) makes it timely to provide an edited volume that brings together in one place a number of studies that shed further light on this issue.

The goal of this edited volume is to bring together a variety of contributors who can cover the topic of alloparenting from widely different perspectives. It contains chapters from anthropologists, psychologists, animal behaviourists, evolutionary ecologists, economists and sociologists who study the provision of offspring care within a wide range of human societies as well as in other mammalian species. Reflecting the myriad disciplines represented in this volume, the style of writing of each chapter is also reflective of traditions in those disciplines ranging from the qualitative – informal narratives that are typified by Helen Penn in Chapter 9, Alma Gottlieb in Chapter 6 and Margaret Robinson, Lesley Scanlan and Ian Butler in Chapter 16 – to the more quantitative, formal presentation of econometric models from Gillian Paull in Chapter 7 and multi-level modelling of data from the Gambia in Chapter 3 by Rebecca Sear and Ruth Mace. Despite this variation, however, each chapter incorporates valuable lessons on the topic of alloparental care.

From a comparative perspective across species, it is clear that human life histories are unique in a number of ways. Raising human offspring is unusually costly: human mothers have relatively short birth intervals compared to other apes of similar body mass, childhood is long, mothers have to care for many dependent children at the same time (whereas other apes raise only one at a time), infant mortality is quite high in natural fertility–mortality populations, and human females have a long post-reproductive lifespan. All these feature conspire to raise the cost of child-rearing. Mothers frequently defray these costs by using paternal help (something other ape species generally do not do) although the contribution of fathers is not always enough; in polygynous societies, for example, spousal loyalties may be divided between several wives. There is growing evidence that grandmothers, elder siblings, other kin, or indeed society as a whole, also help to lower the huge costs of childcare, both in our evolutionary past and in contemporary societies (Hill and Hurtado 1996; Hawkes, O'Connell et al. 1997; Sear, Mace et al. 2000; Lee and Kramer 2002; Pavard, Gagnon et al. 2005; Voland, Chasiotis et al. 2005).

Structure and Content

The volume is divided into two sections. The first section views alloparental strategies from the perspective of both the parent and alloparent: why do we use alloparents, how might alloparental care have evolved, why do we adopt children, what are the economic and other pressures that cause us to rely on alloparents, how does society step in when parents die or fail to take care of their children, and how does this vary across cultures? In parts of the world with access to reproductive technologies, other questions raise themselves, such as why do some women opt to act as surrogate mothers? The second section of the book deals with alloparenting from the child's perspective: what is the impact of the loss of a parent, how do children respond physiologically, behaviourally and emotionally to such stress? Which forms of childcare lead to beneficial (or least harmful) outcomes?

Both sections take a fully cross-disciplinary approach, using case studies from a range of cultures and other species; many are grounded in evolutionary theory, including Sarah Hrdy's Prologue to this volume. For example, Nancy Solomon and Loren Hayes (Chapter 2) provide a thorough survey of alloparental strategies in other species as well as the variety of evolutionary theories advanced to explain the emergence of this phenomenon. Karen Kramer (Chapter 4) adopts an evolutionary perspective to explain the contribution of children and siblings to family production and reproduction in rural Mexico. Rebecca Sear and Ruth Mace (Chapter 3) examine how predictions from evolutionary theory accord with findings of child health in the Gambia depending on who has provided alloparental care. David Howe (Chapter 10) discusses adoption and how this may, or may not, conflict with evolutionary theory.

The variety of approaches to childcare covered in this book should make the reader question whether there is any typical pattern to allocaring in humans. Indeed, this controversial issue is raised by both Helen Penn and Alma Gottlieb (in Chapters 9 and 6 respectively). They challenge the models for appropriate child-rearing that are considered typical and normative in our own Western (or Northern) societies, where, as Penn notes, 'a good parent is one who provides a safe, stable and predictable two-parent family environment, who focuses on the child's individuality and verbal self-expression and ensures material prosperity and surrounds the child with possessions.'

Moreover, Penn argues that this normative model is being 'globalized'. She describes her son-in-law's extended and fluid household in South Africa, where patterns of childcare using a multiplicity of familial carers differ substantially from the typical nuclear family in the U.S. and U.K. Gottlieb's chapter also points to the 'collective' as opposed to 'individual' nature of the child-rearing enterprise among the Beng in the Côte d'Ivoire of West Africa where a large number of allocarers help mothers. (This social picture may be reassuring for comparison against institutional nurseries in Western societies which use a similar range of multiple carers). In addition, the Beng actively encourage babies and young children to accept allocare and to feel comfortable with strangers, all part of efforts to ensure that mothers who have heavy agricultural and household workloads will be able to pursue this work comfortably while their children are with other temporary (and often changing) caregivers. One can find many parallels here with working mothers in industrialized countries.

The collective nature of allocaring in many African societies is underscored by Lorraine van Blerk and Nicola Ansell (Chapter 12) in the context of high rates of HIV/AIDS infection in sub-Saharan Africa. The authors refer to the insurance policy that wide-ranging attachments and allocare ensure for children in environments (even without HIV prevalence) where morbidity and mortality are high due to several endemic infectious and parasitic diseases. In Malawi and Lesotho, the two countries providing the focus of van Blerk and Ansell's chapter, infection rates for HIV/AIDS are 14.2 per cent and 28.9 per cent respectively, and orphan rates are correspondingly high.

There are several other cross-cultural examples of how child-rearing and alloparental care vary in different societies. For example, Claudia Valeggia (Chapter 5) documents how childcare practices are changing with acculturation and urbanization among the Toba of Argentina, who used to be foragers. With increasing urbanization, young children are spending more time with their mothers and, where allocare is required, time with their fathers rather than with multiple care givers. This situation is more akin to the norm in Western societies, confirming perhaps the globalization of childcare referred to by Penn.

The Effects of Allocaring

These cross-cultural studies underscore the fact that multiple allocarers are a common feature in many societies and that this pattern of childcare appears to work. In Western contexts, we are less sure about the benefits of this pattern, complicated also by the institutionalized settings in which it tends to occur. For example, in Chapter 15, Jay Belsky (using the NICHD Study of Early Child Care) points out the long-term detrimental effects, at least in the U.S., of both the amount of time spent in institutionalized alloparenting situations by children prior to school age (five years) and the quality of that childcare. Those children who spent more time in childcare displayed more aggressive and anti-social behaviour when they attended primary school. However, better quality childcare was also associated with enhanced cognitive and linguistic development. Results from the NICHD study are replicated in a similar large-scale study of children aged three and upwards conducted in England.

Belsky does not speculate about the potential causes of an increase in aggressive and anti-social behaviour among the five-year olds studied. Is it possible that increased stress during periods of separation, or increased insecurity among children in alloparental situations, lead to negative behaviours in later life? Or is this more negative behaviour related to lack of effective supervision and/or discipline in nonparental settings? Or, perhaps, aggressive behaviours in young children may be adaptive within group childcare settings where competition for attention and facilities are likely to be greater than in the family home? It would be interesting to know more about the potential causes of the apparently more adverse behaviours in children who have experienced non-parental childcare in the particular Euro-American cultural settings examined here.

Joachim Bensel's (Chapter 14) and Mark Flinn and David Leone's (Chapter 13) studies among widely disparate societies (Bensel in Germany, Europe and Flinn and Leone in the Caribbean island of Dominica) also raise the question of whether early separation experiences among human children have negative repercussions for optimal development. Bensel introduces a number of studies undertaken on mammals where early separation from parents and the resulting stress leads to permanent neurological changes in the offspring that affects behaviour and cognition in later life. Similarly, Flinn and Leone refer to permanent alterations in the hypothalamic-pituitary-adrenal axis in humans that can be caused by high levels of the stress hormone cortisol in early life, and that leads to altered immune and other functions as adults.

Bensel's conclusions about allocare early in life lean decidedly towards the negative; but perhaps they apply exclusively to institutional settings where multiple care givers act as alloparents to infants and young children, and where substitute parental figures may not be consistent. Bensel, for example, points to a number of studies that show increased susceptibility to infections among young children from eight months to two years of age when placed in novel childcare situations, reflecting an increase in stress levels and a compromise of their immune function. In Germany, this has led to the introduction of more gradual and gentle transitions to childcare situations where parents are actively encouraged to spend more time with their offspring at childcare centres during the initial period of alternative childcare (Bensel, Chapter 14).

Similarly, Flinn and Leone demonstrate the physiological and psychological impact of parental loss and substitute parenting among children in Dominica by measuring salivary cortisol levels and associated growth and health data. In households with step-parents, children with access to multiple allocarers in fact do better than those without this help, results that contrast rather startlingly with those of Bensel. The difference between the German and Dominican experience, however, may lie with the specific allocarers in question. Where grandparents (and particularly maternal grandmothers) provide allocare, Dominican children fare best compared to those without such allocare. In the absence of institutionalized care in Dominica, children in any case are only likely to receive alternative care from extended family members. Doubtless, European children would also probably fare better with such related allocarers compared to non-related carers within an institutionalized setting. And, indeed, as pointed out by Gillian Paull (Chapter 7) and others, relatives often provide high levels of unmeasured and informal allocare to parents in Euro-American settings.

Van Blerk and Ansell's chapter on the impact of HIV/AIDS on creating orphans and new ways of alloparenting in southern Africa also covers issues of the inevitable social and emotional stress that must accompany major family disruptions. Their work, however, focuses less on the psychological and hormonal consequences of these stresses, but rather on the social dislocations and breakdown of inter-generational family contracts that have traditionally characterized societies in Malawi and Lesotho. Using narratives provided by orphaned children, they highlight the flexible, and often difficult, patterns of allocare arrangements created and utilized in societies meeting an unprecedented level of parental mortality and family disintegration. These can include cases of children moving on to the streets involving integration into social structures markedly different from typical extended family households. In addition, young orphaned children are frequently expected to provide more labour than would otherwise be the case in order to support both themselves and their adopting relatives.

The important role of grandparents is underscored in Chapter 16 by Margaret Robinson, Lesley Scanlan and Ian Butler in the case of divorced or divorcing parents where the levels of emotional and practical support to the children in such families is highlighted in moving narratives by the children themselves. In addition, maternal grandmothers often step in to provide alloparental care to orphans in Malawi and Lesotho (and probably other areas affected by HIV/AIDS mortality) as pointed out by Lorraine van Blerk and Nicola Ansell (Chapter 12), even where traditional cultural rules previously favoured patrilineality and patrilocality/virilocality.

Sear and Mace (Chapter 3) also talk about how family composition (and whether familiar allocare is maternal or paternal) can have positive, neutral, or negative effects on the health of young children. Children in the Gambian villages studied in this case, like in Dominica, do better in terms of health and growth where *maternal* grandmothers and elder sisters help out, but do not benefit from help from paternal relatives (other studies, such as Voland and Beise 2002, have shown a negative impact of paternal relatives' allocare). Sear and Mace interpret these findings within the context of evolutionary theory where kin selection favours more effective alloparenting from the maternal side due to known biological relatedness of offspring. By this evolutionary reckoning, children who are cared for by unrelated individuals, or strangers, should fare worse than children who are not. And indeed this is often true, as shown by the classic studies undertaken by Daly and Wilson (e.g., Daly and Wilson 1988)

Exceptions exist though in the context of adopted children, who, as pointed out by David Howe in Chapter 10, frequently have better developmental experiences with their adopted parents than they would do with their biological parents (depending of course on the reason for adoption). Howe speculates on the causes of why infertile parents would opt to act as alloparents since this appears to be maladaptive from an evolutionary perspective. He points to the selected behavioural repertoires common to human infants that elicit strong nurturing responses from adults and children alike. He also mentions that children adopted earlier (particularly as infants) are often more closely bonded to their adopted parents than children adopted at later ages. But there are other potential reasons for adopting children that may be adaptive, including the economic and emotional factors (depending on the particular society in question) that accompany parenthood.

Alloparenting and New Reproductive Technologies

If adoption brings with it potential problems for child-rearing, recent technologies that permit surrogacy open fascinating and disturbing new arenas for research into alloparenting. Emma Lycett, in Chapter 11, covers many of the issues that can accompany the journey on this path towards parenthood including feelings of parental inadequacy, excessive stress and tension in a relationship between parental spouses, as well as the difficulties that arise later in explaining to children their complicated parental heritage. Lycett's findings, however, in a study of forty-two surrogate families are highly positive. Surrogate parents reported lower levels of stress and lower depression among mothers compared to fifty-one parents where the egg was donated but gestated by the mother, and eighty parents experiencing natural conception. The surrogate families also had higher scores for attachment-related behaviours towards their children and expressed greater satisfaction with the parental experience. Moreover, the surrogate children did not differ in social, emotional or cognitive development from naturally conceived children. Of course, surrogate families are highly selected to want parenthood since they have expended a great deal more time, money and effort to achieve this state compared to individuals who conceive naturally. This may explain the very positive results from this study, but also bodes well for the children resulting from these alloparental arrangements. The main negative finding from this study was that difficulties can arise in the relationship with the surrogate mother, the risks of which are lessened, however, where she is related to the commissioning family.

Siblings as Alloparents

Many of the cross-cultural studies in this book raise questions about what other issues need to be factored into an equation that measures developmental outcomes based on childcare options that might not be considered in Western contexts. For example, in the Gambia, child growth was negatively affected by the number of older brothers present in the household. While Western families tend to be smaller than highly fertile Gambian or Mexican ones, the presence, gender and ages of other siblings within households might be important confounding factors to individual child development. Interestingly, Robinson, Scanlan and Butler (Chapter 16) found that siblings were generally not a preferred source of emotional support for children experiencing parental divorce; instead, friends were a very critical source of support.

Karen Kramer in Chapter 4 talks about the *positive* effects of siblings among Xculoc Mayan subsistence agriculturalists in actively providing allocare for hardworking families. Using time allocation scan sampling techniques, Kramer calculated that juveniles aged between seven and eighteen years could provide as much as between 82 per cent and 93 per cent of their own economic costs as well as contributing between 35 and 52 per cent of total family consumption. Of course, the particular circumstances of these Mayan families differ substantially from those of the average

Western family, particularly since the Mayan children in question do not attend school regularly. However, older siblings can and often do provide valuable alloparental care to younger children.

Schools and the State as Alloparents

What happens to older children attending school in Euro-American settings? In Chapter 8, Berry Mayall presents a historical and sociological perspective on the purported role of British schools in taking further the socialization process of children begun by their parents or, in historical parlance, by *mothers* specifically. In recent years, she argues, the school is not so much the place for providing happy environments for children and furthering their individual talents (although some obviously do) but more the scene for a continued social moulding of individuals who can contribute economically, socially and morally to the desired cultural milieu of the particular society and nation state in which they are embedded.

In this sense, there is a conflict then, particularly for teachers of younger children, between the desire to fulfil a more nurturing role and the state requirement to fulfil the obligations of an increasingly more structured and dictated curriculum (at least in the U.K.) And data show that as children get older, relationships with teachers are even more distant, with teachers adopting more authoritarian roles. Mayall also documents a decline in health and nutritional provisions for school children in the U.K. from the 1980s onwards as the government became increasingly concerned with issues of the curriculum and standards of academic achievement. Perhaps most importantly, Mayall presents the views of children on their teachers. The former explicitly reject the idea of teachers as alloparents; instead they are providers of knowledge or facts. That teachers are not viewed as satisfactory emotional alloparents is underscored by Robinson, Scanlan and Butler in Chapter 16 where children in divorced families almost unanimously preferred not to discuss their problems with their teachers at school.

Chapter 7 by Gillian Paull continues the theme of childcare being embedded in the economic concerns of the state, although in this case the concern is with how women become incorporated into the work place and negotiate alloparental care as a result. Of far less concern to economists, as Paull notes, is the actual quality of childcare provision. Her chapter then also has clear links with those of Bensel and Belsky, where early alloparental care for infants and young children has expanded in line with the increasing participation of postpartum women in the labour force. However, Paul shows the attempts by economists to model more formally the various factors that play into the decision to use alloparental care, such as the hours that a woman works, her rate of pay versus the cost of childcare, and the quality of the potential childcare. Paull also provides statistics for the prevalence of alloparental care (at least in the U.K.), namely 70 per cent for families where the mother is working full-time, and 62 per cent for families with mothers working part-time. This compares to 47 per cent among families where the mothers are not in paid employment. What is striking here is the high percentage of alloparental use among mothers who are presumably able to look after their own children, although probably the hours of alloparenting in this context are low. Certainly, statistics support the notion that the time spent with allocarers is significantly longer for children with mothers who work longer hours themselves. Single mothers tend to fall in this latter category.

Conclusion

If there is to be one take-home lesson to be learned from the chapters in this volume, it is perhaps that there is no one 'right' way in which to provide either parental or alloparental care. Instead we are presented with a variety of approaches and methods that are highly dependent on specific cultural, economic and ecological conditions. Several authors (e.g., Penn, Valeggia), in fact, provide useful summaries of the history and range of alternative theories on 'appropriate' child-rearing with particular cultural examples that fit these theories. That there are better and worse ways of alloparenting, however, within these contexts, is evidently true. There can also sometimes be role reversal in parental care as is illustrated by Robinson, Scanlan and Butler (Chapter 16), where the authors discuss the frequent emotional support and care provided to divorced parents by their children. And certainly, older children, as outlined by Kramer, may often be net producers and not require much allocare themselves.

It seems, however, that alloparenting is a necessary but flexible phenomenon for humans that may have co-evolved with other life-history traits such as our larger brain size, short birth-intervals, long life spans and extended juvenile period. The heavy investment of parenting typical for humans whose offspring need nurturing for several years has led to the evolution of multiple patterns of allocare and parenting strategies which shape themselves around the particular ecological circumstances of societies. What works well in one context, or for one family may not for another, but the most important outcome is the long-term well-being and health of the next generation.

References

Daly, M., and Wilson, M., 1988. *Homicide*. New York: Aldine de Gruyter.

Hawkes, K., O'Connell, J.F., et al., 1997. Hadza women's time allocation, offspring provisioning and the evolution of long postmenopausal life spans. *Current Anthropology* 38(4), 551–78.

Hill, K., and Hurtado, A.M., 1996. *Ache Life History: The Ecology and Demography of a Foraging People*. New York: Aldine de Gruyter.

Hrdy, S.B., 1999. *Mother Nature: A History of Mothers, Infants and Natural Selection*. New York: Pantheon.

Lee, P.C., 1989. Family structure, communal care and female reproductive effort. In V. Standen and R.A. Foley, *Comparative Socioecology: The Behavioural Ecology of Humans and other Mammals*. Oxford: Blackwell, 323–40.

Lee, R.D., and Kramer, K.L., 2002. Children's economic roles in the Maya family life cycle: Cain, Caldwell, and Chayanov revisited. *Population and Development Review* 28(3), 475–499.

Panter-Brick, C.P.B., and Smith, M.S., 1990. *Abandoned Children*. Cambridge: Cambridge University Press.

Pavard, S., Gagnon, A., et al., 2005. Mother's death and child survival: the case of early Quebec. *J. Biosoc. Sci.* 37(2), 209–27.

Sear, R., Mace, R., et al., 2000. Maternal grandmothers improve the nutritional status and survival of children in rural Gambia. *Proceedings of the Royal Society B* 267, 461–67.

Solomon, N.G., and French, J.A., eds., 1997. *Cooperative Breeding in Mammals*. Cambridge: Cambridge University Press.

Stacey, P.B., and Koenig, W.D., 1990. *Cooperative Breeding in Birds*. Cambridge: Cambridge University Press.

Voland, E., and Beise, J., 2002. Opposite effects of maternal and paternal grandmothers on infant survival in historical Krummhorn. *Behavioral Ecology and Sociobiology* 52(6), 435–43.

Voland, E., Chasiotis, A., et al., eds., 2005. *Grandmotherhood: The Evolutionary Significance of the Second Half of Life*. Rutgers: Rutgers University Press.

Woolfenden, G.E., and Fitzpatrick, J.W., 1984. *The Florida Scrub Jay: Demography of a Cooperative-Breeding Bird*. Princeton: Princeton University Press.

PART I

● ● ●

Alloparental Strategies

• 2 •

The Biological Basis
of Alloparental Behaviour
in Mammals

Nancy G. Solomon and Loren D. Hayes

An Evolutionary Perspective on Human Behaviour

The study of human behaviour is typically conducted by social scientists, who emphasize cultural influences on behaviour. An alternative approach, the evolutionary perspective, assumes that social interactions are influenced by heritable predispositions to act in ways that were adaptive to humans in the past (Emlen 1997). The evolutionary perspective attempts to predict which specific behaviours were favoured in different social contexts, and whether the same predictions can be used to explain human behaviour seen today.

The evolutionary perspective is based on three assumptions, as discussed by Emlen (1997). First, we assume that many social behaviours in animals have been shaped, at least in part, by natural selection. Individuals that are best able to make optimal decisions will be favoured by natural selection, i.e., produce the most surviving offspring that share these heritable predispositions with their parents.

The second, more controversial, assumption is that human behaviour also has been shaped by natural selection. As recently as two decades ago, some social scientists thought that only cultural factors determined patterns of human behaviour. Genetic influences were either considered to be unimportant or only of minor importance. Now with data accumulating from molecular studies, including the human genome project, it is more widely realized that most behaviour patterns result from an interaction of a genetic predisposition and the physical, social and biological environment (Winterhalder and Smith 1992).

The third assumption is that organisms that live in similar types of social circumstances are most likely to have evolved similar behaviours, i.e., convergent evolution (Emlen 1997). Animals faced with problems similar to those of our ancestors are most likely to display the same or similar behavioural patterns as humans.

It has been suggested that early humans lived in social groups consisting of multiple generations of family members (Emlen 1997). Mature offspring continued to live at home and reproduce in their natal family groups, which contained their parents and siblings. Therefore, animals living in similar types of social groups would be the most likely to provide insight into genetic predispositions of ancestral humans. These types of comparative studies can be quite useful in generating predictions about human behaviour.

It is common to find comparisons between humans and our closest phylogenetic relatives, the great apes, or between humans and other primates. In general, few primates live in extended family groups, where breeders form pair bonds and males provide care to young. For these reasons, primates are not the best animal models for studying all types of human behaviours, such as alloparental behaviour discussed here.

Better comparisons can be found in birds or other species of mammals which form extended family groups. In these groups, breeders often form pair bonds, males generally contribute significantly to care of young, and multiple generations (parents, offspring and even grandparents) continue to live together (Brown 1987; Stacey and Koenig 1990; Hayes 2000). In addition to the similarities in social organization, many of these species have more poorly developed cognitive abilities than primates. Therefore, cultural influences would have a minimal influence on social behaviour.

Introduction to Alloparental Care

Alloparental behaviour or 'helping at the nest' is parent-like behaviour directed toward offspring that are not the genetic offspring of the individual (Brown 1987). Alloparental behaviour appears to be paradoxical because there is likely to be a cost to care of offspring that are not one's own and this cost may decrease an individual's ability to produce or rear its own offspring. For this reason, biologists have been interested in species where members of the social group assist in rearing young that are not their own offspring. Even Charles Darwin (1859) was puzzled by the assistance performed by sterile workers in eusocial insects (ants, bees, and wasps) and was concerned that this apparently altruistic behaviour, where there is a cost to the donor but a benefit to the recipient, might undermine his theory of natural selection.

Nearly sixty years later, Alexander Skutch (1935) first described feeding of young birds by more than two adults. Since some of these individuals could not be the parents, he referred to them as helpers. Prior to the advent of W.D. Hamilton's seminal paper on inclusive fitness (1964), biologists were not very concerned with helping behaviours because these types of behaviour were assumed to be for the good of the group (as in Wynne-Edwards' 1962 ideas on group selection). Therefore, ornithologists generally ignored his paper for decades since this behaviour was not a topic of interest at that time.

W.D. Hamilton (1964) provided the major impetus for the study of alloparental behaviour by suggesting that individuals may engage in this apparently altruistic behaviour because they can gain fitness benefits indirectly by helping rear kin. These benefits may compensate for the loss of *direct fitness* (production of one's own offspring) due to lack of reproduction. These benefits are referred to as *indirect* because they result from the increased survival and/or reproduction of non-descendent kin, i.e., individuals with genes shared by common descent. Thus, an individual can increase its *inclusive fitness* (the sum of its direct and indirect fitness) by helping to rear non-descendent kin. Investigations of alloparental behaviour were the original test case for the ability of inclusive fitness theory to explain the evolution of apparently altruistic behaviours.

Originally eusocial insects were the major focus of study for inclusive fitness theory since the theory was developed by an entomologist (Hamilton) and popularized by entomologists (e.g., Wilson 1975; Oster and Wilson 1978). Although these studies provided a number of insights, the application of these investigations to the study of alloparental behaviour in vertebrates was limited by the biological differences between insects and vertebrates, particularly with respect to differences in the mode of inheritance and degree of reproductive suppression or lack of reproduction by helpers. In social insects, workers are haploid and sterile (Wilson 1971). In contrast, vertebrate helpers are diploid and do not typically breed while they remain at their natal nest but are capable of becoming reproductive rapidly when removed from their families (see French 1997; Brant et al. 1998; Bennett and Faulkes 2000 for details on reproductive suppression of alloparents).

In vertebrates, alloparental care occurs only in a small percentage of birds (Brown 1987; Stacey and Koenig 1990; Cockburn 1998), fishes (Taborsky and Limberger 1981; Balshine et al. 2001; Brouwer et al. 2005) and mammals (Hrdy 1976; Gittleman 1985; Jennions and Macdonald 1994; Solomon and French 1997; Hayes 2000; Roulin 2002). The conceptual framework concerning alloparental behaviour has primarily resulted from avian studies (Skutch 1961; Brown 1987; Stacey and Koenig 1990; Koenig and Dickinson 2004). Although studies on alloparental behaviour in mammals began about the same time (see early papers on 'aunting' by Rowell et al. 1964; Hrdy 1976 in primates), there has been much less attention given to mammalian alloparental behaviour previously, possibly due to the difficulty of studying many of these mammalian species (but see Jennions and Macdonald 1994).

Although the theory on alloparental behaviour developed from avian studies applies to mammalian cooperative breeders, there are some fundamental differences between these two classes of vertebrates (Mumme 1997). Birds are oviparous (lay eggs) while most mammals are viviparous (give birth to live young). Additionally, parental care in birds involves incubating and feeding young, behaviours that can be performed by all family members. In contrast, since female mammals lactate, only the breeding female(s) can provide nutrition to unweaned offspring (only rarely do non-breeding females lactate: e.g., Creel et al. 1991). Therefore, we might expect to see differences in alloparental behaviour due to these basic biological differences between taxa.

Alloparental care is seen in two types of social groupings, and early models proposed separate routes for the evolution of these (Brown 1987; Figure 2.1). One route is analogous to the subsocial route proposed for eusocial insects (Wilson 1971, 1975) in which natal philopatry results in groups consisting of overlapping generations. In some species or populations within a particular species, we may see groups with only one breeding female (singular breeders). In these groups with high reproductive skew, one female dominates breeding and the others do not reproduce. These singular breeding groups are usually family groups where young remain with their parents past the typical age of dispersal, and help care for offspring born to the breeding female. Therefore, individuals within groups are often close relatives (e.g., parents and offspring). We would place naked mole-rats (Jarvis 1981; Lacey and Sherman 1991) and most wild canids (Macdonald et al. 2004) at this end of the continuum. In contrast, formation of groups from related or unrelated females that share a nest is similar to the parasocial route proposed for eusocial insects (Wilson 1971, 1975). In mammals these are referred to as plural breeders. In plural breeding groups, multiple females reproduce and communally care for offspring born into the group (Lewis and

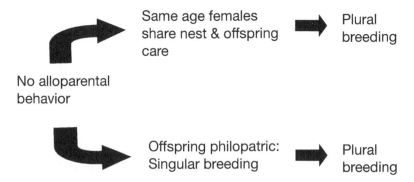

Figure 2.1. Routes to alloparental care of young.
There have been two possible routes proposed that lead to alloparental care of young. Upper arrow: The most widely recognized way occurs when young remain philopatric, which results in an extended family group. Lower arrow: The other way is when females that are usually closely related like sisters, share a nest (or are found in the same group). These females do not behave aggressively toward each other and each participates in alloparental care of the other female's offspring.

Pusey 1997). These breeding females are most often mother and daughters or two or more sisters, but it is possible that they may be unrelated. In these groups, there is no or low reproductive skew and breeding is more equitable. We would place house mice, lions, bat-eared foxes, and banded mongooses at this end of the continuum (Wilkinson and Baker 1988; Lewis and Pusey 1997; Maas and Macdonald 2004; Gilchrist 2006). We are not trying to suggest that all species that engage in alloparental care can be dichotomized into one of these two groups, but that they could be placed somewhere along a continuum defined by the percentage of female group members that are breeding (reproductive suppression or skew; Sherman et al. 1995; Creel and Waser 1997). Interestingly, a few species of carnivores, e.g., dwarf mongooses (Creel et al. 1991), meerkats (Scantlebury et al. 2002), and Ethiopian wolves (Sillero-Zubiri et al. 2004) can be placed off centre but toward the plural side of the continuum because non-breeding females begin to lactate spontaneously after offspring are present in the social group. These females also engage in alloparental care.

As mentioned previously, alloparental behaviour varies among species as well as among populations within species and groups within a population. We may see populations in which singular and plural breeding groups may occur at the same time or the percentage of each type of group may vary over time due to ecological factors and the degree of relatedness among group members. Unrelated females or males may also be present in either of these two types of groups. The presence of unrelated individuals in groups versus those composed solely of closely related family members can drastically change the dynamics in these groups (Emlen 1995) and may affect alloparental behaviour of group members. For example, alloparents that are not related to the breeders or offspring can not benefit through increases in indirect fitness. If they accrue benefits from alloparental care, these benefits may be either current or future direct benefits, possibly associated with living in a group. Unrelated alloparents may also benefit through a process called reciprocal altruism (Trivers 1971). According to this hypothesis, alloparents provide care to young and they receive a benefit from unrelated group members in return. This benefit may occur currently if unrelated female breeders reciprocate by nursing the offspring of the alloparent. Alternatively, the benefit may be returned at a later time if these offspring help the alloparent with subsequent care of her own offspring. Reciprocal altruism may provide a sufficient explanation for alloparental behaviour between unrelated individuals in social groups where individuals repeatedly interact with each other.

In this chapter, we will initially discuss the factors proposed to provide the context for the evolution of alloparental behaviour. We will then focus on the proximate (mechanistic) and ultimate (evolutionary) basis for alloparental behaviour. In order to fully understand alloparental behaviour, we need to know the answers to four major questions (Tinbergen 1963): two mechanistic questions dealing with how this behaviour occurs (i.e., the causal basis for alloparental behaviour and the physiological mechanisms involved in alloparental behaviour), and two dealing with ultimate questions (i.e., why this behaviour occurs from a functional point of view as well as from a historical or evolutionary perspective). In this chapter, we will focus on both mechanistic questions and the first functional question.

Philopatry: Setting the Stage for Helping in Most Singular Breeders

Although our focus is on alloparental behaviour, it is important to preface that discussion by a brief mention of factors that predispose individuals to help rear offspring belonging to other individuals. As Hamilton (1964) suggested, individuals may accrue inclusive fitness benefits if they help rear kin. One way that this occurs is in groups where offspring delay dispersal from their natal nest (i.e., remain philopatric) beyond the age when individuals normally become independent breeders. The presence of older offspring at the nest where parents continue to breed sets the stage for alloparental behaviour to occur.

There are three factors that may predispose individuals to remain philopatric: ecological factors, benefits of philopatry, and life-history factors. In areas where there are more individuals looking for breeding territories than there are high quality territories, offspring may delay dispersal and remain at their natal nest (Koenig and Pitelka 1981; Emlen 1982; Koenig et al. 1992; Solomon 2003; Schradin and Pillay 2005; Lucia et al. 2008). The occurrence of numerous competitors for each high quality territory can occur when breeders have high survival rates (see subsequent discussion of life-history traits). Augmentation of group size and the subsequent benefits that result from large group size, e.g., protection from predators, is another way that philopatric individuals may increase their direct fitness (Brown 1987; Kokko et al. 2001). In many instances, philopatric offspring do not breed (French 1994; Brant et al. 1998; Bennett and Faulkes 2000). The lack of reproduction by young individuals that are old enough to be capable of breeding has been referred to as reproductive suppression. These non-breeding alloparents can only accrue current indirect fitness benefits by helping kin. If philopatric individuals breed and contribute to care for all young in the extended family group, they may gain both direct benefits from their own personal reproduction as well as indirect fitness benefits from assisting close kin.

Benefits and costs of philopatry likely differ among species. Lacey (2004) has posited that direct fitness costs may be greater in species where opportunities for dispersal are extremely limited, and females remain philopatric for life (see also Keller and Reeve 1994). Data on direct fitness of black-tailed prairie dogs and colonial tuco-tucos (a subterranean South American rodent) support this hypothesis (Hoogland 1995; Lacey 2004).

Life-History Factors Associated with Alloparental Care

Recent analyses have suggested that life-history variables may be extremely important in the evolution of philopatry (Arnold and Owens 1999; Hatchwell and Komdeur 2000). Those models predict that philopatry should be seen in species with slow rates of development or where residents have high survival rates. Other analyses predict that plural breeding should occur when individuals give birth to litters instead of a single offspring and when group sizes are small (Lewis and Pusey 1997).

Rate of Development

Dispersal may be delayed in species with slow rates of development because juveniles may need extended parental care or more time to reach adult size. Thus we may be able to determine which species are more likely to display philopatry by comparing rates of development in these species. Blumstein and Armitage (1999) proposed that large species with relatively short growing seasons need more time to mature than small-bodied species with longer growing seasons. Therefore, natal dispersal in marmots does not occur until after the first hibernation, since the growing season is short and they would not have sufficient time for maturation (Blumstein and Armitage 1999). In contrast, woodchucks live in areas with longer growing seasons compared to other marmot species. Thus woodchucks should be able to achieve sufficient body mass to survive the first hibernation alone and, therefore, disperse during their first year. Burda (1990) also argued that species of mole-rats with the slowest rates of development show philopatry while other species that develop faster do not. Comparison of the age of eye opening in social mole-rats with solitary species of subterranean rodents supports Burda's contention that social bathyergids tend to develop more slowly than other subterranean rodents (cf. Bennett et al. 1991). Social mole-rats have much slower growth rates as compared to solitary mole-rats (Bennett et al. 1991) although this difference is not as clear when timing of weaning is compared between social and solitary mole-rats (Burda 1990; Bennett and Faulkes 2000).

In contrast to the interspecific comparisons in marmots and mole-rats, the rate-of-development hypothesis is not supported by comparisons among populations of the same species. Intraspecific comparisons of dispersal in woodchucks suggest that there is variability within and among populations in the timing of dispersal, with some woodchucks delaying dispersal despite the length of the growing season and therefore, differences in body mass (Maher 2006).

A possible correlate of the rate-of-development hypothesis is that dispersal may be delayed until offspring have a reasonable chance of success in winning contests with adults over limiting resources, such as high-quality territories (P.M. Waser, personal communication). If this is the case, we would assume that territorial vacancies occur too infrequently for a particular individual to be likely to fill a vacancy. Where competition for territories is important, individuals may disperse only after they are full grown. In species with slower growth rates, this could lead to delayed dispersal.

Survival

Survival is another life-history variable proposed to influence philopatry. Kokko and Lundberg (2001) modelled the relative importance of survival and other variables affecting philopatry. In their model, they assumed that the habitat was saturated (there was a high proportion of occupied territories) but varied the degree of saturation, quality of the habitat, cost of philopatry to the resident, and survival rates. They found that the degree of habitat saturation and number of competitors for each territory were more important than habitat saturation per se. Kokko and Lundberg (2001) concluded that if other factors were equal, philopatry should increase when there is more competition for territories. Of these factors, survival rate determined when competition increased. Therefore, instead of determining whether all territories are occupied, it may be better to focus on the number of competitors per territory and turnover rate of breeding positions (cf. Waser 1988). As Kokko and Lundberg (2001) suggested, the latter two are influenced by survival of breeders and offspring.

Litter Size, Group Size, and Allonursing

Allonursing, seen in plural breeders, is more often found in mammals with larger litters. In species that give birth to litters, females may be more tolerant of non-descendent offspring because the costs of nursing an additional young decrease with increasing litter size (Packer et al. 1992). In contrast, there would be a large increase in cost for allonursing in species that give birth to a single offspring. Mammals that engage in allonursing also are often found in relatively small social groups (e.g., lions) although this behaviour is sometimes seen in larger herd animals (African buffalo, antelope: Lewis and Pusey 1997) and occasionally in bats (Eales et al. 1988). This result is consistent with models of cooperation stemming from kin selection or reciprocal altruism. In groups where offspring remain philopatric, the average degree of relatedness is highest in small groups (Wilkinson 1987). Reciprocal altruism and mutualism are also most likely to evolve in small groups (Boyd and Richardson 1988).

Proximate Mechanisms Involved in Alloparental Behaviour

Development of Responsiveness to Infants

In some species of callitrichid monkeys and voles, juveniles show high levels of responsiveness toward younger individuals. There are no detailed data on the development of responsiveness to infants in callitrichids. Data from studies of prairie voles show that if juveniles are continually housed with parents and infants, they are responsive to infants and do not attack them (Solomon 1991; Lonstein and De Vries 2001). When voles are about 21 days of age, around the age of weaning, both males and females are also highly responsive toward unfamiliar infants (Roberts et al. 1998; Lonstein and De Vries 2001). By approximately day 24–42, nonbreeding males are more likely to behave alloparentally toward unfamiliar infants than are non-reproductive females (Bales et al. 2004; but see Kirkpatrick and Kakoyannis 2004). Unlike the males, 24–42-day-old female prairie voles are more likely to attack unfamiliar infants. This sexually dimorphic pattern is also seen at day 60, where males are likely to engage in alloparental care of unfamiliar conspecific infants and females show a reduction in the tendency to huddle over and retrieve unfamiliar infants and an increased tendency to attack them (Roberts et al. 1998). Female responsiveness continues to decline until less than 20 per cent of 90-day-old females respond positively toward pups (Lonstein and De Vries 2001). It is not clear why young naïve females, but not males, behave aggressively toward conspecific young after about 24 days of age but it is likely that neurophysiological factors influence alloparental behavior in young prairie voles.

Physiological Basis for Alloparental Behaviour

Hormonal patterns may facilitate alloparental care of offspring. These can be effects, occurring prior to or around the time of birth and setting up the anatomy of sexually dimorphic nuclei in the brain, or activational effects, occurring around the time of puberty and influencing subsequent behaviour. Most studies in which the hormonal mechanisms underlying alloparental behaviour have been investigated have focused on hypothalamic or pituitary hormones including prolactin or oxytocin, and steroid hormones, such as corticosterone or testosterone.

Organizational Effects of Hormones

Variations in early social experience or the hormonal environment can have dramatic effects on alloparental behaviour. There is not much available data concerning organizational effects on alloparental behaviour but hypotheses have been proposed based on prior experiments with breeding females and males. It has been suggested that oxytocin can affect the regulation of the hypothalamic-pituitary-adrenal axis, emotional reactivity, anxiety, and responses toward novel stimuli (Fleming and Leubke 1981; Fleming et al. 1989; Fleming et al. 2002). It is common for rats and sheep that have not given birth to display an aversion to or even fear of novel stimuli such as newborns. Oxytocin could influence an individual's response to young by reducing anxiety (Bales et al. 2004) and brief exposure to an oxytocin antagonist might disrupt behaviours influenced by oxytocin. When 21-day old male, but not female, prairie voles, were treated neonatally with an antagonist to block oxytocin, they showed a significant decrease in alloparental behaviour and increased attacks on pups (Bales et al. 2004). By day 60, treatment had no significant effect on either male or female responsiveness to pups. These results suggest that an oxytocin antagonist may alter development of the neuroendocrine system involved in alloparental behaviour in males.

Roberts et al. (1996) showed that treatment with corticosterone at day 6 after birth decreased alloparental behaviour in female, but not male, prairie voles. In contrast, prenatal administration of corticosterone had no effect on alloparental responsiveness in 24- or 42-day-old male or female prairie voles that were exposed to unfamiliar pups.

Prenatal exposure to testosterone causes changes in brain structure resulting in a male-like pattern in the sexually dimorphic mammalian brain (Nelson 2000). Although prenatal administration of testosterone did not affect alloparental behaviour in 24- or 42-day-old male or female prairie voles that were exposed to pups, administration of testosterone at postnatal day 6 decreased alloparental behaviour only in males (Roberts et al. 1996).

Activational Effects of Hormones in Non-Reproductive Alloparents

Corticosterone is released as a response to a stressor and is also involved in carbohydrate metabolism (Nelson 2000). Additionally, increased levels of glucocorticoids may enhance foraging and food intake (Koch et al. 2002) as well as attention, alertness, and the formation of social preferences (Fleming et al. 1997). Furthermore, and perhaps more importantly for this discussion, small increases in corticosterone may enhance infant care through the sensitivity to infant cues (Storey et al. 2000; De Vries 2002). Therefore, corticosteroid secretion may enhance alloparental behavior in a number of ways. While there is not much data on corticosterone levels in cooperatively breeding mammals, the ability to determine corticosterone from fecal samples should permit investigators to collect more data, without disturbing animals, in the near future.

During the breeding season, reproductive female as well as philopatric non-breeding male and female striped mice had significantly higher levels of corticosterone than breeding adult males (Schradin 2008). There was no difference in levels of corticosterone among the former three groups. Furthermore, if non-hormonal factors, prolactin, testosterone and cortisol are included in an analysis, cortisol levels are more strongly associated with levels of pup feeding in meerkats than are levels of prolactin or testosterone (Carlson et al. 2006a).

Testosterone is a hormone that is at high levels when males are engaging in sexual behaviour but data from avian studies suggest that testosterone levels decrease during the time of paternal care (e.g., Ketterson and Nolan 1994). There is much less data from mammals. Although a number of correlational studies suggest that testosterone levels decrease in male mammals during the time when paternal behaviour occurs (Brown et al. 1995; Wynne-Edwards 2003), there is still some question regarding the hormonal regulation of paternal care (Wynne-Edwards and Timonin 2007). Mean plasma testosterone levels were lower in paired male common marmosets with infants but these levels were not significantly lower than in paired males without infants (Dixson and George 1982).

There is no clear pattern in the relationship between levels of testosterone and alloparental behaviour in males. Levels of testosterone were similar in dominant (breeding) and subordinate (alloparental) males in a number of species (naked mole-rats: Bennett and Faulkes 2000; dwarf mongooses: Creel et al. 1993; canids: Creel and Creel 2002; and callitrichid monkeys: Baker et al. 1993) but were not related to either babysitting or pup feeding in alloparental male meerkats (Carlson et al. 2006a and b). In contrast, breeding males had significantly higher testosterone levels than non-breeding philopatric male striped mice in a natural population (Schradin 2008).

Prolactin is involved in many functions relating to reproduction such as milk letdown, as well as being one of a number of hormones that effects the initiation and maintenance of parental care (Nelson 2000). Previous studies show a positive relationship between prolactin and alloparental care in birds (Brown and Vleck 1998; Khan et al. 2001). Prolactin might also be involved in mammalian alloparental care although the existing data shows mixed support for this hypothesis. In a number of studies, investigators found low prolactin levels in alloparents in cooperatively breeding primates (Ziegler et al. 1996; Schradin et al. 2003; Schradin and Anzenberger 2004). In contrast, non-breeders show elevated prolactin levels in gray wolves (Kreeger et al. 1991) and common marmosets (Mota and Sousa 2000; Mota et al. 2006). Both male and female alloparental marmosets showed increased levels of prolactin when carrying infants compared to levels when not carrying or prior to birth of young (also see Roberts et al. 2001a). These correlational data do not allow us to determine whether increased prolactin levels are a response to contact with infants or if increased levels of prolactin facilitate alloparental behaviour as is seen in birds (Ziegler 2000). More recently, Carlson et al. (2006b) showed that male meerkat helpers showed increased prolactin levels before spending the day babysitting infants, suggesting that the increase in prolactin facilitates this aspect of alloparental care. In addition, Roberts and colleagues (2001b) administered bromocriptine, which blocks prolactin secretion, and found that the number of infant marmosets retrieved and carried decreased. In those individuals that continued to respond to infants, the latency to retrieve them was longer and carrying duration was shorter compared to controls. This is the first experimental manipulation showing that prolactin affects responsiveness to infants and, in conjunction with correlational studies, indicates that prolactin stimulates alloparental behaviour in common marmosets. Studies with other species of cooperative breeders are needed to determine the generality of the hypothesis that prolactin influences alloparental care in mammals, especially in light of results showing that when cortisol is included in the analysis, the effect of prolactin is less important (Carlson et al. 2006a). Since increased levels of circulating cortisol can stimulate prolactin secretion (Freeman et al. 2000), it is difficult to distinguish between causal influences versus a potential by-product of the association between cortisol and alloparental behavior (Carlson et al. 2006a). Finally, as suggested by Carlson et al. (2006b), different hormones may be related to different aspects of alloparental care.

Functional Significance of Alloparental Behaviour

A number of potential benefits can accrue to alloparents. Non-breeding alloparents may gain direct benefits if they increase the probability of their own future reproduction or, in plurally breeding groups, breeding females can increase their own reproductive success. Benefits may be indirect if alloparents increase the fitness of non-descendent kin. In the following section, we discuss some of the proposed direct and indirect fitness benefits to alloparents. Since allonursing may have some unique benefits and costs associated with it, we discuss them separately.

Direct Fitness Benefits to Non-breeding Males and Females

Individuals may gain direct fitness benefits by remaining philopatric and continuing to live with their family (group fitness effects, Gittleman 1985 or through group augmentation Kokko et al. 2001). These benefits may include increases in fitness due to improved foraging, decreased risk of predation by increased vigilance or the dilution effect (safety in numbers that comes from swamping the consumption capacity of predators, Krause and Ruxton 2002), and group defense of territory or resources (Clode 1993). These benefits are due to increased group size but not directly to effects of alloparental care of young. Sometimes helpers also reproduce (e.g., meerkats, dwarf mongooses, callitrichids or wild dogs) but this may be another benefit of philopatry. Although some biologists have discussed the benefits gained from philopatry together with the benefits from alloparental care, group fitness effects can also occur in social animals that are not cooperative breeders (Jennions and Macdonald 1994). Therefore, we will focus only on fitness effects that directly accrue to alloparents from helping to raise non-descendent offspring.

Direct benefits to non-breeders from alloparental care may include: (i) recruitment of future helpers, (ii) learning to be a better parent, i.e., practice in feeding young and building nests (Lancaster 1971), or (iii) gaining social prestige and increasing opportunities to acquire a mate (Zahavi 1990). We discuss the evidence for and against these proposed direct benefits of mammalian alloparental care by non-breeders.

Recruitment of Future Helpers

A future direct benefit from helping is based on delayed reciprocity (Ligon and Ligon 1978; see also reciprocal altruism Trivers 1971). Investigators have suggested that offspring that received alloparental care repay this care by acting as helpers in the future when the alloparents breed. This hypothesis has not received much empirical study in either birds or mammals (but see Ligon and Ligon 1983) but it is possible that delayed reciprocation could evolve due to extensive interactions and individual recognition. In contrast, cheating, in the form of refusing to help while a non-breeding group member but later accepting help as a breeder, should not occur (Kokko et al. 2001). For this type of direct benefit to evolve, individuals (alloparents and offspring) do not have to be related.

Learning to Parent

In singularly breeding groups, alloparents may benefit directly by learning to be good parents (Lancaster 1971). This hypothesis has been used in the mammalian literature to refer to experience gained by females, but in biparental species males may also benefit, although possibly to a lesser extent. This hypothesis predicts that alloparental care would be seen in young inexperienced individuals and in species where individuals raise a limited number of offspring within their reproductive life span. In addition, alloparental care should be seen in species where young require a prolonged or intensive period of parental investment (e.g., Armitage 1981). The learning-to-parent hypothesis also predicts that experience as an alloparent allows an individual to practice its parental skills, which should enhance its future reproductive success (production and survival of offspring).

The best data in support of this hypothesis comes from primate studies. In general, multiparous mothers are more competent in caring for offspring than are primiparous females. For example, infant tamarins born to primiparous females suffer higher mortality than those born to multiparous mothers (Nicholson 1991). In some instances, immature females handle infants belonging to conspecific females so awkwardly that their behaviour has been described as 'aunting to death' (Gartlan 1969; Hrdy 1976). In callitrichid monkeys, younger individuals, particularly females, are seen carrying infants more frequently than other family members (Baker 1991, cited in Bales et al. 2000). Evidence also suggests that primates learn some aspects of infant care (Lancaster 1971; Hrdy 1976), so alloparental care provides opportunities for learning at a low cost to the alloparent's direct fitness. In laboratory settings, experience with infants tends to result in increased infant survival (Pryce 1993, see also Table 2 in Tardif 1997). For example, female vervet monkeys that spent more time carrying infants when they were juveniles were more likely to raise a surviving infant when they became primiparous mothers (Fairbanks 1990).

It is not known if experience as an alloparent is correlated with improved reproductive success in primates as predicted by the learning-to-parent hypothesis. However, there is some evidence from rodent studies that experience as an alloparent results in changes in maternal responsiveness. Wang and Insel (1996) observed that primiparous female prairie voles with previous alloparental experience displayed higher levels of maternal behaviour (i.e., spent more time in the nest with pups) than primiparous females without such experience.

The best evidence that males may benefit is from Salo and French (1989) who showed that alloparental experience influenced reproductive performance, pup growth, and pup development in Mongolian gerbils. Pairs with at least one experienced alloparent produced their first litters significantly sooner than pairs in which neither parent had any previous alloparental experience. Pup growth was also affected by previous alloparental experience. When both parents had previous alloparental experience, pups from the first litter weighed 17.8 per cent more on day 20 than pups from pairs in which only the mother had alloparental experience. Pup development, as indexed by the age of eye opening, showed the same pattern. Pups whose fathers had alloparental experience opened their eyes slightly but significantly sooner than pups raised by inexperienced males. Salo and French suggested that pups whose fathers had previous alloparental experience benefited because males were able to compensate for the poor-quality nests built by inexperienced females and help maintain body temperature of pups.

In conclusion, data from previous studies are primarily correlational and can not be used to establish a causal relationship. Some studies suggest that alloparental experience in certain rodent and primate species may influence adult maternal behaviour but is probably not critical for the occurrence of maternal behaviour in primiparous females (Numan and Insel 2003). Other factors might also have influenced infant survival. For example, the more successful females may have been as successful even without previous experience (Numan and Insel 2003).

Based on the existing evidence, alloparental experience is likely to have the same effect as adult maternal experience on subsequent maternal care (Numan and Insel 2003). In species where opportunities to engage in alloparental behaviour occur, this experience may substitute for the effects of a primiparous maternal experience. In species where reproduction is delayed, individuals may benefit by acquiring maternal experience through alloparental care. They should be more successful rearing their own offspring than they would have been if they lacked any experience with young. The lifetime reproductive success of these individuals should be enhanced by gaining experience prior to producing their first offspring but this remains to be tested.

Mating Opportunities

Zahavi (1990) proposed that alloparental care is assumed to act as a handicap because it is costly. Thus, only high-quality healthy individuals should be able to engage in this costly behaviour. Individuals may, therefore, engage in alloparental behaviour to gain 'social prestige'. In the Arabian babblers studied by Zahavi, an individual makes a special vocalization when it comes to feed young at the nest. This vocalization attracts the attention of other group members (Zahavi 1990). Thus, these individuals are advertising their quality or social status.

If participation in alloparental care is potentially prestigious, it can enhance reproductive opportunities by influencing mate choice or increasing a male's access to a breeding female (Price 1990; Emlen 1991; but see Tardif 1997; Tardif and Bales 1997). Price (1990) suggested that infant carrying by potential breeding males might function as a type of courtship by demonstrating that these males are competent caretakers. The only evidence supporting this hypothesis was provided by Price (1990), who observed that male cotton-top tamarins were more likely to mate successfully when they were carrying infants than when they were not. The interpretation of these data is problematic because data were collected during the entire period of infant development. Thus, the age of infants might affect the amount of carrying by adult males (Tardif 1997). In contrast, there was no difference in the amount of time spent carrying infants by dominant and subordinate golden lion tamarins even though the dominant male monopolized females when they were in estrus (Baker et al. 1993). Thus, there is no strong evidence that infant carrying is related to gaining mating opportunities (Baker et al. 1993).

Indirect Fitness to Non-breeding Males and Females

Alloparental care by non-breeding adults may increase indirect fitness by: (i) increasing the survival and future reproduction of related breeders, (ii) enhancing the production of non-descendent kin, and (iii) enhancing the quality of non-descendent offspring of kin. Although we discuss these benefits separately, we want to emphasize that they may not be mutually exclusive. For example, aid provided by an alloparent may improve the condition of a breeder, thus increasing the number, growth, and survival of offspring produced by the recipient breeder (e.g., Russell et al. 2003a). In this review, we discuss investment in current non-descendent offspring, physical condition, survival, probability of future reproduction, and timing of reproduction.

Increased Survival and Future Reproduction of Related Breeders

Assistance provided by alloparents may increase the survival and reproductive opportunities for breeders (Ross and MacLarnon 2000), increasing the future indirect fitness of alloparents (Solomon and Getz 1997; Cockburn 1998). There are a number of ways in which alloparents could improve the physical condition of breeders and therefore increase breeders' reproductive rate and lifetime reproductive success.

Alloparents may benefit breeders by decreasing the time that breeders spend with offspring. In laboratory studies of rodents, fathers appeared to benefit from the presence of alloparents. In the Mongolian gerbil, both parents, but particularly fathers, decreased nest-building activity in the presence of alloparents (J.A. French, personal communication). In addition, breeding male, but not female, prairie voles spent more time out of the nest feeding, drinking, and foraging when alloparents were present in the family (Solomon 1991). Males may use this time to maintain or improve their physical condition, guard territories and repel conspecifics to ensure mate fidelity or to engage in extra-pair copulations that increase their direct fitness (Solomon and Getz 1997). There are no data yet that show whether or not males benefit from increased time away from offspring, i.e., reduced paternal investment.

In contrast to laboratory studies on rodents, field studies suggest that mothers gain greater benefits than fathers due to the assistance of alloparents. In some species of carnivores, non-reproductive individuals participate in hunting, provisioning mothers that remain at the natal site to protect and nurse their young (e.g., wild dogs, Malcolm and Marten 1982). More commonly, non-reproductive individuals baby-sit offspring at the natal nest (Clutton-Brock et al. 1998; Courchamp et al. 2002). By taking on babysitting duties, alloparents free parents from these duties (Courchamp et al. 2002), allowing females to forage longer (e.g., sperm whales, Whitehead 1996) or more efficiently (e.g., callitrichid monkeys, Tardif 1997, see also Cockburn 1998). In at least one species, the meerkat, help by non-breeders decreases the energetic demands of lactation by breeding females (Scantlebury et al. 2002). Scantlebury and colleagues (2002) estimated that for every ten helpers, breeding females reduce their energetic demands during peak lactation by an energetic equivalent of the cost to produce one more offspring. In subsequent studies, Russell and colleagues (2002,

2003a) demonstrated that helpers also indirectly improve the weight gain of offspring by improving the physical condition of mothers.

Reduced maternal investment and/or increased maternal physical condition may translate into increases in survival of mothers or offspring or decreases in the time between successive parturitions (inter-birth intervals). There are currently no published data on the effects of helpers on the survival of breeding females but there is some evidence that alloparents allow breeding females to reduce inter-birth intervals (prairie voles, Solomon 1991; pine voles, Powell and Fried 1992). In addition, a meta-analysis on the effects of alloparental care showed that breeders from species with alloparental care have shorter inter-birth intervals than breeders from species without alloparental care (callitrichids, Mitani and Watts 1997). Subsequently, Ross and MacLarnon (2000) determined that primate species with greater alloparental care have higher birth rates than species with less alloparental care.

Alloparental care, primarily in the form of infant carrying, reduces the weight loss and increases the subsequent fitness of breeding primates (Sánchez et al. 1999; Achenbach and Snowdon 2002). For example, there is an inverse relationship between the percent weight loss of adult male cotton-topped tamarins and the number of alloparents helping to carry offspring (Achenbach and Snowdon 2002). In at least one species, reduced infant carrying due to help from alloparents resulted in an increased reproductive tenure for fathers (Bales et al. 2000).

Enhanced Current Indirect Fitness through the Production of Non-Descendent Offspring

In mammals, there is some evidence that alloparental care is more likely to be directed towards kin than non-kin (Owens and Owens 1984; Tardiff 1997; but see Clutton-Brock et al. 2001). For example, male brown hyenas give more food to closely related non-descendent offspring than they do to more distantly related non-descendent offspring (Owens and Owens 1984). Similarly, male golden lion tamarins prefer to carry closely related offspring than distantly related offspring (Tardiff 1997). Alloparental care directed towards close kin by non-breeders could enhance the production and survival of non-descendent kin (Emlen 1995; Cockburn 1998) and thus, would increase the current indirect fitness of alloparents.

To our knowledge, there is little evidence that alloparental care by non-breeders directly affects the number of offspring born to mothers in a single reproductive bout (Jennions and Macdonald 1994; Figure 7.12 in Creel and Creel 2002), though non-breeders may improve the condition of mothers, allowing them to produce larger litters (Russell et al. 2003a). Furthermore, laboratory studies do not support the prediction that indirect benefits may occur by reducing offspring mortality. Neither the presence of alloparents nor increased number of alloparents influenced litter sizes at weaning (pine voles, Fried 1987; Mongolian gerbils, French 1994; common marmosets, Rothe et al. 1993) even under environmentally challenging conditions (prairie voles, Solomon 1991). A number of studies have shown a positive correlation between the number of adult male group members, but not total number of helpers, and surviving infants (e.g., common marmosets, Koenig 1995; golden lion tamarins, Baker et al. 1993). The amount of care was not quantified in these studies so it is not clear if males provided more care than other group members.

In contrast, results from field studies show that alloparental care results in increased survival of offspring (but see Malcolm and Marten 1982; Sillero-Zubiri et al. 2004). In African wild dogs, a minimum number of helpers are required for offspring to survive (Courchamp and Macdonald 2001). In other species such as blackbacked jackals and meerkats, the number of surviving offspring at weaning is correlated with the number of helpers (Moehlman 1979; Russell et al. 2003a). Alloparental care by non-breeders also improves the survival of offspring in alpine marmots. In a population in Germany, nearly 25 per cent of offspring living only with parents died over winter (Arnold 1990). In contrast, only 5 per cent of offspring living with parents and full siblings died, presumably due to the thermal benefits of having extra individuals in the group (Arnold 1990). Babysitting is also proposed to protect offspring in sperm whales (Whitehead 1996) but there are no quantitative data to support this claim.

Future Indirect Fitness through the Increased Quality of Non-Descendent Offspring

In some mammals, the quality of offspring that breeders produce is an important predictor of their subsequent fitness (Lindstrom 1999). Offspring that gain more weight between birth and weaning live longer and experience greater reproductive success than lighter conspecifics (Clutton-Brock et al. 2001; also see Lindstrom 1999 and Metcalfe and Monaghan 2001 for reviews on the importance of early postnatal growth).

There is some evidence from laboratory and field studies that alloparental care by non-breeders enhances the weight gain of offspring (e.g., Solomon 1991; Mitani and Watts 1997; Ross and MacLarnon 2000; Hodge 2005). Under environmentally challenging conditions in the laboratory, prairie vole offspring reared by their parents and offspring from the previous litter gained significantly more weight than offspring reared only by their parents (Solomon 1991; for similar results in pine voles, see Powell and Fried 1992). Solomon (1991) also observed that heavier offspring were more likely to survive from weaning until reproductive maturity, suggesting that alloparents may help increase the fitness of recipient offspring in the wild. Field studies providing correlative data suggest that this may be the case (Getz et al. 1997; McGuire et al. 2002; Hodge 2005; Russell et al. 2007). Although most studies have looked at short-term benefits to offspring, these short-term benefits, such as increased growth, can result in an increased probability of gaining lifetime reproductive success as was found in meerkats (Russell et al. 2007). With meerkats, this effect may result, in part, from a significantly increased probability of acquiring alpha status (Clutton-Brock et al. 2002) and breeding at a younger age compared to offspring that weighed less at the age of independence (Russell et al. 2007). Studies that examine growth of offspring within a litter that receive different amounts of alloparental care may help disentangle these factors (Hodge 2005).

In contrast to Solomon (1991), Wang and Novak (1992) and Hayes and Solomon (2004) observed that offspring reared in singularly breeding groups with helper(s) did not gain significantly more weight than offspring reared by parent(s). These studies were conducted under standard laboratory conditions. Thus, the effect of alloparental care on the weight gain of offspring may vary with environmental conditions (Clutton-Brock 2006).

Two meta-analyses suggested that alloparental care affects the quality of non-descendent offspring. Mitani and Watts (1997) determined that among callitrichid monkeys, species with higher levels of alloparental care produced offspring that grew more than species with lower levels of alloparental care when allometry and phylogeny were controlled. Similarly, Ross and MacLarnon (2000) reported that among primates, offspring in species with greater alloparental care grew faster post-natally and were weaned earlier than offspring in species with less alloparental care.

While the aforementioned studies provided insights into the relationship between offspring growth and alloparental care, carefully designed experimental studies are needed to determine the causal relationship between alloparental care and offspring quality. Designing these studies will be a challenge because there are numerous confounding variables that may affect the growth of offspring reared in singular breeding groups, including the quality of the territory, quality of the parents (Clutton-Brock 1991), foraging success of alloparents (Clutton-Brock et al. 2001), sex of the alloparent and offspring (Brotherton et al. 2001), and birth weight of the offspring. Additionally, determining if alloparental care directly affects the growth of non-descendent kin or works indirectly, by improving the condition of parents, is difficult to determine. For example, alloparental meerkats improve the weight gain of offspring (Russell et al. 2003a). The effect appears to be indirect because alloparents improve the quality of parents, possibly decreasing the energetic demands on lactating females (Scantlebury et al. 2002; Russell et al. 2003a). Studies that distinguish between these affects, while difficult, are critically needed to understand the effect of alloparental care on the quality of current offspring. Finally, even if short-term effects are not found, increased fitness of offspring may only be evident in long-term studies (Russell et al. 2007).

Inclusive Fitness Benefits of Allonursing

Although allonursing has been documented in most mammalian families (Packer et al. 1992), we focus on allonursing in plurally breeding groups. In these groups, the benefits of allonursing may differ depending on the degree of relatedness among lactating females (König 1994; Gerlach and Bartmann 2002) or the degree of reciprocity among unrelated females (Lewis and Pusey 1997). Allonursing between kin may increase both the current indirect and direct fitness of mothers. In contrast, when mothers nurse offspring born to unrelated females, mothers may only gain direct fitness through reciprocity (Roulin 2002).

To date, most empirical data on reproductive success of allonursing females in mammals comes from studies of rodents (but see Macdonald et al. 2004 for canid examples). In plurally breeding groups, females may increase their direct and/or indirect fitness by: (i) enhancing the production of offspring (non-descendent and own), (ii) enhancing the quality of offspring, and (iii) sharing and reducing nursing loads, thus, increasing the survival and reproduction of all females.

Enhanced Production of Non-Descendent Offspring

In groups with more than one breeding female, there is conflicting evidence regarding the effects of allonursing on production of offspring. It has been hypothesized that one benefit of allonursing is increasing the amount of nutrition for all offspring, which may result in an increased number of offspring. Evidence supporting this hypothesis is found only in laboratory studies of rodents. Early studies reported that offspring were nursed indiscriminately by both female house mice in communal nests (Sayler and Salmon 1969; Werboff et al. 1970). The best evidence of inclusive fitness benefits from allonursing comes from König's studies on house mice. Allonursing females had a higher probability of reproducing (König 1997). Offspring reared by allonursing females survived longer than offspring reared by single mothers (König 1997; see also Manning et al. 1995). Thus, in house mice, allonursing seems to maximize the inclusive fitness of females.

In contrast, studies on cavies (Kunkele and Hoeck 1995), deer mice (Wolff 1994), fat dormice (Pilastro 1992; Pilastro et al. 1996), white-footed mice (Wolff 1994), and wood mice (Gerlach and Bartmann 2002) indicated that allonursing females and solitary mothers produce a similar number of offspring and these offspring do not survive any better in groups with allonursing females (Pilastro et al. 1996). Whether these differences are species-specific or due to differences in experimental design is not known.

Quality of Offspring

Like alloparental care involving non-breeders, allonursing in plurally breeding groups may improve the weight gain of offspring (Sayler and Salmon 1969; Hayes and Solomon 2004; but see Gerlach and Bartmann 2002) possibly by reducing the time between suckling bouts (König 2006). To date, the best evidence for beneficial effects of communal nursing by plural breeders on the quality of offspring is from rodent studies conducted in the laboratory. In these studies, litters reared by multiple mothers gained significantly more weight than litters reared by one mother (house mice, Sayler and Salmon 1969; Norway rats, Mennella et al. 1990). More recently, Hayes and Solomon (2004) observed that offspring reared by plurally breeding prairie vole mothers gained significantly more weight than offspring reared in singularly breeding groups (one lactating female and one non-breeding female) or by solitary mothers. Prairie vole offspring raised in plurally breeding groups may receive more milk than offspring reared in other social units and may be left alone less than offspring reared in other types of social units (Hayes and Solomon 2006), improving the thermal conditions for optimal weight gain.

Immunological benefits to pups may influence their weight gain, survival and reproduction. For example, since milk is rich in antibodies (Newman 1995) offspring that suckle from multiple mothers may have improved immune capabilities (Roulin and Heeb 1999). If one mother were deficient in a critical immunoglobin, allonursing would ensure that her offspring would receive the immunoglobin and develop normally (Roulin 2002). Additionally, offspring that suckle from multiple mothers may gain antibodies specific to each mother, improving their immune response (Roulin and Heeb 1999).

There are few studies that test this hypothesis and results are mixed. There is only limited evidence that degu pups acquired antibodies from conspecific lactating females (Becker et al. 2007). Also there was no difference in immunoglobin concentrations of house mouse pups reared by females with the same versus a different major histocompatibility complex (MHC – involved in the immune response) but there was a difference in white-blood cell concentration (also involved in the immune response) in pups reared by mothers that differed in MHC versus those that did not. Pups reared by mothers that differed in MHC did not grow any faster than pups reared by lactating females that had the same MHC type (cited in König 2006). The importance of this potential function of allonursing may depend on relatedness between females, group size (and thus, rate of pathogen transfer; Jennions and Mac-Donald 1994), and recency of pathogen outbreaks (Roulin 2002).

Benefits to Mothers

To date, there are several hypotheses for benefits to mothers, which could increase lifetime direct fitness. For example, Wilkinson (1992) proposed that allonursing allows evening bat mothers to reduce their weight before flight. Allonursing may also function to maintain social relationships (as in Murphey et al. 1991). Although these are interesting adaptive hypotheses, to our knowledge there are no data to support them. More likely, allonursing may reduce the work loads of mothers, freeing time for foraging and body maintenance (Malcolm and Marten 1982; König 1997) and reducing energetic demands (Scantlebury et al. 2002).

The benefits of allonursing may vary considerably between plurally breeding females rearing offspring in the same group or nest (Hayes 2000). These relative benefits would depend on relatedness between females (Pusey and Packer 1994), the age difference between lactating females (Gerlach and Bartmann 2002), the age difference between offspring from different litters (Bertram 1975; Mennella et al. 1990), local conditions (e.g., population density, Wolff 1994; Hayes 2000; Gerlach and Bartmann 2002), and possibly the health of mothers (Roulin and Heeb 1999). We will examine the first three of these factors more closely.

Relatedness

In some plurally breeding species, female group members live with close relatives (e.g., lions, Pusey and Packer 1994; grey mouse lemurs, Eberle and Kappeler 2006;

fat dormice, Marin and Pilastro 1994; house mice, Wilkinson and Baker 1988; Manning et al. 1992) suggesting that females may choose to nest with relatives rather than with unrelated individuals. The finding that females live close to relatives is, by itself, insufficient evidence to conclude that female kin groups form due to indirect benefits. More convincing evidence comes from observations that related pairs of house mouse females also wean significantly more offspring than pairs of unrelated females (König 1994). In these studies, allonursing females gain inclusive fitness benefits by helping to rear closely related offspring as well as their own offspring, consistent with the kin selection hypothesis. In contrast, in the only field study in which reproductive success was determined, allonursing did not benefit lion mothers and offspring, suggesting that allonursing may be a unselected by-product of group living in this species (Pusey and Packer 1994), a hypothesis that has been proposed for other species (e.g., Manning et al. 1995; Hayes 2000). Estimates of reproductive success from additional species living in their natural environment are needed before we know if this difference is species-specific or due to the difference between studying alloparental care in the lab versus the field.

Age Difference among Females

Benefits and costs of allonursing may differ depending on the age differences among female group members. For example, Gerlach and Bartmann (2002) observed that nursing effort was not equitable within wood mouse groups containing mothers and daughters. In these groups, daughters nursed pups significantly longer than did their mothers, possibly explaining the delay that daughters experienced in the production of the subsequent litter (Gerlach and Bartmann 2002).

In wood mice and fat dormice, young females may join a communal group when conditions for solitary breeding are unfavourable (Pilastro et al. 1996; Gerlach and Bartmann 2002) causing some to argue that females form plurally breeding groups only when population density is high (Wolff 1994 but see Emlen 1995). Thus, benefits to these females are not expected, and older females should only allow younger females to join the group if they benefit or if there is no cost to them and their offspring (Emlen 1995).

The difference between the costs of allonursing to females within communal groups may be reduced if females are of similar age. For example, Hayes and Solomon (2004) observed that in pairs of same-aged prairie vole sisters, the weight gain of offspring produced by both females was similar, suggesting that when females were the same age, pups in both litters benefited equally.

Age Difference between Offspring

The age difference between offspring in communal litters could explain variation in the reproductive consequences of allonursing to communal females. There is some evidence suggesting that allonursing maximizes the benefits to mothers only when litters are produced synchronously (Gilchrist 2006). For example, approximately 70 per cent of Norway rat pups born in communal nests with 15–28-day-old pups already present died by 5 days of age (Mennella et al. 1990). In contrast, the mortality of pups born in communal nests with 0–14-day-old pups already present was only approximately 5 per cent (Mennella et al. 1990; see also Bertram 1975 for similar results in allonursing lions). These results suggest that when litters are produced asynchronously, there is a greater risk of infanticide (Pilastro et al. 1996; Gerlach and Bartmann 2002) and/or greater asymmetry in the competitive abilities of offspring from different litters (Bertram 1975; Mennella et al. 1990). These results have led some investigators to argue that natural selection could act on females to produce litters synchronously in the wild (e.g., Mennella et al. 1990).

Costs of Alloparenting

Although benefits of alloparental care have received much attention, the costs of alloparental care per se are not as well documented in mammals (Heinsohn and Legge 1999). Forms of alloparental care that may be costly to alloparents include babysitting (Clutton-Brock et al. 1998), infant carrying (Bales et al. 2000), food provisioning (Brotherton et al. 2001), huddling (Arnold 1990), and allonursing (Pilastro et al. 1996). First, we discuss evidence for costs of babysitting, infant carrying, food provisioning, and huddling with offspring. These activities may result in energetic costs or increased exposure to predation, leading to short-term (reduced body condition) and long-term (decreased survival, reduced future fecundity) costs to individuals (Heinsohn and Legge 1999; Gilchrist 2007). Since allonursing may have very different costs and benefits than other forms of alloparental care, we discuss costs of allonursing separately.

Costs of Alloparental Behaviour: Reduced Body Condition

Alloparental care can be energetically costly to non-breeders (Clutton-Brock et al. 1998; Heinsohn and Legge 1999), resulting in loss of physical condition. Weight loss may result from reduced opportunities to forage due to babysitting (Clutton-Brock et al. 1998), social hibernation (Arnold 1990), or infant carrying (Sánchez et al. 1999). Although there are previous theoretical treatments on the effect of helping on the physical condition of alloparents (Heinsohn and Legge 1999; Heinsohn 2004), there are only a few good empirical examples, primarily of short-term costs. We briefly describe three examples for which there is empirical evidence for weight loss.

In most marmot species, individuals hibernate in social groups (Armitage 1999), possibly to reduce the energetic stress and weight loss associated with hibernation in the cold (Arnold 1988). In one species, the alpine marmot, there is evidence that alloparents that assist with thermoregulation of young experience a cost to their physical condition. During hibernation, alloparental alpine marmots lose increasingly more weight with increasing number of infants in a group (Arnold 1990). In contrast, in groups without infants, the weight loss of non-breeders during hibernation is unaffected by group size (Arnold 1990). Arnold (1990) argued that a potential long-term cost of this weight loss is a reduced ability to maintain a territory during the subsequent breeding season, which would reduce direct fitness.

The carrying of infants results in significant costs to the physical condition of primate parents. In captivity, non-breeding cotton-topped and saddle-backed tamarins spend less time feeding while carrying infants compared to times when they are not carrying infants (Price 1992; see Table 2.2 in Tardif 1997; see also Sánchez et al. 1999). Although the amount of infant carrying is correlated with weight loss by adult male (Achenbach and Snowdon 2002) and subadult male cotton-topped tamarins (but not subadult female, Sánchez et al. 1999), the long-term effect of this weight loss on survival and reproduction is not known.

In the wild, non-breeding meerkats babysit offspring for as long as twenty-four hours (Clutton-Brock et al. 1998). Babysitting comes at a cost of foregoing opportunities to forage with the group. Consequently, a babysitting meerkat loses 1.3 per cent of its body weight during a 24-hour shift (Clutton-Brock et al. 1998). In contrast, other group members that are able to forage gain 1.9 per cent of their weight during the same time (Clutton-Brock et al. 1998). Likewise, during the rearing period, babysitters lose more weight with increasing babysitting loads (Clutton-Brock et al. 1998). Although some weight loss may be attributable to other behaviours during time spent babysitting, the most likely explanation for the weight loss is reduced opportunities to forage. Interestingly, the amount of helping provided is related to weight (Clutton-Brock et al. 2002). Meerkats that spend a lot of time babysitting minimize the long-term costs by increasing their foraging rates subsequently (Russell et al. 2003b). Not surprisingly, the amount of time that individual meerkats spend babysitting decreases with an increase in the number of potential helpers in a group (Clutton-Brock et al. 1998).

Although helping has a cost, it is not clear how significant the cost is to helpers. For example, meerkat helpers are less likely to reproduce while still subordinates but there is no effect of helping on survival (Russell et al. 2003b).

Increased Risk of Predation

Alloparents caring for offspring may be at greater risk of predation if they become more conspicuous or less vigilant with respect to predators (König 1997). Moreover, when alloparental care results in reduced weight, as has been observed in meerkats (Clutton-Brock et al. 1998), alloparents may need to intensify foraging to compensate for this loss at a greater risk of predation (as in Metcalfe and Monaghan 2001). Empirical evidence of increased predation risks is limited.

In primates, alloparents that carry infants may experience increased energetic demands (see Tardif 1997 for a review) that may put them at a greater risk of predation than conspecifics that do not carry infants. Indeed, there is some evidence that infant carrying decreases leaping ability in primates. Schradin and Anzenberger (2001) showed that alloparental callitrichid primates experience a 17 per cent reduction in leaping ability while carrying infants in captivity. Although decreased leaping ability associated with infant carrying would likely reduce an individual's ability to escape predators (Schradin and Anzenberger 2001), a relationship between leaping ability and predation has not been demonstrated.

Costs of Allonursing

To understand the potential costs of allonursing, we must first understand that lactation is the most energetically expensive form of maternal investment in mammals (Clutton-Brock et al. 1989). The production of milk requires an input of water, nutrients, energy, and antibodies from mothers (Roulin and Heeb 1999). Lactation is a depreciable form of investment, i.e., energy and resources in milk are lost to mothers during suckling (Clutton-Brock et al. 1989 but see Alberts and Gubernick 1983). As offspring grow and require more milk, lactation becomes increasingly costly to mothers in some species (Lochmiller et al. 1982). As a result of these costs, mothers may be at a greater risk of mortality (Clutton-Brock et al. 1989) or have lower future fecundity (Huber et al. 1999) than non-lactating females. To compensate for these costs, mothers either feed heavily before nursing, rely on fat stores as fuel during lactation, or increase foraging while nursing offspring (Bowen et al. 2001). Regardless of strategy, increased foraging associated with lactation can be costly to mothers (Lima 1998).

Despite the high costs of lactation, mothers allow conspecific offspring to nurse in several species of mammals (Pusey and Packer 1994, Plesner-Jensen et al. 1999; Hayes 2000, see Packer et al. 1992 for a review). Allonursing could reduce fitness if unrelated young steal milk (Packer et al. 1992) or if females misdirect the allocation of milk to unrelated young. Mothers that share milk with non-descendent offspring may experience a reduction in their fitness unless the recipient offspring are closely related or allonursing is reciprocated (see Hayes 2000 and Roulin 2002 for reviews). Similarly, allonursing may result in competition for milk, particularly when there is a large age difference between litters, decreasing the milk intake and, most likely, fitness of offspring. We review two potential costs of allonursing: i) costs to mothers' current offspring, and ii) costs to mothers' survival and future fecundity.

Costs to a Mother's Current Offspring or Litter

The benefits of allonursing may be decreased by behavioral tension between lactating females especially in instances where communal nursing is due to a failure of reproductive suppression (Macdonald et al. 2004). There is evidence from a number of studies that allonursing can be costly to mothers' current direct fitness, even when nest mates are related. Plesner-Jensen and colleagues (1999) observed that warthog groups where females allonursed each other's offspring as well as their own had nearly one fewer juvenile per nursing female compared to groups without allonursing. Similarly, survival of Ethiopian wolf pups from birth to weaning was significantly less when pups were nursed by two lactating females versus pups nursed by only one lactating female (Sillero-Zubiri et al. 2004). The decrease in pup survival with increased number of lactating females was also seen in Mednyi Island Arctic foxes (cited in Macdonald et al. 2004), bat-eared foxes (Maas and Macdonald 2004), and prairie voles (McGuire et al. 2002; Solomon and Crist 2008).

In large social groups, mothers that allonurse are at a greater risk of obtaining (Jennions and MacDonald 1994) and possibly transferring more parasites to their own offspring than mothers nursing offspring alone or in small groups (Roulin and Heeb 1999; Roulin 2002). Additionally, antibodies ingested during allonursing may retard the maturation of the offspring's immune system (Carlier and Truyens 1995) or react with the offspring's red blood cells, causing haemolytic diseases (Roulin and Heeb 1999). Although these hypotheses are very interesting, they have not been tested to our knowledge.

Costs to Mothers' Survival and Future Fecundity

Mothers that nurse more offspring or nurse offspring for a longer time may be at greater risk of mortality than mothers with reduced nursing loads (as in Clutton-Brock et al. 1989). Thus, allonursing may be costly to a mother if the reciprocating females do not participate equally in allonursing. Several studies on allonursing indicate that mothers do not share nursing loads equally (Pusey and Packer 1994; Plesner-Jensen et al. 1999; Gerlach and Bartmann 2002; Hayes and Solomon 2004). In some rodents younger mothers have heavier nursing loads than older mothers (Gerlach and Bartmann 2002). Other factors, such as the relatedness of mothers and timing of litter production may also affect nursing effort (Gerlach and Bartmann 2002; Hayes and Solomon 2004).

Females that nurse conspecific young may also risk receiving pathogens from non-descendent offspring against which they have little immunological resistance (see Roulin and Heeb 1999). The transfer of pathogens from conspecific young to mothers could lead to infection or may reduce the quality of milk that mothers produce.

Conclusion

In this chapter, we have reviewed the biological basis of alloparental care, summarizing proximate (mechanistic) and ultimate (functional) explanations for alloparental care in mammals. Can these hypotheses apply to alloparental care in humans? We argue that many of the proposed proximate and ultimate explanations can be applied to human behaviour. We make this statement based on three assumptions: (1) social behaviour in animals has been shaped by natural selection, (2) human behaviour has also been shaped, at least in part, by natural selection, and (3) animals that live in similar circumstances are most likely to have evolved similar behaviours (Emlen 1997). We have taken an evolutionary perspective based on the postulate that much of our current behaviour results from heritable adaptations that were advantageous in the ancestral human environment (Emlen 1997). Thus, species of cooperatively breeding mammals are likely to provide useful comparative data for examining human alloparental care because we should be able to identify the biological basis for alloparental care in societies that lack cultural overlays. If we find convergence in behavioural patterns in a variety of species, it is likely that they exemplify biological tendencies that are also present in humans.

Other chapters in this volume attest to the benefits gained from an evolutionary approach to studying human behaviour. Only by understanding that human behaviour has a biological basis and that human behaviour can be affected by natural selection, in the same way as seen in other animals, can we begin to understand the complexity of human social interactions. Developing this understanding may have far-reaching benefits to a wide range of issues that humans currently face, including governmental policy, family planning, economic decision making, and human health.

References

Achenbach, G.G., and Snowdon, C.T., 2002. Costs of caregiving: weight loss in captive adult male cotton-top tamarins (*Saguinus oedipus*) following the birth of infants. *International Journal of Primatology* 23, 179–89.

Alberts, J.R., and Gubernick, D.J., 1983. Reciprocity and resource exchange: a symbiotic model of parent–offspring relations. In L. Rosenblum and H. Moltz, eds., *Symbiosis in Parent–Offspring interactions.* New York: Plenum Press, 7–44.

Armitage, K.B., 1981. Sociality as a life-history tactic of ground squirrels. *Oecologia* 48, 36–49.

——— 1999. Evolution of sociality in marmots. *Journal of Mammalogy* 80, 1–10.

Arnold, W., 1988. Social thermoregulation during hibernation in alpine marmots (*Marmota marmota*). *Journal of Comparative Physiology B* 158, 151–56.

——— 1990. The evolution of marmot sociality: II. Costs and benefits of joint hibernation. *Behavioral Ecology and Sociobiology* 27, 239–46.

Arnold, K.E., and Owens, I.P.F., 1999. Cooperative breeding in birds: the role of ecology. *Behavioral Ecology* 10, 465–71.

Baker, A.J. 1991. Evolution of the Social System of the Golden Lion Tamarin (*Leontopithecus rosalia*): Mating Systems, Group Dynamics ad Cooperative Breeding. PhD thesis, University of Maryland.

Baker, A.J., Dietz, J.M., and Kleiman, D.G., 1993. Behavioural evidence for monopolization of paternity in multi-male groups of golden lion tamarins. *Animal Behaviour* 46, 1091–1103.

Bales, K., Dietz, J., Baker, A., Miller, K., and Tardif, S.D., 2000. Effects of allocare-givers on fitness of infants and parents in callitrichid primates. *Folia Primatologica* 71, 27–38.

Bales, K.L., Pfeifer, L.A., and Carter, C.S., 2004. Sex differences and developmental effects of manipulations of oxytocin on alloparenting and anxiety in prairie voles. *Developmental Psychobiology* 44, 123–31.

Balshine, S., Leach, B., Neat, F., Reid, H., Taborsky, M., and Werner, N., 2001. Correlates of group size in a cooperatively breeding cichlid fish (*Neolamprologus pulcher*). *Behavioral Ecology and Sociobiology* 50, 134–40.

Becker, M.I., De Ioannes, A.E., León, C., and Ebensperger, L.A., 2007. Females of the communally breeding rodent, *Octodon degus,* transfer antibodies to their offspring during pregnancy and lactation. *Journal of Reproductive Immunology* 74, 68–77.

Bennett, N.C., and Faulkes, C.G., 2000. *African Mole-rats: Ecology and Eusociality.* Cambridge: Cambridge University Press.

Bennett, N.C., Jarvis, J.U.M., Aguilar, G.H., and McDaid, E.J., 1991. Growth and development in six species of African mole-rats (Rodentia: Bathyergidae). *Journal of Zoology, London* 225, 13–26.

Bertram, B.C.R., 1975. Social factors influencing reproduction in wild lions. *Journal of Zoology, London* 177, 463–82.

Blumstein, D.T., and Armitage, K.B., 1999. Cooperative breeding in marmots. *Oikos* 84, 369–82.

Bowen, W.D., Iverson, S. J., Boness, D.J. and Oftedal, O.T. 2001. Foraging effort, food intake and lactation performance depend on maternal mass in a small phocid seal. *Functional Ecology* 15, 325–34.

Boyd, R., and Richardson, P., 1988. The evolution of reciprocity in sizeable groups. *Journal of Theoretical Biology* 132, 337–56.

Brotherton, P.N.M., Clutton-Brock, T.H., O'Riain, M.J., Gaynor, D., Sharpe, L., Kansky, R., and McIlrath, G.M., 2001. Offspring food allocation by parents and helpers in a cooperative mammal. *Behavioral Ecology* 12, 590–99.

Brant, C.L., Schwab, T.M., Vandenbergh, J.G., Schaefer, R.L., and Solomon, N.G., 1998. Behavioural suppression of female pine voles after replacement of the breeding male. *Animal Behaviour* 55, 615–27.

Brouwer, L., Heg, D., and Taborsky, M., 2005. Experimental evidence for helper effects in a cooperatively breeding cichlid. *Behavioral Ecology* 16, 667–73.

Brown, J.L., 1987. *Helping and Communal Breeding in Birds: Ecology and Evolution.* Princeton: Princeton University Press.

Brown, J.L., and Vleck, C.M., 1998. Prolactin and helping in birds: has natural selection strengthened helping behavior? *Behavioral Ecology* 9, 541–45.

Brown, R.E., Murdoch, T., Murphy, P.R., and Moger, W.H., 1995. Hormonal responses of male gerbils to stimuli from their mate and pups. *Hormones and Behavior* 29, 474–91.

Burda, H., 1990. Constraints of pregnancy and evolution of sociality in mole-rats. *Zeitschrift fur Zoologische Systemmatik und Evolutionsforschung* 28, 26–39.

Carlier, Y., and Truyens, C., 1995. Influence of maternal infection on offspring resistance towards parasites. *Parasitology Today* 11, 94–99.

Carlson, A.A., Manser, M.B., Young, A.J., Russell, A.F., Jordan, N.R., McNeilly, A.S., and Clutton-Brock, T., 2006a. Cortisol levels are positively associated with pup-feeding rates in male meerkats. *Proceedings of the Royal Society B* 273, 571–77.

Carlson, A.A., Russell, A.F., Young, A.J., Jordan, N.R., McNeilly, A.S., Parlow, A.F., and Clutton-Brock, T., 2006b. Elevated prolactin levels immediately precede decisions to babysit by male meerkat helpers. *Hormones and Behavior* 50, 94–100.

Clode, D., 1993. Colonially breeding seabirds: predators or prey? *Trends in Ecology and Evolution* 8, 336–38.

Clutton-Brock, T.H., 1991. *The Evolution of Parental Care.* Princeton: Princeton University Press.

——— 2006. Cooperative breeding in mammals. In Van Schaik, eds., *Cooperation in Primates and Humans.* Berlin: Springer-Verlag, 173–90.

Clutton-Brock, T.H., Albon, S.D., and Guinness, F.E., 1989. Fitness costs of gestation and lactation in wild mammals. *Nature* 337, 260–62.

Clutton-Brock, T.H., Gaynor, D., Kansky, R., MacColl, A.D.C., McIlrath, G., Chadwick, P., Brotherton, P.N.M., O'Riain, J.M., Manser, M., and Skinner, J.D., 1998. Costs of cooperative behaviour in suricates *(Suricata suricatta). Proceedings of the Royal Society B* 265, 185–90.

Clutton-Brock, T.H., Brotherton, P.N.M., O'Riain, M.J., Griffin, A.S., Gaynor, D., Kansky, R., Sharpe, L., and McIlrath, G.M., 2001. Contributions to cooperative rearing in meerkats. *Animal Behaviour* 61, 705–10.

Clutton-Brock, T.H., Russell, A.F., Sharpe, L.L., Young, A.P., Balmforth, Z., and Mcilrath, G.M., 2002. Evolution and development of sex differences in cooperative behavior in meerkats. *Science* 297, 253–56.

Cockburn, A., 1998. Evolution of helping behavior in cooperatively breeding birds. *Annual Review of Ecology and Systematics* 29, 141–77.

Courchamp, F., and Macdonald, D.W., 2001. Crucial importance of pack size in the African wild dog *Lycaon pictus. Animal Conservation* 4, 169–74.

Courchamp, F., Rasmussen, G.S.A., and Macdonald, D.W., 2002. Small pack size imposes a trade-off between hunting and pup-guarding in the painted hunting dog *Lycaon pictus. Behavioral Ecology* 13, 20–27.

Creel, S., and Creel, N.M., 2002. *The African Wild Dog: Behavior, Ecology, and Conservation.* Princeton: Princeton University Press.

Creel, S.R. and Waser, P.M., 1997. Variation in reproductive suppression among dwarf mongooses: interplay between mechanisms and evolution. In N.G. Solomon and J.A. French, eds., *Cooperative Breeding in Mammals.* New York: Cambridge University Press, 150–70.

Creel, S.R., Monfort, S.L., Wildt, D.E., And Waser, P.M., 1991. Spontaneous lactation is an adaptive result of pseudopregnancy. *Nature* 351, 660–62.

Creel, S., Wildt, D.E., and Monfort, S.L., 1993. Aggression, reproduction, and androgens in wild dwarf mongooses: a test of the challenge hypothesis. *American Naturalist* 141, 816–25.

Darwin, C.R., 1859. *On the Origin of Species by Means of Natural Selection, or the Preservation of Favoured Races in the Struggle for Life.* John Murray: London.

De Vries, A.C. 2002. Interaction among social environment, the hypothalamic–pituitary–adrenal axis, and behavior. *Hormones and Behavior* 41, 405–13.

Dixson, A.F., and George, L., 1982. Prolactin and parental behaviour in a male New World primate. *Nature* 299, 551–53.

Eales, L.A., Bullock, D.J., and Slater, P.J.B., 1988. Shared nursing in captive pipistrelles (*Pipistrellus pipistrellus*). *Journal of Zoology, London* 216, 584– 87.

Eberle, M., and Kappeler, P.M., 2006. Family insurance: kin selection and cooperative breeding in a solitary primate (*Microcebus murinus*). *Behavioral Ecology and Sociobiology* 60, 582–88.

Emlen, S.T., 1982. The evolution of helping. I. An ecological constraints model. *American Naturalist* 119, 29–39.

———— 1991. Evolution of cooperative breeding in birds and mammals. In J.R. Krebs and N.B. Davies, eds., *Behavioural Ecology: An Evolutionary Approach*. Oxford: Blackwell, 301–37. Third edition.

———— 1995. An evolutionary theory of the family. *Proceedings of the National Academy of Sciences* 92, 8092–99.

———— 1997. The evolutionary study of human family systems. *Social Science Information* 36, 563–89.

Fairbanks, L.A., 1990. Reciprocal benefits of allomothering for female vervet monkeys. *Animal Behaviour* 40, 553–62.

Fleming, A.S., and Leubke, C., 1981. Timidity prevents the virgin female rat from being a good mother: emotionality differences between nulliparous and parturient females. *Physiology and Behavior* 27, 863–68.

Fleming, A.S., Cheung, U., Myhal, N., and Kessler, Z., 1989. Effects of maternal hormones on 'timidity' and attraction to pup-related odors in female rats. *Physiology and Behavior* 46, 449–53.

Fleming, A.S., Kraemer, G.W., Gonzalez, A., Lovic, V., Rees, S., and Melo, A., 2002. Mothering begets mothering: the transmission of behavior and its neurobiology across generations. *Pharmacology, Biochemistry and Behavior* 73, 61–75.

Fleming, A.S., Steiner, M., and Corter, C., 1997. Cortisol, hedonics, and maternal responsiveness in human mothers. *Hormones and Behavior* 32, 85–98.

Freeman, M.E., Kanyicska, B., Lerant, A., and Nagy, G., 2000. Prolactin: structure, function, and regulation of secretion. *Physiological Reviews* 80, 1523–631.

French, J.A., 1994. Alloparents in the Mongolian gerbil: impact on long-term reproductive performance of breeders and opportunities for independent reproduction. *Behavioral Ecology* 5, 273–79.

French, J.A., 1997. Proximate regulation of singular breeding in callitrichid primates. In N.G. Solomon and J.A. French, eds., *Cooperative Breeding in Mammals*. New York: Cambridge University Press, 34–75.

Fried, J.J., 1987. *The role of juvenile pine voles (Microtus pinetorum) in the caretaking of their younger siblings*. MSc thesis, North Carolina State University, Raleigh.

Gartlan, J.S., 1969. Sexual and maternal behaviour of the vervet monkey, *Cercopithecus aethiops: Journal of Reproduction and Fertility Supplement* 6, 137–50.

Gerlach, G., and Bartmann, S., 2002. Reproductive skew, costs, and benefits of cooperative breeding in female wood mice, (*Apodemus sylvaticus*). *Behavioral Ecology* 13, 408–18.

Getz, L.L., Simms, L.E., McGuire, B., and Snarski, M.E., 1997. Factors affecting life expectancy of the prairie vole, *Microtus ochrogaster*. *Oikos* 80, 362–70.

Gilchrist, J.S., 2006. Reproductive success in a low skew, communal breeding mammal: the banded mongoose, *Mungos mungo*. *Behavioral Ecology and Sociobiology* 60, 854–63.

Gilchrist, J.S., 2007. Cooperative behaviour in cooperative breeders: costs, benefits, and communal breeding. *Behavioural Processes* 76, 100–105.

Gittleman, J.L., 1985. Functions of communal care in mammals. In P.J. Greenwood, P.H. Harvey and M. Slatkin, eds., *Evolution: Essays in Honour of John Maynard Smith*. Cambridge: Cambridge University Press, 187–205.

Hamilton, W.D., 1964. The genetical evolution of social behaviour. *Journal of Theoretical Biology* 7, 1–52.

Hatchwell, B.J., and Komdeur, J., 2000. Ecological constraints, life history traits and the evolution of cooperative breeding. *Animal Behaviour* 59, 1079–86.

Hayes, L.D., 2000. To nest communally or not to nest communally: a review of rodent communal nesting and nursing. *Animal Behaviour* 59, 677–88.

Hayes, L.D., and Solomon, N.G., 2004. Costs and benefits of communal rearing to female prairie voles (*Microtus ochrogaster*). *Behavioral Ecology and Sociobiology* 56, 585–593.

——— 2006. Mechanisms of maternal investment by communal prairie voles (*Microtus ochrogaster*). *Animal Behaviour* 72, 1069–80.

Heinsohn, R.G., 2004. Parental care, load-lightening, and costs. In W. Koenig and J.L. Dickinson, eds., *Ecology and Evolution of Cooperative Breeding in Birds*. Cambridge: Cambridge University Press, 67–80.

Heinsohn, R., and Legge, S., 1999. The cost of helping. *Trends in Ecology and Evolution* 14, 53–57.

Hodge, S.J., 2005. Helpers benefit offspring in both the short and long-term in the cooperatively breeding banded mongoose. *Proceedings of the Royal Society B* 272, 2479–84.

Hoogland, J.L., 1995. *The Black-Tailed Prairie Dog : Social Life of a Burrowing Mammal*. Chicago: University of Chicago Press.

Hrdy, S.B., 1976. Care and exploitation of nonhuman primate infants by conspecifics other than the mother. *Advances in the Study of Behavior* 6, 101–58.

Huber, S., Millesi, E., Walzl, M., Dittami, J., and Arnold, W., 1999. Reproductive effort and costs of reproduction in female European ground squirrels. *Oecologia* 121, 19–24.

Jarvis, J.U.M., 1981. Eusociality in a mammal: cooperative breeding in naked-mole-rat colonies. *Science* 212, 571–73.

Jennions, M.D., and Macdonald, D.W., 1994. Cooperative breeding in mammals. *Trends in Ecology and Evolution* 9, 89–93.

Keller, L., and Reeve, H.K., 1994. Partitioning of reproduction in animal societies. *Trends in Ecology and Evolution* 9, 98–102.

Ketterson, E.D., and Nolan, V. Jr., 1994. Male parental behavior in birds. *Annual Review of Ecology and Systematics* 25, 601–28.

Khan, M.Z., McNabb, F.M.A., Walters, J.R., and Sharp, P.J., 2001. Patterns of testosterone and prolactin concentrations and reproductive behavior of helpers and breeders in the cooperatively breeding red-cockaded woodpecker (*Picoides borealis*). *Hormones and Behavior* 40, 1–13.

Kirkpatrick, B., and Kakoyannis, A., 2004. Sexual dimorphism and the NMDA receptor in alloparental behavior in juvenile prairie voles (*Microtus ochrogaster*). *Behavioral Neuroscience* 118, 584–89.

Koch, K. A., Wingfield, J.C., and Buntin, J. D., 2002. Glucocorticoids and parental hyperphagia in ring doves (*Streptopelia risoria*). *Hormones and Behavior*, 41, 9–21.

Koenig, A., 1995. Group size, composition, and reproductive success in wild common marmosets (*Callithrix jacchus*). *American Journal of Primatology* 35, 311–17.

Koenig, W.D., and Dickinson, J.L., eds., 2004. *Ecology and Evolution of Cooperative Breeding in Birds*. Cambridge: Cambridge University Press.

Koenig, W.D., and Pitelka, F.A., 1981. Ecological factors and kin selection in the evolution of cooperative breeding in birds. In R.D. Alexander and D.W. Tinkle, eds., *Natural Selection and Social Behavior: Recent Research and New Theory*. New York: Chiron Press, 261–80.

Koenig, W.D., Pitelka, F.A., Carmen, W.J., Mumme, R.L., and Stanback, M.T., 1992. The evolution of delayed dispersal in cooperative breeders. *Quarterly Review of Biology* 67, 111–50.

Kokko, H., and Lundberg, P., 2001. Dispersal, migration, and offspring retention in saturated habitats. *American Naturalist* 157, 188–202.

Kokko, H., Johnstone, R.A., and Clutton-Brock, T.H., 2001. The evolution of cooperative breeding through group augmentation. *Proceedings of the Royal Society B* 268, 187–96.

König, B., 1994. Components of lifetime reproductive success in communally and solitarily nursing house mice – a laboratory study. *Behavioral Ecology and Sociobiology* 34, 275–83.

——— 1997. Cooperative care of young in mammals. *Naturwissenschaften* 84, 95–104.

——— 2006. Non-offspring nursing in mammals: general implications from a case study on house mice. In P.M. Kappeler and C.P. van Schaik, eds., *Cooperation in Primates and Humans*. Berlin: Springer-Verlag, 191–205.

Krause, J., and Ruxton, G.D., 2002. *Living in Groups*. Oxford: Oxford University Press.

Kreeger, T.J., Seal, U.S., Cohen, Y., Plotka, E.D., and Asa, C.S., 1991. Characterization of prolactin secretion in gray wolves (*Canis lupus*). *Canadian Journal of Zoology* 69, 1366–74.

Kunkele, J., and Hoeck, H.N., 1995. Communal suckling in the cavy *Galea musteloides*. *Behavioral Ecology and Sociobiology* 37, 385–91.

Lacey, E.A., 2004. Sociality reduces individual direct fitness in a communally breeding rodent, the colonial tuco-tuco (*Ctenomys sociabilis*). *Behavioral Ecology and Sociobiology* 56, 449–57.

Lacey, E.A., and Sherman, P.W., 1991. Social organization of naked mole-rat colonies: evidence for divisions of labor. In P.W. Sherman, J.U.M. Jarvis and R.D. Alexander, eds., *The Biology of the Naked Mole-rat*. Princeton: Princeton University Press, 275–336.

Lancaster, J.B., 1971. Play-mothering: the relations between juvenile females and young infants among free-ranging vervet monkeys (*Cercopithecus aethiops*). *Folia Primatologica* 15, 161–82.

Lewis, S.E., and Pusey, A.E., 1997. Factors influencing the occurrence of communal care in plural breeding mammals. In N.G. Solomon and J.A. French, eds., *Cooperative Breeding in Mammals*. New York: Cambridge University Press, 335–63.

Ligon, J.D., and Ligon, S.H., 1978. Communal breeding in green woodhoopoes as a case for reciprocity. *Nature* 276, 496–98.

———— 1983. Reciprocity in the green woodhoopoe (*Phoeniculus purpureus*). *Animal Behaviour* 31, 480–89.

Lima, S.L., 1998. Stress and decision making under the risk of predation: recent developments from behavioral, reproductive, and ecological perspectives. *Advances in the Study of Behavior* 27, 215–90.

Lindström, J., 1999. Early development and fitness in birds and mammals. *Trends in Ecology and Evolution* 14, 343–48.

Lochmiller, R.L., Whelan, J.B., and Kirkpatrick, R.L., 1982. Energetic cost of lactation in *Microtus pinetorum*. *Journal of Mammalogy* 63, 475–81.

Lonstein, J.S., and De Vries, G.J., 2001. Social influences on parental and nonparental responses toward pups in virgin female prairie voles (*Microtus ochrogaster*). *Journal of Comparative Psychology* 115, 53–61.

Lucia, K.E., Keane, B., Hayes, L.D., Lin, Y.K., Schaefer, R.L. and Solomon, N.G., 2008. Philopatry in prairie voles: an evaluation of the habitat saturation hypothesis. *Behavioral Ecology*, 19, 774–783.

Maas, B., and Macdonald, D.W., 2004. Bat-eared foxes 'insectivory' and luck: lessons from an extreme canid. In D.W. Macdonald and C. Sillero-Zubiri, eds., *Biology and Conservation of Wild Canids*. Oxford: Oxford University Press, 227–42.

Macdonald, D.W., Creel, S., and Mills, M.G.L., 2004. Canid society. In D.W. Macdonald and C. Sillero-Zubiri, eds., *Biology and Conservation of Wild Canids*. Oxford: Oxford University Press, 85–106.

Maher, C.R., 2006. Social organization in woodchucks (*Marmota monax*) and its relationship to growing season. *Ethology* 112, 313–24.

Malcolm, J.R., and Marten, K., 1982. Natural selection and the communal rearing of pups in African wild dogs (*Lycaon pictus*). *Behavioral Ecology and Sociobiology* 10, 1–13.

Manning, C.J., Wakeland, E.K., and Potts, W.K., 1992. Communal nesting patterns in mice implicate MHC genes in kin recognition. *Nature* 360, 581–83.

Manning, C.J., Dewsbury, D.A., Wakeland, E.K., and Potts, W.K., 1995. Communal nesting and nursing in house mice, *Mus musculus domesticus*. *Animal Behaviour* 50, 741–51.

Marin, G., and Pilastro, A., 1994. Communally breeding dormice, *Glis glis*, are close kin. *Animal Behaviour* 47, 1485–87.

McGuire, B., Getz, L.L., and Oli, M.K., 2002. Fitness consequences of sociality in prairie voles, *Microtus ochrogaster:* influence of group size and composition. *Animal Behaviour* 64, 645–54.

Mennella, J.A., Blumberg, M.S., McClintock, M.K., and Moltz, H., 1990. Inter-litter competition and communal nursing among Norway rats: advantages of birth synchrony. *Behavioral Ecology and Sociobiology* 27, 183–90.

Metcalfe, N.B., and Monaghan, P., 2001. Compensation for a bad start: grow now, pay later? *Trends in Ecology and Evolution* 16, 254–60.

Mitani, J.C., and Watts, D., 1997. The evolution of non-maternal caretaking among anthropoid primates: do helpers help? *Behavioral Ecology and Sociobiology* 40, 213–20.

Moehlman, P.D., 1979. Jackal helpers and pup survival. *Nature* 277, 382–83.

Mota, M.T., and Sousa, M.B.C., 2000. Prolactin levels of fathers and helpers in relation to alloparental care in common marmosets, *Callithrix jacchus*. *Folia Primatologica* 71, 22–26.

Mota, M.T., Franci, C.R., and Sousa, M.B.C., 2006. Hormonal changes related to paternal and alloparental care in common marmosets (*Callithrix jacchus*). *Hormones and Behavior* 49, 293–302.

Mumme, R.L., 1997. A bird's eye view of mammalian cooperative breeding. In N.G. Solomon and J.A. French, eds., *Cooperative Breeding in Mammals*. New York: Cambridge University Press, 364–88.

Murphey, R.M., Paranhos Da Costa, M.J.R., Lima, L.O.S., and Duarte, F.A.M., 1991. Communal suckling in water buffalo (*Bubalus bubalis*). *Applied Animal Behavior Science* 28, 341–52.

Nelson, R.J., 2000. *An Introduction to Behavioral Endocrinology*, Second Edition. Sunderland, MA: Sinauer Associates, Inc.

Newman, J., 1995. How breast milk protects newborns, some of the molecules and cells in human milk actively help infants to stave off infection. *Scientific American* 273, 76–79.

Nicholson, N.A., 1991. Maternal behavior in human and nonhuman primates. In J.D. Loy and C.B. Peters, eds., *Understanding Behavior: What Primate Studies tell us about Human Behavior*. New York: Oxford University Press, 17–50.

Numan, M., and Insel, T.R., 2003. *The Neurobiology of Parental Behavior*. New York: Springer-Verlag.

Oster, G.F., and Wilson, E.O., 1978. *Caste and Ecology in the Social Insects*. Princeton: Princeton University Press.

Owens, D.D., and Owens, M.J., 1984. Helping behaviour in brown hyenas. *Nature* 308, 843–45.

Packer, C., Lewis, S., and Pusey, A., 1992. A comparative analysis of non-offspring nursing. *Animal Behaviour* 43, 265–81.

Pilastro, A., 1992. Communal nesting between breeding females in a free-living population of fat dormouse (*Glis glis* L). *Bollettino di Zoologia* 59, 63–68.

Pilastro, A., Missiaglia, E., and Marin, G., 1996. Age-related reproductive success in solitarily and communally nesting female dormice (*Glis glis*). *Journal of Zoology, London* 239, 601–8.

Plesner-Jensen, S., Siefert, L., Okori, J.L.L., and Clutton-Brock, T.H., 1999. Age-related participation in allosuckling by nursing warthogs (*Phacochoerus africanus*). *Journal of Zoology, London* 248, 443–49.

Powell, R.A., and Fried, J.J., 1992. Helping by juvenile pine voles (*Microtus pinetorum*), growth and survival of younger siblings, and the evolution of pine vole sociality. *Behavioral Ecology* 3, 325–33.

Price, E.C., 1990. Infant carrying as a courtship strategy of breeding male cotton-top tamarins. *Animal Behaviour* 40, 784–86.

———— 1992. The costs of infant carrying in cotton-top tamarins. *American Journal of Primatology* 26, 23–33.

Pryce, C.R., 1993. The regulation of maternal behaviour in marmosets and tamarins. *Behavioural Processes* 30, 201–24.

Pusey, A.E., and Packer, C., 1994. Non-offspring nursing in social carnivores: minimizing the costs. *Behavioral Ecology* 5, 362–74.

Roberts, R.L., Zullo, A., Gustafson, E.A., and Carter, C.S., 1996. Perinatal steroid treatments alter alloparental and affiliative behavior in prairie voles. *Hormones and Behavior* 30, 576–82.

Roberts, R.L., Miller, A.K., Taymans, S.E., and Carter, C.S., 1998. Role of social and endocrine factors in alloparental behavior of prairie voles (*Microtus ochrogaster*). *Canadian Journal of Zoology* 76, 1862–68.

Roberts, R.L., Jenkins, K.T., Lawler, T., Wegner, F.H., Norcross, J.L., Bernhards, D.E., and Newman, J.D., 2001a. Prolactin levels are elevated after infant carrying in parentally inexperienced common marmosets. *Physiology and Behavior* 72, 713–20.

———— 2001b. Bromocriptine administration lowers serum prolactin and disrupts parental responsiveness in common marmosets (*Callithrix j. jacchus*). *Hormones and Behavior* 39, 106–12.

Ross, C., and Maclarnon, A., 2000. The evolution of non-maternal care in anthropoid primates: a test of the hypotheses. *Folia Primatologica* 71, 93–113.

Rothe, H., Darms, K., Koenig, A., Radespiel, U., and Juenemann, B., 1993. Long-term study of infant-carrying behaviour in captive common marmosets (*Callithrix jacchus*): effect of nonreproductive helpers on the parents' carrying performance. *International Journal of Primatology* 14, 79–93.

Roulin, A., 2002. Why do lactating females nurse alien offspring? A review of hypotheses and empirical evidence. *Animal Behaviour* 63, 201–8.

Roulin, A., and Heeb, P., 1999. The immunological function of allosuckling. *Ecology Letters* 2, 319–24.

Rowell, T.E., Hinde, R.A., and Spencer-Booth, Y., 1964. 'Aunt'-infant interaction in captive rhesus monkeys. *Animal Behaviour* 12, 219–26.

Russell, A.F., Clutton-Brock, T.H., Brotherton, P.N.M., Sharpe, L.L., McIlrath, G.M., Dalerum, F.D., Cameron, E.Z., and Barnard, J.A., 2002. Factors affecting pup growth and survival in co-operatively breeding meerkats *Suricata suricatta*. *Journal of Animal Ecology* 71, 700–9.

Russell, A.F., Brotherton, P.N.M., McIlrath, G.M., Sharpe, L.L., and Clutton-Brock, T.H., 2003a. Breeding success in cooperative meerkats: effects of helper number and maternal state. *Behavioral Ecology* 14, 486–92.

———— 2003b. Cost minimization by helpers in cooperative vertebrates. *Proceedings of the National Academy of Sciences, U.S.A.* 100, 3333–38.

Russell, A.F., Young, A.J., Spong, G., Jordan, N.R., and Clutton-Brock, T.H., 2007. Helpers increase the reproductive potential of offspring in cooperative meerkats. *Proceedings of the Royal Society B* 274, 513–20.

Salo, A.L., and French, J.A., 1989. Early experience, reproductive success, and development of parental behaviour in Mongolian gerbils. *Animal Behaviour* 38, 693–702.

Sánchez, S., Peláez, F., Gil-Bürmann, C., and Kaumanns, W., 1999. Costs of infant-carrying in cotton-top tamarins (*Saguinus oedipus*). *American Journal of Primatology* 48, 99–111.

Sayler, A., and Salmon, M., 1969. Communal nursing in mice: influence of multiple mothers on the growth of the young. *Science* 164, 1309–10.

Scantlebury, M., Russell, A.F., McIlrath, G.M., Speakman, J.R., and Clutton-Brock, T.H., 2002. The energetics of lactation in cooperatively breeding meerkats *Suricata suricatta*. *Proceedings of the Royal Society B* 269, 2147–53.

Schradin, C., 2008. Seasonal changes in testosterone and corticosterone levels in four social classes of a desert dwelling sociable rodent. *Hormones and Behavior* 53, 573–79.

Schradin, C., and Anzenberger, G., 2001. Costs of infant carrying in common marmosets, *Callithrix jacchus*: an experimental analysis. *Animal Behaviour* 62, 289–95.

————— 2004. Development of prolactin levels in marmoset males: from adult son to first-time father. *Hormones and Behavior* 46, 670–77.

Schradin, C., and Pilay, N., 2005. Intraspecific variation in the spatial and social organization of the African striped mouse. *Journal of Mammalogy* 86, 99–107.

Schradin, C., Reeder, D.M., Mendoza, S.P., and Anzenberger, G., 2003. Prolactin and parental care: comparison of three species of monogamous New World monkeys (*Callicebus cupreus, Callithrix jacchus,* and *Callimico goeldii*). *Journal of Comparative Psychology* 117, 166–75.

Sherman, P.W., Lacey, E.A., Reeve, H.K., and Keller, L., 1995. The eusociality continuum. *Behavioral Ecology* 6, 102–8.

Sillero-Zubiri, C., Marino, J., Gottelli, D., and Macdonald, D.W., 2004. Afroalpine ecology, solitary foraging, and intense sociality amongst Ethiopian wolves. In D.W. Macdonald and C. Sillero-Zubiri, eds., *Biology and Conservation of Wild Canids*. Oxford: Oxford University Press, 311–22.

Skutch, A.F., 1935. Helpers at the nest. *Auk* 52, 257–73.

————— 1961. Helpers among birds. *Condor* 63, 198–226.

Solomon, N.G., 1991. Current indirect fitness benefits associated with philopatry in juvenile prairie voles. *Behavioral Ecology and Sociobiology* 29, 277–82.

————— 2003. A reexamination of factors influencing philopatry in rodents. *Journal of Mammalogy* 84, 1182–97.

Solomon, N.G., and Crist, T.O., 2008. Estimates of reproductive success for group-living prairie voles, *Microtus ochrogaster,* in high density populations. *Animal Behaviour* 76, 881–892.

Solomon, N.G., and French, J.A., 1997. *Cooperative Breeding in Mammals*. New York: Cambridge University Press.

Solomon, N.G., and Getz, L.L., 1997. Examination of alternative hypotheses for cooperative breeding in rodents. In N.G. Solomon and J.A. French, eds., *Cooperative Breeding in Mammals*. New York: Cambridge University Press, 199–230.

Stacey, P.B., and Koenig, W.D., eds., 1990. *Cooperative Breeding in Birds: Long Term Studies of Ecology and Behaviour*. Cambridge: Cambridge University Press.

Storey, A.E., Walsh, C.J., Quinton, R.L., and Wynne-Edwards, K.E., 2000. Hormonal correlates of paternal responsiveness in new and expectant fathers. *Evolution and Human Behavior* 21, 79–95.

Taborsky, M., and Limberger, D., 1981. Helpers in fish. *Behavioral Ecology and Sociobiology* 8, 143–45.

Tardif, S.D., 1997. The bioenergetics of parental behavior and the evolution of alloparental care in marmosets and tamarins. In N.G. Solomon and J.A. French, eds., *Cooperative Breeding in Mammals*. New York: Cambridge University Press, 11–33.

Tardif, S.D., and Bales, K., 1997. Is infant-carrying a courtship strategy in callitrichid primates? *Animal Behaviour* 53, 1001–7.

Tinbergen, N., 1963. On the aims and methods of ethology. *Zeitshrift fur Tierpsychologie* 20, 410–33.

Trivers, R.L., 1971. The evolution of reciprocal altruism. *Quarterly Review of Biology* 46, 35–57.

Wang, Z., and Insel, T.R., 1996. Parental behavior in voles. *Advances in the Study of Behavior* 25, 361–84

Wang, Z., and Novak, M.A., 1992. Influence of the social environment on parental behavior and pup development of meadow voles (*Microtus pennsylvanicus*) and prairie voles (*M. ochrogaster*). *Journal of Comparative Psychology* 106, 163–71.

Waser, P.M., 1988. Resources, philopatry, and social interactions among mammals. In C.N. Slobodchikoff, ed., *The Ecology of Social Behavior*. San Diego: Academic Press Inc., 109–30.

Werboff, J., Steg, M., and Barnes, L., 1970. Communal nursing in mice: strain-specific effects of multiple mothers on growth and behavior. *Psychonomic Science* 19, 269–71.

Whitehead, H., 1996. Babysitting, dive synchrony, and indications of alloparental care in sperm whales. *Behavioral Ecology and Sociobiology* 38, 237–44.

Wilkinson, G.S., 1987. Altruism and cooperation in bats. In M.B. Fenton, P.A. Racey and J.M.V. Rayner, eds., *Recent Advances in the Study of Bats*. Cambridge: Cambridge University Press, 299–323.

——— 1992. Communal nursing in the evening bat, *Nycticeius humeralis*. *Behavioral Ecology and Sociobiology* 31, 225–35.

Wilkinson, G.S., and Baker, A.E.M., 1988. Communal nesting among genetically similar house mice. *Ethology* 77, 103–14.

Wilson, E.O., 1971. *The Insect Societies*. Cambridge, MA: Belknap Press.

——— 1975. *Sociobiology*. Cambridge, MA: Belknap Press.

Winterhalder, B., and Smith, E.A., 1992. Evolutionary ecology and social sciences. In E.A. Smith and B. Winterhalder, eds., *Evolutionary Ecology and Human Behavior*. New York: Aldine de Gruyter, 3–23.

Wolff, J.O., 1994. Reproductive success of solitarily and communally nesting white-footed and deer mice. *Behavioral Ecology* 5, 206–9.

Wynne-Edwards, K.E., 2003. From dwarf hamster to daddy: the intersection of ecology, evolution, and physiology that produces paternal behavior. *Advances in the Study of Behavior* 32, 207–61.

Wynne-Edwards, K.E., and Timonin, M.E., 2007. Paternal care in rodents: weakening support for hormonal regulation of the transition to behavioral fatherhood in rodent animal models of biparental care. *Hormones and Behavior* 52, 114–21.

Wynne-Edwards, V.C., 1962. *Animal Dispersion in Relation to Social Behaviour.* Edinburgh: Oliver and Boyd.

Zahavi, A., 1990. Arabian babblers: The quest for social status in a cooperative breeder. In P.B. Stacey and W.D. Koenig, eds., *Cooperative breeding in birds: long term studies of ecology and behaviour.* Cambridge: Cambridge University Press, 103–30.

Ziegler, T.E., 2000. Hormones associated with non-maternal infant care: a review of mammalian and avian studies. *Folia Primatologica* 71, 6–21.

Ziegler, T.E., Wegner, F.H., and Snowden, S.T., 1996. Hormonal responses to parental and nonparental conditions in male cotton-top tamarins, *Saguinus oedipus*, a New World primate. *Hormones and Behavior* 30, 287–97.

• 3 •

Family Matters

Kin, Demography and Child Health in a Rural Gambian Population

Rebecca Sear and Ruth Mace

The Evolutionary Basis of Alloparental Care

Alloparental care is a rare phenomenon (Clutton-Brock 1991). The costs of investing in another individual's offspring usually outweigh any potential benefits gained through inclusive fitness (increasing one's reproductive success by helping genetically related individuals survive and reproduce) or reciprocation (where the benefits derive from the recipient of the helping behaviour returning the favour in the future). But the human species appears to be one of the few mammalian examples where alloparenting is common. In traditional societies, mothers often receive help from their relatives in raising children. In post-industrial societies, help is often bought in or provided by the state. In this study, we focus on a traditional society, and assume inclusive fitness arguments largely provide an explanation for allocare. Hamilton's rule states that help will be provided to recipients by their relatives, provided that the costs of helping are less than the benefits to the recipient, discounted by the degree of relatedness between recipient and donor:

$$rb>c$$

where r represents the coefficient of relatedness (the probability that any gene will be shared by recipient and donor), b the benefits of helping and c the costs (Hamilton 1964). For allocare to become common between a given set of relatives, the benefits of allocare (b) must be relatively high, the costs (c) relatively low, or both.

The particular features of human life history mean that the benefits of helping are likely to be relatively high, while the costs are relatively low. Human infants are altricial compared to other primates, and require many years of investment before they become self-sufficient in food production. Any help provided by relatives to the mother may therefore yield large benefits both in terms of the survival and well-being of the child, and in enabling the mother to speed up her reproductive rate. The unusual human female life history may also make the costs of helping relatively low. The long pre-reproductive and, in particular, the long post-reproductive period of women's lives means that there is a large pool of potential helpers who are available to help. These non-reproductive helpers will face no conflicts of interest in helping raise another woman's offspring since they are unable to have children of their own.

Note that in the last paragraph we have discussed the help that human *mothers* receive from kin in raising offspring, rather than human parents. Strictly speaking, paternal care is not considered alloparenting since fathers are also parents of the child. But paternal care is unusual, particularly among mammals, and requires explanation (Clutton-Brock 1991). In the majority of primate species, mothers receive little or no help from males in raising their young (though there are exceptions, such as siamang and callitrichids: Chivers 1974; Goldizen 1987). The human species is often cited as an example where paternal investment is high (e.g., Geary 2000). But given the cross-cultural variation in paternal involvement (Draper and Harpending 1982; Hewlett 1992), we do not take paternal care for granted, and for the remainder of the chapter will discuss allomaternal, rather than alloparental, care.

We have suggested that allomaternal care has large benefits and low costs in the human species because of the peculiarities of the human life history. But an idea of long-standing influence is that the causal arrow may point in the opposite direction: rather than allomaternal care arising because of the features of human life history, it is the human life history that has been shaped by the benefits of allomaternal care. The large brain of the human baby, necessitating an altricial birth and long period of dependence, has required human mothers to rely on other relatives in order to raise children successfully to adulthood. This help then allowed to women to have relatively short inter-birth intervals, compared to the other great apes (Galdikas and Wood 1990), since they could delegate the care of weaned children to other individuals. For many years the dominant hypothesis was that paternal provisioning with high calorie meat has shaped human life histories, by relieving women of the burden of feeding so many dependent children simultaneously (Washburn and Lancaster 1968; Lovejoy 1981). More recent research has suggested that behaviours such as hunting, which were initially interpreted as paternal investment, may be mating effort instead and that men contribute relatively little to raising children (Hawkes 1990). Direct childcare by fathers is certainly rare, though there is some cross-cultural variation, and frequently dwarfed by the amount of childcare done by the mother's female relatives (Waynforth 2002). This leads us to the alternative hypothesis that has been proposed to explain the unusual features of human female life history: that it can be explained by help from the mother's relatives, particularly their own mothers and elder daughters. The 'grandmother hypothesis' suggests that the long post-reproductive lifespan of women evolved so that older women could invest in their grandchildren (e.g., Alvarez 2000; Hawkes 2003). This hypothesis simultaneously explains both the short inter-birth intervals of human females, and the most unusual feature of human female life history – menopause. Pre-reproductive offspring may also act as 'helpers at the nest' enabling women to raise more children than they would be able to support alone (Lee and Kramer 2002; Kramer, this volume).

Though these ideas about the importance of kin to the evolution of human life history have been around for several decades (Williams 1957; Hamilton 1966), only relatively recently has empirical investigation of the impact of kin on demographic outcomes begun in earnest. If kin do contribute significantly to childcare or child provisioning, then this leads to the testable predictions that child survival and growth rates and/or female fertility rates should be higher in the presence of fathers, grandmothers or other helpers. During the late 1980s and 90s this prediction began to be tested in contemporary populations by evolutionary ecologists (see Turke 1988 and Hill and Hurtado 1991 for early examples). Among the pioneers of this research, Hawkes and colleagues, working with Hadza hunter-gatherers in Tanzania, have been influential in promoting the idea that grandmothers have important roles to play in provisioning children (Hawkes, O'Connell and Blurton Jones 1989, 1997; Hawkes, O'Connell and Jones 2001). Hill and Hurtado, working on Ache hunter-gatherers in South America, broadly represent the 'men matter' point of view, having found little evidence that grandmothers make a difference to demographic patterns (Hill and Hurtado 1991, 1996). Investment from the father does not necessarily preclude investment from female relatives, or vice versa. Both fathers and female kin may help mothers out, though the roles they play may differ. Marlowe, for example, has suggested that men may enable forager women to increase their fertility rates, though they may have no impact on child survival (Marlowe 2001). These hunter-gatherer studies have led to a recent explosion of interest investigating the effects of kin on various demographic outcomes across a variety of ecological niches (Bereczkei 1998; Sear, Mace and McGregor 2000; Crognier, Baali and Hilali 2001; Quinlan 2001; Sear et al. 2002; Sorenson Jamison et al. 2002; Voland and Beise 2002; Waynforth 2002; Reher and González-Quiñones 2003; Sear 2008; Sear, Mace and McGregor 2003; Lahdenpera et al. 2004; Leonetti and Nath 2004; Tymicki 2004; Beise 2005; Leonetti et al. 2005).

Here we draw together research we have conducted over the last few years to investigate the effects of relatives on demographic outcomes, using an unusually rich database from a farming community in rural Gambia. This database, which includes a combination of demographic, anthropometric and genealogical data, has allowed us to analyse the effects of kin on a number of life history characteristics, including both child outcomes and fertility patterns. We demonstrate that kin are important to all the components of reproductive success that we have looked at, but that different relatives have different roles to play in a woman's reproductive life.

A Unique Long-term Database from Rural Gambia

The data we use here were collected by Ian McGregor under the auspices of the U.K. Medical Research Council (McGregor and Smith 1952; McGregor 1991). The main focus of this research program was to study tropical disease, but McGregor's holistic approach to research resulted in the collection of an impressive array of data from the inhabitants of four villages in rural Gambia. The longitudinal nature of this project makes it a particularly useful data source. Demographic data have been continuously collected since 1950, and McGregor conducted anthropometric surveys at least annually between 1950 and 1980. He also collected genealogical information, which allows us to match individuals with their parents, grandparents, siblings, children and other relatives.

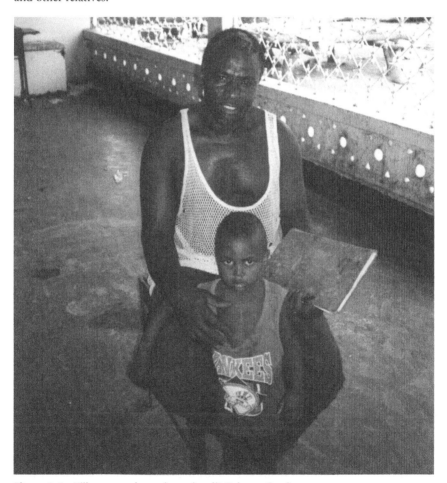

Figure 3.1. Village recorder and son (credit Rebecca Sear).

Between 1950 and 1974 this was a natural fertility population which had little access to medical care or contraception, though McGregor (a medical doctor) did treat individuals as necessary during the annual surveys. Both fertility and mortality were high during this period. Women gave birth to around seven children on average, but almost 50 per cent of these children died before the age of five years (Billewicz and McGregor 1981). In 1975, a permanent research station was set up by the MRC Dunn Nutrition Unit, who began to conduct research in this area in that year. Though data collection continues at this research station today, we have restricted our analysis to the earlier, natural fertility period between 1950 and 1974 (with a single exception, noted below). The permanent research station, which provides free medical services to all villagers, has had significant effects on both the demography and economy of these villages (Lamb et al. 1984; Weaver and Beckerleg 1993; Beckerleg, Austin and Weaver 1994; Sear 2001).

The villagers were patrilineal, patrilocal, Muslim and predominantly of the Mandinka ethnic group. Polygyny was widespread, and divorce and remarriage were also common, so that women as well as men may have had a number of marital partners during their reproductive lives (Thompson 1965). Though women did eventually move to their husbands' compounds after marriage, they often remained in their natal homes until after the birth of a child or two. Most women married within their village of birth (80 per cent), or one of the neighbouring villages (11 per cent), so that both their own parents, as well as their spouse's parents, would have been readily available during the marriage. Ethnographic evidence suggests that mothers did receive help in raising children in this society (Thompson and Rahman 1967). Older women and pre-adolescent children helped women out with direct childcare. Fathers did no childcare, but could potentially contribute to child well-being through productive work.

This was primarily a subsistence agriculture community. Women were responsible for a substantial proportion of subsistence farming. Men did some subsistence farming and a little cash-cropping of groundnuts. The environment was highly seasonal. Villagers suffered considerably from outbreaks of infectious and parasitic disease during the rainy season, which was also the season of low food availability and hard subsistence labour. These Gambian individuals were relatively short and light compared to Western standards. Women were 158 cm tall and weighed 51 kg on average; men averaged 168 cm and 58 kg. The growth (and growth faltering) of the children in these villages has been well documented both by McGregor and by the MRC Dunn Nutrition Unit (e.g., McGregor et al. 1968; Billewicz and McGregor 1982; Poskitt, Cole and Whitehead 1999).

How Do We Estimate Whether Kin Are Helpful?

We have conducted statistical analysis comparing child growth and survival rates in the presence and absence of various categories of kin in order to infer patterns of helping behaviour in this population. We also want to know whether kin have effects on other reproductive outcomes. So we have examined the effects of kin on female reproduction in this community: comparing age at first birth and female fertility rates in the presence and absence of kin. The measures used and the statistical techniques employed are outlined below.

Child Survival

We used event history analysis (EHA) to analyse the effects of kin on child survival over the first five years of the child's life (see Sear et al. 2000, 2002 for further details). Relatively few children died after the age of five years, so we were unable to identify any effects of kin after this age. EHA models the probability of an event happening over time, and is particularly useful for this analysis as it allows the inclusion of time-dependent covariates, such as the presence or absence of kin (Allison 1984). Multi-level discrete-time EHA was performed using MLwiN (Rasbash et al. 2000). Most mothers had several children entered into the analysis, and the survival probabilities of siblings are known to be correlated (e.g., Curtis and Steele 1996). Multi-level models were necessary to control for this non-independence of datapoints. The models controlled for sex of child, maternal age, parity, length of preceding and succeeding birth intervals, village of birth and whether the child was lastborn.

The determinants of child mortality change over the first five years of the child's life: endogenous causes predominate in the first year of life, exogenous causes after infancy. Relatives are also likely to be important at different ages: mothers being of paramount importance while children are still dependent on breastmilk, but other relatives having opportunities to take over the care of older children. To control for these potential confounds, we divided the first five years into three periods: infancy (under 12 months), toddlerhood (12–23 months) and older childhood (24–59 months) and ran the analysis separately on each age group. Sample sizes for the infant, toddler and childhood analyses were 2,294, 1,664 and 1,341 children respectively.

We analysed the effects of the following relatives on child mortality: mothers, fathers, maternal grandmothers and grandfathers, paternal grandmothers and grandfathers, elder sisters and elder brothers of the child. For parents and grandparents, we entered the survival status of each category of kin into each model as a time-dependent categorical variable: kin were coded as alive until the point that they died, and were coded as dead after that point. We also included a dummy variable for missing data for each category of kin. Though we are describing these variables as the 'survival status' of kin, we are effectively constructing variables for the presence or absence of kin in the child's village or one of the neighbouring three villages. We only have information on those individuals who lived in these four villages at some time between 1950 and 1974. 'Missing' relatives are therefore likely to be either those who died before 1950 or who are living in a village some distance from the child's village. Those relatives coded as 'alive' are thus only those who were alive and living in the same or nearby village as the child.

The elder sisters and elder brothers' variables were included as time-dependent dichotomous variables, coded for whether or not the child had any sisters or brothers who were at least ten years older than the child. We restricted this variable to siblings at least ten years older as these siblings are likely to be the most useful carers of the child, and are less likely to be in competition with the child for parental resources than siblings closer in age.

We also tested whether the mother's remarriage to a new husband increased a child's mortality risk, as step-parents have been shown to be a risk factor for child death in other studies (Daly and Wilson 1988; but see Temrin, Nordlund and Sterner 2004). This variable was only included in the later childhood model as few remarriages occurred when women had very young children.

Child Anthropometric Status

The death of a child is an extreme outcome and may be a relatively crude measure of allomaternal investment. Analysing other child outcomes, such as anthropometric status, may allow a more sensitive investigation of the effects of alloparents on child health. Analysing this measure of child health also allows us to investigate the effects of kin beyond the first five years of life. We used multi-level linear regression to determine the effects of relatives on three measures of child anthropometric status: height, weight and haemoglobin level. All three measures should indicate the child's level of health: children who are poorly nourished and suffer frequent infections will be shorter, lighter and should have lower haemoglobin levels than those in better health (McGregor et al. 1966; Rowland, Cole and Whitehead 1977). All three models controlled for: age, sex, whether the child was a twin, village, season and cohort of birth, maternal age and parity. The height model controlled for both maternal and paternal height, the weight model for maternal and paternal weight and the haemoglobin model for maternal and paternal haemoglobin.

Because of the longitudinal nature of the dataset, most individuals have a number of measurements taken at different ages. We included all measurements in our models, and performed multi-level models to control for these repeated measurements, as measurements from the same individual will be highly correlated. We tested whether mothers, fathers, maternal grandmothers and grandfathers, and paternal grandmothers and grandfathers had any impact on child anthropometric status. We also included variables for the number of living elder sisters and brothers, and whether the mother had remarried a new husband. In each analysis, approximately 28,000 measurements were included from 3,960 children.

Age at First Birth

EHA was used to model the probability of a woman having a first birth between the ages of thirteen and twenty-five years (no woman had a first birth earlier than thirteen, and first births after the age of twenty-five were considered unlikely given that women were married at menarche in this population. See Allal et al. 2004 for further details). For all the EHA analyses we have measured time in months, rather than years, in order to increase the sensitivity of the analysis. This means that for the first birth analysis, we needed to know both the woman's date of birth and her age at first birth by month and year. We only have this information on month of birth for women born in 1950 or later, so for this analysis only we included all data collected by the MRC to 2001 in order to obtain a reasonable sample size. Age at first birth has not been as dramatically affected as child mortality by the presence of the permanent research station, but has started to decline in recent years. We have included a variable for birth cohort in the model to control for this effect. This model also controls for the woman's anthropometric status, which is strongly related to age at first birth, as well as village and season of birth. 437 women were included in the analysis. For this analysis, we tested for any effects of the woman's mother, father and elder brothers and sisters on her age at first birth.

Reproductive Rate

Finally, we investigated the effects of kin on female reproductive rates. Again, we used discrete-time EHA. In this case we modelled the probability of a birth over time since a previous birth, effectively investigating the impact of kin on the length of birth intervals (Sear et al. 2003). Multi-level models were again used as most women had several different birth intervals included in the analysis, and women are known to differ in their fecundability. This model controlled for the following factors known to affect fertility: survival status of the index child (born at the start of the interval), maternal age and parity. We tested for the effects of the woman's mother and father, her husband's mother and father, whether the women herself had elder living brothers and sisters, and whether she had living daughters and sons at least ten years older than the index child. 2,532 birth intervals from 765 women were included in the analysis.

Which Kin Matter?

The Effects of Kin on Child Survival

Relatives are clearly important to child survival over the first five years of the child's life, but different relatives are important at different ages. Table 3.1 shows the results of the multi-level models of infant, toddler and child mortality. For the parent and grandparent 'dead' category, the odds ratios illustrate the risk of death for a child whose relative has died, compared to the risks for children with a living relative. In infancy, mothers are the only relative to exert any impact on child survival rates. Mothers are vitally important at this age: of the 13 children who lost their mothers before reaching the age of one year, 12 died (the only survivor was 11 months old when she lost her mother – all the others lost their mothers at an earlier age). This is reflected in the highly statistically significant relationship between mother's death and infant death. During the first year of life, children who have lost their mothers have risks of dying which are more than six times greater than those with living mothers.

Table 3.1. Results of multi-level event history analysis showing effects of kin on child mortality (separate models shown for infant, toddler and later childhood mortality).

Variable	Infant			Toddler			Later childhood		
	Estimate	(SE)	Odds ratio	Estimate	(SE)	Odds ratio	Estimate	(SE)	Odds ratio
Constant	−3.35	(0.35)**		−5.02	(0.58)**		−3.52	(0.47)**	
Mother:									
Dead	1.82	(0.51)**	6.2	1.66	(0.61)**	5.2	0.35	(0.56)	1.4
Alive	0		1.0	0		1.0	0		1.0
Father:									
Dead	0.13	(0.61)	1.1	−0.73	(0.73)	0.5	−0.33	(0.39)	0.7
Alive	0		1.0	0		1.0	0		1.0
Maternal grandmother:									
Dead	0.13	(0.19)	1.1	0.55	(0.27)*	1.7	−0.09	(0.26)	0.9
Alive	0		1.0	0		1.0	0		1.0
Paternal grandmother:									
Dead	−0.25	(0.19)	0.8	−0.17	(0.24)	0.8	−0.05	(0.23)	0.9
Alive	0		1.0	0		1.0	0		1.0
Maternal grandfather:									
Dead	0.07	(0.18)	1.1	0.28	(0.26)	1.3	0.01	(0.24)	1.0
Alive	0		1.0	0		1.0	0		1.0
Paternal grandfather:									
Dead	0.28	(0.16)	1.3	−0.05	(0.38)	0.9	−0.29	(0.21)	0.7
Alive	0		1.0	0		1.0	0		1.0
Living sisters 10+ years older:									
Yes	−0.03	(0.18)	1.0	−0.07	(0.25)	0.9	−0.48	(0.24)*	0.6
No	0		1.0	0		1.0	0		1.0
Living brothers 10+ years older									
Yes	0.06	(0.19)	1.1	−0.22	(0.26)	0.8	−0.30	(0.24)	0.7
No	0		1.0	0		1.0	0		1.0
Mother remarried:									
Yes	−	−		−	−		0.65	(0.27)*	1.9
No									1.0
Mother level variance	0.39*	0.16		0.36	0.28		0.44*	0.12	

* p < 0.05, ** p < 0.01. All models control for sex of child, maternal age, parity, length of preceding and succeeding birth intervals, village of birth and whether the child was lastborn

Figure 3.2. Mother and son (credit Nadine Allal).

Mothers are also important during the second year of the child's life, though the odds ratio is slightly lower (5.2). But at this age, maternal grandmothers also have a significant impact on child survival (Figure 3.3). Children without maternal grandmothers are 1.7 times more likely to die than children with maternal grandmothers. Neither the loss of the mother nor maternal grandmother appears to affect child survival after the age of two years, but elder sisters are able to improve child survival rates between 2–5 years. Children with living elder sisters at least ten years older have risks of dying which are only 0.6 times as great as those without sisters. This effect is independent of the sex of the child (an interaction term between elder sisters and sex of child is not significant – results not shown). Fathers, paternal grandmothers, elder brothers and grandfathers do not have any impact on child survival at any age. However, remarriage of the mother to a new husband did increase the risk of mortality for children between 2–5 years.

The Effects of Kin on Children's Anthropometric Status

Table 3.2 shows the results of the analysis of child height, weight and haemoglobin level. Here a negative parameter estimate indicates the anthropometric status is lower in the absence of a particular relative. These analyses provide further evidence that mothers, maternal grandmothers and elder sisters are important for improving child outcomes. The absence of a mother or maternal grandmother results in lower anthropometric status for children in all three models, though for both categories of kin this is only significant in the case of height. There is a consistently positive effect of the

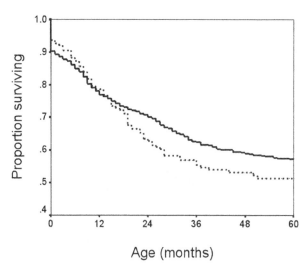

Figure 3.3. Kaplan–Meier plot showing the effect of maternal grandmothers on child mortality. Solid line shows children with living maternal grandmothers, dotted line children without maternal grandmothers.

Figure 3.4. Grandmother and grandson (credit Rebecca Sear).

Figure 3.5. Children playing (credit Rebecca Sear).

number of elder sisters on child height, weight and haemoglobin. This is significant for height at the 5 per cent level, and marginally significant (p<0.1) for haemoglobin level. Height is a measure indicating long-term anthropometric status, less susceptible to fluctuations due to temporary food shortage or illness than either weight or haemoglobin. Kin effects on weight and haemoglobin may be washed out by other fluctuations in these measurements, at least when the whole fifteen-year period of childhood is considered in a single model.

There is little evidence that male and paternal kin are beneficial for child health. Fathers, paternal grandmothers and grandfathers have inconsistent effects on child growth across the three measures of anthropometric status. Fathers and paternal grandmothers have no significant effects on anthropometric status in any model. The lack of a paternal grandfather has a significant positive effect on height (i.e. children without paternal grandfathers are significantly taller than those with paternal grandfathers), but non-significant and negative effects on weight and haemoglobin level. The lack of the maternal grandfather also has a significant positive effect on height but a significant negative effect on weight, and a negative but non-significant effect on haemoglobin level. There appear to be no detrimental effects of remarriage to a new husband on child anthropometric status, when all fifteen years of childhood are considered.

Table 3.2. Results of multi-level regression models showing effects of kin on child anthropometric status (separate models shown for child height, weight and haemoglobin level)

Variable	Height Estimate	(SE)	Weight Estimate	(SE)	Haemoglobin Estimate	(SE)
Constant	7.05	(3.33)**	–8.49	(0.42)**	6.85	(0.31)**
Mother dead	–0.63	(0.29)*	–0.11	(0.10)	–0.09	(0.09)
Father dead	–0.25	(0.19)	–0.04	(0.06)	0.09	(0.06)
Maternal grandmother dead	–0.55	(0.19)*	–0.02	(0.06)	–0.05	(0.05)
Paternal grandmother dead	0.18	(0.18)	–0.02	(0.06)	–0.03	(0.05)
Maternal grandfather dead	0.39	(0.17)*	–0.27	(0.06)*	–0.03	(0.05)
Paternal grandfather dead	0.65	(0.22)*	-0.08	(0.07)	–0.18	(0.06)
Living sisters	0.19	(0.09)*	0.02	(0.03)	0.04	(0.02)†
Living brothers	–0.20	(0.09)*	–0.07	(0.03)*	–0.01	(0.02)
Mother remarried	0.18	(0.34)	0.02	(0.11)	–0.09	(0.08)
Child level variance	17.91	0.52**	1.87	(0.06)**	0.75	(0.03)**

† $p < 0.1$, * $p < 0.05$, ** $p < 0.01$. All models control for age, sex, whether the child was a twin, village, season and cohort of birth, maternal age and parity, and parental anthropometric status

The number of elder brothers has a consistent negative effect on child growth, significantly so in the case of both height and weight. The effects of both elder brothers and elder sisters were independent of the sex of the child. Interactions between the elder sibling variables and child sex were included in initial models, but dropped because they were not significant. Note that the elder sibling variables are coded as number of elder siblings rather than as a dichotomous variable, as with the other categories of kin (so that a positive estimate means a positive relationship between the number of elder siblings and anthropometric status).

Do Kin Affect Age at First Birth?

In contrast to the analysis of child outcomes, female kin don't appear to make any difference to the age at which a woman has her first birth. Table 3.3 shows the results of the EHA of women's first births. In this table, the odds ratios for parents indicate

Table 3.3. Results of event history analysis showing effects of kin on female age at first birth (adapted from Allal et al 2004)

Variable	Odds ratio
Mother:	
Dead	1
Alive	0.95
Father:	
Dead	1
Alive	1.27[†]
Elder siblings:	
None	1
More sisters than brothers	0.95
More brothers than sisters	1.48*
Same number brothers and sisters	0.90
Missing data on birth order	0.96
Missing data on sibling sex	0.60*

[†] $p < 0.1$, * $p < 0.05$. Model controls for birth cohort, anthropometric status, village and season of birth

the likelihood of having a first birth per unit time if the parent is living compared to cases where the parent is dead. Higher odds ratios therefore mean a younger age at first birth, lower odds ratios an older age at first birth. There is no significant effect of mothers, but there is a marginally significant (p=0.062) effect of fathers: women with living fathers have earlier first births than those without. Elder brothers also matter for women's age at first birth. Women with more elder brothers than sisters have relatively early first births compared to women with no elder siblings.

Do Kin Affect Fertility Rate?

Once again, kin matter for this reproductive outcome. Table 3.4 shows the results of the fertility EHA. Parameter estimates and standard errors only, and not odds ratios, are presented in Table 3.4. When performing EHA it is important to test for significant interactions between each variable of interest and time (in this case, time since last birth) to ensure that the assumption these models make of proportional hazards is not violated. These interactions were not significant in previous analyses so were dropped from the final models. A number of interactions with time were significant in this fertility model, so were retained in the final model. These interactions make the odds ratios hard to interpret, so they have not been presented here. Time in this analysis was modelled as a quadratic function, so interactions with both time (which is indicated by the 'month' variable) and time squared were included.

Table 3.4. Results of multi-level event history analysis showing the effects of kin on female fertility

Variable	Estimate	SE
Constant	–9.86	(0.27)**
Mother alive	–0.01	(0.15)
Mother*month	–0.04	(0.02)*
Mother*month^2	0.001	(0.0003)*
Father alive	0.08	(0.08)
Husband's mother alive	0.21	(0.08)**
Husband's father alive	–0.80	(0.11)*
Husband's father*month	0.10	(0.03)**
Husband's father*month^2	–0.002	(0.0008)**
Elder brothers	–0.22	(0.09)*
Elder sisters	0.06	(0.09)
Living sons at least 10 yrs older than index child	0.68	(0.19)**
Sons*month	–0.03	0.006)**
Living daughters at least 10 yrs older than index child	–0.49	(0.13)**
Daughters*sex of child	0.44	(0.16)**
Woman level variance	0.27	(0.04)*

* $p < 0.05$, ** $p < 0.01$. Model controls for survival status of the index child (born at the start of the interval), maternal age and parity

There are no significant effects of having either a living mother or father on the probability of birth. There is a significant interaction between having a living mother and time suggesting the effects of the mother vary over time since last birth, but no main effect of having a living mother. Having a mother-in-law speeds up a woman's fertility rate (in Table 3.4 a positive parameter estimate indicates a higher probability of birth per unit time, and therefore shorter birth intervals). This effect is independent of time since last birth. There is a significant effect of having a living father-in-law, and also a significant interaction between this variable and time. The main effect of fathers-in-law is negative, but the interaction with time alters the interpretation of the estimate. Figure 3.6 plots out model predictions of the probability of birth over time for women with and without living fathers-in-law, both for cases when the child at the start of the birth interval, or index child, was alive and when the index child was dead (the strongest determinant of the length of birth intervals). These plots indicate that in most cases, the presence of the father-in-law increased, rather than

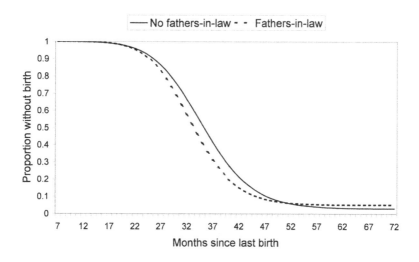

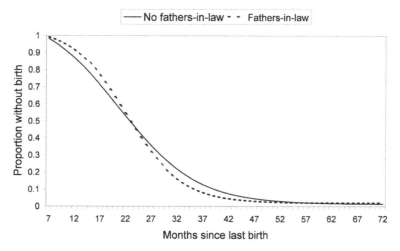

Figure 3.6. Survival plot using model predictions of the effect of the husband's father on probability of birth for cases where the index child was alive (a) and cases where the index child was dead (b). Model was fitted using reference categories for all other variables but maternal age and parity (model was fitted at mean maternal age of twenty-seven years and mean parity of four).

decreased, fertility. The effects of both parents-in-law are small but highly statistically significant. This analysis demonstrates the effects of kin over a single birth interval. The cumulative effect of the presence of parents-in-law on overall fertility is likely to be larger.

Having elder sisters makes no difference to a woman's fertility rate, but having elder brothers decreases her fertility rate. Both elder daughters and sons have significant effects on fertility rate but these relationships are more likely to be explained by parental investment strategies rather than any helping behaviour from older children. Having elder sons and elder daughters slows down, rather than speeds up, a woman's birth rate (though the effect of elder daughters is seen only if the index child is a girl). This suggests women may be slowing down their reproductive rate once a desired family size and composition is achieved.

Why Do Different Kin Have Different Effects?

We have shown that relatives matter for all the outcomes we have investigated for this project, but that different relatives matter for different reproductive outcomes. Children without mothers clearly suffer a penalty of poorer growth and higher mortality rates, and have little chance of survival if they lose their mothers during infancy. Perhaps surprisingly, mothers do not have an impact on child survival after the second year of life, but this may be because other relatives are picking up some of the burden of childcare. Maternal grandmothers and elder sisters become important for child survival in toddlerhood and later childhood. The results of the analysis of anthropometric status confirm that maternal grandmothers and elder sisters are beneficial for children, at least in terms of child height (which is perhaps the best long-term measure of child growth).

Both the mortality and anthropometric status analysis suggest that male and patrilineal kin matter little to children, with the exception of elder brothers. Fathers and paternal grandmothers are irrelevant to child growth and survival as they have no significant impact on any indicator of anthropometric status or mortality rates at any age. Grandfathers also make no difference to child mortality. The results of the anthropometric models for grandfathers are hard to interpret given their inconsistency across different measures, but we certainly don't see the consistently positive effect we observe for female, matrilineal kin. Elder brothers even seem to be detrimental to child growth (for both sexes), though this does not show up in increased mortality rates. We may be observing competition between siblings for parental resources here. This is a patrilineal society, and early born sons will have the highest status amongst a family's children, which is likely to result in preferential treatment in terms of food and healthcare allocation.

The Importance of Female Kin

The mortality analysis suggests maternal grandmothers are most important around the time of weaning (which occurs between eighteen and twenty-four months in this population). In this community, maternal grandmothers are known to have an important role around this time in a child's life. Women usually send their toddlers away to another relative to 'forget the breast' when they want to wean a child, and the preferred relative for this task is the woman's own mother (Thompson 1965). Maternal grandmothers are traditionally supposed to prepare high energy foods, such as peanut mashes, for weanlings at this stage, and children without maternal grandmothers may suffer more from the stress of weaning than those whose maternal grandmothers are available to provide such good quality care.

An alternative explanation is that the mortality of children and their grandmothers could be positively associated because of genetic or environmental correlations. Some families could be healthier than others, because of fortunate genetic or environmental endowments, which would lead to a correlation between the survival of different family members. We do not think this is an adequate explanation in this case for the following reasons. Firstly, the effect is specific to the maternal grandmother. If genetic or environmental factors were important, we would expect to see this relationship with other grandparents (particularly as the child is more likely to live with his paternal than his maternal relatives). Secondly, the mortality effect is specific to the period around weaning, and is not seen in early or later childhood. If the correlation were due to genetic or environmental effects, then we would expect to see it at all ages. Finally, we have a plausible mechanism: we know that maternal grandmothers have a role to play in childcare that is particularly important around the time of weaning.

We find that elder sisters are also important for child anthropometric status and survival, regardless of the child's sex. Elder sisters have a role to play in childcare in the Gambia, as is common in other traditional societies (Weisner and Gallimore 1977; Borgerhoff Mulder and Milton 1985; Bove, Valeggia and Ellison 2002). Weaned children are allocated a nursemaid, preferably an elder sister of the child (though other young female relatives or occasionally brothers may be co-opted into this duty). Nursemaids are responsible for looking after small children while their mothers are busy in the fields, or with other chores (Thompson and Rahman 1967). Again, our analysis suggests that the quality of care provided by elder sisters is sufficient to show up as improved child anthropometric status, and improved mortality rates for children between the ages of two and five years. The effects on mortality and growth are independent of sex, and should not be confounded by birth order since this is controlled for in the model. The effect therefore seems unlikely to be due to parental investment strategies. It also seems unlikely that phenotypic correlations are causing the relationship, since we have controlled for differences in mortality experience between women, and because we do not see the same positive correlation between elder brothers and mortality or growth. In fact, for anthropometric status the relationship with elder brothers is negative.

Implications for the Evolution of Menopause

In the earlier part of this chapter, we described the grandmother hypothesis for the evolution of menopause. This hypothesis states that, as the costs of giving birth to one's own children increase with age, it becomes adaptive for women to switch to investing in their existing children and grandchildren rather than continuing to risk giving birth themselves (Hawkes et al. 1998). More recently the hypothesis has been re-phrased to emphasise that it is long post-reproductive survival that is the derived trait that needs to be explained, rather than menopause itself (Hawkes 2003). Which-ever way this hypothesis is framed, it predicts that children will have higher survival rates in the presence of grandmothers, exactly the pattern we see in this Gambian society. However, despite recent claims to the contrary (Hawkes 2004; Lahdenpera et al. 2004), finding positive effects of grandmothers on child survival or other com-ponents of reproductive success in a single society does not allow us to come to any conclusions about the evolution of menopause. Menopause may have evolved so that grandmothers could switch to investing in their grandchildren, or grandmothers could be investing in their grandchildren because menopause makes them unable to continue having children of their own (and investing in grandchildren is better than investing in nothing at all).

One way to try to understand the evolution of menopause is to build math-ematical models which can be used to investigate theoretically the costs and benefits of menopause or long post-reproductive life (Rogers 1993; Shanley and Kirkwood 2001; Lee 2003). Our collaborators at the University of Newcastle, Daryl Shanley and Tom Kirkwood, have built a model based on parameters estimated from this Gambian population to do just this (Shanley et al. 2007). Their model finds impor-tant support for the contribution of the grandmother effect to the evolution of meno-pause, although the optimal age at last birth is predicted to be a little later than the average age at menopause. The loss of the mother has a much stronger detrimental effect on child survival than the loss of the grandmother, but the loss of the mother is a rare event. The loss of the grandmother, therefore, has a more important effect on the costs and benefits of menopause than the loss of the mother, and may help explain the evolution of this phenomenon.

Do Men Matter?

Contrary to the hypothesis that it is male provisioning and care which is a distin-guishing feature of human life history, fathers make absolutely no difference to child anthropometric status and survival in this society. There is marked division of labour by sex in this community: fathers are not involved in direct childcare, and mothers produce a substantial proportion of the food consumed by children. This is a highly polygynous society, and men may direct their labour towards acquiring resources which can be used to marry other wives, rather than invest in their existing children. However, we do find a negative effect of divorce and remarriage on child survival rates. The mother's divorce and remarriage means that the child will either move to a new (and unrelated or distantly related) man's compound, or be left behind in the father's compound without the mother. Either event is likely to increase stress and disruption (see Flinn and England 1995; also Flinn, this volume, for increased stress in children with step-parents), apparently increasing mortality rates (we have never come across any suggestion in the ethnographic literature or elsewhere that step-fathers may be involved in deliberate infanticide of children in the Gambia). The mother's widowhood, on the other hand, may frequently involve less disruption to the life of a child than is the case in some societies. This society practises the levirate (widows being inherited by their husband's brother), and patrilineally related men often live together in the same compounds in the Gambia. The death of a father may then mean little change to the child's life, as well a step-father who is closely geneti-cally related.

Male and patrilineal kin do seem to be more important for a woman's fertility than her female, matrilineal kin, however. There is some suggestion that fathers do matter for a woman's age at first birth, though this is not a particularly strong ef-fect: women without fathers have later first births than those with fathers. Fathers are responsible for arranging women's marriages, and women without fathers may have slightly delayed marriages if they have to rely on other relatives to perform this task. This contrasts with studies in other ecologies which have found the presence of fathers inhibits their daughters' sexual and reproductive behaviour (Flinn 1988; Ellis et al. 2003; but see Waynforth 2002 for a similarly positive effect of fathers on their daughters' first births). Having elder brothers also speeds up a woman's first birth. Girls are useful to their mothers in terms of childcare and other domestic tasks, and mothers may be reluctant to let a daughter marry and leave home until her brothers have brought in wives to replace her: having many older brothers therefore may speed up a woman's marriage, since at least some are likely to have already brought in wives by the time she is of marriageable age. Additionally, families with elder brothers may be keen to see their daughters married off quickly, as the brideprice a daughter brings in can be used to buy wives for her brothers.

Conflicts of Interest between Women and Their Husband's Kin

While the lack of a father-effect on child growth or survival might be explained by the division of labour in this society, that paternal grandmothers also do not provide care for their grandchildren perhaps needs more explaining, especially as children are more likely to live with their paternal than their maternal grandmothers in this patrilocal society. Grandmothers may invest their limited time and energy in their daughters' children rather than their sons' children, because investing in the matri-lineal line is a safer genetic bet. Their daughter's children will certainly be related to them; their sons' (putative) children might not be. We have no quantitative estimates of paternity uncertainty in this population, but a few cases of children being fathered by men other than the mother's husband were reported by McGregor. The large age differences between spouses in this society, polygyny, and the late age at which men marry might suggest some opportunity for uncertain paternity.

A simpler explanation may be that the large age differences between husbands and wives in this community mean that grandmothers are younger and healthier when their daughters' children need care than by the time their sons have children. However, controlling for grandparents' age in both the child mortality and anthropometric status models made no difference to the results. Other studies have shown that the presence of paternal grandmothers is either less beneficial to their grandchildren than that of maternal grandmothers or it may even increase the mortality rates of their grandchildren (Sorenson Jamison et al. 2002; Voland and Beise 2002). This has been attributed to conflict between women and their mothers-in-law, which results in higher mortality rates of young children, and may increase the risk of the woman herself dying (Skinner 1997).

There are clearly conflicts of interest between men and women in their reproductive strategies, particularly so in a highly polygynous society such as this, where men's reproductive strategies are very different from women's. Men in the Gambia desire much larger family sizes than do women (Ratcliffe, Hill and Walraven 2000). These conflicts of interest may spill over onto the relationships between a woman and her husband's kin, as a woman's in-laws will be attempting to maximize the reproductive success of their own kin rather than that of his wife. Our study found that the presence of a mother- or father-in-law speeds up a woman's fertility rate, while her own relatives have no impact on her reproductive rate. As both the husband's father and mother have this effect, it seems unlikely that it can all be explained by any helping effect of parents-in-law reducing the energetic burden on women (by taking over some childcare or subsistence duties) and thus allowing them to conceive earlier. Instead, we suggest husband's parents may put social pressures on women to give birth to many children, to maximise their son's reproductive success. Such social pressures may be less likely to come from a woman's own family, as giving birth to many closely spaced children can be detrimental to women's health (Jelliffe and Maddocks 1964; Tracer 1991). Women are not genetically related to their husbands' parents, so that in-laws may emphasise a woman's reproductive duties even at the expense of her own health, as daughters-in-law are to some extent replaceable should they become ill or die. Elsewhere, mothers-in-law have been found to have stronger desires for their daughters-in-law to continue reproducing than did the women themselves, and these views tended to coincide with their sons' opinions on family size (Kadir et al. 2003). Such conflicts of interest may, in some cases, result in the increased mortality rates of women and children described above (see the paper by Voland and Beise [2005] entitled "'The husband's mother is the devil in the house'" for a more detailed discussion of this topic).

Are Humans Cooperative Breeders?

We have conducted a detailed investigation of the effects of relatives on various components of reproductive success in a single society, and found significant effects of kin on all the life history characteristics that we have investigated. But can these results be generalised to draw useful conclusions? Given the wide variety of social and ecological environments the human species inhabits, it is dangerous to extrapolate from the study of a single society to the human species as a whole. As evolutionary ecologists, we believe research such as this is most useful when it can be considered alongside similar studies which have been conducted in different socio-ecological environments. Generalisable conclusions can then be drawn from a comparison of the similarities and differences in the helping behaviour of kin across a variety of populations. The growing body of research investigating the effects on kin on aspects of reproductive success has been carried out across a variety of environments and subsistence strategies including: South American hunter-gatherers (Hill and Hurtado 1991; Hurtado and Hill 1992; Waynforth 2002); farmers in historical Europe, Canada and Japan (Sorenson Jamison et al. 2002; Voland and Beise 2002; Lahdenpera et al. 2004; Beise 2005); contemporary populations in Eastern Europe, North Africa and Asia (Bereczkei 1998; Crognier et al. 2001; Griffiths, Hinde and Matthews 2001; Leonetti and Nath 2004; Leonetti et al. 2005; Sear 2008).

In recent reviews of this research, we found a number of common themes, but concluded that ecological context is also important in determining the importance of kin to demographic outcomes (Mace and Sear 2005; Sear and Mace 2008). Of most importance to this symposium was the finding that in all populations there were beneficial effects of at least one relative (apart from the mother) on child survival. This suggests that alloparenting is an adaptive strategy, and that mothers are disadvantaged if they cannot co-opt other individuals into helping them raise their children. But we find some variation between societies in which relatives are beneficial. A common theme is that maternal grandmothers are good for child survival, whereas paternal grandmothers are somewhat less important (though there are exceptions: see Sear 2008 for an example of paternal grandmothers who are more beneficial than maternal, and Beise 2005 for an example where both paternal and maternal grandmothers improve child survival). The effects of fathers are rather small, in that in only a third of populations do fathers seem to have any impact on child survival rates, suggesting that paternal investment is contingent on environmental conditions (see Hewlett 1992 for cross-cultural perspectives on paternal investment strategies). These results suggest that the Western emphasis on the nuclear family as the most important unit for child well-being may be rather narrow, and that there is a variety of family structures in which children can thrive.

Note

We would like to thank the Gambian Scientific Co-ordinating Committee and Ethical Committee for permission to use the data.

References

Allal, N., Sear, R., Prentice, A.M., and Mace, R., 2004. An evolutionary model of stature, age at first birth and reproductive success in Gambian women. *Proceedings of the Royal Society B* 271, 465–70.

Allison, P.D., 1984. *Event History Analysis: Regression for Longitudinal Event Data.* Newbury Park: Sage Publications.

Alvarez, H.P., 2000. Grandmother hypothesis and primate life histories. *American Journal of Physical Anthropology* 113, 435–50.

Beckerleg, S., Austin, S. and Weaver, L., 1994. Gender, work and illness: the influence of a research unit on an agricultural community in the Gambia. *Health, Policy and Planning* 9, 419–28.

Beise, J., 2005. The helping grandmother and the helpful grandmother: the role of maternal and paternal grandmothers in child mortality in the 17th and 18th century population of French settlers in Quebec, Canada. In E. Voland, A. Chasiotis and W. Schiefenhoevel, eds., *Grandmotherhood: The Evolutionary Significance of the Second Half of the Female Life.* New Brunswick: Rutgers University Press, 215–38.

Bereczkei, T., 1998. Kinship network, direct childcare and fertility among Hungarians and Gypsies. *Evolution and Human Behaviour* 19, 283–98.

Billewicz, W.Z., and McGregor, I.A., 1981. The demography of two West African (Gambian) villages, 1951–75. *Journal of Biosocial Science* 13, 219–40.

——— 1982. A birth-to-maturity study of heights and weights in two West African (Gambian) villages, 1951–75. *Annals of Human Biology* 9, 309–20.

Borgerhoff Mulder, M., and Milton, M., 1985. Factors affecting infant care in the Kipsigis. *Journal of Anthropological Research* 41, 231–62.

Bove, R.B., Valeggia, C.R., and Ellison, P.T., 2002. Girl helpers and time allocation of nursing women among the Toba of Argentina. *Human Nature* 13, 457–72.

Chivers, D.J., 1974. *The Siamang in Malaysia.* Basel: Karger.

Clutton-Brock, T.H., 1991. *The Evolution of Parental Care.* Princeton: Princeton University Press.

Crognier, E., Baali, A., and Hilali, M.K., 2001. Do 'helpers at the nest' increase their parents' reproductive success? *American Journal of Human Biology* 13, 365–73.

Curtis, S.L., and Steele, F. 1996. Variations in familial neonatal mortality risks in four countries. *Journal of Biosocial Science* 28, 141–59.

Daly, M., and Wilson, M., 1988. *Homicide.* New York: Aldine de Gruyter.

Draper, P., and Harpending, H., 1982. Father absence and reproductive strategy: an evolutionary perspective. *Journal of Anthropological Research* 38, 255–73.

Ellis, B.J., Bates, J.E., Dodge, K.A., Fergusson, D.M., Horwood, L.J., Pettit, G.S., and Woodward, L., 2003. Does father absence place daughters at special risk for early sexual activity and teenage pregnancy? *Child Development* 74, 801–21.

Flinn, M.V., 1988. Parent-offspring interactions in a Caribbean village: daughter guarding. In L. Betzig, M. Borgerhoff Mulder and P.W. Turke, eds., *Human Reproductive Behaviour.* Cambridge: Cambridge University Press, 189–200.

Flinn, M.V., and England, B.G., 1995. Childhood stress and family environment. *Current Anthropology* 36, 854–66.

Galdikas, B.M.F., and Wood, J.W., 1990. Birth spacing patterns in humans and apes. *American Journal of Physical Anthropology* 83, 185–91.

Geary, D.C., 2000. Evolution and proximate expression of human paternal investment. *Psychological Bulletin* 126, 55–77.

Goldizen, A.W., 1987. Tamarins and marmosets: communal care of offspring. In B. Smuts, D.L. Cheney, R,M. Seyfarth, R.W. Wrangham and T.T. Struhsaker, eds., *Primate Societies*. Chicago: University of Chicago Press, 34–43.

Griffiths, P., Hinde, A., and Matthews, Z., 2001. Infant and child mortality in three culturally contrasting states of India. *Journal of Biosocial Science* 33, 603–22.

Hamilton, W.D., 1964. The genetical evolution of social behaviour I. *Journal of Theoretical Biology* 7, 1–16.

———— 1966. The moulding of senescence by natural selection. *Journal of Theoretical Biology* 12, 12–45.

Hawkes, K., 1990. Why do men hunt? Benefits for risky choices. In E. Cashdan, ed., *Risk and Uncertainty in Tribal and Peasant Economies*. Boulder, Colorado: Westview Press, 145–66.

———— 2003. Grandmothers and the evolution of human longevity. *American Journal of Human Biology* 15, 380–400.

———— 2004. Human longevity – the grandmother effect. *Nature* 428, 128–29.

Hawkes, K., O'Connell, J.F., and Blurton Jones, N.G., 1989. Hardworking Hadza grandmothers. In V. Standen and R.A. Foley, eds., *Comparative Socioecology: The Behavioural Ecology of Humans and Other Mammals*. Oxford: Blackwell, 341–66.

———— 1997. Hadza women's time allocation, offspring provisioning and the evolution of long postmenopausal life spans. *Current Anthropology* 38, 551–78.

Hawkes, K., O'Connell, J.F., Blurton Jones, N.G., Alvarez, H., and Charnov, E.L., 1998. Grandmothering, menopause and the evolution of human life histories. *Proceedings of the National Academy of Sciences* 95, 1336–39.

Hawkes, K., O'Connell, J.F., and Jones, N.G.B., 2001. Hunting and nuclear families: some lessons from the Hadza about men's work. *Current Anthropology* 42, 681–709.

Hewlett, B.S., 1992. *Father-Child Relations: Cultural and Biosocial Contexts*. New York: Aldine de Gruyter.

Hill, K., and Hurtado, A.M., 1991. The evolution of premature reproductive senescence and menopause in human females: an evaluation of the 'grandmother hypothesis'. *Human Nature* 2, 313–50.

———— 1996. *Ache Life History: The Ecology and Demography of a Foraging People*. New York: Aldine de Gruyter.

Hurtado, A.M., and Hill, K.R., 1992. Paternal effect on offspring survivorship among Ache and Hiwi hunter-gatherers: implications for modelling pair-bond stability. In B.S. Hewlett, eds., *Father-Child Relations: Cultural and Biosocial Contexts*. New York: Aldine de Gruyter, 31–55.

Jelliffe, D.B., and Maddocks, I., 1964. Notes on ecologic malnutrition in the New Guinea Highlands. *Clinical Pediatrics* 3, 432–38.

Kadir, M.M., Fikree, F.F., Khan, A., and Sajan, F., 2003. Do mothers-in-law matter? Family dynamics and fertility decision-making in urban squatter settlements of Karachi, Pakistan. *Journal of Biosocial Science* 35, 545–58.

Lahdenpera, M., Lummaa, V., Helle, S., Tremblay, M., and Russell, A.F., 2004. Fitness benefits of prolonged post-reproductive lifespan in women. *Nature* 428, 178–81.

Lamb, W.H., Lamb, C.M.B., Foord, F.A., and Whitehead, R.G. 1984. Changes in maternal and child mortality rates in three isolated Gambian villages over ten years. *Lancet 2* (8408), 912–14.

Lee, R.D., 2003. Rethinking the evolutionary theory of aging: transfers, not births, shape social species. *Proceedings of the National Academy of Sciences* 100, 9637–42.

Lee, R.D., and Kramer, K.L., 2002. Children's economic roles in the Maya family life cycle: Cain, Caldwell, and Chayanov revisited. *Population and Development Review* 28, 475–99.

Leonetti, D.L., and Nath, D.C., 2004. Do women really need marital partners for support of their reproductive success? The case of the matrilineal Khasi of NE India. *Research in Economic Anthropology* 23, 151–74.

Leonetti, D.L., Nath, D.C., Hemam, N.S. and Neill, D.B., 2005. Kinship organisation and the impact of grandmothers on reproductive success among the matrilineal Khasi and patrilineal Bengali of Northeast India. In E. Voland, A. Chasiotis and W. Schiefenhoevel, eds., *Grandmotherhood: The Evolutionary Significance of the Second Half of Female Life.* New Brunswick: Rutgers University Press, 194–214.

Lovejoy, C.O., 1981. The origin of man. *Science* 211, 341–50.

Mace, R., and Sear, R., 2005. Are humans cooperative breeders? In E. Voland, A. Chasiotis and W. Schiefenhoevel, eds., *Grandmotherhood: The Evolutionary Significance of the Second Half of Female Life.* New Brunswick: Rutgers University Press, 143–59.

Marlowe, F., 2001. Male contribution to diet and female reproductive success among foragers. *Current Anthropology* 42, 755–60.

McGregor, I.A., 1991. Morbidity and mortality at Keneba, the Gambia, 1950–75. In R.G. Feacham and D.T. Jamison, eds., *Disease and Mortality in Sub-Saharan Africa.* Oxford: Oxford University Press, for the World Bank, 306–24.

McGregor, I.A., Rahman, A.K., Thompson, B., Billewicz, W.Z., and Thomson, A.M., 1968. The growth of young children in a Gambian village. *Transactions of the Royal Society of Tropical Medicine and Hygiene* 62, 341–52.

McGregor, I.A., and Smith, D.A., 1952. A health, nutrition and parasitological survey in a rural village (Keneba) in West Kiang, Gambia. *Transactions of the Royal Society of Tropical Medicine and Hygiene* 46, 403–27.

McGregor, I.A., Williams, K., Billewicz, W.Z., and Thomson, A.M., 1966. Haemoglobin concentration and anaemia in young West African (Gambian) children. *Transactions of the Royal Society of Tropical Medicine and Hygiene* 60, 650–67.

Poskitt, E.M.E., Cole, T.J., and Whitehead, R.G., 1999. Less diarrhoea but no change in growth: 15 years' data from three Gambian villages. *Archives of Disease in Childhood* 80, 115–19.

Quinlan, R.J., 2001. Effect of household structure on female reproductive strategies in a Caribbean village. *Human Nature* 12, 169–89.

Rasbash, J., Browne, W., Goldstein, H., Yang, M., Plewis, I., Healy, M., Woodhouse, G., Draper, D., Langford, I., and Lewis, T., 2000. *A User's Guide to MLwiN*. London: Institute of Education.

Ratcliffe, A.A., Hill, A.G., and Walraven, G., 2000. Separate lives, different interests: male and female reproduction in the Gambia. *Bulletin of the World Health Organization* 78, 570–79.

Reher, D.S., and González-Quiñones, F., 2003. Do parents really matter? Child health and development in Spain during the demographic transition. *Population Studies* 57, 63–75.

Rogers, A.R., 1993. Why menopause? *Evolutionary Ecology* 7, 406–20.

Rowland, M.G.M., Cole, T.J., and Whitehead, R.G., 1977. Quantitative study into the role of infection in determining nutritional status in Gambian village children. *British Journal of Nutrition* 37, 441–50.

Sear, R., 2008. Kin and child survival in rural Malawi: are matrilineal kin always beneficial in matrilineal societies? *Human Nature* 19, 277–293.

———— 2001. *Evolutionary Demography of a Rural Gambian Population*. PhD Thesis, University College London.

Sear, R. and Mace, R., 2008. Who keeps children alive? A review of the effects of kin on child survival. *Evolution and Human Behavior* 29, 1–18.

Sear, R., Mace, R., and McGregor, I.A., 2000. Maternal grandmothers improve the nutritional status and survival of children in rural Gambia. *Proceedings of the Royal Society B* 267, 461–67.

———— 2003. The effects of kin on female fertility in rural Gambia. *Evolution and Human Behavior* 24, 25–42.

Sear, R., Steele, F., McGregor, I.A., and Mace, R., 2002. The effects of kin on child mortality in rural Gambia. *Demography* 39, 43–63.

Shanley, D.P., and Kirkwood, T.B.L., 2001. Evolution of the human menopause. *Bioessays* 23, 282–87.

Shanley, D.P., Sear, R., Mace, R., and Kirkwood, T.B.L., 2007. Testing evolutionary theories of menopause. *Proceedings of the Royal Society B* 274, 2943–49.

Skinner, G.W., 1997. Family systems and demographic processes. In D.I. Kertzer and T. Fricke, eds., *Anthropological Demography: Toward a New Synthesis*. Chicago: University of Chicago Press, 53–95.

Sorenson Jamison, C., Cornell, L.L., Jamison, P.L., and Nakazato, H., 2002. Are all grandmothers equal? A review and a preliminary test of the 'Grandmother Hypothesis' in Tokugawa Japan. *American Journal of Physical Anthropology* 119, 67–76.

Temrin, H., Nordlund, J., and Sterner, H., 2004. Are stepchildren overrepresented as victims of lethal parental violence in Sweden? *Proceedings of the Royal Society B* 271, S124–26.

Thompson, B., and Rahman, A.K., 1967. Infant feeding and child care in a West African village. *Journal of Tropical Pediatrics* 13, 124–38.

Thompson, E.D.B., 1965. Marriage, Childbirth and Early Childhood in a Gambian Village: A Socio-Medical Study. PhD Thesis, University of Aberdeen.

Tracer, D.P., 1991. Fertility-related changes in maternal body composition among the Au of Papua New Guinea. *American Journal of Physical Anthropology* 85, 393–405.

Turke, P.W., 1988. Helpers at the nest: childcare networks on Ifaluk. In L. Betzig, M. Borgerhoff Mulder and P. Turke, eds., *Human Reproductive Behaviour: A Darwinian Perspective.* Cambridge: Cambridge University Press, 173–88.

Tymicki, K., 2004. The kin influence on female reproductive behaviour: the evidence from the reconstitution of Bejsce parish registers, 18th–20th centuries, Poland. *American Journal of Human Biology* 16, 508–22.

Voland, E. and Beise, J., 2002. Opposite effects of maternal and paternal grandmothers on infant survival in historical Krummhörn. *Behavioural Ecology & Sociobiology* 52, 435–43.

————— 2005, 'The husband's mother is the devil in the house': data on the impact of the mother-in-law on stillbirth mortality in historical Krummhörn (C18–19 Germany) and some thoughts on the evolution of postgenerative female life. In E. Voland, A. Chasiotis and W. Schiefenhoevel, eds., *Grandmotherhood: The Evolutionary Significance of the Second Half of the Female Life.* New Brunswick: Rutgers University Press, 239–55.

Washburn, S.L., and Lancaster, J., 1968. The evolution of hunting. In R.B. Lee and I. Devore, eds., *Man the Hunter.* Chicago: Aldine, 293–303.

Waynforth, D., 2002. Evolutionary theory and reproductive responses to father absence: implications of kin selection and the reproductive returns to mating and parenting effort. In C.S. Tamis-Lemonda and N. Cabera, eds., *Handbook of Father Involvement: Multidisciplinary Perspectives.* Lawrence Earlbaum Associates, 337–57.

Weaver, L.T., and Beckerleg, S., 1993. Is health sustainable? A village study in the Gambia. *Lancet* 341, 1327–30.

Weisner, T.S., and Gallimore, R., 1977. My brother's keeper: child and sibling caretaking. *Current Anthropology* 18, 169–90.

Williams, G.C., 1957. Pleiotropy, natural selection and the evolution of senescence. *Evolution* 11, 398–411.

• 4 •

Does It Take a Family to Raise a Child?

Cooperative Breeding and the Contributions of Maya Siblings, Parents and Older Adults in Raising Children

Karen L. Kramer

Introduction

The human life history pattern of short birth intervals, relatively high child survival and a long dependency period means that mothers are often in the position of supporting multiple dependents of various ages simultaneously. Because infants, young children and older children each require different kinds of time and energy investments, mothers are posed with an allocation problem throughout much of their reproductive career: how to provide childcare without compromising time spent in economic activities that provide food and other resources for older children (Hewlett 1991; Hill and Kaplan 1988; Hrdy 1999; Hurtado et al. 1992; Lee 1979; LeVine 1977; Panter-Brick 1989). How mothers resolve this trade-off has led to provocative debate in anthropology about the evolution of the rapid pace of human reproduction and the human pattern of what biologists refer to as cooperative breeding.

Cooperative breeding is a reproductive strategy in which non-parental members of a social group help to raise young (Brown 1987; Clutton-Brock 2002; Emlen 1991; Skutch 1935, 1987). While relatively rare, cooperative breeding has been documented across diverse taxa, predominantly among some 2–3 per cent of bird and 2 per cent of mammalian species: primarily wild canids, mongoose, rodents and several species of primates (Brown 1987; Emlen 1984).[1] Across human populations, parents commonly rely on the help of others to raise children (Cain 1977; Draper and Harpending 1987; Hames 1988; Hawkes et al.1995, 1998; Ivey 2000; Lee and Bulatao 1983; Reynolds 1991; overview in Hrdy 1999). Help from others redistributes the cost of raising offspring and may benefit mothers by having a positive effect on reducing birth intervals, raising maternal fertility, or child survival. For example, among the Ifaluk, Micronesian islanders, women who bear female children, who are valuable helpers to their mothers, early in their reproductive careers had greater completed fertility than mothers whose first born children were boys (Turke 1988, 1989). Since Turke's seminal study introduced cooperative breeding into anthropology, attention has centered on the importance of grandmothers (Hawkes et al. 1989, 1997), male parental investment (Kaplan et al. 2000; Lancaster et al. 2000) and children (Hrdy 1999, 2005a; Kramer 2005a, b) as alternate strategies to help provision young.

This chapter uses time allocation data to observe first how Maya mothers resolve the allocation trade-off of investing in childcare and economic activities that support older children, and second, the role that fathers, children and older adults play in subsidizing the cost of reproduction. The Maya are an ideal population to examine the relative contribution of different classes of helpers since they are a natural fertility population, have large families, and mothers draw on help from a number of individuals. Emphasis is placed on cross-cultural comparison. Societies discussed here are limited to natural fertility, subsistence populations because family planning and economic options available to raise children, which affect maternal allocation trade-offs, the need for help and the cost of helping, are very different in contracepting, market-economy populations. In contracepting populations, parents can solve the competing demands of providing for children of different ages by delaying first birth, extending birth intervals and limiting family size. Parents in market economies can also smooth fluctuations in the time and resources needed to support dependents by banking funds for the future, paying for childcare or relying on loans and state subsidies.

The Maya Study Population and Data Collection

Maya time allocation and reproductive history data are used to examine the comparative contributions of mothers, fathers, children and older adults to raising children in a pre-market-economy, natural-fertility population. These data were drawn from a year-long study in a Maya village (Xculoc) of 316 residents in the interior of Yucatan Peninsula, Mexico. The Xculoc Maya are subsistence farmers; each household grows its own food and furnishes the labour to provision the household. The majority of calories come from maize, and to lesser extent from cultivated beans, squash, sweet potatoes, peanuts and other fruits and vegetables. Domesticated turkeys, ducks, chickens and pigs are raised for occasional consumption, and forest animals are hunted to supplement their diet. Honey is collected for sale from hives maintained in the forest and small quantities of maize may be exchanged in the village store for limited commodities such as vegetable oil, eggs, and candles. Otherwise, no cash crops are grown for sale. When the baseline time allocation data used here were collected in 1992–93, the village had no running water or electricity and because of its remoteness and the long distances to market towns, villagers participated minimally in wage labour and the market economy.

Although parents are interested in having their children learn to read and write, school teachers rarely make the trip to Xculoc and classes are infrequently held. Consequently, schooling has little impact on children's labour. Older children are eligible to attend boarding school in towns some distance from the village. These schools, however, are not free and few children attend them. Children's education is not more widely pursued because there is little associated economic benefit due to the community's isolation and the limited access to skilled wage labour.

Maya children live and work in their parents' household until they marry and begin families of their own in their late teens and early twenties. Men may intermittently leave the village for a few days at a time to engage in wage labour to finance the purchase of basic household items such as cloth, needles and thread, medicine, or simple building materials. Women and children were not involved in wage labour or other income producing activities and in 25 per cent of village households, men never participate in wage labour.

Upon marriage, most young couples stay in the village and establish fields of their own. Few villagers either marry a spouse from another village or leave the village to marry: of married adults, 97 per cent were born in Xculoc. Under the *ejido* land tenure system that was instituted following the Mexican Revolution, the communal lands allotted to each village are by law insoluble, neither owned nor heritable. This immutability assuages competition for arable land and wealth stratification, which has important consequences in minimizing variance in access to resources and nutritional status among villagers. The village's deeded *ejido* allotment of some 5, 200 hectares has been adequate to support the village's growing population.

Demographic data were collected by asking all village residents the names, ages and birth dates of themselves, their parents, siblings and children, whether living or dead. Fertility is relatively high, and has been from at least the early decades of the twentieth century. Median completed family size for mothers 46 and older is 7.3 in 2000. Birth spacing is relatively short, with a median birth interval of 2.2 years (Kramer and McMillan 1998, 2006).

This level of fertility, while not sustainable in the long term, has been feasible because only now is the local Maya population recovering from colonial-era decimation and returning to pre-European-contact population levels. Low population density over the past several hundred years, coupled with an absence of large-scale agricultural production in this part of Yucatan and an ample allotment of *ejido* lands has meant that established households as well as young couples have adequate access to the means of production and the resources necessary for reproduction.

Mothers have their last child in their late thirties to early forties, when the parents have the maximum number of dependents living at home. Firstborn children begin to leave home and marry a few years later and the lastborn child marries when parents are in their early sixties. Death dates and age at death of deceased spouses and other relatives were recorded as part of the original survey. Although the accuracy of life expectancy calculated from retrospective interview data in the absence of birth and death records is difficult to ascertain, when demographic data were recollected in 2001 it was possible to track the life span of older adults alive during the 1992–93 census. The average age at death among those adults who survived to age 50, was 67.8.

How household members allocate their time was collected from a subsample of the village population that included 19 of the village's 52 households. Individual time allocation budgets were gathered using behavioural scan sampling and focal follow techniques (Altmann 1974; Borgerhoff Mulder and Caro 1985; Hames 1992). Scan samples were recorded for each participant every other week for an observation period of three to four hours. During an observation period, an individual's activity was recorded every 15 minutes. The following analyses include 112 individuals ages 0 to 65 and draws on over 17,000 scan samples recorded over the course of a year. Every effort was made to ensure that all individuals were sampled equally, and a mean of 154 scan samples per person was recorded (Kramer 1998, 2005a). Scan sampling is advantageous as a behavioural observation method because it gives a detailed and accurate profile of the proportion of time that an individual spends in a wide variety of activities (Dunbar 1976).

Where time allocation is discussed relative to consumption, the proportion of time that an individual allocates to work is transformed into an estimate of his or her production. This conversion is necessary so that how much an individual produces and consumes is comparable, a) in a common currency and b) across age and sex classes. Work includes agricultural tasks (ground preparation, planting, weeding, harvesting, transporting field goods), domestic tasks (food processing, preparation, cooking, serving, running errands, hauling water, chopping firewood, washing, cleaning, tending animals) and wage labour in the case of those males who participate.

To account for differences in the work activity of adults compared to children and of males relative to females, two adjustments are made in converting the simple proportion of time that an individual spends working to an estimate of production. First, some activities are more strenuous and require greater caloric expenditure than others. For example, chopping firewood is more energetically demanding than swinging in a hammock while minding a child. To compensate for this variation (Becker 1981), the time allocated to strenuous tasks is weighted more heavily than less strenuous tasks. The scale for ranking tasks is based on published experimental studies that monitor the rate of an individual's energy expenditure while performing a wide variety of domestic and field activities (Astrand 1971; Durnin and Passmore 1967; Uliajasek 1995). The second adjustment weights for differential efficiency across age and sex classes. For example, if a father and son spend an hour harvesting maize, the father may harvest 10 kg of maize per hour while his young son yields 2 kg. To account for this, the time an individual spends in a task is weighted by differences in the return rates of adults relative to children and of females relative to males.

Two steps are made to express an individual's consumption as time. Based on observed time allocation budgets, 80 per cent of Maya household production is related to food: the labour spent to cultivate food, process, prepare and cook food, fetch wood and water, tend animals, maintain bee hives and to hunt. An individual's consumption of these food-related activities is estimated to be proportional to his or her daily caloric requirements. For example, if a household spends an average of 40 person hours a day working, 80 per cent (or 32 hours) is estimated to be related to the production, processing and preparation of food. If an eight-year-old girl's daily caloric requirement is 10 per cent of the household's total caloric requirements, she is estimated to consume 3.2 daily hours of household work (32 * .1 = 3.2) that is related to food. The remaining 20 per cent of household production is time spent washing, cleaning, sewing, building and maintaining structures and other domestic tasks. An individual household member's consumption of these non-food-related activities is estimated on a per capita basis. If the eight-year-old girl is one of five household members, she is estimated to consume an additional hour of work per day (40 * .2 / 8 = 1) that is not related to food production. Her total consumption is then 4.2 hours. While it can not be known for certain how domestic production is allocated among its members, this method has the advantage of expanding the definition of consumption beyond simply food consumption (Kramer 2005a; Lee and Kramer 2002).

How Do Maya Mothers Allocate Their Time across the Family Life Cycle?

As children mature they require different kinds of investments. Infants rely on mother's milk. Young children require specialized, calorie-rich, yet easily digestible and low volume food during childhood, the period of time following weaning until the eruption of permanent molars and completed brain growth. As children transition from childhood to juvenility and develop mature dentition and digestive tracts, they begin to consume adult foods.

If a mother raised one dependent at a time, the predominant primate pattern, she could shift her investment from nursing, to providing weaning food to adult food as a child developed from infancy to childhood to juvenility. However, because human mothers often have an infant, as well as older dependents to care for at the same time, they are faced with a tradeoff about where to direct their parental effort. Since child mortality is greatest during the first several years of life and exacerbated by the death of a mother, Hurtado et al. (1992) proposed that a mother would allocate her time to activities that do not compromise competent primary childcare (also see Voland 1988). Corollary to this hypothesis is the expectation that *maternal allocation should vary with the age structure of her dependents as their probability of survival changes and the demand for food production and other activities that support older children increases.*

The family life cycle, then, should be an important source of variation in determining how Maya mothers allocate their time to balance the competing demands of younger and older children. Subsequently, the demand for helpers should also change across the family life cycle.

The time Maya mothers allocate to childcare varies with nursing status (Figure 4.1) and, not surprisingly, mothers spend significantly more time in direct childcare when infants are less than a year old. (Direct childcare includes nursing, feeding, carrying, holding and grooming (dressing, bathing, delousing, minor medical); indirect childcare includes playing with, walking or laying in a hammock with a child, talking to or teaching a child). The time mothers allocated to domestic work changes little with nursing status. Domestic tasks occur in the village and are logistically compatible with primary care.

However, the time mothers allocate to field work does vary with nursing status. Fields are located some distance from the village, and nursing mothers with infants less than a year old spend no time in field work, regardless of whether they have older children. Mothers with no young children (0 to 6) spend more than twice as much time in field work than do nursing mothers and mothers with young children (see Figure 4.2).

The Maya pattern is in keeping with the few studies that report quantitative data on how mothers spend their time relative to nursing status. Comparable time budget data suggest that mothers with nursing children balance the increased demands on their time through a reduction in time spent in either domestic activities, foraging ac-

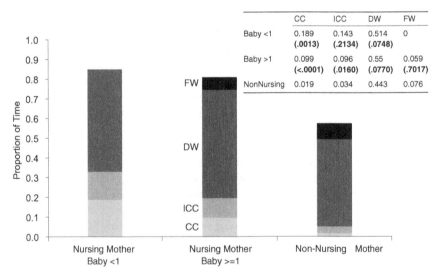

	CC	ICC	DW	FW
Baby <1	0.189 (.0013)	0.143 (.2134)	0.514 (.0748)	0
Baby >1	0.099 (<.0001)	0.096 (.0160)	0.55 (.0770)	0.059 (.7017)
NonNursing	0.019	0.034	0.443	0.076

Figure 4.1. The proportion of time that Maya mothers (n = 18) allocate to direct childcare (CC), indirect childcare (ICC), domestic work (DW) and field work (FW) over an eleven-hour observation day stratified by nursing status. P values shown for differences between means by nursing status.

tivities or field work (for exception see Hawkes et al 1997: 557). For example, among the Ye'kwana, neotropical agriculturalists, mothers are challenged to simultaneously care for infants while also maintaining a normal amount of garden work and other economic activities that help feed older children. Mothers with very young, dependent children, spend less time in economic activities, such as garden work, but do not compromise the time allocated to childcare (Hames 1988). Among the Hiwi and Ache, South American forager/horticulturalists, nursing mothers decrease their foraging effort relative to non-nursing mothers (Hurtado et al. 1985, 1992). Likewise, Maya mothers throughout their reproductive career drop out as field workers when they have young nursing children. These studies suggest that mothers balance the demands on their time to provide competent childcare through a reduction in time spent in foraging, domestic, or field work: activities that benefit older children.

Redistributing the Cost of Raising Children

Human mothers are seldom the sole caretakers of their young children. As mothers cross-culturally, Maya mothers receive childcare help primarily from female relatives: daughters, aunts and grandmothers (Table 4.1). Among non-human primates, mothers who receive help carrying infants, which alleviates constraints on their foraging efficiency, have shorter birth intervals (Mitani and Watts 1997). However, this

Table 4.1. Mean percentage of direct childcare received by an infant.

	Mothers	Fathers	Siblings	Grand-mothers	Other Related/Unrelated
Yekwana Hames 1988: 245	49%	2.7%	♂ 16.7% ♀ 1.9%	11.2%	20.6%
Agta Goodman et al. 1985: 1206	51.7%	4.4%	♂ 10.2% ♀ 1.1%	7.6%	
Maya	46.1%	1.6%	♂ 31.6% ♀ 4.6%	1.2%	11.2% [b] 2.8%
Alyawara[a] Denham 1974: 264	53%	<1%	31%		16%
Toba Valeggia, this volume	50%		♂ 33% ♀ 4%	12.5%	

[a] Values reported for carrying children only.
[b] Related individuals shown on the top of which aunts comprise 8.4%.
Note: In the Alyawara case, values for male and female children were reported as an aggregate. A blank indicates data not reported for category.

fertility benefit can be offset by increased infant mortality due to carelessness and mistreatment by helpers, especially among lower-ranked females (Fairbanks 1990). In humans this cost of allocare appears mollified. Borgerhoff Mulder and Milton's (1985) study of childcare among the Kipsigis, sub-Saharan agro-pastoralists, found that the quality of care provided by mothers and helpers was similar, and children were no more likely to be distressed when in the care of helpers or their mother. This is supported by cross-cultural time-allocation data, which show that infants typically receive only about 50 per cent of care from mothers. This regularity in part may reflect that no one can substitute maternal time spent nursing, which in the Maya case accounts for 38 per cent of mothers' childcare observations, and that mothers can only downwardly adjust allocation to primary childcare so far, regardless of the availability of helpers. This follows with Bove et al.'s (2000) finding that helpers have no effect on the time that nursing mothers spend in childcare.

Help from Fathers

Although maternal work effort reflects changes in family age structure, mothers work effort alone does not meet their children's consumption needs (Figure 4.2). Male parental investment is common in a number of cooperative breeding species (Asa 1997; Woolfenden and Fitzpatrick 1984), including non-human primates (Bales et al. 2000; Goldizen 1987; McKenna 1987). Among humans the level of paternal assistance varies widely. Males may assist relatively little in childcare (see Table 4.1), but their contribution to economic production is vital to raising young in many tradi-

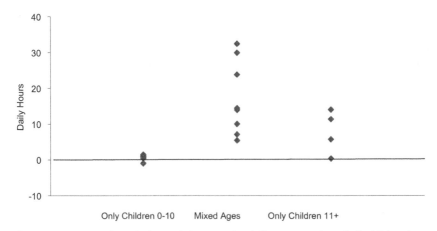

Figure 4.2. Can mothers do it on their own? The daily consumption of all children in a Maya household (n = 18) minus their mother's daily work effort stratified by household age composition. Each point indicates the number of hours in excess of a mother's work effort needed to meet a household's daily consumption.

tional societies (Draper and Hames 2000; Hewlett 1988; Hurtado et al. 1992; Irons 1983; Lancaster and Lancaster 1987).[2]

Maya fathers allocate more time to food production than do mothers (and less time to domestic production) during all stages of the family life cycle (Figure 4.3). But fathers spend almost twice as much time in field work when the family age structure is such that all their children are over the age of six.

Mothers and fathers increase their work effort at different points in the family life cycle. Maternal work effort increases during early parities and reaches a maximum early in the family life cycle, while paternal work effort increases and plateaus later in the family life cycle. This staggered increase in parental work effort appropriately reflects sex differences in the kinds of care mothers and fathers provide their children. Time spent in domestic work, which women fund and is a large component of their total work effort, increases sharply during early parities when mothers have multiple dependents and no children old enough to assist them. Their work effort then plateaus; from about marriage year five to twenty, a Maya mother will have more or less the same number of young dependents living in her household – one child is born as one reaches productive age. On the other hand, fathers spend the most time working when families mature and the number of older children to feed increases. Reflecting this, fathers spend almost twice as much time in field work (37 per cent) when all their children are over the age of six, but only 19 per cent of their time is spent in field work when they have children under the age of six living at home.

To observe vicissitudes in parents' shortfall to meet their dependent children's consumption, parental production is plotted relative to consumption across the family's demographic life cycle. To model demographic changes, the typical Maya family life cycle is constructed using the average age at marriage, which is twenty-two for

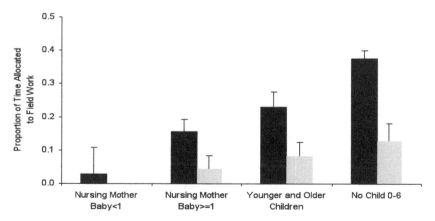

Figure 4.3. The proportion of time that Maya fathers (left n = 18) and mothers (right n = 18) allocate to field work over an eleven-hour observation day by family composition. Bars show standard error.

Maya males and nineteen for females, average birth interval at each parity and the average Maya family size of seven children.[3] A life table appropriate to village mortality is then superimposed to calculate the age distribution of surviving members.[4] Average age- and sex-specific levels of production and consumption derived from the time allocation data are then folded into these demographic changes so that consumption demand relative to labour supply can be observed across the family life cycle (Lee and Kramer 2002). Figure 4.4 shows mother's and father's production (domestic work, field work and wage labour for those males who work for wages) relative to their family's consumption from the onset of a marriage union, to the birth of the first child, the birth of the last child and the departure of the first and last child. The deficit in parental production relative to family consumption increases during early parities, but is greatest after the last child is born when most children are living at home. The most difficult time for parents and the greatest deficit in parental production relative to family consumption is when children are older, not younger.

Help from Children

Although Maya children are dependent on others, they are also a potential source of help (Kramer 2005a, b). The proportion of time that co-residential male and female children allocate to economic activities (domestic work, field work and wage labour for older males) increases throughout the juvenile period (Figure 4.5). The age patterning of childcare differs from economic activities in that it is younger, not older children, who allocate the most time to childcare. Children who are young enough to still receive childcare also care for their younger siblings.[5] This pattern has been both anecdotally noted and formally documented (Flinn 1988: 220; Hames 1988: 246; Nag et al. 1978: 294–6; Weisner 1987; Weisner and Gallimore 1977; Whiting and Edwards 1988).

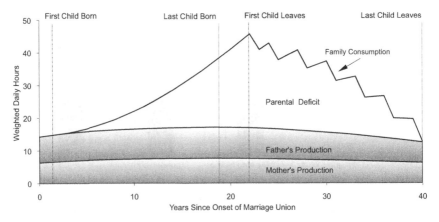

Figure 4.4. Where do parents fall sort? Maya mother's and father's production relative to family consumption across the typical family life cycle.

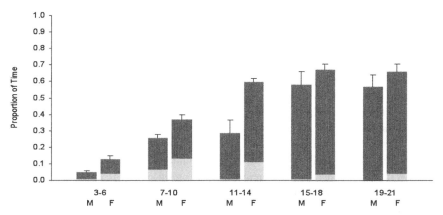

Figure 4.5. The proportion of time that coresidential Maya male and female children (n = 76) allocate daily to childcare (bottom) and economic production (domestic and field work; top) over an eleven-hour observation day. Standard errors bars shown for economic production.

In all age groups, Maya children allocate more time to economic activities than to childcare. This is also the case cross-culturally. Children across subsistence agricultural populations proportionally allocate substantially more time to economic activities compared to childcare (Figure 4.6). This is an important point because much of the research on the helping behaviour of children has focused on the effect that allo-*childcare* has on alleviating maternal time budgets. Yet it is economically that children make the greatest contribution.

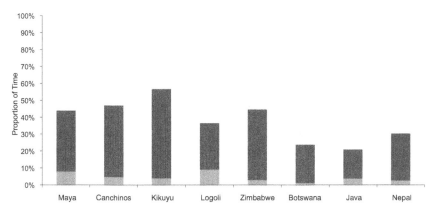

Figure 4.6. Proportion of time that agricultural children allocate cross culturally to childcare and other work. Sources: Maya (Kramer 2002); Canchicos (Munroe et al. 1983: 360); Kikuyu (Munroe et al. 1983: 360); Logoli (Munroe et al. 1983: 360); Zimbabwe (Reynolds 1991: 63); Botswana (Bock 1995: 101); Java (Nag et al. 1978: 294–5); Nepal (Nag et al. 1978: 295–6).

But here lies an analytic problem. To quote from Reynolds' monograph on children's labour among subsistence agriculturalists in Zimbabwe: 'Labour is notoriously difficult to measure. Women's labour, especially domestic labour, has been dubbed invisible because it is so hard to record. Children's labour is mercurial' Reynolds 1991: 41–42). While we may be able to record children's labour activities, analytically children's contributions can appear mercurial because, although children may spend considerable time working, they are also consumers.

To assess whether children's help actually offsets constraints on maternal time, the effects of children as *both* consumers and producers have to be taken into account. Figure 4.7 plots the relative share of children's help (P/C ratio) as a group across the family life cycle. Children as a group produce more than half of what they consume after the thirteenth year of the family life cycle, when the mother is still in her prime reproductive years. By the twentieth year of the family life cycle, children as a group produce 80 per cent of what they consume. Starting around the twenty-eighth year of the family life cycle, children as a group produce virtually all of what they consume. The economic contributions of Maya children offset a considerable portion of their own consumption costs. Children's contributions, importantly, play a substantial role during the peak economic squeeze in the mid-family life cycle when the greatest number of children is living at home and parents face bottlenecks in their ability to support multiple dependent young.

When the P/C ratio is calculated for the relative contribution that young children (3–6), juveniles (7–18) and sexually mature children (19 and older) make as a group, juveniles fund between 82 per cent and 93 per cent of their own costs and between 35 and 52 per cent of the family's total consumption during the mid-family cycle.

Figure 4.7. Maya children's gross production and consumption across the family life cycle.

Help from Older Adults

Among some groups of foragers, grandmothers help their daughters resolve the competing demand of providing competent childcare and food for older children by caring for young children while their daughters spend time away from camp foraging. In other forager contexts, mothers with newborns spend less time foraging and grandmothers' assistance in food collection is critical to subsidizing weaned dependents (Hawkes et al. 1989, 1997, 1998; Hurtado et al. 1992). For example, among the Hadza, foragers in sub-Saharan Africa, children's weight is correlated with mother's foraging effort, but only for non-nursing mothers. With the birth of a new child, children's weight is correlated with foraging effort of older adults (O'Connell et al. 1999).

The few studies for which time allocation data are reported specifically for older adults, indicate that they remain hard workers until late in life (Hawkes et al. 1989, 1997; Kaplan 1994; Kramer 2005a; Turke 1988). Likewise, although Maya adults in their fifties begin to produce less as the number of children living at home decreases, most adults remain net producers throughout their life span (Figure 4.8). A comparative time allocation study of the Piro and Machiquenga, two groups of South American horticulturalists, and the Maya shows that a high proportion of older adults produce more than they consume (Table 4.2). As net producers these older adults not only continue to support themselves, but also produce a surplus that can be transferred to help subsidize others (Lee et al. 2002). However, it is less clear who the recipients are of their surplus labour.

Across the family life cycle, as Maya mothers age and their older children leave home, mothers' production surplus stays more or less constant. If their production surplus does not decline in step with the number of children living at home, is it be-

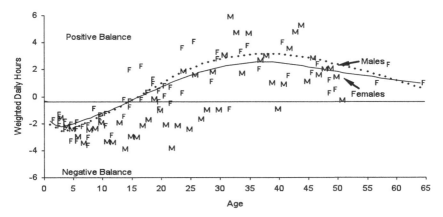

Figure 4.8. Net production balance (production minus consumption) across the Maya life course. Markers showing individual values for males and females. Dotted line showing average values for males and solid line average values for females.

Table 4.2. Proportion of adults fifty and older who maintain a positive production balance in three natural fertility populations (Lee, Kaplan and Kramer 2002).

| | Percent of Net Producers over Age 50 | |
	Male	Female
Machiquenga	75%	67%
Piro	100%	80%
Maya	75%	100%

cause these mothers have older dependent children who consume more than younger children, or because they are subsidizing grandchildren? Because of large family size and long reproductive careers, Maya grandmothers are also mothers through much of their post-reproductive lives. Most Maya mothers still have several dependents living at home when they are well into their post-reproductive years and are already grandmothers themselves. Each of the older adults in the Maya sample is a parent as well as a grandparent, and still has several children living in their household, usually including an older son, his spouse and children. Labour is pooled across these commensal groups, and these grandchildren no doubt benefit from the help of older co-residential adults. Maya grandmothers, for example, are the care givers in 4 per cent of all childcare observations.[6] In most cases, childcare by a grandmother occurs in the situation described above, in extended households where a married son, his wife and children live with his parents. Maya parents are in their early sixties when their last child leaves home and marries.

Several studies have shown that the *presence* of grandmothers *correlates* with child survival (Jamison et al. 2002; Voland and Beise 2002). But demonstrating that it is their help rather than social status or other form of support that is *causally* related to the probability of survival is more problematic. Supporting time allocation data are critical to make this link. However, few time-budget studies document the transfer of a grandmother's labour or resources to her grandchildren and their effect on grandchildren's survival or nutritional status. Exceptions include the well-cited work among the Hadza, which shows that older women's foraging returns covary with weight changes in children (Hawkes et al. 1997) and among the Hiwi and Ache (Hurtado et al. 1985).

The value of grandmothers' help is expected to vary with subsistence ecology and demography. Where grandmothers have many daughters or many grandchildren, the effect of a grandmother's help on any one grandchild, or on a daughter's fertility may be beneficial, but is likely too diffuse to formally model. For example, most older Maya parents have well over twenty grandchildren. One alternative is to model the effect that Maya grandmothers and other helpers have on offsetting maternal time constraints.

Evaluating the Effect of Helpers on Maternal Time Constraints

A logistic nested modelling procedure is used to evaluate the effect that helpers have on the probability that a mother engages in childcare. Logistic regression is advantageous in analysing behavioural data because it maximizes sample size by treating each scan sample, rather than the individual, as a binary observation. A nested, or hierarchical, model selection procedure culls among a set of predictor variables to determine the utility of including an additional term. The utility of the added term is assessed by subtracting the models' deviances, or log-likelihood ratios. The remainder, or drop in deviance, is then compared to a X^2 distribution with one degree of freedom. If the drop in deviance is significant, the inclusion of the term improves the fit of the model (Colette 1991).

After adding a consumer term for the demand on mother's time – in this case the number of co-residential children six and younger – helper terms are sequentially added to the model (Table 4.3; top half). The sample includes 2447 scan observa-

Table 4.3. Results of fitting nested logistic models for the probability of a mother engaging in childcare.

Terms Fitted to Nested Model		Deviance	DF
Intercept		2143	2446
# of children 0–6		2090	2445
# of children 0–6, mother living in village		2082	2444
# of children 0–6, mother living in village, # female children 11–18		2075	2443
# of children 0–6, mother living in village, # female children 11–18, # female in-laws in household		2008	2442

Best Fit Model	Parameter Estimate	Wald Chi Sq	p value
Intercept	–2.0183	88.47	<.0001
# of children 0–6	0.3906	30.68	<.0001
mother living in village	–0.2976	6.26	.0123
# female children 11–18	–0.8307	56.17	<.0001
# female in-laws in household	–0.2214	7.57	.0059

Deviance is the -2 log likelihood of the current model and DF is the number of observations minus the number of parameters. Sample inclusion criteria included mothers who have a children under the age of seven (2447 observations on 15 mothers).

tions for 15 mothers. Mothers who have a mother living in the village and the number of co-residential daughters aged eleven to eighteen are significant when added to the model. The drop in deviance is most significant when the number of female in-laws that a mother has living in her household is added to the model. (Sons and daughters over the age of eighteen, who allocate much less time in childcare than do younger daughters, were not significant when added to the model). The parameter estimates generated from the best fit model are the predicted log odds of an increase or decrease in y for an increase in x (Table 4.3; bottom half). Exponentiation transforms a parameter estimate into a more interpretable adjusted odds ratio. Adjusted odds ratios from the best fit model show that a variety of helpers reduce the probability of a mother allocating time to childcare. A mother is .74 ($e^{-.2976}$) less likely to engage in childcare when her mother lives in the village, .8 ($e^{-.2214}$) less likely if she has one daughter eleven to eighteen and half as likely ($e^{-.2214(3)}$) if she has several daughters ages eleven to eighteen. If a mother has a co-residential female in-law, it reduces her probability of allocating time to childcare by half ($e^{-.8307}$).

Maya mothers may benefit from different age classes of helpers at different points in their reproductive careers. Early in her reproductive career, a mother is mostly likely to have a living mother. Newlyweds not uncommonly live in the male's natal household for several years until they establish a household of their own. Proximity to female in-laws may be an important source of childcare help to a young mother. Later in their reproductive careers, when mothers are most pressed by the competing demands of supporting both younger and older children, they no longer live in their husbands' natal households. During this mid-family life cycle mothers are less likely to have a surviving mother, but most likely to have productive-aged daughters.

Conclusion

Because children's ability to support themselves falls below their consumption, in all human societies children are subsidized by others throughout much of their growth and development. Mothers, however, have a finite time and resource budget out of which various competing expenditures must be funded: taking care of themselves, providing primary care to younger children, and food and other resources to older children. Under natural fertility conditions, since mothers often have multiple dependents of different ages, they are faced with an allocation problem. In recognition of this, a number of seminal discussions in anthropology have centered on allocare strategies to provision children.

When mothers reach bottlenecks in the time and resources that they have available to support multiple dependents, they have several options to redistribute the cost of raising children. They can increase their own labour effort, or draw on help from some combination of spouses, co-residential children, older female adults or other related and non-related individuals.[7] The Maya study suggests that mothers both increase production as the number of dependents grows over the family life cycle, and receive help from a variety of family members.

Several points are made in conclusion. First, although Maya mothers do increase production as the number of dependents grows over the family life cycle, they are most stretched to meet their family's consumption when their children are older, not younger, when they require food and other investments, not childcare. The time that mothers and fathers allocate to economic production is similar, albeit with an emphasis on different kinds of activities. Fathers spend time in food production, but provide little help with childcare. Mothers receive the most help in childcare first from their children, then from their sisters, their spouse and their mother. Second, while children assist in childcare, their most important contributions are toward alleviating the time mothers spend in food production and domestic tasks. Third, Maya parents have enough hours in the day to support about four children. If mothers alone were responsible, they would be able to support even fewer children. Because four children is the very lowest limit of family size in natural fertility populations (Bentley et al.1993), it suggests that alloparenting has been an aspect of human reproductive strategies for as long as mothers have sustained this level of fertility. Hrdy's (1999, 2002, 2005b) work has been important in emphasizing the ancestry of cooperative breeding as a gateway condition to other human life history attributes.

Lastly, for the few populations for which age-specific production and consumption data are available, older adults clearly remain net producers and help to subsidize others until late in life. The duration of the life stage when older women are economically unencumbered by the conflicting interests of providing for their own children, or helping grandchildren, is affected by the timing of births, child survivorship and female adult mortality rates. Under pre-industrial mortality schedules, the likelihood of a mother having a surviving productive-aged child, older sister or mother varies over the family life cycle, and different age classes of helpers would be important at different points in a woman's reproductive career.

Allomaternal care is an important human reproductive strategy both as a buffer to child mortality and in underwriting fertility. In a theoretic multivariate model, for example, Crognier et al. (2001: 372) show that sibling allocare augments maternal reproductive success primarily through an increase in child survival. Other studies have shown that helpers allow mothers to raise more children than they might otherwise be able to by having either a positive effect on shortening birth interval length, lengthening reproductive span or fertility (Bereczkei 1998; Flinn 1989; Kramer 2002). The chapter by Sear and Mace (this volume; Sear et al. 2000) shows that the presence of a maternal grandmother is associated with improved child survival, but patrilineal kin is important to fertility. The effect of helpers on *both* mortality and fertility was likely critical to the demographic success of humans relative to other primates (Kramer 2005b).

The traditional view of past population growth was that gains in fertility were kept in check by high child mortality. Recent models of past population growth, however, suggest that, rather than a stable pattern of high fertility and high mortality, rates varied. This oscillation rendered the net effect of low population growth until the modern demographic transition (Boone 2002; Keckler 1997). If past population growth occurred in fits and starts, human mothers had to successfully negotiate a variety of demographic conditions and their effect on the availability of helpers to subsidize the cost of raising children.

The distribution of the cost of reproduction appears key to holding the human life history combination of a relatively fast reproductive rate and a long duration of juvenile dependence in balance. Unlike other great apes, prolonging investment in offspring occurred without compromising maternal reproductive success. Flexibility in allomaternal strategies would have been crucial to alleviate constraints in maternal time and resource budgets throughout the family life cycle and under variable demographic conditions.

Notes

1. Two recent overviews estimate higher percentages for cooperative breeding in birds of 8–17 per cent (Cockburn 1998; Heinsohn and Double 2004).
2. There is some ambivalence in the cooperative breeding literature about where to place the help of fathers. In avian studies, where ideas about cooperative breeding were developed, traditionally the help of fathers is considered male parental investment, not allocare per se. When genetic testing opened up the possibility of ascertaining paternity, it became clear that many male helpers were not fathers at all. In recent cooperative breeding studies, to avoid making assumptions about paternity, male assistance in raising young is often considered an extension of allocare.
3. Median birth interval in each parity (1–7) varies between 2.0 and 2.2 years, with a range of one to seven years (Kramer and McMillan 2006).
4. The Coale–Demeny Model West female life table with a life expectancy of 70 was selected based on the close fit between table parameters and the age distribution and mortality rates of the village population. A life expectancy of 70 is equivalent to about four deaths per 1000 per year, or 1.26 deaths per year in Xculoc. With all village members accounted for, there were 12 deaths between the 1992 and 2003 census, or 1.2 deaths per year.
5. Maya children under the age of two receive 80 per cent of all childcare observations, and children six and younger, 98 per cent of childcare observations.
6. Table 4.1 reports that a Maya infant *receives* 1.2 per cent of its childcare from a grandparent. The time allocation study included a sample of village residents and did not necessarily include all of a child's grandparents or all of a grandparent's grandchildren. Unless the sample included all possible caregivers and all possible children, there will be slight differences in percentage values depending on whether childcare is viewed from the point of view of the giver or the receiver.
7. A third option is to decrease consumption. Because the Maya live at subsistence level, mothers are expected to reduce consumption only under dire circumstances.

References

Altmann, J., 1974. Observational study of behaviour: sampling methods. *Behaviour* 49, 227–67.

Asa, C., 1997. Hormonal and experiential factors in the expression of social and parental behaviour in canids. In N. Solomon and J. French, eds., *Cooperative Breeding in Mammals*. Cambridge:Cambridge University Press, 129–49.

Astrand, I., 1971. Estimating the energy expenditure of housekeeping activities. *The American Journal of Clinical Nutrition* 24, 1471–75.

Bales, K., Dietz, J., Baker, A., Miller, K., and Tardif, S., 2000. Effects of allocare-givers on fitness in infants and parents of Callitrichid primates. *Folia Primatologica* 71, 27–38.

Becker, G.S., 1981. *A Treatise on the Family*. Cambridge: Harvard University Press.

Bentley, G., Goldberg, T., and Jasienska, G., 1993. The fertility of agricultural and non-agricultural societies. *Population Studies* 47, 269–81.

Bereczkei, T., 1998. Kinship network, direct childcare, and fertility among Hungarians and Gypsies. *Evolution and Human Behaviour* 19(5), 283–98.

Bock, J., 1995. The Determinants of Variation in Children's Activities in a Southern African Community. Ph.D. thesis, Department of Anthropology, University of New Mexico.

Boone, J.L., 2002. *Subsistence strategies and early human population history: An evolutionary ecological perspective*. World Archaeology 34(1), 6–25.

Borgerhoff Mulder, M., and Caro, T.M., 1985. The use of quantitative observational techniques in anthropology. *Current Anthropology* 26, 323–35.

Borgerhoff Mulder, M., and Milton, M., 1985. Factors affecting infant care in the Kipsigis. *Journal of Anthropological Research* 41(3), 255–60.

Bove, R.B., Valeggia, C.R., and Ellison, P.T., 2002. Girl helpers and time allocation of nursing women among the Toba of Argentina. *Human Nature* 13(4), 457–72.

Brown, J.L., 1987. *Helping and Communal Breeding in Birds*. Princeton: Princeton University Press.

Cain, M., 1977. The economic activities of children in a village in Bangladesh. *Population and Development Review* 3, 201–27.

Clutton-Brock, T.H., 2002. Breeding together: kin selection and mutualism in cooperative vertebrates. *Science* 296, 69–72.

Cockburn, A., 1998. Evolution of helping behavior in cooperatively breeding birds. *Annual Review of Ecology and Systematics* 29, 141-77.

Collett, D., 1991. *Modelling Binary Data*. London: Chapman and Hall.

Crognier, E., Baali, A., and Hilali, M.K., 2001. Do 'helpers at the nest' increase their parents' reproductive success? *American Journal of Human Biology* 13, 365–73.

Denham, W.W., 1974. Infant transport among the Alyawara tribe, Central Australia. *Oceania* 64(4), 253–77.

Draper, P., and Hames, R., 2000. Birth order, sibling investment and fertility among Ju/Hoansi (!Kung). *Human Nature* 11(2), 117–56.

Draper, P., and Harpending, H., 1987. Parental investment and the child's environment. In J. Lancaster, J. Altmann, A. Rossi, and L. Sherrod, eds., *Parenting across the Lifespan: Biosocial Dimensions*. New York: Aldine Press, 207–35.

Dunbar, R.I.M., 1976. Some aspects of research design and their implications in the observational study of behaviour. *Behaviour* 58(1–2), 58–78.

Durnin, J.V., and Passmore, R., 1967. *Energy, Work and Leisure.* London: Heinemann Educational Books.

Emlen, S.T., 1984. The evolution of cooperative breeding in birds and mammals. In J.R. Krebs and N.B. Davies, eds., *Behavioural Ecology. An Evolutionary Approach,* Second Edition. London: Blackwell Scientific Publications, 305–39.

———— 1991. Evolution of cooperative breeding in birds and mammals. In J.R. Krebs and N.B. Davies eds. *Behavioural Ecology. An Evolutionary Approach,* Third Edition. London: Blackwell Scientific Publications, 301–37.

Fairbanks, L., 1990. Reciprocal benefits of allomothering for female vervet monkeys. *Animal Behaviour* 40, 553–62.

Flinn, M.V., 1988. Parent-offspring interactions in a Caribbean village: daughter guarding. In L. Betzig, M. Borgerhoff Mulder and P. Turke, eds., *Human Reproductive Behaviour: A Darwinian Perspective.* Cambridge: Cambridge University Press, 189–200.

———— 1989. Household composition and female reproductive strategies in a Trinidadian village. In A. Rasa, C. Vogel and E. Voland, eds., *Sociobiology of Sexual and Reproductive Strategies.* London: Chapman and Hall, 206–33.

Goldizen, A.W., 1987. *Tamarins* and marmosets, communal care of offspring. In B. Smuts, D. Cheney, R. Seyfarth, R.Wrangham and T. Struhsaker, eds., *Primate Societies.* Chicago: University of Chicago Press, 34–43.

Goodman, M., Griffin, P., Estioko-Griffin, A., and Grove, J., 1985. The comparibility of hunting and mothering among the Agta hunter-gatherers of the Philippines. *Sex Roles* 12, 1199–209.

Greaves, R., n.d. Fishing strategies and technology. Ethnoarchaeological research strategies for Pumé foragers.

Hames, R., 1988. The allocation of parental care among the Ye'Kwana. In L. Betzig, M. Borgerhoff Mulder and P. Turke, eds., *Human Reproductive Behaviour: A Darwinian Perspective.* Cambridge: Cambridge University Press, 237–51.

———— 1992. Time allocation. In E.A. Smith and B. Winterhalder, eds., *Evolutionary Ecology and Human Behaviour.* New York: Aldine De Gruyter, 203–35.

Hawkes, K., O'Connell, J. and Blurton Jones, N., 1989. Hardworking Hadza grandmothers. In V. Standen and R.A. Foley, eds., *Comparative Socioecology: The Behavioural Ecology of Humans and Other Mammals.* London: Basil Blackwell, 341–66.

———— 1995. Hadza children's foraging: juvenile dependency, social arrangements, and mobility among hunter-gatherers. *Current Anthropology* 36(4), 688–700.

———— 1997. Hadza women's time allocation, offspring provisioning and the evolution of long postmenopausal life spans. *Current Anthropology* 38(4), 551–77.

Hawkes, K., O'Connell, J., Blurton Jones, N., Alvarez, H., and Charnov, E., 1998. Grandmothering, menopause and the evolution of human life histories. *Proceedings of the National Academy of Sciences* 95, 1336–39.

Heinsohn, R., and Double, M. C., 2004. Cooperative or speciate: new theory for the distribution of passerine birds. *Trends in Ecology and Evolution* 19(2), 55-60.

Hewlett, B., 1988. Sexual selection and paternal investment. In L. Betzig, M. Borgerhoff Mulder and P. Turke, eds., *Human Reproductive Behaviour: A Darwinian Perspective.* Cambridge: Cambridge University Press, 263–76.

———— 1991. Demography and childcare in preindustrial societies. *Journal of Anthropological Research* 47(1), 1–37.

Hill, K., and Kaplan, H., 1988. Tradeoffs in male and female reproductive strategies among the Ache, part 1 and 2. In L. Betzig, M. Borgerhoff Mulder and P. Turke, *Human Reproductive Behaviour: A Darwinian Perspective.* Cambridge: Cambridge University Press, 277–305.

Hrdy, S.H., 1999. *Mother Nature.* New York: Pantheon Books.

———— 2002. On why it takes a village: cooperative breeders, infant needs and the future. In *The Tanner Lectures on Human Values* 23, 57–110. Salt Lake City: University of Utah Press.

———— 2005a. Comes the child before the man: how cooperative breeding and prolonged postweaning dependence shaped human potential. In B.S. Hewlett and M.E. Lamb, eds., *Hunter-Gatherer Childhoods.* New Brunswick: Transaction Publishers, 65–91.

———— 2005b. Evolutionary context of human development: the cooperative breeding model. In C.S. Carter, L. Ahnert, K.E. Grossman, S.B. Hrdy, M.E. Lamb, S.W. Porges and N. Sachser, eds., *Attachment and Bonding: A New Synthesis.* Cambridge: M.I.T. Press, 9–32.

Hurtado, M., Hawkes, K. Hill, K., and Kaplan, H., 1985. Female subsistence strategies among Ache hunter-gatherers of eastern Paraguay. *Human Ecology* 13, 1–28.

———— 1992. Trade-offs between female food acquisition and child care among Hiwi and Ache foragers. *Human Nature* 3(3), 1–28.

Irons, W., 1983. Human female reproductive strategies. In S. WASSER, ed., *Social Behaviour of Female Vertebrates.* New York: Academic Press, 169–213.

Ivey, P.K., 2000. Cooperative reproduction in Ituri Forest hunter-gatherers: who cares for Efe infants? *Current Anthropology* 41(5), 856–66.

Jamison, C.S., Cornell, L.L., Jamison, P.L., and Nakazato, H., 2002. Are all grandmothers equal? A review and a preliminary test of the 'Grandmother Hypothesis' in Tokugawa Japan. *American Journal of Physical Anthropology* 119, 67–76.

Kaplan, H., 1994. Evolutionary and wealth flows theories of fertility: empirical tests and new models. *Population and Development Review* 20(4), 753–91.

Kaplan, H., Hill, K., Lancaster, J., and Hurtado, A.M., 2000. A theory of human life history evolution, diet, intelligence, and longevity. *Evolutionary Anthropology* 9(4), 156–85.

Keckler, C.N.W., 1997. Catastrophic mortality in simulations of forager age-at-death: where did all the humans go? In R.R. Paine, ed., *Integrating Archaeological Demography, Multidisciplinary Approaches to Prehistoric Populations.* Carbondale, Il.: Center for Archaeological Investigations, Occasional Paper No. 24, 205–28.

Kramer, K.L., 1998. Variation in Children's Work among Modern Maya Subsistence Agriculturalists. PhD Thesis. Department of Anthropology, University of New Mexico.

———— 2002. Variation in juvenile dependence, helping behaviour among Maya children. *Human Nature* 13(2), 299–325.

———— 2004. Reconsidering the cost of childbearing: the timing of children's helping behaviour across the life cycle of Maya families. In M. Alvard, ed., *SocioEconomic Aspects of Human Behavioral Ecology*, Research in Economic Anthropology, Volume 23, Amsterdam: Elsevier, 335–53.

——— 2005a. *Maya Children, Helpers at the Farm*. Cambridge: Harvard University Press.

——— 2005b. Children's help and the pace of reproduction: cooperative breeding in humans. *Evolutionary Anthropology* 14(6), 224–37.

Kramer, K.L., and McMillan, G.P., 1998. How Maya women respond to changing technology: the effect of helping behaviour on initiating reproduction. *Human Nature* 9(2), 205–23.

——— 2006. The effect of labor saving technology on longitudinal fertility changes. *Current Anthropology* 47(1), 165–72.

Lancaster, J., Kaplan, H., Hill, K., and Hurtado, A.M., 2000. The evolution of life history, intelligence and diet among chimpanzees and human foragers. In F. Tonneau and N.S. Thompson, eds., *Perspectives in Ethology. Evolution, Culture and Behaviour*, Volume 13. New York: Kluwer Academic, 47–72.

Lancaster, J., and Lancaster, C., 1987. The watershed: change in parental-investment and family-formation strategies in the course of human evolution. In J. Lancaster, J. Altmann, A. Rossi and L. Sherrod, eds., *Parenting Across the Life Span*. New York: Aldine De Gruyter, 187–205.

Lee, R.B., 1979. *The !Kung San: Men, Women and Work in a Foraging Society*. Cambridge: Cambridge University Press.

Lee, R.D., and Bulatao, R.A., 1983. The demand for children: a critical essay. In R.A. Bulatao and R.D. Lee, eds., *Determinants of Fertility in Developing Countries*, Volume 1. New York: Academic Press, 233–87.

Lee, R.D., and Kramer, K.L., 2002. Children's economic roles in the Maya family life cycle, Cain, Caldwell and Chayanov revisited. *Population and Development Review* 28(3), 475–99.

Lee, R.D., Kramer, K.L., and Kaplan, H., 2002. Children and the elderly in the economic life cycle of the household: a comparative study of three groups of horticulturalists and hunter-gatherers. Paper presented at the Annual meeting of the Population Association of America, Atlanta, Georgia.

Levine, R.A., 1977. Child rearing as cultural adaptation. In S. Leiderman, R. Tulking, and A. Rosenfeld, eds., *Culture and Infancy: Variations in the Human Experience*. New York: Natural History Press, 15–27

McKenna, J.J., 1987. Parental supplements and surrogates among primates: cross-species and cross-cultural comparisons. In J. Lancaster, J. Altmann, A. Rossi, and L. Sherrod, eds., *Parenting Across the Life Span*. New York: Aldine De Gruyter, 143–84.

Mitani, J.C., and Watts, D., 1997. The evolution of non-maternal caretaking among anthropoid primates: Do helpers help? *Behavioural Ecology and Sociobiology* 40, 213–20.

Munroe, R., Koel, A., Munroe, R., Bolton, R., Michelson, C., and Bolton, C., 1983. Time Allocation in Four Societies. *Ethnology* 22, 355–70.

Nag, M., White, B., and Peet, R., 1978. An anthropological approach to the study of the economic value of children in Java and Nepal. *Current Anthropology* 19(2), 293–306.

O'Connell, J.F., Hawkes, K., and Blurton Jones, N.G., 1999. Grandmothering and the evolution of *Homo erectus. Journal of Human Evolution* 36, 461–85.

Panter-Brick, C., 1989. Motherhood and subsistence work: the Tamang of rural Nepal. *Journal of Biosocial Science* 23, 137–54.

Reynolds, P., 1991. *Dance Civet Cat: Child Labour in the Zambezi Valley.* Athens: Ohio University Press.

Sear, R., Mace, R., and McGregor, I.A., 2000. Maternal grandmothers improve the nutritional status and survival of children in rural Gambia. *Proceedings of the Royal Society B* 267, 461–67.

Skutch, A.F., 1935. Helpers at the nest. *Auk* 52, 257–73.

——— 1987. *Helpers at Birds' Nests. A Worldwide Survey of Cooperative Breeding and Related Behaviour.* Iowa City: University of Iowa Press.

Turke, P.W., 1988. Helpers at the nest: childcare networks on Ifaluk. In L. Betzig, M. Borgerhoff Mulder and P. Turke, eds., *Human Reproductive Behaviour: A Darwinian Perspective.* Cambridge: Cambridge University Press, 173–88.

——— 1989. Evolution and demand for children. *Population and Development Review* 15(1), 61–90.

Ulijaszek, S., 1995. *Human Energetics in Biological Anthropology.* Cambridge: Cambridge University Press.

Voland, E., 1988. Differential infant and child mortality in evolutionary perspective. In L. Betzig, M. Borgerhoff Mulder and P. Turke, eds., *Human Reproductive Behaviour: A Darwinian Perspective.* Cambridge: Cambridge University Press, 253–61.

Voland, E., and Beise, J., 2002. Opposite effects of maternal and paternal grandmothers on infant survival in historical Krummhörn. *Behavioural Ecology and Sociobiology 52*, 435-43.

Weisner, T., 1987. Socialization for parenthood in sibling caretaking societies. In J. Lancaster, J. Altmann, A. Rossi and L. Sherrod, eds., *Parenting across the Lifespan: Biosocial Dimensions.* New York: Aldine De Gruyter, 237–70.

Weisner, T., and Gallimore, R., 1977. My brother's keeper: child and sibling caretaking. *Current Anthropology* 18, 169–90.

Whiting, B.B., and Edwards, C.P., 1988. *Children of Different Worlds. The Formation of Social Behaviour.* Cambridge: Harvard University Press.

Woolfenden, G.E., and Fitzpatrick, J.W., 1984. *The Florida Scrub Jay: Demography of a Cooperative-Breeding Bird.* Princeton: Princeton University Press.

• 5 •

Flexible Caretakers

Responses of Toba Families in Transition

Claudia R. Valeggia

Alloparenting in Foraging Societies

The study of allomothering has received increasingly more attention from anthropologists and evolutionary biologists during the last decade. It is now well established that, compared to other primates, human children require extensive maternal care or investment. Considerable evidence shows that they also require non-parental investment as well if they want to improve their chances of survival. Furthermore, it has been hypothesized that allomaternal help was essential during human evolution (Hrdy 1999, 2005). According to the cooperative breeding hypothesis, childcare provided by people other than the mother played a pivotal role in shaping our species (Hrdy 2005). Allomothering would have allowed women to have energetically expensive babies and shorten inter-birth intervals without jeopardizing child survival. A special case of this line of reasoning is known as the 'Grandmother Hypothesis', developed by Kristen Hawkes and her colleagues (Hawkes et al. 2001; Hawkes et al. 1998; O'Connell et al. 1999). This hypothesis proposes that help provided by post-reproductive female kin, particularly maternal grandmothers, was critical for child survival and a major driving force in human evolution. However, childcare practices do not leave fossils. Thus, we do not really know, and probably never will, what the exact childcare pattern or variety of patterns were the norm in the Pleistocene. However, evidence derived from extant foraging societies can give us some clues on the variables that may have had an impact on the way children were raised, allowing us to attempt a reconstruction of the history of the human family.

A quick review of the best-studied hunter-gatherer societies reveals a considerable variability in the degree of use of allomothers around the world. For an extensive review of childcare patterns in hunter-gatherer groups, readers should consult Konner's reevaluation of the hunter-gatherer childhood model (Konner, 2005). In Table 5.1, I present examples of the variability in allomothering practices in eight foraging societies from around the world. This spectrum takes us from no use of allomothers among the Aché of Eastern Paraguay, to intermediate use among the Hadza of Tanzania and the Hiwi of the Venezuelan llanos, to the Efe of the Ituri Forest: the most extreme example of allomothering in a foraging population. Among the Aché, childcare seems to take priority over all other maternal activities, including foraging. Aché mothers carry infants and toddlers all the time; they even sleep in a sitting position, cross-legged with the infant on their laps (Hill and Hurtado 1996). Quite oppositely, Efé infants as young as three weeks old spend almost 40 per cent of their time in

Table 5.1. Comparison of use of allomothering in selected foraging populations.

Ethnic group	Local ecology	Degree of use of allomaternal infant care	Who allocares?	References
Aché	Neotropical forests	No use of allomothers	No one	Hill & Hurtado 1996
Yąnomamö	Neotropical forests	Very low	Female kin (if ever)	Kuzara & Hames 2004
!Kung	Dry savannah	Intermediate-low	Girls, multi-age peer group	Konner 2005
Shipibo	Neotropical forests	Intermediate	Female kin preferentially, siblings, other relatives	Hern 2004
Hiwi	Neotropical savannah	Intermediate	Kin women, kin men, older sibling	Hurtado et al. 1992
Hadza	Dry savannah	Intermediate	Grandmothers, fathers (dry season)	Marlowe 2005
Aka	Tropical forest	Substantial	Fathers, other kin	Hewlett B. 1991; Hewlett & Lamb 2005
Efe	Tropical rain forest	Very high	Kin boys and girls, kin men, kin and nonkin women	Ivey 2000; Ivey et al, 2005; Tronick et al. 1987

physical contact with individuals other than their mothers and by five months of age, babies spend more time with allomothers than with their own mother (Ivey Henry et al. 2005; Tronick et al. 1987). In between these two extremes we find a whole range of childcare practices. There is also variation, but to a lesser extent, in the identity of the alternative caretakers in those societies that do show alloparenting care. Female kin, particularly grandmothers and sisters, are more frequently engaged as caretakers than other sex and age categories. Two common features emerge from the analysis of childcare patterns in different societies. First, regardless of the degree of use of allomothering, the mother is still the primary caretaker ('maternal primacy', Konner 2005). Second, although not all studies evaluate age of the baby, there is a marked tendency to rely more on allomothers as the child grows. This tendency most likely reflects breastfeeding and subsistence work patterns in each society.

Several hypotheses, at different levels of analysis and from different perspectives, have been advanced to explain the high variation in use of alternative caretakers in foraging societies. Paula Ivey (Ivey 2000) summarizes evolutionary explanations of allomothering behaviour in three major, not mutually exclusive, groups: nepotism, reciprocity, and learning-to-mother. In a nutshell, assuming that most cases of allomothering involve close kin, allomothers would act nepotistically because they would increase their own genetic representation by helping parents rearing close relatives. Other reasons for explaining the evolution of alloparenting involve reciprocal altruism. In small human groups, with frequently interacting individuals (even if unrelated), allocare could be considered a cooperative behaviour, such as food sharing: 'today I help you, tomorrow you help me'. Finally, the learning-to-mother hypothesis proposes that allomothers gain personal, but delayed benefits through skills acquired from caring for someone else's offspring. The general observation that young girls are frequently observed as alternative caretakers seems to support this hypothesis. The 'helping-at-the-nest' behaviour (Emlen, 1984) exhibited by older sisters would combine the first and last of these evolutionary explanations of allomothering. By caring for their younger siblings, girls would increase their parents' reproductive success, increasing their own inclusive fitness (Crognier et al. 2001; Crognier et al. 2002; Turke 1988; but see Hames and Draper 2004) and, at the same time, they would acquire critical mothering skills for future reproductive attempts.

At another level of analysis, we find hypotheses that evaluate the proximate causes of allomothering behaviour. Variation in childcare patterns has been associated with demographic variables such as number of adult women without children present in the village, density of the settlement, fertility and mortality patterns, and sex and age distribution in camp (Hewlett 1991; Hewlett and Lamb 2005; but see Ivey 2000 for contrasting evidence). Following this model, the degree of use of allomothers would be directly related to the availability of caretakers. The more women without children present in the group, the more allomothering that population would exhibit. Meehan (2005) found that, among the Aka of the Central African Republic, residential locality had an effect on alloparental behaviour. In this foraging group, there was a significant variation in the identity of the allomother depending on whether the residence was uxorilocal or patrilocal. Fathers provided more care when the couple resided with paternal kin than when they resided with maternal kin. Also associated with allomothering is the flexibility in schedules and degree of leisure time in each society: the hunter-gatherer lifestyle would be more permissive of multiple caregiving behaviour than the more rigorous farmer or herder schedule (Hewlett and Lamb 2005).

Other lines of research have stressed the local ecological context of the population (Crittenden 2003). A general ecological model would propose that childcare patterns are the result of infants and caretakers employing strategies that are shaped by ecological factors (Hewlett 1988; Tronick et al. 1985). According to one of these ecological explanations, the more dangerous the environment is for infants/toddlers, the less alloparenting a population will exhibit (Hurtado et al. 1992). For example, the lush forests of Eastern Paraguay pose many threats to young Aché children (snakes, poisonous insects, jaguars, poor visibility of the underbush, among others). It is to be expected that alloparenting, especially that provided by young siblings, will not be common in foraging people inhabiting those forests. More benign environments, such as the open plains or the African savannahs would allow mothers to safely leave their children under someone else's care (including less experienced girls) while they engage in productive or reproductive tasks. Allomothering, then, would be more common in these environments. To that respect, Hurtado et al. (1992) proposed a useful construct that allows the comparison of different environments in terms of their degree of HIA, i.e., health insults (to offspring) that a parent can avoid by doing their own childcare. In the previous examples, the Paraguayan forests have a high degree of HIA, whereas savannah environments, in general, have a lower degree of HIA. Allomothering would be directly related to the HIA: the higher the HIA, the lower the use of alternatives caretakers and vice versa. The degree of HIA would also be directly related to women's acquisition rates and time spent foraging. The trade-off between women's economic contribution and childcare in foraging societies has been the focus of several excellent behavioural ecology studies (Hames 1988; Hill and Hurtado 1996; Hurtado et al. 1992; Panter-Brick 1989; and Kramer, this volume), which contributed to a better understanding of life history strategies in human populations. The same topic has been analysed from an economic perspective by Gillian Paull in this volume (Chapter 7).

Assuming that alloparenting evolved as an adaptive response to the demands of the environment, what would happen if the ecological context in which a foraging group is immersed were drastically altered? Evidence, by now quite substantial, seems to indicate that alloparenting behaviour is facultative and the entire childcare system of a society could be flexible, reflecting variation both within and between groups. From that perspective, which aspects of childcare would be the most prone to be modified? Would the amount and timing of alloparenting change? Would the identity of allomothers be different? The Toba of the South American Gran Chaco offer us an excellent opportunity to answer these questions. In the next sections I briefly summarize the ethnohistory of these Amerindian groups, describe their current situation, and analyse the past and present use of allomothers during infancy. I will conclude by evaluating whether a radical change in subsistence activities correlates with changes in childcare patterns.

The Toba of Argentina

The Toba are one of the eighteen linguistically different indigenous groups inhabiting the Gran Chaco. The Toba belong to the Guaycurúan linguistic family. There are written references to the Gran Chaco Indians from European soldiers from as early as the mid 1500s (Schmidel 1970). These groups successfully resisted Spanish colonization and Argentine expansion policies until the late 1800s. Chacoan Indians, particularly the Toba, who adopted the horse complex, had a reputation of being fierce warriors (Martinez Sarasola 1992). Despite considerable language variation, all Chacoan indigenous groups shared similar subsistence economies. The groups were traditionally nomadic or semi-nomadic hunter-gatherers, with occasional horticulture (Braunstein and Miller 1999; Mendoza and Wright 1989). Female gathering played a major role in Chaco economies, complementing the almost exclusively male activities of hunting, fishing, and honey collecting. They organized themselves in exogamous bands led by family chiefs (Braunstein and Miller 1999). Monogamy was, and still is, the norm.

Mendoza (1994) defines a Toba residential unit as 'a family unit culturally defined by relatedness, genealogy, and co-residency, where people developed specific tasks related to production, distribution, and transmission of knowledge and to the reproduction of the members' (ibid: page 243, my translation). The most frequent residential unit was the matrilocal, extended family. This unit consisted of an adult pair, their offspring, the woman's parents and, eventually, her bachelor siblings.

There is little information on alloparenting practices in Chacoan hunter-gatherers. Interviews with elders suggest that both men and women spent time foraging and left infants with post-reproductive women or young female relatives (unpublished field notes). Some also reported that ten to twelve-year-old girls were also recruited as allomothers. During the *algarroba* fruiting season, a period of intense collection in the hottest months of the year, women left infants preferably with grandmothers or great aunts. In the absences of those, they used to take with them girl relatives (daughters, sisters) to mind the baby while they collected the *algarroba* fruits (Marcela Mendoza, pers. comm.). Fathers, or other men, were never mentioned as being possible caretakers, not even during the fruit collection season, which was said to be the time 'for men to rest and women to work'. It is notable that Toba elders always mention alloparenting in relation to women's foraging activities.

Until the 1930s most communities still relied on foraging for their subsistence. During the last century, disruptions to their traditional lifestyle (e.g., through missionisation, state limitation of their mobility) and ecological deterioration of the habitat forced many communities to migrate to urban centres and become sedentarised. At present, indigenous communities in the Gran Chaco fall along an acculturation continuum which goes from the more traditional, living in rural, isolated areas, to the more Westernized communities living in the periphery of most non-indigenous towns in the Gran Chaco and in the city of Rosario and Buenos Aires (Miller 1999). This variability of settlement patterns provides a good opportunity for a long-term study of the role of local ecology and economics on alloparenting structure, fertility, and gender relations.

Alloparenting in a Rural Toba Community

As part of the Chaco Area Reproductive Ecology (C.A.R.E.) program, our research team is currently conducting a long-term study of the reproductive ecology of the Western Toba, a group of 7–10 communities living in a remote, rural area of the dry Chaco, about 500 km west of the city of Formosa, Northern Argentina. A total of 1500 people live in a 35,000-ha., community-owned property. Although there is a certain degree of mobility both within the property and between the property and a more urbanized town located 50 km away, most families are sedentary and have been so for the last thirty years.

These groups still rely considerably on hunting, gathering, and fishing for their subsistence. Depending on the season, the average percentage of foraged items varies between 25 and 75 per cent (Gordillo 1995, and unpublished data). In this highly seasonal environment, the months of October to February are the bountiful months. Women collect several kinds of fruits (*algarroba, chañar, mistol*), and wild legumes during the early good season. Men collect honey and hunt rabbits, small deer, peccaries, and armadillos. March and April are the months of fish abundance, but a poor season for hunting and collecting. Families eat mainly fish and honey. Some families even move to a temporary camp closer to the wetlands in order to be closer to the fishing places. The following months (May to July) are dry and cold and resources from the forest are scarce (Valeggia et al. 2005).

During this part of the year these rural communities also tend small, low-maintenance gardens that yield melons, watermelons, and various types of squash. Most families supplement their diet with store-bought food, such as noodles, wheat flour, rice, eggs, and beef. Cash to purchase such items comes from different sources: government subsidies for large families or for unemployment (both men and women), temporary jobs men take in the nearby towns (men), permanent jobs such as health agents and school teaching assistants paid by the provincial government (very few men), and returns from the sale of weavings and handicrafts to travellers and merchants from Formosa city (women).

We conducted a series of interviews aimed at estimating the daily time allocation and diet composition of Western Toba adult men and women at different times of the year during one calendar year (2002–3). We interviewed approximately 102 men and

98 women, ages fifteen to sixty years old (Valeggia et al. 2005). From these interviews we were able to glean information about the performance and frequency of childcare activities in men and women of different ages. Only two men, aged twenty-five and thirty-six, reported minding children as an activity, and both of them did it during the time of fruit gathering. Both men were married and they reported having taken care of their own infants. As expected, all nursing mothers indicated that they provided care to their infants. Across all seasons, an average of 52 per cent of postmenopausal women indicated having performed childcare activities. A similar percentage (49 per cent) was found for nulliparous women aged fifteen to nineteen years old.

As part of a study of time allocation and subsistence activities, we also conducted day-long observations of families in which there was at least one infant (< 24 months old). We visited twenty-four families from dawn to dusk and recorded, every fifteen minutes, who was taking care of the infant. These observations confirmed that adult men seldom provided infant care: they were in charge of the infants in less than 2 per cent of the observation points (Figure 5.1). We found that the mother was the main caretaker in about 60 per cent of the observation points. Older sisters and maternal grandmothers were the two categories that most contributed to allomaternal care, followed by aunts and female cousins.

Ad libitum observations (unpublished) also suggest that it is mostly young, related girls who are the main providers of alloparenting care, at least for nursing infants. During the fruit-gathering season, mothers usually take their nursing infants with them, but they also take along older daughters, young sisters, or nieces that carry the baby when they are actively gathering fruits in the forest. Weaned children (approximately two to four years old) usually join older children's groups and roam around the community with them, only going to their mothers when they are sleepy or hungry.

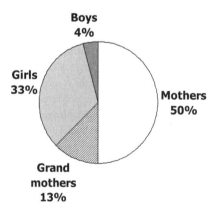

Figure 5.1. Mean percentage of observation points by caregiver category in a rural Toba community.

Alloparenting in a Peri-urban Toba Community

Our C.A.R.E. Program studies extended to Namqom, a peri-urban village located 11 km north of the city of Formosa, northern Argentina. A population of approximately 2,500 people is distributed in an area of 120 ha. Since their settlement in 1972, the community has been growing rapidly because of a high fertility rate (TFR = 6.7, Valeggia and Ellison 2004) and massive immigration from rural communities. The degree of mobility in this community is quite low and current lifestyle can be characterized as sedentary.

The Toba of Namqom rely mainly on the wage labour of men and on government subsidies for their subsistence. Most men are hired as temporary workers in Formosa city or by development programs. Some men work on a permanent basis for state organizations receiving a stable monthly pay. Women's activities include household chores, care taking of children, and basket weaving. Some women are employed as cooks, teaching assistants, or housemaids, while others receive unemployment subsidies and must devote some hours to community work. Women sell their handicrafts door-to-door in the city and it is common to see them, accompanied by several children, walking along city streets selling baskets or asking for hand-outs from non-indigenous people.

In the context of a longitudinal study of breastfeeding and fertility (Valeggia and Ellison 2004), we collected data on childcare practices in this population. We observed a group of seventy-five breastfeeding mothers and their infants (aged zero to eighteen months) longitudinally for an average of eleven months. We visited each of the mother–infant pairs twice a month and observed the interaction between the infant and any available caregiver.

Caring for their infants was the activity in which Toba mothers spent most time (Figure 5.2). On average, they spent 34 per cent of their waking time tending their babies. Mothers were the infant's primary caregivers most of the time (77 per cent of the observation points). The average 22 per cent of allomothering in this population is accounted for by the participation in care taking of close relatives of the baby (non-related allomothers accounted for only 0.8 per cent of the observation points, Figure 5.3). The use of alloparents increased with age of the infant ($F_{1,771} = 14.8$, $p < 0.001$) from 17.3 per cent at 0 to 3 months of age to 41.7 per cent for infants older than 18 months. Allomothering was not related to the age of the mother nor her parity (all $p > 0.10$), although mothers with many children tended to use alternative caretakers more often.

In contrast to the rural Toba population, fathers were the most frequent allomothers. The father's involvement in childcare increased with the infant's age ($R^2 = 0.2$, $p = 0.02$). In a couple of cases, the father was the only caretaker during the entire observation period. In a preliminary study, we found that babies whose fathers were present during the first two years of life spent fewer months in sub par nutritional status than babies whose father was absent (Ellis and Valeggia 2003). However, babies of single mothers had fewer respiratory infections than babies of married mothers.

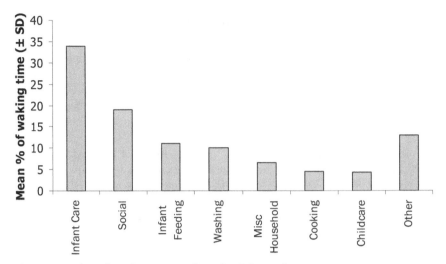

Figure 5.2. Time allocation pattern of nursing Toba mothers.

Interestingly, married and single mothers did not differ in the amount of alloparenting use. We did not find differences in any other health variable between children of married mothers and children of single mothers. Care provided by others in single-mother homes even if it does not differ in frequency or degree from married-mother homes seems to compensate for lack of paternal help.

The other important categories of alloparents are female relatives, mainly older sisters, grandmothers, and aunts (Figure 5.3). Even if the amount of alternative care from other females is relatively low, mothers with more women relatives in the household relied more on alloparenting than mothers who had fewer relatives ($\rho = -0.3$, $p = 0.012$). Grandmothers and aunts, when available, provided care regardless of

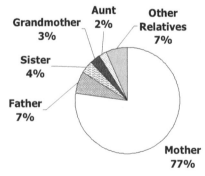

Figure 5.3. Mean percentage of observation points by caregiver category in a peri-urban Toba population.

the age of the baby. On the other hand, girl helpers were not involved in care giving when the infant was young and only became part of the 'alternative care staff' when the baby was older (fifteen months and older). In fact, in a study of the influence of girl helpers on their nursing mother's time allocation, we did not find differences in infant care activities between mothers with older daughters and mothers without daughters (Bove et al. 2002). Women with girl helpers spent more time in social activities and less time in domestic work.

Allomothering in Transition Times: A Conclusion

Along the acculturation continuum currently exhibited by Chacoan indigenous populations, the ecological context of rural Toba populations seems to be the most similar to the conditions of their traditional past. Although they have changed their nomadic lifestyle for a more sedentary one, the general environment (both physical and social) resembles what early ethnographers had described for these populations. Our observations of rural communities suggest that few changes in the local ecology are related to few changes in the traditional pattern of alloparenting. Mothers still recruit helpers quite often, mainly during the demanding fruit season. These helpers are, as in the past, related post-reproductive and non-reproductive female kin.

In contrast, the peri-urban population is undergoing a drastic lifestyle change, with important demographic, nutritional, and epidemiological consequences. Families do not forage any more and rely heavily on subsidies from the government. Several demographic variables that may have a direct impact on availability of allomothers have been changing rapidly in the last few decades. Both age at first birth and interbirth intervals are steadily declining, while total fertility rate is increasing (Sanchez-Ocasio 2003; Sanchez-Ocasio and Valeggia 2005). As a result, there is a great overlap of generations. Grandmothers still have nursing infants of their own and therefore are not available as allomothers. Unemployed or partially employed husbands are present at home a considerable portion of the day. Our study suggests that, in response to a less demanding subsistence lifestyle and a changing social context, alloparenting practices changed among the Toba. Unlike their more traditionally living relatives, peri-urban mothers rely less on others for taking care of their nursing infants. And when they do, it is husbands more than other relatives who collaborate.

These findings agree well with what Barry Hewlett found for other hunter-gatherer societies (Hewlett and Lamb 2005). He proposed that variability in multiple care-giving practices could be explained by differences in demographic factors. For example, a high adult-to-child ratio would favour allomothering. With higher fertility rates than before, this ratio is nowadays quite low in Namqom, explaining some of the differences with the rural population. In addition, as Hewlett again proposed, the amount of leisure time is also having an impact on who cares for the baby and how much. Adult men have more free time available than adult women, who are busy raising their own children.

However, availability of alternative caregivers does not explain the differences found in our studies. Given Namqom's high fertility rates, we would expect larger families, with more availability of older sibling care. Although in fact families are larger and there are plenty of opportunities for 'helping at the nest', girls do not provide direct infant sibling care as much. A possible explanation would be that in this peri-urban setting, girls attend school and, thus, are not at home to participate in their sibling's care. Still, school hours are 7:30 AM to 12:00 PM and most girls do not engage in school-related activities in the afternoon (Bove et al. 2002). Older daughters do help, but not with infant care. Childcare seems to be a priority for women in Namqom. The amount of time nursing mothers spent in infant care (approximately 35 per cent) is considerable and it exceeds the normative 10 per cent of women's time allocated to childcare in other cultures (Ware 1981). This pattern is not at all infrequent and has been documented in other foraging and non-foraging cultures (Gallimore et al. 1974; Hill and Hurtado 1996).

Because of its marginalization from mainstream economic activities as well as from traditional subsistence activities, Namqom offers little opportunity for women's work outside the home. In addition, the kind of domestic work required in the household does not require sophisticated skills or demanding physical activity (Valeggia and Ellison 2004). In this situation, domestic work, a time-demanding task that can be delegated to helpers, might be deemed the responsive variable while care of infants is the constant priority for mothers. It is important to note that this study was focused on infants who were still nursing (exclusively and semi-exclusively). As seen many other societies, it is possible that weaned children receive more allomothering care than nursing infants. In fact, the most frequent sight in Toba villages is the multi-age sets of children playing in common areas (streets, plazas) and going from household to household (Mendoza 1994). These multi-age sets include toddlers usually carried by older siblings. On many occasions, when asked about where her last child was during an interview, the mother would reply that she did not really know, that the child must be with 'sus hermanos' (his/her siblings), apparently not giving much thought to it. The presence of an older sister in the multi-age group would potentially be beneficial since she could provide the weanling with closer attention than other less-related or younger children in the group would. Given the high mortality at weaning in Toba populations (23 per cent, Programa Nacional de Nacimientos y Defunciones 2000), it is likely that sisters can make an important contribution to their young sibling's health.

The effects on childcare of changing lifestyles in hunter-gatherer groups have been recently analyzed for the Baka of southeastern Cameroon (Hirasawa 2005). Originally a foraging nomadic society, the Baka are now settled and rely mainly on farming for their subsistence. Hirasawa's data suggest that, as is the case for the Toba, many childcare behaviours change when foragers settle down. In contrast to the Toba, however, the settled Baka are shown to depend more on children (mainly siblings) for childcare than foragers. Time in direct physical contact and age at weaning are other child-rearing characteristics that seem to have decreased as they became settled. This change is most likely related to the shift in subsistence patterns (from foraging to time-demanding farming).

In conclusion, this study suggests that allomothering practices are responsive to changes in the social and physical environment, and, as such, are flexible and dynamic. There seems to be a constellation of biocultural factors affecting whether, from whom, and when to allocare. Looking back into evolutionary times, the study of how those factors impacted on childcare practices in traditional societies can shed some light on our understanding of the evolution of the human family. This study adds to the increasingly stronger evidence which points to childcare being a *time allocation* problem for women in traditional (and non-traditional) societies. Thus, the use of allomothers would be in direct relation to the woman's economic contribution to the family. Looking forward, the study of childcare practices in societies in transition can help us to understand better the mechanics of enculturation, i.e., the process by which children learn their culture. How will the change in time devoted to childcare by the mother affect the way children perceive gender relations and roles in the family? In just one or two generations, a shift from being brought up by several (mostly female) caregivers in a mobile community to being raised by just the mother plus sometimes the father can deeply affect the modal personality of the population (Kelly 1995), and, therefore, the process of cultural evolution.

References

Bove, R.M., Valeggia, C., and Ellison, P.T., 2002. Girl helpers and nursing women's activities among the Toba of Argentina. *Human Nature* 13, 457–72.

Braunstein, J., and Miller, E., 1999. Ethnohistorical Introduction. In E. Miller, ed., *Peoples of the Gran Chaco.* Westport, CT: Bergin & Garvey.

Crittenden, A.N., 2003. Female Subsistence Strategies and the Energetic Constraints of Motherhood: Implications for the Evolution of the Sexual Division of Labor in Hominids. MA Thesis. University of California, San Diego.

Crognier, E., Baali, A., and Hilali, M-K., 2001. Do 'helpers at the nest' increase their parents' reproductive success? *American Journal of Human Biology* 13, 365–73.

Crognier, E., Villena, M., and Vargas, E., 2002. Helping patterns and reproductive success in Aymara communities. *American Journal of Human Biology* 14, 372–79.

Ellis, P., and Valeggia, C., 2003. Father vs. nonpaternal allomothering effects on child health among the Toba of northern Argentina. *American Journal of Physical Anthropology Supplement* 38, 78.

Emlen, S.T., 1984. Cooperative breeding in birds and mammals. In J.R. Krebs and N. Davies, eds., *Behavioural Ecology: An Evolutionary Approach.* Sunderland, MA: Sinauer, 245–81.

Gallimore, R.J., Boggs, J.W., and Jordan, C., 1974. *Culture, Behaviour, and Education: A Study of Hawaiian Americans.* Beverly Hills, CA: Sage.

Gordillo, G., 1995. La subordinación y sus mediaciones: Dinámica cazadora-recolectora, relaciones de producción, capital comercial y estado entre los Tobas del oeste de Formosa. In H. Trinchero, ed., *Producción doméstica y capital: estudios desde la antropología económica.* Buenos Aires: Biblos.

Hames, R.B., 1988. The allocation of parental care among the Ye'kwana. In L. Betzig, M.B. Mulder and P. Turke, eds., *Human Reproductive Behaviour: A Darwinian Perspective.* Cambridge: Cambridge University Press, 237–51.

Hames, R.B., and Draper, P., 2004. Women's work, child care, and helpers-at-the-nest in a hunter-gatherer society. *Human Nature* 15, 319–41.

Hawkes, K., O'Connell, J.F., and Blurton Jones, N.G., 2001. The evolution of human life histories: primate tradeoffs, grandmothering socioecology, and the fossil record. In P. Kappeler, and P. Pereira, eds., *The Role of Life Histories in Primate Socioecology.* Chicago: University of Chicago Press, 204–227.

Hawkes, K., O'Connell, J.F., Blurton Jones, N.G., Alvarez, H., and Charnov, E.L., 1998. Grandmothering, menopause, and the evolution of human life histories. *Proceedings of the National Academy of Sciences* 95, 1336–39.

Hern, W.M., 2004. Shipibo. In: C.R Ember and M. Ember, eds. *Encyclopedia of Medical Anthropology.* New York: Kluwer Academic, 947–956.

Hewlett, B.S., 1988. Multiple caretaking among African pygmies. *American Anthropologist* 91(1):186–191.

——— 1991 Demography and childcare in preindustrial societies. *Journal of Anthropological Research* 47, 1–37.

Hewlett, B.S., and Lamb, M., 2005. *Hunter-Gatherer Childhoods: Evolutionary, Developmental and Cultural Perspectives.* New Brunswick: Aldine Transaction.

Hill, K.R., and Hurtado, A.M., 1996. *Ache Life History: The Ecology and Demography of a Foraging People.* New York: Aldine de Gruyter.

Hirasawa, A., 2005. Infant care among the sedentarized Baka hunter-gatherers in southeastern Cameroon. In: B.S. Hewlett and M. Lamb, eds., *Hunter-Gatherer Childhoods: Evolutionary, Developmental and Cultural Perspectives.* New Brunswick: Aldine Transaction, 365–84.

Hrdy, S.B., 1999. *Mother Nature: A History of Mothers, Infants, and Natural Selection.* New York: Pantheon Books.

Hrdy, S.B., 2005. On why it takes a village: cooperative breeders, infant needs, and the future. In: R.L.Burgess and K. MacDonald, eds. *Evolutionary perspectives on human development.* Thousand Oaks: Sage Publications, 167-188.

Hurtado, A.M., Hill, K.R., Kaplan, H., and Hurtado, I., 1992. Trade-offs between female food acquisition and child care among Hiwi and Ache foragers. *Human Nature* 3, 185–216.

Ivey Henry, P.K., Morelli, G.A., and Tronick, E.Z., 2005. Child caretakers among Efe foragers of the Ituri Forest. In B.S. Hewlett and M. Lamb, eds., *Hunter-Gatherer Childhoods: Evolutionary, Developmental and Cultural Perspectives.* New Brunswick: Aldine Transaction, 191–213.

Ivey, P.K., 2000. Cooperative reproduction in Ituri Forest hunter-gatherers: who cares for Efe infants? *Current Anthropology* 41, 856–66.

Kelly, R.L., 1995. *The Foraging Spectrum: Diversity in Hunter-Gatherer Lifeways.* Washington DC: Smithsonian Institution Press.

Konner, M.J., 2005. Hunter-gatherer infancy and childhood: the !Kung and others. In B.S. Hewlett and M. Lamb, eds., *Hunter-Gatherer Childhoods: Evolutionary, Developmental and Cultural Perspectives.* New Brunswick: Aldine, 19–64.

Kuzara, J., Hames, R., 2004. Yąnomamö. In: C.R. Ember and M. Ember, eds. *Encyclopedia of Medical Anthropology.* New York: Kluwer Academic/Plenum, 1017–1028.

Marlowe, F., 2005. Who tends the Hadza children? In: B.S. Hewlett and M. Lamb, eds. *Hunter-Gatherer Childhoods: Evolutionary, Developmental and Cultural Perspectives.* New Brunswick: Aldine Transaction, 177–190.

Martinez Sarasola, C., 1992. *Nuestros Paisanos los Indios.* Buenos Aires: Emece.

Meehan, C.L., 2005. The effects of residential locality on parental and alloparental investment among the Aka foragers of the Central African Republic. *Human Nature* 16, 58–80.

Mendoza, M., 1994. Tecnicas de observación directa para estudiar interacciones sociales infantiles entre los Toba. *RUNA* xxi, 241–62.

Mendoza, M., and Wright, P.G., 1989. Sociocultural and economic elements of the adaptation systems of the Argentine Toba: the Nacilamolek and Taksek cases of Formosa Province. In S.J. Shennan, ed., *Archaeological Approaches to Cultural Identity.* London: Routledge, 242–57.

Miller, E., ed., 1999. *Peoples of the Gran Chaco.* Westport, CT: Bergin & Garvey.

O'Connell, J.F., Hawkes, K., and Blurton Jones, N.G., 1999. Grandmothering and the Evolution of *Homo erectus. Journal of Human Evolution* 36, 461–85.

Panter-Brick, C., 1989. Motherhood and subsistence work: the Tamang of rural Nepal. *Journal of Biosocial Science* 23, 137–54.

Programa Nacional De Nacimientos Y Defunciones, 2000. Programa NacyDef: Informe interno sobre estadísticas vitales de la Provincia de Formosa para el año 2000. Formosa: Derpartamento de Vigilancia Epidemológica. Formosa: Ministerio de Desarrollo Humano.

Sanchez-Ocasio, K., 2003. A Fork in Fertility: The Demographic Transition and Factors Mediating a Fertility Decline among the Indigenous Toba of Argentina. B.A. (Hons) Thesis. Harvard University, Cambridge, MA.

Sanchez-Ocasio, K., and Valeggia, C., 2005. Fertilidad y transición demográfica entre los Toba del Gran Chaco Argentino: Factores mediadores. (Fertility and Demographic transition among the Toba of the Argentine Gran Chaco: Mediating Factors.) Anales del XXIV *Encuentro de Geohistoria* 24, 167–78.

Schmidel, U., 1970. *Viaje al Río de la Plata.* 1534–54. Buenos Aires: Plus Ultra.

Tronick, E.Z., Morelli, G.A., and Winn, S., 1987. Multiple caretaking of Efe Pygmy infants. *American Anthropologist* 89, 96–106.

Tronick, E.Z., Winn, S., and Morelli, G.A., 1985. Multiple caretaking in the context of human evolution: why don't the Efe know the Western prescription for child care? In M. Reite and T. Field, eds., *Psychobiology of Attachment.* New York: Academic Press.

Turke, P., 1988. Helpers at the nest: childcare networks on Ifaluk. In L. Betzig, M. Borgerhoff Mulder and P. Turke, eds., *Human Reproductive Behaviour: A Darwinian Perspective.* Cambridge: Cambridge University Press, 173–88.

Valeggia, C., and Ellison, P.T., 2004. Lactational amenorrhea in well nourished Toba women of Formosa, Argentina. *Journal of Biosocial Science* 36, 573–95.

Valeggia, C.R., Lanza, N.A., and Córdoba, L.I., 2005. Fuentes de variación en la alimentación actual de los toba-pilagá del oeste formoseño. (Sources of variation in the current diet of Toba-Pilaga people in Western Formosa.) *Actas del Quinto Congreso de Americanistas, Sociedad Argentina de Americanistas* 5, 123–42.

Ware, H., 1981. *Women, Demography and Development.* Canberra: Australian National University Press.

• 6 •

Who Minds the Baby?

Beng Perspectives on Mothers, Neighbours and Strangers as Caretakers

Alma Gottlieb

Introduction

In the contemporary middle class of many post-industrialized societies, families are constructed, at least discursively if not in actual fact, as what we call 'nuclear', and babies are raised – again, at least discursively if not in actual fact – so exclusively by one person, generally the mother, that many are convinced that this must be a 'natural' phenomenon with deep roots in biological structures (see Helen Penn, this volume). Yet at the same time that this discourse has firmly taken hold, anthropologists and other researchers have quietly but strikingly been documenting a notable array of caretaking strategies across time and space for even the youngest of children – strategies that diverge significantly from those that hold at least discursive sway in the contemporary post-industrialized West. Elsewhere, these caretaking strategies routinely involve more than just the mother (or a single mother-substitute).

A small but growing literature now explores the multiple options for caretaking of infants that exist in numerous societies across the globe and through time. Indeed, the model of a mother being the exclusive or even major caretaker of her own young children – a model that still exists as normative in the American public imagination, for example, and that is still enacted in at least some middle-class American families (e.g., Richman et al.1988) – is of decreasing relevance even in middle-class, Euro-American society (Harkness and Super 1992). It is far less relevant in other American sub-groups, as well as in many other societies (Weisner and Gallimore 1977). From Pygmies in Central Africa (e.g., Hewlett 1991; Tronick et al. 1987) and peasants in

Cameroon (Nsamenang 1992) to the highlands of Ecuador (Stansbury et al. 2000) to small-town residents in central Italy (New 1988), data are accumulating that the relatively recent, normative Euro-American model of 'mother taking more-or-less exclusive care of her young children' may be something of a statistical anomaly. In West Africa, the Beng pattern of caretaking fits in with this growing awareness that in many societies, the care of infants is more a collective than an individual (mother's) responsibility.[1]

First, a few brief words about the Beng. A small ethnic minority of some twelve thousand in the West African nation of Côte d'Ivoire, the Beng have been sidelined by the Ivoirian state and remain severely impoverished. Precolonially they farmed, hunted, and made some crafts items that had regional appeal, attracting long-distance traders to their villages. Cash-cropping was introduced by the colonial French about a century ago, and – ironically – is responsible for much of their current poverty (Gottlieb 2004: 266–305). Most recently the Beng region has been invaded by rebels in the continuing civil war, who have caused many to flee the region and have kept those who have remained virtually hostage in their own villages.[2] In this chapter I discuss the situation before the current disruptions.

Multiple Caretakers

The waking – and sleeping – hours of Beng infants are marked by a high level of active social interactions with a large number of people. Young children learn to feel physically and emotionally comfortable with a wide array of relatives and neighbours, many of whom serve as (often impromptu) caretakers; they also learn to feel comfortable with strangers. I begin this discussion by exploring the multiple social ties that Beng infants forge with a large range of familiar Others and then investigate the striking case of 'strangers' who form part of the social universe of village-dwelling Beng babies. Throughout the chapter, I aim to demonstrate that the Beng child-rearing agenda emphasizes as a major goal the teaching of the value of sociability. The strategy has foundations most obviously in women's labour practices but also, perhaps even more interestingly, in religious ideology.

At somewhere between two and four months of age, a (relatively healthy) Beng baby starts to range out from the household fairly regularly. It is then that a post-partum woman (assuming she has recovered normally from the delivery) starts returning to work in the fields. By three to four months post-partum, she is generally back at her agricultural labour full time. For her part, the baby spends much of the day in a vertical position on someone's back, often napping (see Gottlieb 2004: 165–84). Sometimes this back belongs to the baby's mother. But undertaking very demanding physical labour with a baby attached to her back is not considered optimal for a new mother's own health and can also seriously reduce her work productivity. For these reasons, a mother often tries to find a regular babysitter, or *leŋ kuli*, for her infant. This is especially important if a woman has other young children whom she is taking care of, or if her fields are far and she would have to walk long distances carrying her baby on her back while carrying crops, firewood and tools on her head. A *leŋ kuli* can hold the baby while the mother walks to the fields balancing a heavy head load of crops, farm tools, cooking pots, or firewood.

A lucky new mother will be able to commandeer the baby-carrying services of a relative (see Gottlieb 2004: 136–64). A girl between the ages of seven and fourteen is ideal: old enough to have the strength to carry an infant, but not so old that she is working full time in her own field. Women usually choose girls rather than boys for babysitters because boys generally accompany their fathers to work in the fields. But if a competent boy is available, he will not be overlooked as a babysitter.

Figure 6.1. This young Beng girl holds a baby on her back as long as her strength allows.

Mothers also try to find someone with a 'good character' (*sie geŋ*). In some cases, the baby may grow quite attached to a young caretaker. An older child may point to the now grown woman and reminisce warmly, 'She was my *leŋ kuli*'.

Nevertheless, not all babysitters can work full time. For one thing, the younger the child caretaker, the more likely that she will tire quickly, and the baby will not last long on her youthful babysitter's aching back. For their part, adult women and even teenagers have their own fields to farm. And babies themselves may fuss in ways that adults interpret as a request for a change of carrier. Beng adults attribute a high degree of both cognition and volition to infants, due to a conception that they have recently been living another life in a place the Beng call *wrugbe* (or, the afterlife) (Gottlieb 2004: 79–104). Thus the claim that infants may request a change of carrier is consistent with a broader model of infant intelligence, memory, and emotion, and babies tend to pass quite often from one back to another on any given day.

Figure 6.2. This Beng grandmother regularly takes care of her grandson while her daughter works.

Recognizing this likelihood, many Beng mothers of infants try to create a reliable network of several potential *lɛŋ kuli* who can care for their infants intermittently while they do their work. They make the children as physically attractive as possible in order to attract a wide pool of potential baby holders. Thus mothers typically spend an hour or so every morning grooming their babies, including applying herbal medicine in attractive designs, and cleaning jewelry (Gottlieb 2004: 105–35). The morning bath routine is partly designed to 'seduce' potential babysitters into offering their caretaking services to an irresistibly beautiful baby.

Typically, a baby will not spend more than an hour or two with a given person. In a quantitative study that I conducted, the commonest length of time that infants remained with a given caretaker was a mere five minutes (see Table 6.1). The next commonest duration for remaining with a single caretaker was ten minutes. After that, the next three most common durations were fifteen, twenty and twenty-five minutes (the latter two times were tied for fourth place). During the forty-one two-and-a-quarter-hour sessions that we observed, the babies were engaged with an average of 2.2 people, but in many cases they were engaged with three to four people, and in two cases they were engaged with five or six people (see Table 6.2).[3]

The quality of Beng caretaking is as intense as its quantity is dense. When adults and older children are around infants, it is common for them to engage actively with

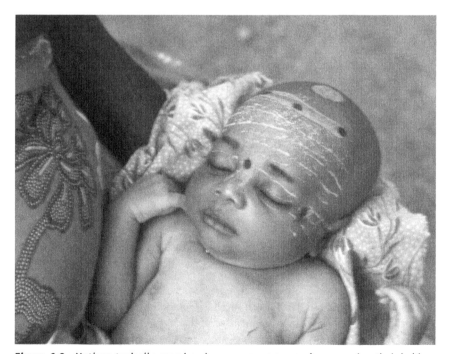

Figure 6.3. Mothers typically spend an hour or so every morning grooming their babies.

Table 6.1. Number of minutes spent with a given caretaker.

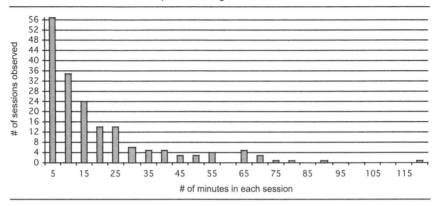

Table 6.2. Number of people with whom babies interacted during forty-one 2½-hour periods of observation. (Average 2.2 people per baby.)

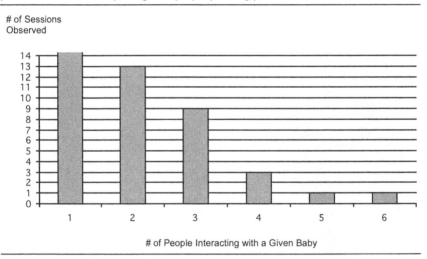

the babies. Traditionally, infants enjoyed any number of body-oriented games and songs (but see Gottlieb 2004 266–305 for recent changes). There is much face-to-face engagement, and frequent changes of the faces in the baby's line of vision, at any given moment. Babies often play together and with toddlers in their family or in neighbouring compounds, with much social stimulation for much of the day.

Babies also change position frequently. Adults and older children may place infants in moving positions in which they gain a great deal of physical as well as social stimulation – such as being enthusiastically dragged about for a rough ride in an old

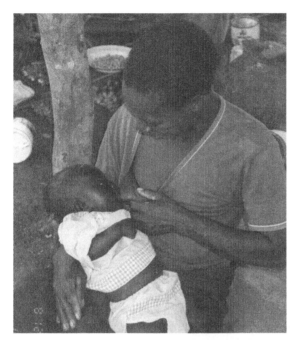

Figure 6.4. This Beng grandmother offers her empty breast to her grandson—who is content to suck on it as a pacifier for some time while awaiting his mother's return.

Figure 6.5. Beng infants benefit from much face-to-face engagement. This mother, Tahan, is enjoying her infant son, Sassandra.

box by an older sibling, or sitting on the handlebars of a bicycle for a playful ride around the courtyard with a favourite uncle. Through the abundance of caretakers and the common pattern of actively playing with and talking to them, Beng babies learn early to value sociability.

After infancy, this casual passing among a large and fluctuating group of caretakers takes on new dimensions. My notebooks are replete with examples of the casual movements of toddlers, as adults care for them in rotation. To provide the flavor of such practices, I quote from three typical entries from my field notes regarding a single child, not-quite-three-year-old Chantal and her mother, M'Akwe:

13 July 1993

Today M'Akwe brought Chantal along with her to the fields. But when she got to her sister Véronique's fields, she left Chantal with her brother's son, Kouakou Alphonse, to serve as the girl's *lεŋ kuli* for the day. Alphonse was weeding the fields of his father's sister, Véronique [who was there with another of Chantal's aunts], and myself. For her part, M'Akwe was going to work in a field that's very far away, helping her cross-cousin Akissi harvest rice. Chantal could not walk the long distance to the fields, nor would M'Akwe want to carry her all that way. It would be even more difficult to carry Chantal back to the village while also carrying a heavy load of rice on her head.

Chantal spent the morning contentedly grilling forest snails and playing around her various older relatives working in her aunt's fields. But at noon, when two of her aunts and I mentioned that we were getting ready to return to the village, Chantal decided to come along. At not-quite-three, she had already learned that she might join any number of caretaking groups, and when there were reasonable alternatives, the adults in her life generally allowed Chantal to choose her preferred option at any given moment.

8 August 1993

This morning, M'Akwe went off to [the somewhat distant Beng village of] Manigbe to work in the fields with a friend from the village. The friend has parents living in Manigbe, and it's their fields that M'Akwe will be weeding with her friend. Because she'll be too busy working, she left Chantal in Asagbe for the day. [Chantal moved casually between many caretakers during the course of the day.]

9 August 1993

Today, M'Akwe went to the fields and left Chantal behind in the village. She is left in the care of whoever is in the courtyard. [Once again, Chantal moved casually between many caretakers during the course of the day.]

In the middle-class sector of the post-industrialized nations, such casual comings and goings of young children might easily be taken as a 'risk factor'. But the anthropologist Mary Douglas and her colleagues have argued that the concept of 'risk' is as much a matter of cultural perception as it is pharmacological or physical reality (Douglas 1966, 1970, 1992: 3–121; Douglas and Wildavsky 1982; also see Gottlieb 2004: 105–35; Rizzini and Dawes 2001: 316). Thus, in the Beng context, casual comings and goings of even very young children are meant to convey to the children themselves a feeling of safety, not one of risk. Indeed, they should have the effect of socializing young children to feel comfortable with most transfers of caretaking responsibility over them. Adults view children's lives as normatively somewhat peripatetic, and they do not consider this a risk for healthy emotional development. Mothers take this overall child-rearing strategy farther in teaching their children to feel comfortable not only with a broad array of relatives and neighbours, but even with strangers.

Strangers in a Beng Land

Following Mary Douglas, I suggest that the ways in which members of a society conceive of dangers – as localized internally or externally, for example, or as sited in tangible or invisible loci – says much about how they imagine the notion of community, and how they imagine their ideal model for relations among neighbours. Thus it is significant that the generalized fear of the Stranger-as-Dangerous-Other occurs in contemporary societies in which the bonds of family are themselves often strikingly attenuated. Concomitantly, child development researchers working largely in Western (and Westernized) countries have noted that infants and young children in these nations tend to establish a relatively small number of emotionally intense relationships, or 'attachments' – generally to those in their nuclear families, and especially to their mothers. Accordingly, the bulk of the voluminous 'attachment' literature in the field of psychology still remains decidedly matricentric, although some contemporary developmental psychologists and other scholars are endeavouring to forge a culturally nuanced model of emotional attachment by expanding the focus of their research to include infants' emotional 'attachments' to fathers, day care teachers, and other adults.[4]

In any case, unlike many middle-class Euro-Americans, Beng adults do not socialize their youngest members to fear strangers, with the goal of defining the very category of 'stranger' as socially/symbolically/legally threatening. Instead, Beng adults train children to view 'strangers' as friendly.

'Strangers' in Beng Infants' Lives

Let us start with the local meanings of the concept of 'stranger' itself. By Beng definition, a stranger, or *tiniŋ*, is neither (intrinsically) morally good nor bad, neither threatening nor protecting.[5] However, far more often than not, *tiniŋ* are seen in a positive light. To refer to most *tiniŋ* who enter a Beng village, 'visitor' or 'guest' would be a better English translation than 'stranger'. Yet in some contexts, the English 'stranger', with its typically negative connotations, does fit well. For it is true that some *tiniŋ* do in the end turn out to be unwelcome, occasionally even threatening. But on initial encounters, the benefit of the doubt regarding the character of the *tiniŋ* is routinely accorded, and 'strangers' are generally assumed innocent unless proven guilty.

That *tiniŋ* occupy a categorically valued social space in Beng thought is revealed in architectural practice. While building a new house, a homeowner often incorporates one log of a particular tree somewhere in the construction. People refer to this as the *tiniŋ yrí*, or 'stranger/visitor/guest/tree' because this arboreal species is said to house benevolent spirits (*bɔŋzɔ*) that, when incorporated into a house frame, will attract numerous strangers/guests to the home. Rural Beng women are careful never to chop down these trees as firewood, otherwise the resident spirits would curse the offending woman by never allowing *tiniŋ* to visit her home.

Moreover, in most situations, strangers don't remain 'strangers' for more than a few moments at most.[6] Beng hosts and hostesses welcoming a stranger exhibit a range of behaviours that 'de-strangerize', we might say, the stranger. For example, they use a formulaic welcoming greeting that is repeated in all such encounters, which itself puts a familiar linguistic frame around the unfamiliar.[7] In the course of this greeting sequence, adults may initiate eye contact and usually shake hands; and the host(ess) inevitably offers the visitor both a chair and a drink of water. Beng infants witness such predictable behaviours regularly. This predictability may incline infants to interpret encounters with strangers in a manner that reduces or obviates any anxiety that a newcomer might otherwise produce. Observing that adults in the compound are exhibiting friendly and familiar behaviour to a visitor should key a young child into the friendly status of the guest – as psychologists have noted occurs in Western experimental situations (e.g., Clarke-Stewart 1978: 115–19).

If Beng villagers attempt to familiarize the stranger, many middle-class Euro-Americans often attempt to do the opposite: to estrange the familiar. Nowadays, websites with write-in advice are replete with the pleas of adults who are torn between whether or not to intervene when they perceive neighbors' or strangers' children acting unhappily, or even being neglected or abused (http://episteme.arstechnica.com/eve/forums/a/tpc/f/34709834/m/288004007931); lamenting the sort of non-community-oriented society we live in that can produce extreme neglect and abuse that goes unnoticed by neighbours (http://www.shoutdaily.com/2008/08/do-we-ignore-our-neighbors-too-much/); and, by contrast, bemoaning meddlesome adults who inappropriately attempt to discipline their friends' and neighbours' 'misbehaving' children (http://www.cafemom.com/answers/106825/When_is_it_okay_for_a_friend_neighbor_to_discipline_your_Child_ren). Although some adults might well intervene in cases of strangers' or neighbours' children being abused or neglected, and some might elegantly defend their right to discipline others' misbehaving children, there is a widespread perception among Euro-Americans that child-rearing is now, for better or worse, the nearly-exclusive domain of the parents, and especially of the mother. The law formalises this perception. Consider the following commentary by a legal scholar examining the American legal basis for absolving people of responsibility to rescue minors who are in grave danger unless they are close relatives or people over whom they have specific, legally constituted authority:

> One judge explained it this way: 'I see my neighbor's two-year-old babe in dangerous proximity to the machinery of his windmill in his yard and easily might, but do not, rescue him. I am not liable in damages to the child for his injuries ... because the child and I are strangers, and I am under no legal duty to protect him.' The judge wrote that in 1897 – over one hundred years ago. And it's still true today (Gajda 1999).[8]

A similar situation in a Beng village would be evaluated quite differently. There, villagers would condemn anyone who did *not* attempt to rescue a young child – or anyone else – who was obviously in grave danger, regardless of their relationship (or non-relationship) to the person at risk. That is, in Bengland, people witnessing a dangerous situation – whether or not they are close kin, neighbours, or even strangers – are considered morally bound to 'attempt a rescue'. Unlike in the American juridical context, the notion of 'stranger' here constricts to the irrelevant.

In Beng villages, other culturally mandated infant care practices teach even very young babies to welcome people who are unfamiliar. The first image the newborn sees is the presence of several people, typically all women, in the birthing room.[9] Of course at this early stage, the newborn knows nothing about kinship and is unable to distinguish between kin and non-kin, stranger and non-stranger. But very soon, the baby will learn that the faces and voices of those first unfamiliar people in the birthing room show up regularly and begin to seem familiar.

At the same time, the newborn's social circle widens dramatically almost immediately following the birth. As soon as a (healthy) infant emerges from the mother's womb and is taken to be washed by one of the older women present, someone from the mother's family announces the baby's arrival to every village household. On hearing the news, people flock to the courtyard to welcome the fresh arrival to the village, and to this life. Within about an hour, a long line forms outside the birthing room. One by one, men and women approach the doorway and address the new mother with a formulaic exchange:

> V(isitor): *ná ka kwàu* [Mother, good afternoon].
> M(other): *àúúúŋ, mú wiyau* [Good afternoon].
> V: *aúŋ. ka n gbà pɔ* [Mm-hmm – what have you given me]?
> M: *leŋɛ* [or] *gɔŋɛ* [A girl (or) A boy].
> V: *kà núwaliaà* [Thank you].
> (The visitor may then toss small change to the mother.)
> M: *aúŋ* [Mm-hmm].

This exchange is repeated over and over as a representative of (ideally) each household arrives to congratulate the new mother. Every village birth I observed or heard about was followed by such a large-scale, ritual greeting.

Of course, Western-trained psychologists would point out that a newborn's memory function is not capable of remembering this point. Yet the general lesson concerning the positive value of a wide range of social contacts, including with strangers, will remain well past the ritual welcoming line, and as the brain develops, the growing child will internalize the lesson.

Over the first few weeks following the birth, the new baby will receive dozens, perhaps hundreds more visits. The new mother should allow each visitor to connect actively with the newborn. Indeed, the newborn is given early instructions in greeting, in which the mother or another caretaker 'speaks for' the baby in encounters with the guest (Gottlieb 2004: 79–104). The typical such encounter involves direct eye contact between the baby and whoever is speaking for him or her – a critical feature for inclining young children to engage in friendly social encounters (e.g. Clarke-Stewart 1978: 121–27).

A Beng baby is frequently introduced to visitors not only visually and verbally but also somatically: normally, someone who travels from another village to visit a new baby should immediately be offered the child to hold. It is considered preferable for the baby to be awake so that the two can be introduced. The mother or an attending kinswoman addresses the baby directly, introducing him or her to the person-who-is-at-first-a-*tiniŋ*. The caretaker points to the guest and then turns to the infant, asking the child directly, 'Who's that?' (*dé kánà?*). If the question is greeted with silence, the caretaker may repeat the question. Depending on the little one's age, the baby may answer with a noise such as 'Mm' or 'Eh'. The caretaker may interpret this as the correct answer, and may then say, pleased, 'Yes, that's your cross-cousin' (*ah-heh, mi pɛnaɛ*) or 'Yes, that's your little mother' (*ah-heh, mi da kroɛ*), and so on, thereby placing the guest in a meaningful social universe.[10] After such a formal introduction, the visitor can now have a face-to-face conversation with the little one.

Of course, such an exchange is problematic if – as happens often in the lives of infants – the baby happens to be sleeping when a guest arrives. In such cases, it is common to awaken the little one. Beng villagers extend the principle behind this practice in a dramatic way. They maintain that in theory, any young child is eligible to be adopted by anyone else in the village, emphasizing the extent to which the bonds of community define many visitors to the household as friendly to the utmost degree.

The contrast with models of appropriate levels of social involvement for newborns that are common in many middle-class, Euro-American households is stark. In the U.S., many middle-class parents are instructed by others around them, including not only their friends and relatives but also professionals such as pediatricians and pediatric nurses, as well as trained advice columnists, that they should pursue a strategy of minimizing – rather than maximizing – social contacts for the newborn and young infant. For example, a recent 'Baby Health & Safety' column in the popular magazine, *Parents,* was subtitled 'Limit visitors to keep baby healthy'. Here, the first-time parent eager for authoritative advice could read:

> It's natural to want to show off your newborn to family and friends. But since even a simple illness is much more worrisome in a young baby than in an older one, try to limit her contact with others – and thus her exposure to bacteria and viruses – for the first four to six weeks, says Thom M. Pantino, M.D., a pediatric urgent-care physician at Egleston Children's Health Care System, in Atlanta. 'There's no harm in stopping by the office or your neigh-bour's with the baby,' says Pantino. 'Just don't stay more than an hour or so, or expose her to lots of people.' (Parents 1996; emphasis in the original)

A Beng mother would at best be perplexed by this advice, and might even consider it selfish, cruel, or even mad.[11]

In Beng villages, the somatic lessons of sociality extend from holding the baby to breastfeeding. In the Beng setting, breastfeeding is a social act that potentially en-compasses more than the classic duo of lactating mother and child. A casual attitude toward wet nursing offered as an improvizatory feeding strategy produces the possi-bility that Beng babies experience the breast as a site not just of nourishment but also of sociability (cf. Kitzinger 1995: 390).[12]

Now let us look at the broader and longer-term implications of the patterns of early infant care that we have so far explored.

Stranger Anxiety?

In the U.S. today, many middle-class mothers who read popular child development books and articles recognize that the onset of 'stranger anxiety' some time toward the end of the first year of life is somewhat expected (if not necessarily desirable). We can take this question-and-answer column by pediatrician William Sears from the popu-lar magazine, *Parents,* as typical of this abundant literature:

Soothing Stranger Anxiety

Q: How long does stranger anxiety typically last? Our 21-month-old daugh-ter gets upset around unfamiliar people. How can we make her more com-fortable meeting strangers?

A: Stranger anxiety usually begins at around 8 months, and can intensify when a child is 1 to 2 years of age, when she becomes more discerning about who gets close to her. It commonly subsides by the age of 3. Rest assured that this behavior isn't a reflection on parenting skills or an indication that a baby is insecure. In fact, some of the most emotionally secure children go through many months of this common phase before they become comfort-able meeting new people. (Sears 1999: 37)

Popular pediatrician-authors such as Sears take their cue from research conducted by developmental psychologists demonstrating that fear or wariness of strangers by older infants and young toddlers, although not universal, is frequently considered normal. As one influential developmental psychologist specializing in this issue has recently written: 'It is clear that negative stranger reactions are common in infancy' (Sroufe 1996: 111).

Some professional research challenges at least implicitly the universality of the 'stage' of 'stranger anxiety' insofar as its authors argue that the context of particular stranger–infant interactions determines much of a given infant's reaction to a given stranger (e.g., Décarie et al. 1974; Mangelsdorf 1992; Rheingold and Eckerman 1973). Clarke-Stewart wrote early on that 'fear of strangers is neither as predictable nor as universal at any one age as once was thought' (1978: 111). Notwithstanding such important caveats in the professional literature, popular opinion nowadays among the Euro-American middle-class tends to valorize the normalcy of 'stranger anxiety'. Is there a place for the concept of 'stranger anxiety' as a normal stage of development in Beng understandings of young childhood?

The Beng language indeed includes a term that might be translated loosely as 'stranger anxiety'. In describing some babies, Beng mothers use the word gbanɛ, explaining that these babies 'do not go to [other] people' (ŋà ta soŋ klɛ). As with their Western counterparts, Beng infants classified by their mothers as gbanɛ are subject to noticeable wariness of strangers, and they exhibit a strong preference for their mothers over all others. And as with their Western counterparts, these infants first exhibit these qualities some time during the second half of their first year.

But unlike their Western counterparts, Beng mothers maintain that the appearance of any level of 'stranger anxiety' at all is rare, and very few Beng babies are classified as gbanɛ. In a large Beng village (pop. ca. 1,500), only one infant was identified to me as gbanɛ. Although there may well have been a few others whom I did not come to observe, they were certainly not abundant.

Equally important, children who are classified as gbanɛ, even mildly so, are considered by the Beng to be 'difficult' (ŋo sie grégré – 'their character is difficult'). Therefore, they are frequently criticized and derided, and Beng mothers and others actively socialize their babies to avoid this type of behaviour. Mothers of such children view themselves as unfortunate for having to deal with what they consider an excessive attachment to them. How will they get their work done? The mother of the gbanɛ child will have to keep the baby with her at all times, and for a full-time farmer this is quite physically demanding. An excessively gbanɛ baby can threaten the mother's ability to complete all the labour, both agricultural and domestic, that is required for her to run and feed a large household, and may even put at risk the food supply of the household.[13]

Thus a baby who exhibits even the mildest form of 'stranger anxiety' or wariness toward strangers – which might be considered normal and even somewhat expected by many Western parents and developmental psychologists alike – is judged at best a nuisance, and at worst a failure, by Beng standards. That is, some babies who would be categorized as emotionally healthy and securely attached to their mothers by psychologists would instead be categorized by Beng mothers as *gbanε*, hence emotionally unhealthy, as well as socially problematic, and even a threat to the household's economic productivity.[14]

By contrast, most babies are classified by the Beng as 'not *gbanε*', are typically quite independent, and are appreciated by their mothers for it. In explaining to me that none of her children had ever exhibited signs of being *gbanε*, one mother told me proudly, '*ŋo ta soŋ klε -- ŋà gbanε*' ('they go with [other] people, they don't cling/stay attached [to me]').

Most Beng babies seem equally comfortable and happy with their mothers and, generally, with a variety of others, including, often, with strangers. In Beng villages, I watched infants daily being passed from person to person – sometimes to people with whom they were quite familiar, at other times to people who were new to them: *tiniŋ* (including myself). In almost all instances, the babies I observed went willingly to their new (temporary) caretakers, and it was rare for them to cry or otherwise express regret, fear, anxiety or anger when their mothers disappeared from view. Later, when they were reunited with their mothers, babies might smile with mild pleasure at the sight of their mothers – especially if they were hungry and hadn't been able to breastfeed while under their babysitter's care. But that pleasure was fairly quiet, and it almost never involved obvious relief from reducing anxiety at being left in another's charge. Indeed, separating from one's mother to be given to someone else – whether or not that someone else is known to the baby – is expected *not* to induce anxiety but rather should ideally be perceived as a routine event that happens without stress many times over, in a typical Beng baby's day. Accordingly, in the Beng view, a mother's return should not normally be the occasion for major rejoicing.[15] In short, I suggest that the tendency for the vast majority of Beng babies and young toddlers to exhibit little or no anxiety around strangers is due to a dual child-rearing agenda: the efforts that Beng mothers make to train their infants to be, in effect, somewhat minimally attached to them; and the complementary efforts that they make to provide abundant social networks, multiple reliable caretakers, and a high comfort level with strangers.

In addition to the methods we have already considered that Beng mothers use to lessen the chance that their children will become singularly attached to them, there is another particularly striking technique that some mothers employ specifically to ensure that their infants do not become *gbanε*. To explain that strategy, I reproduce part of a conversation I had with my field assistant, Amenan:

Alma: Is it possible to know in advance which [babies] will be *gbanε*? Is there a sign?

Amenan: Those who will become like that [*gbanε*] look [a lot] at their mother [when they are quite young].

Alma: When can a child notice the mother?

Amenan: When he or she is one month old.

Alma: Maybe because the mother is doing something intriguing?

Amenan: Me, when [my] babies look in my eyes, I blow in their face; this way, they don't become *gbanε*. … If you get used to a child, you can't work. There are times to work. You can't, if you have a child [you like too much]. You should give him to somebody else [regularly]. It's not good to like the child too much.

In her own parenting efforts, Amenan deliberately endeavoured to reduce her children's emotional attachments to her, and she used such direct and self-conscious methods as trying to break her infant's gaze at herself. Although not all Beng mothers resort to such a dramatic strategy, Amenan is not alone in her use of this technique. And the technique itself is certainly not disapproved of by other Beng women who do not use it themselves. In Amenan's statement, we see encapsulated an extreme version of a child-rearing agenda that is vastly different from that which is common in many middle-class, Euro-American households today.

Interpreting Strangers and Sociability in Beng Villages

What might account for the distinctive pattern of childcare practices and behaviours that we have traced in this chapter? I would like to suggest three factors – concerning religion, political economy, and history – that together may go some way in accounting for the childcare patterns and behaviours we have observed for the Beng.

First, the practise of welcoming 'strangers' into their midst, and the associated habit of encouraging the creation of a broad variety of social ties and emotional attachments, accords well with Beng religious ideology. As I explore elsewhere (Gottlieb 2004), Beng adults maintain that babies come to this life after a previous existence in an afterlife they call *wrugbe*. Put differently, we might say that the birth of a baby is not seen as the occasion to receive a strange new creature but rather someone who has already been here before and then left, and is now returning as a reincarnated ancestor. I suggest that the ideology of reincarnation provides a template for welcoming the young 'stranger' as a friendly guest with social ties to the community. In turn, the baby-as-stranger being welcomed actively into the village echoes the formal structures for welcoming adult guests to the village. Moreover, the perceived temptation for the baby to 'return' to *wrugbe* must be constantly combated by those who care for the child. The more people embrace an infant – both literally and emotionally – the more welcome to this world the infant will be (Gottlieb 2000). Encouraging high levels of sociability is in effect one means the Beng adopt to combat high rates of infant mortality.

At another level, the pattern of encouraging children to form multiple emotional attachments with a variety of people from the earliest days of infancy works well with the demands of women's labour. As has long been documented for much of rural Africa (e.g., Boserup 1970; Bryceson 1995; Coquery-Vidrovitch 1997: 9–20), Beng women's lives are circumscribed by enormous labour demands. Most obviously, they are all full-time farmers. In addition, Beng women have sole responsibility for chopping and hauling firewood from the forest; fetching water for the household water supply; hand-washing the laundry for a large family; and doing the vast majority of food preparation for that family, including pounding, cooking, and dishwashing – much of this while pregnant or breastfeeding. It is hard to imagine a woman performing all these tasks continually on her own, day in and day out without relief, while taking competent, full-time care of several small children – including, frequently, a baby and a toddler. To keep her household running and the family's food supply intact, virtually every mother must arrange either for a single regular babysitter or a network of potential baby carriers for dependable childcare. In this way, the typical Beng mother's habit of encouraging an infant to be accepting of strangers, to forge satisfying emotional attachments to many people, and to discourage her infant from forming an especially strong and singular emotional attachment to her, makes pragmatic sense as situated in the universe of women's labour.

Finally, there is the obvious question of history. In what sort of historical circumstances would an effort to embrace strangers be a reasonable strategy? Here we are awash in a sea of irony. For at least the brief period for which there is some documented history – barely more than a century – the Beng have appeared to be a relatively remote and insulated group. Yet their apparent isolationism belies a deep social, linguistic, and economic engagement with the neighbouring world and beyond. The precolonial Beng economy included a long-distance trade in kola nuts with Jula traders, and other goods with Baule, Ando and Jimini neighbours (Gottlieb 2004: 62–75). To engage in these transactions, most Beng were (and still are) multilingual. The precolonial Beng were intricately engaged in regional and long-distance networks in both economic and other forms of commerce. In such a setting, perceiving ties with 'strangers' as unwelcome could well disrupt crucial economic links in potentially disastrous ways. By contrast, welcoming those strangers who did appear in the villages – and training their children to do so from the earliest days *ex utero* – would have made supreme economic and political sense.

And of course, from the perspective of the infant, in addition to such true 'strangers' – i.e., adults who are 'strange' not just to the young children of the village but also to the adults – there are, in the early weeks and months after birth, many people who appear 'strange'. Indeed, if we consider such people (from the infant's perspective) as 'strangers', it is ironic that Beng infants probably encounter far more 'strangers' – that is, people who are 'strange' to themselves – than is the case with Euro-American, middle-class infants, who are typically far more protected from social encounters in general. Thus, although there may be fewer absolute 'strangers' entering the lives of village-dwelling Beng infants than is the case for urban-dwelling Western infants, who are sociologically surrounded by 'strangers', the actual Beng infant's experience of interacting with those who (at least initially) seem like 'strangers' is probably far richer than it is for many Western infants.

Moreover, in recent years (before the nation's civil war), economic routes to a wider world were even more open, as many Beng farmers sold crops to (non-Beng) middlemen who came to the villages from Abidjan to buy their harvest; other Beng farmers travelled to nearby towns or distant cities themselves to sell their agricultural wares at a greater profit. Still other Beng villagers hired themselves out as labourers on distant commercial plantations run by members of other ethnic groups, and still others migrated to the cities to seek their fortunes (see Gottlieb 2004: 266–305). In all cases, engaging productively with 'strangers' continued to be critical to their survival.

I began this chapter by mentioning that shared caretaking patterns such as the one I have outlined for the Beng may be far more common around the globe, and through history, than we have realized. While families in post-industrialized societies both shrink and become more isolated and scattered, it is imperative for us to remember that in the rest of the world, and perhaps for most of human history, variations in caretaking have abounded based on alternative family and community structures. The intentionally high levels of sociability and shared caretaking that characterize the lives of Beng infants may be extreme, but they serve as a salutary reminder that the full story and history of human caretaking is not yet written. The other essays collected in this volume constitute an important contribution to that story-in-the-making.

Notes

For support of my field research and writing, I am grateful to the John Simon Guggenheim Memorial Foundation, National Endowment for the Humanities, Wenner-Gren Foundation for Anthropological Research, Social Science Research Council, United States Information Agency, and several units at the University of Illinois (Center for Advanced Study, Research Board, and Center for African Studies). For intellectual support during my field research, I owe a continuing debt, which I always strive in vain to repay, to the Beng community.

Most of this chapter is extracted from Gottlieb (2004), especially Chapter 6. Earlier versions were presented as talks to the joint Africanists Workshop/Human Development Workshop at the University of Chicago; the interdisciplinary Faculty Seminar on the Stranger, and the Brown Bag series of the Center for African Studies, both at the University of Illinois at Urbana-Champaign; and to the conference on Alloparenting (London) organized by Gillian Bentley and Ruth Mace. I am grateful to members of all audiences for their perceptive comments and questions.

1. Two notable exceptions documented in the ethnographic literature are the cases of rural Maya in Mexico and the Dani of Irian Jaya. In both groups, young infants are cared for mostly or exclusively by their mothers and are kept in very quiet, dark places for several

months (Brazelton 1977; Butt 1998). These examples remind us not to generalize about 'the non-Western world', which itself contains a diverse collection of practices overdetermined by historical layers of culture and political economy.

Conversely, some scholars have recently documented contemporary challenges to the traditional non-Western model of collective childcare, due to a variety of both local and, increasingly, global factors (e.g. Swadener et al. 2000). Such sweeping changes have not yet affected Beng village-based child-rearing structures to the extent that they have in some other parts of the world; elsewhere, I discuss other changes that are more pertinent to the Beng context (Gottlieb 2004: 266–305).

2. The 'ethnographic present' of this work is 1993. As in all my published writings to date, my discussion concerns Beng villages, where I have concentrated my research (for general background on Beng society, see Gottlieb 1996; Gottlieb and Graham 1994). My informal observations among the still relatively small group of Beng families now living in towns and cities would suggest a fair amount of continuity in infant care practices with those reported in this work. This accords with the work of a new generation of scholars who argue that rural/urban relations in Africa may be more productively thought of as a continuum than a divide and, moreover, may be far more porous than was previously assumed. Exciting studies of urban migration within Africa as well as the contemporary urban African diaspora in Europe and the U.S. show an often provocative combination of predictable ruptures and surprising continuities between 'traditional' rural practices and new urban lives (e.g., D'Alisera 2004; Hutchinson 2001; Johnson 2001; Stoller 1996, 2002). Among urban Beng families, infant care practices seem to vary depending on a host of factors, especially the mother's education level, whether or not she has married a Beng man, and whether or not she is surrounded by Beng neighbours. Examining to what extent, and in what ways, Beng families now living in cities in Côte d'Ivoire and elsewhere replicate – or challenge – the model I discuss in this chapter requires further field research. The contemporary crisis in Beng families' lives caused by the nation's current civil war is likewise a pressing topic for further investigation.

3. Dieudonné Kwame Kouassi carried out most of the observations in this quantitative portion of the study. In total, we observed 25 babies in 43 observational sessions over a total of 5,745 minutes, or 95.75 hours. Of the 43 sessions, 41 were 135 minutes in duration; 1 was 120 minutes in duration; and 1 was 90 minutes in duration. The babies ranged in age from three months to twenty-four months, with the average age being 11.4 months.

4. On relations with fathers focusing largely on European and other post-industrialized nations, see especially the work of Lamb and his colleagues (e.g., Lamb 1987, 1997, 1999; Lamb et al. 1999). On meaningful emotional attachments between young children (including infants) and their caretakers, including daycare teachers in post-industrialized settings, see, for example, Cummings (1980); Kearsley et al. (1975); Lamb (1999); Lamb et al. (1992); and Sroufe et al. (1983); for helpful overviews of this controversial literature, see Karen (1998: 313–44) and Sroufe (1996). For parallel work looking at the lives and experiences of fathers cross-culturally (mostly conducted by anthropologists), see Hewlett (1993).

I deploy the term 'attachment' in a somewhat looser way than developmental psychologists usually deploy it. I do so deliberately, in order to expand the parameters of discussion to encompass indigenous models of 'attachment' whose content may look somewhat different from how it is represented in the models that have been identified by Western-trained researchers for Western(-ized) populations. Researchers steeped in Western contexts may be surprised to learn of the relatively large number of meaningful emotional 'attachments' that Beng infants, as with many others in West Africa, have with a large array of adults and older children.

In this section, I also link two bodies of work: on the one hand, work by historians, sociologists and other scholars on strangers; on the other hand, work by developmental psychologists on emotional and social attachments as well as on relations of infants to strangers. Concerning the latter, I further combine discussion of two technical bodies of literature in developmental psychology: writings on 'attachment', and writings on fear of, or wariness toward, strangers. In some work by developmental psychologists, these two topics of inquiry have been inextricably linked; in other works they have been considered as independent; and in still others they are seen as related but in complex and not easily predictable ways. I lack space here to expound on the implications inherent in this issue (for one early, thoughtful discussion, see Clarke-Stewart 1978). Briefly, my own perspective is that the two parameters of 'attachment' on the one hand and attitude toward strangers by young children on the other hand are indeed linked, but in compound and subtle ways. In referencing these discrete bodies of literature, I will explore how the issues implicated in these two sets of writing speak to each other in striking ways in Beng villages.

5. This echoes an observation made for the linguistically related northern Mande groups by Jansen: 'A stranger in Mande is, in fact, not "strange" at all; the term "stranger" is as neutral as, for instance, the term "hunter" or "brother"' (1996: 26).

6. The pattern I have described may be common in other villages throughout much of sub-Saharan Africa; for a Ugandan case with certain similarities to what I have described, see Obbo (1979).

7. In Beng, the greeting (which incorporates words from the Baule language) is as follows for a hostess welcoming a male visitor (with minor variations for different gender combinations):

> Hostess: *aba ka kweŋ* [Father, welcome].
> Male guest: *maa, nye wiau.* [OK.]
> Hostess: *aúŋ. blíni ka. we nã ŋo grè?* [OK. Have a seat. Are the folks where you're coming from all well?]
> Male guest: *we nã ŋo myankalo.* [Those folks are all fine.]
> Hostess: *aúŋ. mu wiau.* [OK.]
> Male guest: *màà.* [OK.]

8. For the New Hampshire legal case cited, see Buch v. Amory Mfg Co. (1898).

9. In the case of a very difficult childbirth, a male healer may be called in to administer herbal remedies, and/or a male Master of the Earth may enter to offer prayers and sacrifices.

10. Beng terms for relatives group together individuals of different genealogical categories

to place them in the same conceptual universe according to a combination of complex principles. For instance, two girls or women who are called 'sisters' might be first- or second-degree matrilateral or patrilateral parallel cousins, or even more distantly related clan-mates. The details of this system are not relevant to this discussion. Suffice it to say that in learning that, for instance, a boy is called an 'elder brother', a young girl does not confuse this boy with her own (genealogical) brother but comes to understand that the two boys are of the same generation and gender and may also belong to the same (matri- or patri-)clan as herself. In Beng villages, only children younger than oneself are addressed by name; all others are accorded kinship terms as a sign of respect, whether or not the two people are actually related. From the infant's perspective, this means that virtually every-one the small child meets – including strangers – will be introduced by a kin term and not a name.

11. The tendency to restrict social engagements during an infant's first few months of life is not monopolized by Western societies – some non-Western societies have their own reasons for restricting social contacts to an even greater extent than is common in the contemporary Euro-American middle-class. Writing of the Dani of Irian Jaya (Indonesia), Butt explains that the first three to four months of life the young infant is never exposed to the sun (1998: 119). Instead, the child is almost constantly wrapped up in several lay-ers of net bags, staying in virtual darkness: 'The point is not to stimulate the child, but to sedate through darkness, quiet, routine breastfeeding on demand, and through providing stimulation only when the child [later] comes to demand it' (1998: 15). During these early months, when a mother takes her infant to the gardens she encloses her child under ten or twelve bags to protect her against the sun, where it is so cool and dark that the baby can often sleep for hours. The rationale for this set of practices is well thought out: young babies are said to be frightened easily (ibid: 121) and are also considered vulner-able to spirits' or ancestors' attacks that can sicken the child (ibid.: 121–22); in the face of these culturally constituted risks, Dani parents maintain that babies grow best without too much talking or stimulation (ibid.: 119). It is only by the fourth or fifth month that Dani mothers allow their babies to play with other adults (ibid.: 122).

12. I explore some detailed examples of this pattern elsewhere (Gottlieb 2004: 185–219).

13. For an incisive, comparative analysis of the cybernetic relations among mothers, infants and others in the family from the standpoint of the household food supply, see Popkin et al. (1986). For further discussion of food and Beng infants, see Gottlieb (2004: 185–219).

14. The likelihood that a particular Beng baby who exhibits 'stranger anxiety' would be clas-sified by a developmental psychologist as emotionally healthy and properly 'attached' (to the mother) depends on several factors about which the relevant psychology literature has much to say. A discussion of the nuances and technical details underlying the classifica-tory schema is beyond the scope of this essay; for one clear summary of the relevant issues, see Sroufe (1996: 112–13).

15. These informal situations of separations and reunions that I observed in daily life loosely approximated the 'Strange Situation' test that is administered by 'attachment' research-ers in developmental psychology to test for the degree and kind of infants' attachments

to their mothers (or other primary caretakers). However, I did not administer the formal 'Strange Situation' test as such during fieldwork for a variety of reasons, including the pragmatic consideration that it would not have been possible to replicate the carefully controlled laboratory conditions created for such studies as conducted by most developmental psychologists.

References

Boserup, E., 1970. *Woman's Role in Economic Development.* New York: St. Martin's Press.

Brazelton, T.B., 1977. Implications of infant development among the Mayan Indians of Mexico. In P. H. Leiderman et al., eds., *Culture and Infancy: Variations in the Human Experience.* New York: Academic Press, 151–87.

Bryceson, D.F., ed., 1995. *Women Wielding the Hoe: Lessons from Rural Africa for Feminist Theory and Development Practice.* Oxford: Berg.

Buch V. Amory Manufacturing Co., 1898. Buch v. Amory Mfg Co., 44 A. 809 (N.H. 1898).

Butt, L., 1998. The Social and Political Life of Infants among the Baliem Valley Dani, Irian Jaya. PhD Thesis. McGill University, Montreal.

Clarke-Stewart, K.A., 1978. Recasting the lone stranger. In J. Glick and K.A. Clarke-Stewart, eds., *The Development of Social Understanding.* New York: Gardner Press/Halsted Press/ John Wiley and Sons, 109–76.

Coquery-Vidrovitch, C., 1997 [1994]. *African Women: A Modern History.* Boulder, CO: Westview Press.

Cummings, E.M., 1980. Caregiver stability and day care. *Developmental Psychology* 16: 31–37.

D'Alisera, J., 2004. *An Imagined Geography: Sierra Leonean Muslims in America.* Philadelphia: University of Pennsylvania Press.

Décarie, T.G., et al., 1974. *The Infant's Reaction to Strangers.* New York: International Universities Press.

Douglas, M., 1966. *Purity and Danger.* London: Routledge.

———— 1970. *Natural Symbols.* New York: Pantheon.

———— 1992. *Risk and Blame: Essays in Cultural Theory.* London: Routledge.

Douglas, M., and Wildavsky, A., 1982. *Risk and Culture: An Essay on the Selection of Technological and Environmental Dangers.* Berkeley: University of California Press.

Fogel, A., 1993. *Developing through Relationships: Origins of Communication, Self, and Culture.* Chicago: University of Chicago Press.

Gajda, A., 1999. *Legal Issues in the News* [commentary on 'duty to rescue']. WILL-AM radio (Urbana, IL), 22 March 1999.

Gottlieb, A., 1996 [1992]. *Under the Kapok Tree: Identity and Difference in Beng Thought.* Chicago: University of Chicago Press.

———— 2000. Luring your child into this life: a Beng path for infant care. In J.S. Deloache and A. Gottlieb, eds., *A World of Babies: Imagined Childcare Guides for Seven Societies.* New York: Cambridge University Press, 55–89.

———— 2004. *The Afterlife Is Where We Come from: The Culture of Infancy in West Africa*. Chicago: University of Chicago Press.

Gottlieb, A., and Graham, P., 1994 [1993]. *Parallel Worlds: An Anthropologist and a Writer Encounter Africa*. Chicago: University of Chicago Press.

Harkness, S., and Super, C.M., 1992. The cultural foundations of fathers' roles: evidence from Kenya and the United States. In B.S. Hewlett, ed., *Father-Child Relations: Cultural and Biosocial Contexts*. New York: Aldine de Gruyter, 191–211.

———— 1991. *Intimate Fathers: The Nature and Context of the Aka Pygmy Paternal Infant Care*. Ann Arbor: University of Michigan Press.

Hewlett, B.S., ed., 1993. *Father-Child Relations: Cultural and Biosocial Contexts*. New York: Aldine de Gruyter.

Hutchinson, S., 2001. The Nuer diaspora and the rise of 'segmentary Christianity'. Paper presented at the annual meeting of the African Studies Association, Houston, TX, 15–18 November 2001.

Jansen, J., 1996. The younger brother and the stranger in Mande status discourse. In J. Jansen and C. Zobel, eds., *The Younger Brother in Mande: Kinship and Politics in West Africa*. Leiden: Research School, Center for Non-Western Studies, 8–34.

Johnson, M., 2001. On the road to *Alijana*: reconfiguring Islam and 'Mandinga-ness' in the 'new' African diaspora. Paper presented at the annual meeting of the African Studies Association, Houston, TX, 15–18 November 2001.

Karen, R., 1998 [1994]. *Becoming Attached: First Relationships and How They Shape Our Capacity to Love*. Oxford: Oxford University Press.

Kearsley, R.B., Zelazo, P.R., Kagan, J., and Hartmann, R., 1975. Separation protest in day-care and home-reared infants. *Pediatrics* 55(2), 171–75.

Kitzinger, S., 1995. Commentary: Breastfeeding: biocultural perspectives. In P. Stuart-Macadam and K.A. Dettwyler, ed., *Breastfeeding: Biocultural Perspectives*. Hawthorne, NY: Aldine de Gruyter, 385–94.

Lamb, M.E., 1999. Nonparental child care. In M.E. Lamb, ed., *Parenting and Child Development in 'Nontraditional' Families*. Mahwah, NJ: Lawrence Erlbaum, 39–55.

———— 1997. *The Role of the Father in Child Development,* Third Edition. New York: Wiley.

Lamb, M.E., ed., 1987. *The Father's Role: Cross-Cultural Perspectives*. Hillsdale, NJ: Lawrence Erlbaum.

———— 1999. *Parenting and Child Development in 'Nontraditional' Families*. Mahwah, NJ: Lawrence Erlbaum.

Lamb, M.E. et al., 1999. Parent-child relationships: development in the context of the family. In M.H. Bornstein and M.E. Lamb, eds., *Developmental Psychology: An Advanced Textbook,* Fourth Edition. Mahwah, NJ: Lawrence Erlbaum, 411–50.

Lamb, M.E. et al., eds., 1992. *Child Care in Context: Cross-Cultural Perspectives*. Hillsdale, NJ: Lawrence Erlbaum.

Mangelsdorf, S., 1992. Developmental changes in infant–stranger interaction. *Infant Behaviour and Development* 15, 191–208.

New, R.S., 1988. Parental goals and Italian infant Care. In R.A. Levine, P.M. Miller and M.M. West, eds., *New Directions for Child Development, no. 40. Parental Behaviour in Diverse Societies.* San Francisco: Jossey-Bass, 51–63.

Nsamenang, B.A., 1992. Early childhood care and education in Cameroon. In M.E. Lamb et al., eds., *Child Care in Context: Cross-Cultural Perspectives.* Hillsdale, NJ: Lawrence Erlbaum, 419–39.

Obbo, C., 1979. Village strangers in Buganda society. In W. Shack and E. Skinner, eds., *Strangers in African Societies.* Berkeley: University of California Press, 227–41.

Parents, 1996. Baby health & safety: limit visitors to keep baby healthy. *Parents* 21(11) (November), 47.

Popkin, B.M., Lasky, T., Spicer, D., and Yamamota, M.E., 1986. *The Infant-feeding Triad: Infant, Mother, and Household.* New York: Gordon and Breach.

Rheingold, H.L. and Eckerman, C.O., 1973. Fear of the stranger: a critical examination. In H.W. Reese, ed., *Advances in Child Development and Behaviour, vol. 8.* New York: Academic Press, 185–222.

Richman, A.L., Miller, P.M., and Solomon, M.J., 1988. The socialization of infants in suburban Boston. In A.L. Richman, P.M. Miller and M.M. West, eds., *New Directions for Child Development, no. 40. Parental Behaviour in Diverse Societies.* San Francisco: Jossey-Bass, 65–74.

Rizzini, I., and Dawes, A., 2001. Editorial: On cultural diversity and child adversity. *Childhood* 8(3), 315–21.

Schütz, A., 1944. The stranger: an essay in social psychology. *American Journal of Sociology* 49(6), 499–507.

Sears, W., 1999. Answers from Dr. Sears: soothing stranger anxiety. *Parenting* (May 1999), 37–38.

Sroufe, L.A., 1996. *Emotional Development: The Organization of Emotional Life in the Early Years.* Cambridge: Cambridge University Press.

Sroufe, L.A., Fox, N., and Pancake, V., 1983. Attachment and dependency in developmental perspective. *Child Development* 54, 1615–27.

Stansbury, J.P., Leonard, W.R., and Dewalt, K.M., 2000. Caretakers, child care practices, and growth failure in Highland Ecuador. *Medical Anthropology Quarterly* 14(2), 224–41.

Stoller, P., 1996. Spaces, places, and fields: the politics of West African trading in New York city's informal economy. *American Anthropologist* 98(4), 776–88.

———— 2002. *Money Has No Smell: The Africanization of New York City.* Chicago: University of Chicago Press.

Swadener, B.B., with Kabiru, M., and Njenga, A., 2000. *Does the Village Still Raise the Child? A Collaborative Study of Changing Child-Rearing and Early Education in Kenya.* Albany: State University of New York Press.

Tronick, E.Z., Morelli, G.A., and Winn, S., 1987. Multiple caretaking of Efe (Pygmy) infants. *American Anthropologist* 89(1), 96–106.

Weisner, T.S., and Gallimore, R., 1977. My brother's keeper: child and sibling caretaking. *Current Anthropology* 18(2), 169–90.

• 7 •

Economic Perspectives on Alloparenting

Gillian Paull

Introduction

Public debate over the nature and desirability of alloparenting in the UK has become increasingly vocal in recent decades as rising numbers of mothers have chosen to return to paid employment rather than undertake full-time care of their children. Government policy has sought to enhance the availability and affordability of alloparenting (or 'childcare' to use the term employed in the economics literature)[1] through a variety of financial incentives and direct involvement in the childcare market, with the stated objectives of helping poorer families to escape from poverty and of reducing social and gender inequalities. An economic perspective on alloparenting can provide a fruitful framework for thinking through the complex issues involved in explaining why and how parents use alloparenting and whether such choices can be influenced through policy.

Alloparenting has featured prominently in two streams of economic research: the analysis of the employment of women and the study of child development. In the labour-market literature, childcare has been increasingly studied as a key factor in explaining the gender differences in work behaviour. On the child development issue, economists have analysed the impact of alloparenting on subsequent educational attainment and employment choices, while other researchers have considered the effects on a range of non-economic outcomes. More recent work by economists has sought to recognize the links between these two issues and to develop more complete models which incorporate both motivations for alloparenting.

This chapter endeavours to describe how the economic literature on alloparenting has developed.[2] The next section considers how economists have framed the reasons for alloparenting and derived how economic factors may affect alloparenting decisions. The third section shows that while empirical work has provided substantial evidence on alloparenting choices in the U.K. and identified many key characteristics related to those decisions, finding precise evidence on how these driving forces operate has proved to be a challenge. The fourth section of the paper presents the arguments for government involvement in influencing alloparenting choices and summarises recent childcare policy developments in the U.K. The final section concludes.

Economic Models of Alloparenting

A Basic Model

Two main justifications for alloparenting have been employed in the economics literature. First, alloparenting is seen as a means to an end by allowing parents childfree time, particularly in permitting mothers to undertake formal paid employment where they cannot simultaneously care for children. Second, alloparenting may be desirable in itself for the educational and development opportunities that non-maternal childcare may offer children. Taken independently, either of these scenarios can be handled reasonably straightforwardly within traditional economic frameworks. Once the motivations are combined, modelling becomes far more complex.

The first justification has been considered extensively in research on the labour supply of mothers,[3] although only a few studies have analysed models based exclusively on the first reason for alloparenting.[4] In models based solely on the need to allow parents to work, the alloparenting choice is linked directly to the work decision. The childcare dimension is easily incorporated into the labour supply model as an additional work-related cost and can be modelled in a similar way to, say, travel expenses. The alloparenting costs can be both monetary and non-pecuniary, such as the inconvenience of the childcare arrangement. These models highlight how the decision to alloparent depends on the cost of care and on the benefits of working including the wage, the enjoyment of employment and the benefits of furthering the career. For example, a reduction in the price of childcare is equivalent to an increase in the wage rate and will increase the likelihood that a parent works, making alloparenting more likely.[5]

A model of alloparenting driven only by the motivation of the benefits to child development is also relatively straightforward to derive. In this case, alloparenting is treated in the same way as any other consumption good that might be purchased. For example, the higher the price, the less likely it will be purchased or a smaller quantity may be bought. Alternatively, the higher the income of a family, the more likely it can afford to alloparent, or will purchase a greater quantity.

Combining the two motivations generates a much more complicated model. If alloparenting is beneficial for the child, childcare becomes an unusual type of 'good' in economic terms because it requires money to be purchased while also holding the potential to generate income (by allowing the mother to undertake paid employment). The alloparenting decision, therefore, depends on the degree to which it is 'self-financing' or, in other words, the extent of the net cost or income. Against this monetary figure must be weighed the benefits (or detriment) of the non-maternal childcare relative to the mother's care and the displeasure (or pleasure) that the mother may experience from being in formal paid employment rather than caring for the child. The magnitudes of these factors may also change as quantities increase. Initial hours of non-maternal care may be beneficial for the child while very long hours may be detrimental (and similarly for the benefit to mothers of paid employment). An additional pound of income may be valued more highly at lower levels when necessities are being purchased and hold less value for the purchase of luxuries at higher levels.

To illustrate the issues involved, the following model incorporates both justifications for alloparenting and is similar to the type presented in Ribar (1995). The model is a static model in the sense that decisions are made without consideration to the future. Parents are assumed to care about the quality of care received by the child (denoted as Q), the mother's work-free time (denoted as L for leisure) and the family's total consumption (denoted as C). Mathematically, this can be written as parents maximizing a utility function:

$$U = U(Q, C, L)$$

It is assumed that maternal care is equal to the mother's leisure time, that is, alloparenting is used for every hour that the mother is in paid employment but not at any other time. It is also assumed that there are only two types (and two corresponding qualities) of non-maternal care: paid formal care and free informal care. The total quality of care received by the child depends on the amount of maternal care (L), on whether formal or informal childcare is used if the mother works (where F indicates the use of formal care) and on the family's consumption (C):

$$Q = Q(L, F, C)$$

This flexible function says nothing about the relative qualities of maternal, informal and formal care. For example, the function Q may allow for the first hour of formal childcare a week to be good for a child, but the sixtieth hour in a week to be bad. Informal care is assumed to be free, but formal childcare has a cost P. This cost depends upon the number of hours used, which is equal to the mother's work hours (denoted H) if formal care is used when the mother works:

$$P = P(H).F$$

This allows for a non-linear relationship between weekly childcare cost and weekly hours worked. Denoting the mother's hourly wage as W and net transfers from the tax and benefit system and other family income as N,[6] consumption (assumed equal to net income) can be written as the sum of the mother's gross earnings and other net taxes and income minus any formal childcare costs ('the budget constraint'):

$$C = WH + N - P(H).F$$

The mother's total time (denoted K) is divided between work and maternal care (leisure) so that $K = H + L$. Substituting the expressions for childcare quality, family consumption and the time constraint into the original utility function shows that the family chooses the mothers' hours of formal employment (H) and whether to use formal childcare (F) to maximize utility:

$$U = U(Q(K-H, F, WH + N - P(H).F), WH + N - P(H).F, K-H)$$

This complicated expression highlights the economic factors that play a role in the alloparenting decision: the price of formal care, the mother's wage, other family income and the tax system. It also shows the interactions between the alloparenting and employment choices. However, few useful unambiguous predictions can be derived from the model. For example, if formal childcare is beneficial for the child, higher family income (captured in N) may increase the likelihood that formal care is used because the family can afford to spend more on such 'good's, but, on the other hand, it may reduce the likelihood of using formal care because there is less financial need for the mother to work in formal employment. Alternatively, and somewhat unintuitively, a lower price for formal childcare (denoted P) might induce an employed mother to reduce her work hours and use less formal childcare because the family has higher net income and does not need the mother to work so much.

The derivation of this model, even with its simplifying assumptions, illustrates how economists have struggled to derive a useful, applicable model of alloparenting. In addition, analysing data from empirical sources has made it necessary to relax several of these assumptions in order to be consistent with some of the observed facts. These additional complications and extensions to the model are discussed in the following subsections.

The Link between Employment and Childcare

The basic model described above assumes that the hours of alloparenting are set equal to the mother's work hours, but this is unrealistic. Alloparenting hours may be shorter than this, for example, if the father covers some of the mother's work hours or school time provides some hours of care. It is also noticeable, empirically, that a significant proportion of employed mothers with pre-school children report that they do not use any alloparenting, suggesting an ability to simultaneously work and care for children in some circumstances. Hours may also be longer than the mother's work hours if the mother requires travel-to-work time or desires childfree time for reasons other than formal employment. Indeed, many mothers not in paid employment use significant amounts of paid childcare each week.[7]

Hence, it is necessary to relax the assumption of equality between the mother's hours of work and the hours of alloparenting. In this situation, the family now makes three rather than two choices: the mothers' hours of formal employment (H), the hours of childcare (denoted as A for alloparenting) and whether to use formal childcare (F). The objective function becomes:

$$U = U(Q(A, F, WH + N - P(A).F), WH + N - P(A).F, K-H)$$

It should be noted that the degree to which the hours of alloparenting can vary from the mother's employment hours will depend upon her alternative sources of care (such as whether the child is at school) and how easily employment and maternal care can be combined. For non-working mothers, this extended model allows the alloparenting hours (A) to be positive even if H is zero.

Quality of Childcare

An underlying problem for the economic modelling of childcare is the uncertainty of whether alloparenting is a 'good' or a 'bad' relative to maternal care. Childcare may be purchased in order to allow parents to work even if it is directly unbeneficial. On the other hand, the use of significant amounts of alloparenting by non-working mothers shows that assuming alloparenting is purely a 'bad' may be unrealistic.[8] The issue is further complicated by the recognition that there are also degrees of quality of care. In the economics literature, the term 'quality' of care has been used to mean both the direct impacts on children, such as cognitive and social development, as well as other aspects of the care that are valued by parents, such as convenience and proximity to home. Variation in such quality is likely to be positively related to the cost of care in the formal market, both because it may cost more to produce higher-quality care and because providers may profit from parents' willingness to pay more for better-quality options.

Allowing alloparenting quality to vary by degrees introduces further complexity into the basic model described above. Not only do parents have an additional choice variable of the quality of care (denoted q), but the cost of formal care may depend on the quality level as well as the hours of care. Hence, the family now makes four choices: the mothers' hours of formal employment (H), the hours of childcare (A), whether to use formal childcare (F) and the quality of formal or informal alloparenting (q) to maximize the utility function:

$$U = U(Q(A, F, q, WH + N - P(A, q).F), WH + N - P(A, q).F, K-H)$$

Introducing quality variation also raises an econometric challenge. Good measures of the quality of care are typically not available in the data sources used to analyse employment choices. Consequently, the price variables include quality variation which can lead to misleading inferences about the link between the price of childcare and parents' demand for alloparenting. For example, if parents who choose higher quality care also tend to choose longer hours, ignoring the quality dimension may lead to the spurious conclusion that the use of alloparenting increases as the price rises.[9]

Informal Childcare

Economists have distinguished between two main types of alloparenting: formal childcare provided by nurseries, playgroups, crèches, school clubs, childminders, nannies and au pairs in a market environment and informal care provided by family and friends in an essentially non-market setting. From a modelling perspective, this distinction is essential. Formal childcare is provided in return for an observable, well-defined monetary payment and is assumed to be equally available to all families living within a common geographical area defining the local market. The returns to informal care may be far more diverse: monetary payment, favours in kind, the enjoyment of caring or simply altruistic 'helping out'. In addition, the sources of informal care will vary from family to family. However, the availability of informal care to a particular family is typically not observed in most data sources unless the care is actually used, making empirical modelling problematic. Consequently, only a few studies have explicitly recognized the role of informal care in alloparenting and employment choices.[10]

Rationing in the Formal Childcare Market

A final extension to the basic model is to consider the possibility of supply constraints in the childcare market. In the U.K., concerns have frequently been expressed that there is a shortage or rationing of childcare places. Such rationing could be incorporated into the base model as a maximum value on the amount of formal childcare, but most studies have not made any explicit allowance for supply constraints.

In theoretical terms, excess or unmet demand is defined as a situation where parents wish to purchase childcare at the going cost but are unable to obtain a place or a sufficient number of hours.[11] Such unmet demand should create pressure for the price of care to rise, inducing increases in provision or falls in demand until equilibrium in supply and demand is reached. There are several theoretical arguments why prices may not rise and rationing may persist. First, prices could remain low because of statutory price ceilings, although these do not exist in the U.K. Second, childcare providers may not maximise profits and would not raise prices in the face of excess demand. This is more likely to be true for non-profit organisations or childminders who are self-employed. Third, childcare providers may deliberately keep prices low in order to maintain a stable set of users which could reduce their operating costs. Finally, providers may prefer the existence of excess demand because it allows them to choose children, based on the assumptions that the costs of providing care varies across children; that the provider is able to identify these potential differences in costs; and that the provider is unable to pass on the cost differences to parents as differentiated prices. However, none of these scenarios are completely convincing, particularly as it would require only one segment of the market to respond by raising prices and increasing supply to resolve the unmet demand. The theoretical case for persistent rationing in the childcare market therefore appears weak.[12]

Evidence from the U.K.

Economists have studied alloparenting in the U.K. using a variety of data sources.[13] This section provides a brief introduction to this research, but much more extensive analyses can be found in the publications.

Alloparenting Choices

Very few studies have used fully representative samples of families because the most commonly used data sources on childcare tend to be restricted in some way, for example, to mothers in paid employment, or to lone mothers, or to low-income families or to children in a limited age range. An exception to this is the report by La Valle et al. (2000)[14] which presents the findings from a survey of all parents with children aged fourteen and under conducted in 1999. Some 57 per cent of parents with children aged fourteen and under report having used childcare in the past week, while some 86 per cent say they have use alternative care in the past year (La Valle et al. 2000: Table 1.2). However, childcare use is more prevalent among families with mothers in paid employment than those with mothers not in work: childcare usage in the previous week is reported to be 70 per cent and 62 per cent among families with full-time and part-time working mothers compared to 47 per cent among those with mothers not in paid employment (La Valle et al. 2000: Table 8.1). There is also evidence that higher use of informal rather than formal care explains the higher child-care use among mothers in paid employment (La Valle et al. 2000: Table 1.14) and that hours of childcare tend to be longer for children of working mothers (La Valle et al. 2000: Table 8.7).[15] Families with a working mother are also more likely to pay for their childcare than those without a mother in employment (La Valle et al. 2000: Table 6.6) and to pay more, particularly if the mother is working full-time (La Valle et al. 2000: Table 6.15).

For children of mothers in paid employment, extensive childcare information is available in the large nationally representative Family Resources Survey. A summary from this survey of childcare use for families with working mothers (and working lone fathers) for the years 1998–2001 is presented in table 7.1.[16]

When asked whether 'anyone else normally looks after the children because you or your partner are working', 44 per cent of working families (defined as those where all parents are in employment at least sixteen hours each week) respond that they use childcare but only 23 per cent report that they pay for the care. Given that almost three quarters (74 per cent) of these families contain only school-age children, this is not surprising as parents may be able to fit work around school hours or the children may be old enough to look after themselves. Indeed, the majority of working families with pre-school children do use childcare, while around half pay for it. Only 18 per cent of the working families report using formal care, while 31 per cent have used informal care.[17] Almost all formal care is paid for, but only about one third of informal care, and the average weekly cost (for those who pay) is higher for formal

Table 7.1. Childcare Use for Families with No Parent Working Less than 16 Hours Each Week

	Couples				Single Parents				All families
	Pre-school children		Only school children		Pre-school children		Only school children		
	1	2+	1	2+	1	2+	1	2+	
Any type of non-parental care:									
per cent using care	77	72	23	34	85	90	38	47	44
per cent paying for care	50	49	10	15	51	51	16	20	23
average weekly cost	£76	£90	£33	£42	£63	£68	£33	£37	£62
Formal care:									
per cent using care	42	40	7	10	43	39	11	12	18
per cent paying for care	41	39	7	10	40	37	10	11	17
average weekly cost	£80	£97	£35	£46	£68	£71	£35	£44	£69
Informal care:									
per cent using care	47	45	18	26	56	68	31	39	31
per cent paying for care	19	19	5	8	24	25	9	12	11
average weekly cost	£52	£49	£28	£33	£46	£48	£28	£25	£38
Number of families (1000s)	361	419	830	1112	70	54	320	229	3394

Notes: 'Pre-school children' includes families with at least one pre-school child. The average weekly cost is the total cost for all children and is averaged over those paying for care. All monetary values are in approximate April 2003 prices. Formal care includes nurseries, crèches, school clubs, childminders, nannies and au pairs. Informal care is that provided by relatives and friends. The numbers of families have been grossed to the national level.

Source: Table 7.2 from Paull (2003) using Family Resources Survey (1998–99, 1999–2000 and 2000–1)

than informal care. Hence, families using formal childcare tend to spend more than users of informal care, both because they are more likely to pay for it and because, if they do pay, they pay more. In addition, working single parents are more likely to use informal care than working couples with children, while families with only school children are also more likely to rely on informal sources of care than families with at least one pre-school child. Families with more than one child tend to pay less per child for care than those with a lone child.

Figure 7.1 presents the use of formal and informal care by the age of the child. The picture highlights the difference in the use of alloparenting between pre-school and school-age children. This distinction is not as dramatic as might be expected given the provision of effectively 'free and compulsory' childcare during school hours for those children above compulsory school age. The use of informal care declines steadily but not dramatically with age for pre-school children, but remains fairly constant for school children up until age eleven. In contrast, the use of formal modes peaks for ages one to three and drops from 29 per cent for a four-year-old pre-school child to 22 per cent for a four-year-old school child. The proportion of school children using formal care declines markedly with age, falling to 3 per cent for twelve-year-olds. Indeed, use of any type of non-maternal childcare declines rapidly with age for school children and is unusual for children over the age of eleven.[18]

Table 7.2 presents the proportions of children in formal care by type of care. Of all pre-school children using some type of formal care, 44 per cent are in some centre-type care (covering day nurseries, playgroups and crèches), 43 per cent are cared for by childminders, almost 8 per cent are in some other type of care (including nannies

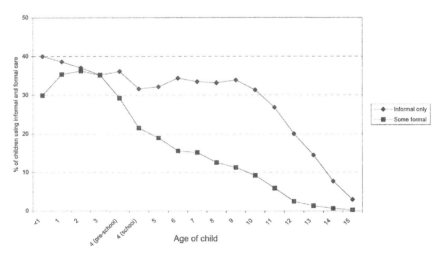

Figure 7.1. Childcare use for children of working mothers. Source: Figure 6.1 from Paull and Taylor (2002) using Family Resources Survey (1994/5 to 1998/9).

Table 7.2. Type of Formal Childcare by Age of Child for Working Mothers

% in care type:	Pre-school children aged:					
	<1	1	2	3	4	All ages
Centre	38.6	36.4	43.0	53.5	45.3	43.8
Childminder	51.8	51.9	47.0	29.3	37.8	43.2
Other	8.5	8.6	6.4	7.5	6.3	7.5
Multiple	1.1	3.1	3.6	9.8	10.6	5.6
% in care type:	School children aged:				
	4–5	6–7	8–9	10–11	All ages
Centre	16.5	12.8	11.5	6.7	12.5
Childminder	61.0	60.0	56.3	62.2	59.7
Other	19.6	24.6	28.7	27.2	24.7
Multiple	2.9	2.5	3.5	3.9	3.1

Notes: Centre care includes day nurseries, playgroups and crèches, but after-school clubs and school holiday clubs are included as a residual in the 'other' category with nannies and au pairs. 'All ages' for school children includes only those under 12.

Source: Table 6.5 from Paull and Taylor (2002) using Family Resources Survey (1994/5 to 1998/9)

and au pairs) and 6 per cent use a mixture of the above. There is a distinct switch in choices at age three, with the proportion using childminders dropping sharply while the share in centre and multiple types of care jumps markedly. This movement towards centre care may reflect greater benefits at the older age from increased socialization and educational content of centre care or may be a response to changes in relative prices for the older children. Of school children using some form of formal childcare, almost 60 per cent are in the care of childminders, while almost 25 per cent use the 'other' type of care (including nannies, au pairs, after-school clubs and holiday schemes). Almost 13 per cent use centre care and only 3 per cent use multiple types of care. The only distinct change in this distribution over the child's age is a decline in the use of centre care and a slight increase in the use of other types of care.

Childcare usage by families with a working mother has also been slowly evolving over time. Over the second half of the 1990s, there was a steady decline in the use of informal care for school children, while the use of centre-based care increased relative to childminders and other types of care for both pre-school and school children using formal care. The amount spent by families on childcare has increased in real terms and the proportion of family income spent on childcare has also risen.[19]

Related Factors

Many of the U.K. studies have estimated the relationships between various demographic and economic variables and alloparenting choices. These analyses have addressed the modelling issues of childcare quality, informal care and potential rationing in various ways and to differing degrees.[20] Table 7.3 presents some of the main results from three studies which use multiple regression techniques to control for the interactions between multiple parameters.

For families with both working and non-working parents, alloparenting is most likely to be used when children are aged 3–4 and is also when formal types of care are particularly likely to be used. Use of childcare is positively related to the parents' working and to the income and social status of the family. For families with a working mother, childcare usage in several dimensions (use, preference for formal care, hours of care, amount spent and the quality of care) is positively related to the need for care in terms of the mother's work hours and to the ability to pay for care in terms of the mother's earnings, family income and the number of children for whom care must be provided. Interestingly, once financial factors are held constant, single working mothers are more likely than those with partners to use more care in all dimensions except for quality, suggesting a lack of alternative care from a partner. Independent of financial constraints, older and more educated mothers also have a stronger preference than other mothers to use childcare, to use formal sources of care and to use longer hours of care. Families of non-white ethnicity are less likely to use childcare, but, if they do use it, use more formal types of care and use longer hours of care.

From an economic perspective, it is especially important to understand how the price of childcare influences its use. This is particularly relevant for considering how childcare subsidies might influence the use of alloparenting. Indeed, much of the research on alloparenting choices outside of the U.K. has focused on the impact of childcare price.[21] For the U.K., the impact of price on childcare choices has been analyzed in Duncan et al. (2001a).[22] Using FRS data for 1994/5 to 1998/9, they employ a method from the hedonic pricing literature to remove quality effects from the observed hourly cost to capture a measure of pure price variation across local authorities. Their findings suggest that higher prices for formal care are related to lower usage for pre-school children, but there is no evidence of a significant relationship between price and the hours of formal care purchased for pre-school or school children. In addition, price is found to be negatively related to the quality of care chosen, suggesting that childcare subsidies might be used to enhance the chosen quality of care as much as the overall usage.

Is Alloparenting Good or Bad for the Child?

Surveys rarely collect information on whether parents use alloparenting because they consider it to be directly beneficial to the child. The argument that something must be good if families are willing to pay for it does not hold up in the case of childcare,

Table 7.3. Factors Related to Alloparenting Choices

Use of childcare

All children	More likely for children aged 3–4, smaller families, whites, and families with all parents working, higher income or higher social class.
Children with a working mother	More likely for smaller families, whites, single mothers, older mothers, mothers working longer hours, mothers with higher earnings, and families with higher other income.

Use of formal (or paid) rather than informal (or unpaid) care

All children	More likely for children aged 3–4, non-whites, and families with fewer adults, higher family income or higher social class.
Children with a working mother	More likely for children aged 2, smaller families, single mothers, older mothers, more educated mothers, mothers working longer hours, mothers with higher earnings and families with higher other income.

Centre-based is preferred type of formal care

Children with a working mother	More likely for smaller families.

Hours of childcare

Children with a working mother	Longer for smaller families, non-whites, single mothers, more educated mothers, mothers working longer hours, mothers with higher earnings and families with higher other income.

Amount spent on childcare

Children with a working mother	Higher for mothers working longer hours, mothers with higher earnings, and families with higher other income.

Proportion of family income spent on childcare

Children with a working mother	Higher for single mothers, mothers with lower earnings, and families with lower other income.

Quality of care

Children with a working mother	Higher for smaller families, mothers with higher earnings and families with higher other income

---

Notes: Smaller and larger families refer to the number of children.

Sources: La Valle et al (2000: 36–44) for all children, Paull and Taylor (2002) for children with a working mother and Duncan et al. (2001a) for the quality of care.

which may be purchased as a means to an end, either to facilitate employment or to permit some childfree non-working time. Research on the direct benefits or costs of alloparenting has spanned a range of outcomes from the short-term socioemotional and cognitive development of the child to longer-term impacts on such variables as employment, earnings, income, crime and delinquency. Analysts have also considered the benefits and ill effects that accrue not only to the child and immediate family but also to the broader society. Much of this work has run beyond the traditional domain of economists and has been addressed by other types of researchers.

Evidence on the direct impacts of childcare on child development in the U.K. is sparse and somewhat inconclusive, as highlighted by the review in Waldfogel (1999).[23] Research from other countries highlights the heterogeneity in potential effects, summarized in Waldfogel's description of the results from the recent NICHD early childcare network in the US as: '[O]ne cannot make sweeping conclusions about whether early childcare harms, or helps, children; rather, the effects of early childcare on a child's attachment, child–mother interactions, and cognitive and behavioural outcomes depend critically on the characteristics of that care (including the quality of care, its continuity, and the number of hours that the child is in care) and the characteristics of the child and family.'[24]

Is Childcare Rationed?

Concern that there is a shortage of affordable, good quality childcare has often featured in the policy debate in the U.K., but finding evidence of pure unmet demand for childcare places has proved difficult. This is perhaps not surprising given that unmet demand is a relatively intangible concept to measure. Three main types of arguments have been made to support the existence of rationing: the variation in childcare availability across the country; survey questions reporting parents' dissatisfaction with the available childcare; and studies attempting to directly measure unmet demand.

Variation in the availability of formal childcare places across the country is illustrated in Table 7.4, which presents average levels of availability, measured as the number of places per 10,000 children, over the five years from 1995–1999. To highlight the diversity across areas, the ratio of availability in the LA with greatest availability to the availability in the LA with lowest availability is presented in the final column. Playgroups have the smallest range in provision, while holiday scheme places have the greatest diversity: some areas have over 200 times as many places per child as other areas. It is clear that childcare provision varies enormously across the country, yet this may reflect differences in the demand for childcare rather than unmet demand in particular areas. The availability of childcare places is also positively related to the proportion of mothers who are in paid employment across different areas of the country,[25] but this correlation could reflect causation in either direction: either low employment rates in some areas generate a low demand for childcare which leads to low provision, or low availability of childcare in some areas prevents some mothers

Table 7.4. Variation in Childcare Availability Across Local Authorities

Type of Childcare	Number of Places Per 10,000 Children			Availability Ratio: Highest LA / Lowest LA
	Average	Highest LA	Lowest LA	
Day Nursery	630	3095	140	22 times
Playgroup	1199	2292	270	8 times
Childminder	704	1623	148	11 times
Out of School club	375	5415	61	89 times
Holiday scheme	1234	6785	31	219 times

Notes: The base child population is children under the age of 5 for day nursery and playgroup places, children under the age of 8 for childminder places and children aged 5 to 7 for out of school club and holiday scheme places. The availability rates are averaged over the 5 years from March 1995 to March 1999. The lowest LA is the LA with the lowest non-zero availability. Holiday scheme places are counted as one per holiday period

Source: Table 1 in Paull and Brewer (2003), summarized from Chapter 5 in Paull and Taylor (2002). The LA data was originally published by the Department of Health and the Department for Education and Employment.

from undertaking paid employment. In itself, neither the variation in childcare availability nor the association with mothers' employment rates can be taken as evidence of rationing in the childcare market.[26]

The second approach has been to *ask* parents whether they have limited childcare options. Several studies have shown that substantial proportions of non-working mothers report that they would like to go to work if suitable childcare were available (Jarvis et al. 2000; La Valle et al. 2000; Ford 1996). Similarly, substantial proportions of mothers working part-time report that they would work longer hours if they had access to adequate care (Jarvis et al. 2000; La Valle et al. 2000; Paull and Taylor 2000). Other work shows that about half of parents believe that there are not enough childcare places in the local area (La Valle 2000; Blake et al. 2001). In contrast, when parents are asked for specific instances when they have wanted or needed childcare and had been unable to get it over the previous year, Chapter 3 of La Valle et al. (2000) shows that the majority of parents (69 per cent) report no 'unmet demand' over that period and only 7 per cent reported problems occurring once a month or more often.[27] More generally, these types of questions to parents do not distinguish families being unable to obtain a suitable childcare place at the going price (rationing in the strict sense) from the desired type of care simply costing too much or the available affordable care being considered of too poor quality. This criticism is particularly poignant when, for example, the question is termed as asking what parents would do if they had access to 'good-quality, convenient, reliable and affordable childcare'.

Finally, other studies have attempted to measure unmet demand more directly. Callender (2000) provides evidence that some care providers have waiting lists, indicating unmet demand. However, it is also true that others have vacancies while a third of all providers have waiting lists and vacancies at the same time, suggesting that both may reflect only frictional turnover. In other work, Chevalier and Viitanen (2002b) find that changes in childcare supply lead to changes in mothers' employment, suggesting that mother's employment is constrained by a lack of childcare. However, the authors concede that their measure of childcare supply may not be perfect: it is proxied by the number of childcare workers, which, as argued above for availability measures, might reflect equilibrium childcare use, rather than childcare supply.

Alloparenting Policies

Should Alloparenting Be a Policy Concern?

The case for government involvement in alloparenting choices is essentially twofold. First, it is argued that childcare policies should be used to encourage mothers to work in formal paid employment in order to reduce gender inequalities in the labour market; to make the best use of the potential labour force and thereby improve economic efficiency; and to reduce the dependence of poorer households on the state. Second, if pre-school children benefit from alloparenting, it is argued to be desirable on equity grounds to ensure that it is available to poorer families. In the absence of government intervention, families may not make the best employment and childcare choices for several reasons: the benefits may be social as well as private; parents may lack complete information or be short-sighted; or parents may be credit-constrained and unable to make investments in childcare. In addition, there may be supply constraints in the provision of childcare due to inefficiencies in the market such as inhibiting regulation or high start-up costs. For these reasons, it may be desirable for government policies to help families with the cost of care and to ensure the smooth functioning of the childcare market.

Recent Policy in the U.K.

Over the last decade, several initiatives have been launched in the U.K. to increase the availability and reduce the cost of the alloparenting options open to families. Initial measures were primarily tied to employment, including the introduction of tax relief for employer-provided workplace childcare in 1990 and a reform in the Family Credit program for working parents in 1994 that allowed some recipients to claim up to £40 per week childcare expenditure deduction from their income assessment. The effectiveness of these measures were limited by the fact that the former applies only to workplace facilities, while the latter only benefited the small minority of the Family Credit caseload who were not already receiving the maximum benefit. However, the replacement of the Family Credit program with the Working Families' Tax Credit

(WFTC) in October 1999 introduced a childcare credit that was far more generous than any previous subsidy for childcare costs. The credit increased benefit entitlement by 70 per cent of registered childcare costs (subject to maximums of £100 per week for parents with one child and £150 per week for parents with two or more children). This credit continued into the Working Tax Credit introduced in April 2003 with some minor modifications.

Other policy initiatives have aimed to encourage the use of formal childcare independent of any work requirement. The childcare voucher scheme was introduced nationwide in April 1997, entitling all four-year-old children to an annual £1,100 childcare voucher towards the cost of a place in a participating childcare institution. The value of this voucher has been regularly uprated and the scheme has subsequently been renamed the Nursery Education Grant. In May 1998, the government launched the National Childcare Strategy with the three central aims of raising the quality of childcare, making childcare more affordable and making childcare more accessible. The Strategy has included measures to increase the number of childcare places and to improve the available information about childcare options.

Impacts of Alloparenting Policies

There has been relatively little direct analysis of the impact of these policies on alloparenting choices. Even the introduction of the WFTC has been analysed mainly for its effect on mothers' employment rather than on childcare use.[28] One study (Duncan et al. 2001b) has attempted to model the simultaneous impacts on childcare and labour supply. Their results suggest that even the generous childcare subsidy in the WFTC had small effects on alloparenting choices: an additional 1.4 per cent of single mothers were estimated to use childcare with the introduction of the WFTC, while the net effect for mothers with partners was negligible. In addition, the low use of the childcare element of the tax credit suggests that it is unlikely to have had a substantial effect on alloparenting. According to official government statistics, 175,100 families benefited from the childcare credit in August 2002, amounting to only 13 per cent of the total WFTC caseload and less than 3 per cent of all families with children (Inland Revenue 2003: Tables 1.3 and 1.1). It has been suggested that the main reason that so few families benefit from the childcare credit is the low usage of *approved* forms of care among families who would otherwise be eligible for the credit (Paull and Brewer 2003).

Conclusion

Economists have spent a great deal of time and effort analysing families' alloparenting decisions and how these choices might be influenced. Historically, this research was mainly driven by a desire to understand women's labour market behaviour but recent work has also been motivated by more direct concerns about the adequate functioning of the childcare market and the availability of alloparenting options. Empirical analysis has provided extensive descriptions of the nature of alloparenting, addressing the question of 'what', 'how much' and 'at what cost' quite well, but the challenges of mastering the unique complexities of the economic modelling of alloparenting has left the questions of 'why' and 'what if' rather unsatisfactorily answered. Intellectual curiosity alone may lead researchers to seek new modelling techniques to provide better answers, but the dual social concerns of raising gender equality in the labour market and ensuring that future generations of children are brought up in the best possible caring environments will surely spur others to further work on alloparenting in an economic context.

Notes

1. The term 'alloparenting' (defined as the provision of childcare by individuals other than the biological parents) would not be immediately recognized by most economists as the literature has used the concept of 'childcare' to capture a range of meaning from any non-parental childcare in the broadest interpretation to formal, paid care in the narrowest definition.

2. It should be noted that the summary in this paper reflects research on childcare in developed market economies. In line with that work, alloparenting is treated to mean care by someone other than the legal parents or guardians rather than someone other than the biological parents.

3. Men's employment choices are largely independent of the presence of children, while women's employment rates depend quite crucially on the need to care for children. Hence, the literature has assumed that alloparenting is only an issue for mother's labour supply and most models incorporating childcare are either applicable to single mothers or to mothers in couples.

4. For example, Averett et al. (1997), Blundell et al. (2000) and Brewer et al. (2003).

5. However, a reduction in the childcare price has an ambiguous effect on the *hours* of work, conditional on employment, because there are offsetting income effects (the family has more money at the same hours and can afford to work less) and substitution effect (the return to each hour of work is greater).

6. N can also be a function of the mother's work hours and the number of alloparenting hours (for example, as under the childcare element of the current Working Tax Credit), but these arguments are omitted for clarity in exposition.

7. For example, see La Valle et al (2000).

8. It could be the case that these parents are alloparenting to allow childfree time for non-employment activities rather than for any direct benefits to the child.

9. This is discussed extensively in Duncan et al. (2001a) and in chapter 7 of Paull and Taylor (2002).

10. For example, in Heckman (1974), Ribar (1995), and Blau and Hagy (1998).

11. It is important to distinguish this from the case where parents are unable to obtain a childcare place because they cannot afford the cost or because the affordable places are not of a satisfactory quality.

12. See below for a summary of the empirical evidence of rationing in the U.K.

13. These data sources include the 1989 UK Lone Parents Survey (Jenkins and Symons 2001); the 1991 and 1998 General Household Surveys (Bridgwood and Savage 1993; Duncan et al. 1995; Duncan and Giles 1996; Bridgwood et al. 2000); the British Social Attitudes Survey (Jarvis et al. 2000); the Survey of Parents of Three and Four Year Old Children and Their Use of Early Years Services (Blake et al. 2001); the PSI/DSS Programme of Research into Low Income Families Surveys (Marsh and McKay 1993; Finlayson at al. 1996; Marsh et al. 2001); the 1999 DfEE/Centre for Social Research Survey of Parents' Demand for Childcare (La Valle et al. 2000); the Family Resources Survey (Duncan et al. 2001a, 2001b; Paull and Taylor 2002; Paull 2003; Paull and Brewer 2003); and the Families and Children Survey (McKay 2002).

14. The studies using the GHS also provide comprehensive samples, but collect only limited childcare information.

15. Some of the comparisons between families with a mother in employment and those where the mother does not work are presented in the original report as a division of two-parent families into 'both parents work', 'one works full-time, one part-time', 'one works full-time' and 'neither works'. The conclusions made here assume that the one parent working is most likely to represent a working father and non-working mother.

16. The remaining presentation in this subsection is derived from Paull and Taylor (2002) and Paull (2003).

17. The use of each type is not mutually exclusive, so the proportions sum to slightly more than the total for any type of childcare.

18. La Valle et al. (2000) present childcare use by age of child for children with both working and non-working mothers (Table 2.4). The picture is very similar to Figure 6.1, with a steep rise in the use of formal care for the three- to four-year-old group, a substantial drop in the use of care at age five and a gradual decline in use, particularly of formal care, after the age of five.

19. See page 187 in Paull and Taylor (2002).

20. There is also a double selection issue that requires the wages of non-workers and the childcare price for those not using childcare to be estimated, but standard econometric techniques have been applied to this problem.

21. For example, see Blau and Robins (1988, 1989), Berger and Black (1992), Leibowitz et al. (1992), Connelly (1992), Michalopoulos et al. (1992), Hofferth and Wissoker (1992), Ribar (1992, 1995), Kimmel (1995, 1998), Averett et al. (1997), Blau and Hagy (1998), Hagy (1998), Anderson and Levine (1999) and Michalopoulos and Robins (1999).

22. This study is also summarised in Chapter 7 of Paull and Taylor (2002).

23. In particular, see footnote 9 on page 7 in Waldfogel (1999). A more recent study in Toroyan et al. (2003) was unable to report any significant impacts on children of being allocated a place at an Early Years centre due to the small sample size and possibly also because children in the control group were able to use formal childcare at other centres.

24. From page 7 of Waldfogel (1999).

25. See Paull and Taylor (2002), Chapter 5.

26. In work in progress, Chevalier and Viitanen (2002a) use statistical exclusion restrictions to identify a group of mothers who are rationed in their use of formal care. They find that the availability variables are significant in explaining parents' use of childcare after controlling for the price of childcare. However, these variables reflect usage rather than supply and may therefore be influenced by demand factors which would invalidate the paper's conclusions.

27. In addition, the reasons for this unmet demand included cases where childcare could not be used because the children were ill, and where parents could not afford the care.

28. Blundell et al. (2000) provide an ex ante evaluation and Brewer et al. (2003) an ex post evaluation of the employment effects alone.

References

Anderson, P.A., and Levine, P.B., 1999. *Child Care and Mothers' Employment Decisions.* National Bureau of Economic Research Working Paper No. 7058. Cambridge, MA.

Averett, S., Peters, E., and Waldman, D., 1997. Tax credits, labor supply, and child care. *Review of Economics and Statistics* 79 (February), 125–35.

Berger, M., and Black, D., 1992. Child care subsidies, quality of care, and the labor supply of low-income single mothers. *Review of Economics and Statistics* 744, 635–42.

Blake, M., Finch, S., Mckernan, A., and Hinds, K., 2001. *4th Survey of Parents of Three and Four Year Old Children and Their Use of Early Year Services Spring 1999 to Spring 2000.* Research Report No. RR247. London: Department for Education and Employment.

Blau, D.M., and Hagy, A., 1998. The demand for quality in child care. *Journal of Political Economy* 106(1), 104–46.

Blau, D.M., and Robins, P.K., 1988. Child-care costs and family labor supply. *Review of Economics and Statistics* 70, 374–81.

———— 1989. Fertility, employment and child care costs. *Demography* 26, 287–99.

Blundell, R., Duncan, A., Mccrae, J., and Meghir, C., 2000. The labour market impact of the working families' tax credit. *Fiscal Studies* 211, 75–104.

Brewer, M., Duncan, A., Shephard, A., and Suárez, M.-J., 2003. *Did WFTC Work? Analysing the Impact of In-work Support on Labour Supply and Programme Participation.* Inland Revenue Working Paper. London: Institute for Fiscal Studies, mimeo, December, 2003.

Bridgwood, A., and Savage, D., 1993. *1991 General Household Survey.* GHS No. 22. London: HMSO.

Bridgwood, A., Lilly, R., Thomas, M., Bacon, J., Sykes, W., and Morris, S., 2000. *Living in Britain: Results from the 1998 General Household Survey.* London: Office for National Statistics.

Callender, C., 2000. *The Barriers to Childcare Provision.* Research Report RR231, October. London: Department for Education and Employment,

Chevalier, A., and Viitanen, T., 2002a. The supply of childcare in Britain: do mothers queue for childcare? Mimeo. Dublin: ISSC, University College, Dublin.

———— 2002b. The causality between female labour force participation and the availability of childcare. *Applied Economics Letters* 914, 915–918.

Connelly, R., 1992. The effects of childcare costs on married women's labor force participation. *Review of Economics and Statistics* 741, 83–90.

Duncan, A., and Giles, C., 1996. Should we subsidise pre-school childcare, and, if so, how? *Fiscal Studies* 17(3), 39-61.

Duncan, A., Giles, C., and Webb, S., 1995. *The Impact of Subsidising Childcare*. Research Discussion Series No. 13. Manchester: Manchester: Equal Opportunities Commission.

Duncan, A., Paull, G., and Taylor, J., 2001a. *Price and Quality in the UK Childcare Market*. IFS Working Paper W01/14. London: Institute for Fiscal Studies.

———— 2001b. *Mothers' Employment and the Use of Childcare in the UK*. IFS Working Paper W01/23. London: Institute for Fiscal Studies.

Finlayson, L., Ford, R., and Marsh, A., 1996. Paying more for childcare, *Labour Market Trends* July, 295–303.

Ford, R., 1996. *Childcare in the Balance: How Lone Parents Make Decisions about Work*. London: Policy Studies Institute.

Hagy, A.P., 1998. The demand for child care quality. *Journal of Human Resources* 33, 683–710.

Heckman, J., 1974. Effects of child-care programs on women's work effort. *Journal of Political Economy* 82 (March/April), S153–61.

Hofferth, S., and Wissoker, D., 1992. Price, quality and income in child care choice. *Journal of Human Resources* 27, 70–111.

Inland Revenue, 2003. *Working Families' Tax Credit Statistics: Quarterly Enquiry: United Kingdom: August 2002.* January 2003. London: National Statistics.

Jarvis, L., Hinds, K., Bryson, C., and Pork, A., 2000. *Women's Social Attitudes, 1983 to 1998: A Report Prepared for the Women's Unit Cabinet Office*. London: National Centre for Social Research.

Jenkins, S., and Symons, E., 2001. Child care costs and lone mothers' employment rates: UK Evidence. *The Manchester School* 69(2), 121–47.

Kimmel, J., 1995. The effectiveness of child-care subsidies in encouraging the welfare-to-work transition of low-income single mothers. *American Economic Review* Papers and Proceedings 85, 271–5.

———— 1998. Child care costs as a barrier to employment for single and married mothers. *Review of Economics and Statistics* 80, 287–99.

La Valle, I., Finch, S., Nove, A., and Lewin, C., 2000. *Parents' Demand for Childcare*. DfEE Research Report No. RR176, March. London: Department for Education and Employment.

Leibowitz, A., Klerman, J., and Waite, L., 1992. Employment of new mothers and child care choice. *Journal of Human Resources* 27, 112–34.

Marsh, A., and Mckay, S., 1993. Families, work and the use of childcare. *Employment Gazette* (August), 361–70.

Marsh, A., Mckay, S., Smith, A., and Stephenson, A., 2001. *Low-income Families in Britain: Work, Welfare and Social Security in 1999*. Research Report No. 138. London: Department of Social Security.

Mckay, S., 2002. *Low/moderate-income Families in Britain: Work, Working Families' Tax Credit and Childcare in 2000.* Research Report No. 161. London: Department for Work and Pensions.

Michalopoulos, C., and Robins, P.K., 1999. Employment and child-care choices in Canada and the United States. Mimeo. Manpower Demonstration Research Corporation and University of Miami, August.

Michalopoulos, C., Robins, P., and Garfinkel, I., 1992. A structural model of labor supply and child care demand. *Journal of Human Resources* 271, 166–203.

Paull, G., and Brewer, M., 2003. *How can Suitable, Affordable Childcare be Provided for All Parents Who Need it to Enable Them to Work?* Briefing Note No. 34, March. London: The Institute for Fiscal Studies.

Paull, G., and Taylor, J., With Duncan, A., 2002. *Mothers' Employment and Childcare Use in the UK.* London: The Institute for Fiscal Studies.

Paull, G., 2003. Chapter 7: Childcare Subsidies. In *The IFS Green Budget: January 2003,* Commentary 92, January. London: The Institute for Fiscal Studies.

Ribar, D., 1992. Child care and the labor supply of married women: reduced form evidence. *Journal of Human Resources* 27, 134–65.

———— 1995. A structural model of child care and the labor supply of married women. *Journal of Labor Economics* 13(3), 558–97.

Toroyan, T., Roberts, I., Oakley, A., Laing, G., Mugford, M., and Frost, C., 2003. Effectiveness of out-of-home day care for disadvantaged families: randomised controlled trial. *British Medical Journal* 327, 906–11.

Waldfogel, J., 1999. *Early Childhood Interventions and Outcomes.* Working Paper No. 21. London: London School of Economics, CASE.

• 8 •

The School as Alloparent

Berry Mayall

Introduction

Does it make sense to think of the school as an alloparent? Clearly schools and teachers share some responsibility with parents for the care and education of children, but a more interesting question is whether schools *behave* like parents, and this is the topic I address here. I argue that, in general, they do not, and that this matters. But there are a number of related issues which also complicate the response. This chapter approaches the topic along a series of avenues. I limit myself mainly to England, since this is where my data originate.

There are perhaps two interlocking central issues to be addressed. The first relates to the purpose of the educational system. As Janet Finch (1984: 4) summarizes, there is always a tension between education as a service which offers opportunities to individuals from which they derive personal benefit, and education as a system for moulding and controlling individuals in the interests of the economy, the state or society. Her survey covers the years from the 1944 Education Act to about 1980, and she notes how varying emphases on these two functions work their way through policy documents. During the war years, planning for the reconstruction of Britain was developed with education as one of the main pillars for this rebuilding along with health and social security measures. A 1943 government White Paper on Educational Reconstruction beautifully identifies these twin goals for a reformed, free universal educational system providing secondary education up to the age of fifteen:

> The government's purpose ... is to secure for children a happier childhood and a better start in life; to ensure a fuller measure of education and opportunity for young people and to provide means for all of developing the various talents with which they are endowed ... In the youth of the nation we have our greatest national asset. Even on the basis of mere expediency,

we cannot afford not to develop this asset to the greatest advantage. It is the object of the present proposals to strengthen and inspire the younger generation. For it is as true today, as when it was first said, that 'the bulwarks of a city are its men'. (quoted in Finch 1984: 196)

As Janet Finch documents, the optimism and idealism of the early post-war years gave way to pessimism, not least because the benefits of education were systematically failing to reach some groups. By the late 1970s, calls for the moulding and controlling functions of education became more strident, and led to the establishment of a more forcibly state-controlled system developed in the wake of the 1988 Education Act.

The second, linked, central issue in this chapter is people's understandings of the functions of parents. Just as for education, so for parenthood! In a welfare state there will always be tension between two basic views of parental functions: that a parent's job is focused on the individual child (her happiness, her abilities and talents); and that the job is to fit the child for the society in which she progressively participates. Since the 1990s, the coinage of the words 'parenting' and 'parenting education' has reflected the state's assumption of responsibility to influence what parents do in the interests of society. The coinage also carries an extremely dubious assumption that there is clear knowledge about what constitutes good parenting and, therefore, the relations between parents' behaviour and child 'outcomes'. I also note initially that there is a tendency at all levels – policy, research, common parlance – to equate parenting with top-down childcare; that is, what adults do to children. In this connection, we should recognize that while many people may think of parenting as one-way traffic from parent to child, other approaches, including modern sociological approaches, consider child–parent relations as two-way traffic, as interactive relational processes whereby both childhood and parenthood are constructed and reconstructed. Children's own experiential knowledge and their participation are crucial here.

In this chapter I take up three main approaches to the school as parent. First, when tackling the issue of education's purpose, we have to take into account a highly influential concept in traditional sociological understandings of childhood and of education, namely socialization. This has been seen as a key explanatory concept for those who do think that schools parent children. But how well does the concept fit circumstances?

Secondly, we should take seriously children's views and experiences and how these provide comment on and challenge adult views as well as how children report their experiences and understandings of parents and parenthood, and of schools and teachers. From my own data and those of others, I would suggest that children see clear differences between the actions of parents and those of teachers and schools. Of intense interest here are child–adult relations, how these are differently understood in the two situations, and how processes in these relations differ.

Thirdly, we must consider new elements in understanding the social character of child–adult relations: the sociology of childhood and the related pressure for children's rights. Here we must also take account of changes in the dominant discipline about children –that is, psychology – away from biological determinism to a vision of interactive learning. Yet the cruder versions of traditional developmental psychological thinking still hold sway in many people's thinking.

This chapter is concerned with inter-generational relations at both macro and micro levels and relations between them. Children and parents – and alloparents – can be seen to be constructed in varying ways, at differing times and places. As Leena Alanen (2001) says, people get positioned as children or as adults, and definitions change over time and according to place. Further, a change in the character of one position must lead to a change in the character of the other, because childhood is relational with adulthood. In this sense, therefore, childhood and adulthood are interdependent. However, in my view, child–parent relations differ critically and fundamentally from child–teacher or child–school relations, across time (and place).

Socialization – A Key Concept

> Education is the influence exercised by adult generations on those that are not yet ready for social life. Its object is to arouse and to develop in the child a certain number of physical, intellectual and moral states which are demanded of him by both the political society as a whole and the special milieu for which he is specifically destined. (Durkheim 1956: 71)

My chapter on the school as parent has sociological underpinnings. Sociology, classically, sets out to explain how the social order works; what holds it together; what contributions social groups make to maintaining the social order and advancing its interests. It also considers what problems threaten its stability or good functioning. Functionalism was a hugely important early approach to these problems and is still influential; it presents a commonsense explanation of how the social order works. In particular, as regards our topic, we must note within this explanation first that the education system is a central agency for ensuring conformity and continuity, and second that children are edited out of the social order: children are regarded as asocial, or pre-social; they are to be prepared for adulthood, which serves as the gold standard for human behaviour. So it is relevant to consider the words of the founding fathers of functionalism, which form the basis of many people's views today, including those of many policy makers (it would seem).

At the turn of the twentieth century, Durkheim (1956) set the scene for conceptualizing the sociology of education within functionalism. Mothers are the first educators, carrying out the simple tasks of socializing children into moral and social norms. School continues this task. Children are not part of the social order, but inhabit a pre-social domain. They are blank slates, empty vessels.

> Society finds itself, with each new generation, faced with a *tabula rasa*, very nearly, on which it must build anew. To the egoistic and asocial being that has just been born it must, as rapidly as possible, add another, capable of leading a moral and social life. (Durkheim 1956: 72)

Durkheim's work was taken up with new enthusiasm by functionalists in the United States from the 1930s (see Giddens 1972: 38). The American selection of Durkheim's work cited here has a Foreword by Talcott Parsons – the high priest of functionalism – who notes that Durkheim, especially in his work on suicide, implies a belief in the psychological notion of internalization. Durkheim and Freud, he says, must be given credit for 'what is undoubtedly one of the most fundamental of all psychological discoveries, namely that of the fact of internalization of culture as part of the structure of the personality itself, not simply as providing an "environment" within which the personality or the organism functioned' (Parsons 1956: 9). Parsons thus establishes links between functionalist ideas about how society works and psychological ideas, standard at the time, about children as beings in a preparatory pre-social domain, where they internalize societal norms. If we add to these twentieth century giants the figure of Piaget, we are provided with a clear schema of how children progress through stages to mature adulthood, during which process they both assimilate experience and modify understandings in the light of experience (for discussion see Jenks 1996: Chapter 1). As Jenks with characteristic verbal elegance puts it, Piaget treats the growth process of the child's cognition 'as if it were impelled towards a prestated structure of adult rationality' (1996: 27).

In this functionalist vision, school staff and school itself emerges as a better-informed parent; school takes up parenting from the simple beginning initiated by mothers (see Musgrave 1965). Within these traditional ideas, we can identify two versions of how socialization takes place at school (Young and Whitty 1977: Chapter 1), that is, how school is a key instrument as agent of reproduction for the wider uses of society (see also for discussion Barton and Walker 1997).

The first version proposes the school as self-determining: actively and positively working for state agendas; self-monitoring; where people – teachers – act to maintain social order; and children learn to conform to the social order, first of school and then of society. This is the standard *consensus* view (as in Parsons).

The second version presents the school as under the overt control of the state: here we have top-down control over curriculum/knowledge. Some versions of this are *conflict*-based (as in Marx). The interests of some sections of society are opposed to state agendas. Sometimes those working within state-controlled institutions revolt, but generally they conform, often under protest.

The argument presented here can itself be sited within the social context of education policy and practice. For observers writing since the 1970s it seems obvious that the second function of education – moulding in state interests – has taken clear precedence over the first – promoting happy childhoods where talents are fostered.

So, if the school is agent of the state, can we think of the state as alloparent? Is the welfare state our Nanny? Can we conceptualize the Prime Minister as Father of his people? Or, possibly more convincing, the Queen as Mother? But that sort of vision perhaps fits best with more traditional, more authoritarian societies – Stalin as Father, or with nation-founders like Washington or Mao? In a well-functioning democracy, are the voters less like dependent children, and more like people on equal terms with politicians? On a key issue of children's rights, our media tell us that the U.K. government will go to extreme lengths to avoid the label 'the Nanny State'; ministers, over many years, have blocked moves to ban adults' rights to hit children.

Clearly, however we may respond to such offhand thoughts, we are concerned here with inter-generational relations at all levels, from national policies to local interactions. And we are concerned with ideas about children: what are children for? Are children for childhood? Is enabling a happy childhood (as proposed in 1943) an appropriate goal for adults, whether teachers or parents? Are children best thought of as social capital for the future? Are they raw material, through moulding by which the state may tackle social inequalities? (Durkheim thought not; he was clear, as the first quotation in this section shows, that educational agendas would differ according to the social station to which groups of children were called ['the rich man in his castle, the poor man at his gate']).

Changing Relations between State, School and Children

Within the educational system in England, in the recent past and present, we see key changes in how generational relations between state, school and children are understood and worked through. These differing emphases provide points of entry into the question: whether the school can be seen as parent

From the establishment in England of universal secondary education under the 1944 Education Act, up to the present day, the big questions have been: how far the school system could help promote a more equal society; how far it reinforces or fights against social ills. Studies using large-scale samples focused first on social class differences in school attainment (Young and Whitty 1977); later on, ethnicity and gender were, and still are, fashionable topics. Essentially, the question whether school reinforces or redresses society's ills links to a broader question: how far is the school an agent of the state, and how far is it an agent with its own agendas, which acts to counterbalance or confront the state?

Beginning in the 1970s, the 'new' sociology of education focused on processes, studies of interaction in the classroom, in order to understand how and why working-class children failed (Barton and Walker 1997). This micro-approach allowed for consideration of relations within the school, between teachers and children, asking how far these were bureaucratic, authoritarian, controlling, and how far they were individualized, supportive, caring (e.g., King 1978; Woodhead and McGrath 1988; Waksler 1991). The general consensus of research was that teacher–child relations became more distant, more bureaucratic, more entrenched in state agendas as the children got older. And that what could look like caring, child-centred practices could also be interpreted as control through psychological régimes of truth (Walkerdine 1984).

The 1980s saw a powerful backlash in education policy: so-called Black Papers dating from the 1970s had attacked what the authors termed progressive, child-centred education, and instead favoured top-down transmission of knowledge; there was increasing rhetoric about the need for higher standards, especially with the aim of competing in the international market place. The 1988 Education Act was a key trigger for changes in the 1990s. Top-down, whole-class teaching, based on a national curriculum and backed by national tests, was the way to raise standards across the board. These proposals were met with considerable resistance by the teachers, who initially refused to implement the tests. Perhaps we have here conflict between state agendas and a profession standing up for the children. Or perhaps we have a profession privileging its own ideas about a child-centred classroom, and fighting for independence from state control.

The 1990s saw the bedding down of the National Curriculum; tests at age seven, eleven and fourteen; competition between schools; and the publication of test results. During this period then, we can see clear control over school agendas by government policies aimed at creating a future work-force. These were based on implicit assumptions (as in Durkheim) that children are empty vessels and that a body of knowledge can be poured into them. In terms of our understandings of relations between the state and the school, we can see competing paradigms: the consensus model and the conflict model, in which teachers can be understood as agents of the state acting, respectively, willingly or unwillingly, to promote state agendas. From the government's point of view, the important thing was and is outcomes – children's fitness to join the labour market. Policies did not regard children as active in learning, nor was their experience of the school regime relevant. In practice, however, some teachers probably maintained more individualized, caring, enabling relations with the children they taught, especially with the youngest ones (Pollard et al 1994).

So, in the traditional sociological vision, we have, most of the time, a clearly prescribed function for the teacher as agent of the state. Teachers have to work with an eye on state requirements as well as on the children in the classroom. As I shall suggest below, the processes of individualized, long-term, child-focused relations common between U.K. parents and children do not fit well with this picture of the tensions in teachers' work. If we think of the triangle of school, state and children, then the school is closely allied to the state; whereas if we think of the triangle of parents, state and children, then parents are more closely allied to the children, even though, as noted earlier, the state may aim to monitor and influence parental behaviour (Donzelot 1980).

In Loco Parentis?

Running alongside these considerations about school as state agent is, however, another (weaker) strand in ideology about schools which is summarized in the phrase *in loco parentis*. In this view, during the hours children are away from parents the school has a duty to look after them, in place of parents. There are perhaps two facets to this duty and this practice: what the teachers do, and what the school provides. And again, we have to keep an eye on the larger picture of state priorities, which largely determine teacher practice.

As to what teachers do, an idea dating from the nineteenth century social world of schools is encapsulated in the phrase 'the mother made conscious' (Steedman 1988). In this view, teachers – who were generally, of course, women – combined middle-class mothers' knowledge and skill with the natural instinctual nurturing kindliness of a working-class mother. There is some evidence that teachers in training have thought of themselves as having motherly caring functions regarding especially younger, primary age, children (Burgess and Carter 1992; Mayall 1994). This includes hands-on comforting and child-sensitive régimes, partly, according to teachers, this was partly in recognition that the youngest children (four or five years old in the English system) are 'only babies really', and also partly as an instrumental measure, in order to ease them sensitively into the social order of the school. But now that teachers are asked to implement a highly structured curriculum, even with the youngest children, motherliness is under threat.

The second facet of the *in loco parentis* function of schools is that, if they are to behave like parents, schools should provide a healthy environment – in the broadest sense – appropriate for the children. Many studies show that maintaining, promoting and restoring the health and well-being of children is a central concern and function of parents, with mothers as the principal responsible adult (e.g., Stacey 1981; Graham 1984; Currer and Stacey 1986; Mayall 1986). In school, this healthy environment would include material provision, the social environment, and preventive and curative care. Material provision would include light, warmth, outdoor play space, lavatories, child-sized chairs and tables, drinking water, milk, school meals and so on (Mayall 1994, 1996, Mayall et al 1996). The social practices of staff are integral to this material health-related provision: how far they take account of children's social and psychological well-being; the pacing of each day, giving breaks, respecting children's active agency, facilitating and encouraging good social relations. Also relevant is the provision of a 'lay' and 'professional' health service, provided by school staff and health service staff, where children can get preventive and curative health care. How far schools actually do provide an appropriate social and healthy environment depends, again, very much on national educational agendas.

In a study of the status of children's health in primary schools in the early 1990s (Mayall et al. 1996), we carried out a national survey (England and Wales), using a one-in-twenty random sample of primary schools (n= 620; 60 per cent response rate) and six case-studies in a range of primary schools. Teachers (in questionnaires and interviews) provided evidence that standards of material provision and standards of care had declined in the 1990s. For instance, teachers said that the physical environment was poorly maintained, there was no time to care for the children, that they had to work the children beyond appropriate limits, and that, specifically, the 1980s deregulation of school meals had had a disastrous effect on nutritional standards and on children's health. Cut-backs in staffing of health services also meant a decline in standards. School doctors and nurses and specialist staff were in short (and variable) supply, and many school staff had inadequate health-related support and advice. In the education system generally, across time, it is probably true to say that the social and health-promoting environment has had much lower political priority than its cognitive developmental function, and that standards are lower than in some neighbouring countries.

We should also note a further feature of the English education system as designed and implemented since the 1988 Education Act. This is the attempt to harness parents as an important resource in the education arena: to increase parental involvement and to define parents as the 'consumers' of education. Thus, the concept of parental choice of schools has been encouraged through inter-schools competition. Parents are to be more important as governors of schools, influencing internal policy, and parents are to agree, through a 'home–school contract' to work with and for school agendas, including taking responsibility for ensuring their children complete their homework. These moves were described in *The Parent's Charter* (Department of Education and Science 1991), which begins:

> This Charter will help you to become a more effective partner in your child's education. As a parent you have important responsibilities. Good schools work better if they have your active support. Your child's education is your concern – and you will want to play your full part at every stage. (Parent's Charter 1991:1).

There are a number of points one could make about this development. Two key ones are made here: first, because of the gendered division of labour encouraged by social policies, it is mothers who are expected to be the active parent; and their relationship with the school is affected by the traditional blame and denigration attached to mothers and motherhood as a social status. If the education system promotes maternal involvement, this will consolidate schools' power in that relationship. Secondly, within this vision of parental involvement, the children themselves are defined as objects of the education system, rather than as active participants. So if we think about the school as alloparent, then the positioning of 'the child' in the education process is as an object of pressure from two sets of adults: the school staff and 'the parent'. This is a very different relationship from the more active, interactive and responsive processes taking place within child–parent relations at home.

It is therefore also appropriate at this point to cite the argument that children at school are an exploited class. Their work in acquiring social and cultural capital is downplayed in comparison with the work of the teachers. This view is supported by the fact that most of the money poured into the state education service goes to teachers' salaries (Oldman 1994). It is their work that counts; and if children achieve then praise goes to teachers (Mayall 2003: 2). Very few financial resources, relatively, go to the provision of an environment which would prioritize children's active engagement with learning. As Susan Isaacs (1973 [1930]) pointed out many years ago, we have failed in our education system to capitalize on children's 'interest in discovery and in the concrete events of the physical and biological world' – and, one might add, the social world. Seriously to enable children to learn 'by doing' would require far better material and social resources both on site and in the immediate neighbourhood; paradoxically it would also require more adults to work as partners with children.

In essence, therefore, there may be a difference of opinion on the school as alloparent according to the kind of education system we think we have, at differing points in its history. But, there may also be a difference of opinion depending on whether one looks at the grand picture (relations between the state, school and children); or whether one looks at the micro-level: what actually takes place in schools, how teachers mediate state policies in their relations with children, and how home–school relations work out in practice.

What Do Children Think about Child–Adult Relations and the Socialization Thesis?

We turn now to another kind of approach to the question whether the school can justifiably be understood as behaving as parents do. Here we are concerned with a uniquely expert view on the question. Children themselves have clear and highly relevant experiences of home and school, and clear and often trenchant views on these two settings. They are indeed uniquely positioned as a social group; they experience parenting and schooling in the here and now. Their views are central to this debate.

I draw here on my own research (Mayall 2002) and make some brief, summary points from my research conversations with children (these outline points are supported by, for example, Cullingford 1991; Morrow 1998; Alderson 1999). The points derive from four studies in England with children in primary and secondary schools, whose ages ranged from five to thirteen years,.

We start with children's experiences and views on child–parent relations.

a) Children do regard parents as *socializers* – parents have a duty to teach morality, as well as customs of the family/culture (see also Montandon 2001).
b) Children rely on parents to provide for them and protect them; it is a *dependent* relationship. Indeed one of the privileges of childhood is the absence of responsibility for provision.
c) Parents also have *distinctive long-term relations* with children and are seen as *supportive and committed*: as being there for them, standing up for them, and being reliable (especially mothers).
d) Parents and children, except in the most extreme authoritarian households, have *interactive relations,* based on trust, affection and knowledge over time.
e) *Both children and parents contribute* to household/family well-being; children do work around the home; they establish, maintain and promote good personal re-

lations; children may care for as well as being cared for. The family is therefore presented as an interdependent joint enterprise – a process.

In sum, children think that parents have a socializing duty, that children are dependent on parents, parents have long-term reliable relations with their children, interact with their children, and that both parents and children contribute to the well-being of the family.

If we take these views as a basis, we may consider how far children think child–school relations resemble child–parent relations. They say:

a) On *socialization*: teachers are not moral teachers, but they have a cognitive or technical function: to teach things – mainly facts – you need to know.
b) Children do not see teachers or the school, in general, as providers and protectors. However teachers do *provide information/knowledge.*
c) Compared to child–parent relations, *children's relations with teachers are more short-term, and more superficial.* (But the class-teacher system in primary school means that children do develop personal relations with the teacher over one year; in secondary school there is much less opportunity for personal relations).
d) On *support and commitment*: children do not assume that teachers are 'for' them, on their side, although some may be, some of the time. They understand that teachers have to teach certain topics as prescribed by the curriculum/government.
e) Relatively, compared to child–parent relations, *child–teacher relations are formal, top-down.*
f) Children think they have little opportunity to contribute to the school as social order or to good child–teacher relations. In particular, *children's participation rights are rejected.*

If we take children's views seriously, then they cast doubt on the school as alloparent. The child–adult relation has distinctive, specific characteristics in the two cases.

Table 8.1. Children's views on characteristics of parent-child and teacher-child relations

	Parents	Teachers
Socialization	social/moral norms	topics prescribed in curriculum
Protection and provision	key responsibilities	provision of knowledge mainly
Longevity of relations	long-term	short-term
Support	reliable over time	less reliable over time
Type of relations	informal, interactive	formal, less interactive
Allows child participation in constructing social order	yes, generally	disputed terrritory

A general point of contrast may be flagged up here derived from children's accounts and also from adult research (e.g., Gardner 1993): the school has traditionally been concerned mainly with one component of the child: cognitive learning. By contrast, parents pay attention to the physiological, emotional, psychological and cognitive components – a holistic approach (for consideration of the finer points of this see Mayall 1994, 1996, 2002).

I also note, for future reference, that children's understandings include implicit reference to the UN Convention on the Rights of the Child. Children think their parents have responsibility for *protecting* them and *providing* for them, and they note that their *participation* as social agents is more honoured at home than it is at school.

On from the 1990s: New Elements in the Equation: The Sociology of Childhood, Children's Rights and the Creativity Movement

In this section of the chapter, I describe these new elements and go on to consider what differences they make to the idea of the school as alloparent.

The Sociology of Childhood

The sociology of childhood was developed and popularized (mainly in Europe) during the 1980s and 1990s. It offers a challenge to traditional sociological formulations of children and childhood. It also offers a complementary set of perspectives to those of the still dominant discipline: developmental psychology.

In brief, in the sociology of childhood, the child is not a being in preparation, living in a pre-social sphere, but is a contributing member of society from her earliest days: thus childhood is a contributory component of the social order (Qvortrup 1985). Qvortrup argues that while children traditionally contributed to household and national economic prosperity through their work in homes, fields and factories, nowadays, in some societies, their work takes place in school. But – and not least because of traditional sociological emphasis on socialization – adult commentators downplay children's contributions to learning at school in favour of emphasis on what teachers do to children.

Further, children are to be understood as social agents, participating in the construction of their childhoods (Alanen 1992). Children have been shown to adopt positive coping strategies to deal with situations where adults commonly regard them merely as victims, such as divorce (Neale 2002). Children, as competent social agents, can be observed in many situations making a real difference. For instance, many children care for sick or disabled parents (Aldridge and Becker 2002). Lorraine van Blerk and Nicola Ansell (this volume) show how children whose parents have died are not only being cared for by grandparents, but are caring for them, and are helping to resource the household through their work. However, we must also identify children as a minority social group, under the control of adults; their participation as social agents therefore depends on the social order organized by adults (Mayall 2002). As I suggest above, school is less accepting of children's participation than home.

Childhood should also be understood as socially constructed (Prout and James 1997 [1990]); we should consider childhood not as a natural phenomenon, but as differently constructed in differing times and places (Hendrick 1997). These points mean taking a critical look at child–adult relations, deconstructing them and thinking about other kinds of child–adult relations – could we and should we rethink childhoods and policies for them?

The sociology of childhood also critiques traditional and still popular psychological formulations about children. Instead of the child programmed to go through certain stages – a child determined – we have the child as social agent, participating in the construction of social relations. In this vision, socialization – with its top-down empty-vessel assumptions – is not an appropriate concept to apply to how children live their childhoods, relationally with each other and with adults, nor to how they learn. It is important to note that studies of childhood in psychology and in sociology have become more similar since about the mid 1980s. Developmental psychology has become less universalistic and more contextualized, notably, via research studies about how children learn (Bruner 1986, 1990; Vygotsky 1978; Faulkner, Littleton and Woodhead 1998). It understands children as people who contribute to their own learning, through interactions with other people (Rogoff 1990; Greene 1999). Social psychological research has taught us the importance of local ideologies and practices, and the importance of intersections between social structures and child–adult relational processes (Kagitcibasi 1996; Penn, this volume).

Nevertheless, developmental psychology remains highly influenced by its traditional concerns. It is future-oriented, wanting to know how small people become big people; it is concerned with difference – with what factors lead to good and bad outcomes; it understands children as highly vulnerable and malleable. Its focus is commonly on the individual and on 'micro' interactions, so that it often presents an apolitical face, although in its assumptions (for instance about the importance of mother–child relations) it is deeply political (and influential). By contrast, the sociology of childhood focuses on the character and quality of childhood now; it understands children as competent and resilient social agents, it is concerned with commonality – what children across a number of 'variables' (class, sex, ethnicity) have in common as a minority social group, and it is in its nature, therefore, a political movement.

The Children's Rights Movement

In relation to the sociology of childhood, the children's rights movement provides a complementary, intertwined set of propositions (Franklin 2002). Under the 1989 UN Convention on the Rights of the Child (UNCRC), children are understood to have rights to protection and provision by adults, and participation rights. Though

England is backward compared to, notably, Nordic countries, yet there has been some implementation of the CRC from the 1990s onwards, with government departments now giving (at least) lip-service to listening to children. A start has been made on the idea of children as participants in constructing the social order of school through the (problematic) introduction of citizenship education (Alderson 2004) and the promotion of school councils. These moves indicate some (minimal) shift away from top-down socialization. Research indicates that, at present, these moves are patchy, token and rarely experienced as genuine by students (Burke and Grosvenor 2003; Linsey and Rayment 2004).

On children's rights, the state of play in England in the first decade of the twenty-first century is broadly that, while not using the term 'rights', policy makers, educators and parents accept adult responsibility to protect children and to provide for them. More difficult – because requiring more sustained effort by adults – is to respect children's participation rights. As regards school, such respect would require radical change in child–adult relations and in understanding the aims and functions of the school system.

Creativity – The New Buzz Word in Education

There is currently in England, in this new century, a third new element in the equation: ideas centring on the term creativity. Currently the educational pendulum is swinging back, with changing rhetoric and some changes in practice, towards notions of active learning (Prentice et al. 2003). Creativity has become a buzz word and provides a new challenge to the socialization thesis; for policy makers have accepted (at least rhetorically) the implications for the education system of the argument that we need flexible thinkers and doers for the twenty-first century (Joubert 2001). Recent government reports and pronouncements have argued for what some regard as incompatible strands in education: an emphasis on creativity is to run in tandem with a government-determined curriculum, with testing and competition. Creativity becomes a tool of the state (see for discussion Turner et al. 2004: 11).

The School as Alloparent?

These three new strands in debates on children's relations with school – the sociology of childhood, the children's rights movement, and the government's emphasis on creativity – complicate even further the picture of the school as alloparent. Within these concepts, children have a right to an education that respects them as active learners. Children within the school system are to be thought of as lending their agile, imaginative, resilient, creative minds and emotions to the construction of knowledge. Furthermore, children have participation rights within the school's social order; these rights can be understood as applying not just to questions of what food should be provided, but to questions of what part children should play in deciding what, how, when and where to learn.

The notion of children as citizens is one that is currently causing some difficulty for English policy makers, given their reluctance to accept children's rights. They have introduced citizenship education as part of the national curriculum, for a whole range of reasons, mainly to do with promoting social inclusion and responsible adulthood (Jeffs 2002; Scott 2002). The emphasis has been on education for future citizenship. But both the sociology of childhood and the children's rights movement have pointed out that children should rightly be understood as citizens now, in the present; and furthermore child citizenship implies that the state education system is a service, not only for the state, but for the benefit of children, respectful of their rights. As citizens, in theory, children enter into a direct relation with the state; they have a right to participate in central decisions about their education. For policy makers this notion is problematic, not only because they favour the socialization thesis, but to the extent that they have defined the education system as a service for parents (as noted earlier). Essentially, therefore, to define (however grudgingly) children as citizens suggests their participation rights should be honoured, but this conflicts with the idea that the state should define and control agendas in school.

So within new thinking about childhood – through sociological and rights lenses – we can understand children as a social group of citizens with a right to an education service, and as active participants in learning. This is a long way from the traditional sociological thesis that schools act as socializing agents, working on people conceptualized as pre-social beings, with empty heads to be filled.

Linking School with Society

The above notes on current dilemmas within the English education system point to some wider issues. In particular, it is relevant to stress that the division of labour and responsibility for children sites children very differently in the two domains – the home and the school. Within the so-called liberal society, the concept of parental responsibility for children has considerable power; children are dependent for protection and provision on parents, though the state helps out through services and financial contributions. As to participation rights, the evidence is that the particular characteristics of the parent–child relationship, as described by children, favour respect for their participation rights at home. The principal state contributions to children's present and future well-being are through the universalistic health service and education service, with welfare services in residual role. Though the school operates a health-related protection and provision service (as suggested above), in practice this is understood and operationalized as a holding operation during the day; for the school – *in loco parentis* – hands back the children to the principal carers: parents. The school's principal function, as understood by policy makers, is in socialization; though this is contested in recent thinking. Thus, as children of parents, children's relations with the state are mediated through their relations with parents. As school children, their relations with the state are more direct, since the state attempts to influence them directly.

We can opt for a more optimistic vision. Looked at from the perspective of new ideas about childhood, rights and school curricula, school and its educational agendas may, perhaps, be seen as an environment where children participate with active engagement in learning. Children are not essentially dependent in relations with teachers (though traditional practices tell us the opposite). Within new understandings of childhood, school could be reconceptualized as a democratic agency where children participate in setting the agendas and work in partnership with teachers.

The rights agenda, if well implemented, could enable children to regard themselves as citizens across home and school. The rights agenda could lead to child–teacher relations being more democratic, interactive, more personal, and more long-term – perhaps more like those of children with their parents. Rethinking children as active learners, as concerned citizens, could also help in demoting the current top-down curriculum with its tests. Preoccupation with outcomes could give way, somewhat, to consideration of process. School would then become less controlling, more enabling and more highly valued by children. Children might be enabled to enjoy school (!) and to respect their teachers as interactive guides to learning. Some schools have moved along these routes (Osler 2000; Linsley and Rayment 2004).

Twenty years after the 1988 Education Act, some of these possibilities are moving towards realization. Though tests remain at age seven and eleven, those at fourteen have been scrapped. An independent review of primary education has emphasized children as active learners and teachers as guides helping children develop intellectual, personal and social resources to enable them to participate as active citizens (eg James and Pollard 2008). And a government-commissioned report proposes broader areas for children to explore, to replace the fact-based 'subjects' set in place in the 1990s (DCSF 2008)

These theoretical and policy-relevant developments may help towards the recognition of education as self-actualization: learning who you are in the world; learning at school so that you can function now and in future in society. While currently many young people see school and schooling as irrelevant in their lives now and for the future, the idea of education in school as self-actualization can provide young people with understandings that they have an active place in society. Such a change would further challenge the concept of socialization – children not as empty vessels, but as active learners, seeking ways of living in society.

Conclusion

In summary, is it helpful to think of school and teachers as acting like parents?

As I have briefly indicated, the frequent shifts in English education policy mean we have to describe and analyse a different picture just about each decade.

Secondly, children's own accounts suggest clear differences between child–parent and child–teacher/school relations at the moment.

Thirdly and more broadly, if the school is an agent of the state, does the state act in ways comparable to parental behaviour? I would say that generally the history of schooling shows clear blue water between parents and the state as regards responsibility for children and as regards goals for children.

Fourthly, the sociology of childhood, the children's rights movement and the latest proposals to put creativity (back) into schools suggest prospects both towards the school as a service to children as citizens, and towards a more equal relation between children and those adults who work in schools. But this would again lead to different relational processes from those between children and parents. I note again, that the dependencies and interdependencies of child–parent relations and parental long-term commitment are not replicated in the child–teacher relation.

References

Alanen, L., 1992. *Modern Childhood? Exploring the 'Child Question' in Sociology.* Research Report 50. Finland: University of Jyväskylä.

——— 2001. Explorations in generational analysis. In L. Alanen and B. Mayall, eds., *Conceptualizing Child-adult Relations.* London: RoutledgeFalmer.

Alderson, P., 1999. *Civil Rights in Schools.* ESRC Research Briefing No 1. Swindon: Economic and Social Research Council.

——— 2004. 'Democracy in schools: myths, mirages and making it happen'. In B. Linsey and E. Rayment, *Beyond the Classroom: Exploring Active Citizenship in 11–16 Education.* London: New Politics Network.

Aldridge, J., and Becker, S., 2002. Children who care: rights and wrongs in debate and policy on young carers. In B. Franklin, ed., *The New Handbook of Children's Rights.* London: RoutledgeFalmer.

Barton, L. and Walker, S., 1997. Sociological perspectives and the study of education. In R. Meighan and I. Siraj-Blatchford, *A Sociology of Educating,* Third Edition. London: Cassell.

Bruner, J. 1986 *Actual Minds, Possible Worlds.* Cambridge MA: Harvard University Press.

Bruner, J. 1990 *Acts of Meaning.* Cambridge MA: Harvard University Press.

Burgess, H., and Carter, B., 1992. 'Bringing out the best in people': teacher training and the 'real' teacher. *British Journal of Sociology of Education* 13(3), 349–59.

Burke, C., and Grosvenor, I., 2003. *The School I'd Like.* London: RoutledgeFalmer.

Cullingford, C., 1991. *The Inner World of the School: Children's Ideas about Schools.* London: Cassell.

Currer, C., and Stacey, M., eds., 1986. *Concepts of Health, Illness and Disease: A Comparative Perspective.* Oxford: Berg.

Department of Education and Science 1991 *The Parents' Charter.* London: DES.

Department for Children, Schools and Families 2008 *The Independent Review of the Primary Curriculum: Interim Report.* London: DCSF.

Donzelot, J., 1980. *The Policing of Families: Welfare Versus the State.* London: Hutchinson.

Durkheim, E., 1956. *Education and Sociology.* New York: Free Press.

———— 1961 [1912]. *Moral Education: A Study in the Theory and Application of the Sociology of Education.* New York: Free Press.

Faulkner, D., Littleton, K. and Woodhead, M. 1998 *Learning Relations in the Classroom.* London: Routledge in association with the Open University.

Finch, J., 1984. *Education as Social Policy.* London: Longman.

Franklin, B., 2002. Children's rights: an overview. In B. Fanklin, ed., *The New Handbook of Children's Rights.* London: RoutledgeFalmer.

Franklin, B., ed., 2002. *The New Handbook of Children's Rights.* London: RoutledgeFalmer.

Gardner, H., 1993. *The Unschooled Child: How Children Think and How Schools Should Teach.* London: Fontana.

Giddens, A., 1972. Introduction. In A. Giddens, ed., *Emile Durkheim: Selected Writings.* Cambridge: Cambridge University Press.

Graham, H., 1984. *Women, Health and the Family.* London: Harvester Press.

Greene, S., 1999. Child development: old themes, new directions. In M. Woodhead, D. Faulkner and K. Littleton, eds., *Making Sense of Social Development.* London: Routledge, in association with the Open University.

Hendrick, H., 1997. Constructions and reconstructions of British childhood: an interpretive survey 1800 to the present. In A. James and A. Prout, eds., *Constructing and Reconstructing Childhood: Contemporary Issues in the Sociological Study of Childhood.* London: Falmer.

Isaacs, S., 1963 [1930]. *Intellectual Growth in Young Children.* London: Routledge and Kegan Paul.

James, M. and Pollard, A. 2008 *Learning and Teaching in Primary Schools: Insights from TLRP.* Primary Review Research Survey 2/4. Cambridge: University of Cambridge Faculty of Education.

Jeffs, T., 2002. Schooling, education and children's rights. In B. Franklin, ed., *The New Handbook of Children's Rights.* London: RoutledgeFalmer.

Jenks, C., 1996. *Childhood.* London: Fontana.

Joubert, M., 2001. The art of creative teaching: NACCCE and beyond. In A. Craft, B. Jeffrey and M. Leibling, eds., *Creativity in Education.* London: Continuum.

Kagitcibasi, C., 1996. *Family and Human Development: A View from the Other Side.* New Jersey: Lawrence Erlbaum.

King, R.A. 1978 *All things Bright and Beautiful? A Sociological Study of Infants' Classrooms.* Chichester: John Wiley and Sons.

Linsey, B., and Rayment, E., 2004. *Beyond the Classroom: Exploring Active Citizenship in 11–16 Education.* London: New Politics Network.

Mayall, B., 1986. *Keeping Children Healthy.* London: Allen and Unwin.

———— 1994. *Negotiating Health: Children at Home and Primary School.* London: Cassell.

———— 1996. *Children, Health and the Social Order.* Buckingham: Open University Press.

———— 2002. *Towards a Sociology for Childhood: Thinking from Children's Lives.* Buckingham: Open University Press.

———— 2003. *Sociologies of Childhood and Educational Thinking*. London: Institute of Education.

Mayall, B., Bendelow, G., Barker, S., Storey, P and Veltman, M. 1996. *Children's Health in Primary School*. London: The Falmer Press.

Montandon, C., 2001. The negotiation of influence: children's experiences of parental education practices in Geneva. In L. Alanen and B. Mayall, eds., *Conceptualizing Child-Adult Relations*. London: RoutledgeFalmer.

Morrow, V., 1998. *Understanding Families: Children's Perspectives*. London: National Children's Bureau.

Musgrave, P.W., 1965. *The Sociology of Education*. London: Methuen.

Neale, B., 2002. Dialogues with children: children, divorce and citizenship. *Childhood* 9(4), 455–76.

Oldman, D., 1994. Childhood as a mode of production. In B. Mayall, ed., *Children's Childhoods: Observed and Experienced*. London: Falmer.

Osler, A., ed., 2000. *Citizenship and Democracy in Schools: Diversity, Identity, Equality*. Stoke on Trent: Trentham Books.

Parsons, T., 1956. Foreword to E. Durkheim, *Education and Sociology*. New York: Free Press.

———— 1964. *Social Structure and Personality*. New York: Free Press.

Pollard, A., Broadfoot, P., Croll, P., Osborn, M., and Abbott, D., 1994. *Changing English Primary Schools: The Impact of the Education Reform Act at Key Stage One*. London: Cassell.

Prentice, R., et al., 2003. Creative development: learning and the arts. In J. Riley, ed., *Learning in the Early Years*. London: Paul Chapman Publishing.

Prout, A., and James, A., 1997 [1990]. A new paradigm for the sociology of childhood? Provenance, promise and problems. In A. James and A. Prout, eds., *Constructing and Reconstructing Childhood: Contemporary Issues in the Sociological Study of Childhood*. London: Falmer.

Qvortrup, J., 1985. Placing children in the division of labour. In R. Close and R. Collins, eds., *Family and Economy in Modern Society*. London: Macmillan.

Reid, I., 1978. *Sociological Perspectives on School and Education*. London: Open Books.

Rogoff, B., 1990. *Apprenticeship in Thinking: Cognitive Development in Social Context*. New York: Oxford University Press.

Scott, C., 2002. Citizenship education: who pays the piper? In B. Franklin, ed., *The New Handbook of Children's Rights*. London: RoutledgeFalmer.

Stacey, M., 1981. *The Sociology of Health and Healing*. London: Routledge.

Steedman, C., 1988. 'The mother made conscious': the historical development of a primary school pedagogy. In M. Woodhead and A. McGrath, eds., *Family, School and Society: A Reader*. London: Hodder and Stoughton, in association with the Open University.

Turner, H., Mayall, B., et al., 2004. *Evaluation of the National Theatre's Drama Work in Primary Schools*. London: Social Science Research Unit.

Vygotsky, L.S. 1978 *Mind in Society*. Cambridge MA: Harvard University Press.

Waksler, F.C., 1991. Dancing when the music is over: a study of deviance in a kindergarten classroom. In F.C. Waksler, ed., *Studying the Social Worlds of Children*. London: The Falmer Press.

Walkerdine, V., 1984. Developmental psychology and the child-centred pedagogy: the insertion of Piaget into early education. In J. Henriques, W. Hollway, C. Urwin,
C. Venn and V. Walkerdine, *Changing the Subject*. London: Methuen.

Woodhead, M. and McGrath, A. eds. 1988 *Family, School and Society*. London: Hodder and Stoughton, in association with the Open University.

Young, M., and Whitty, G., 1977. *Society, State and Schooling*. Lewes: The Falmer Press.

• 9 •

The Parenting and Substitute Parenting of Young Children

Helen Penn

Introduction

Sociobiologists and primatologists, such as Sarah Hrdy (Prologue) have documented the evolutionary roots of primate behaviour. They have emphasized the variability of maternal and paternal behaviour across species. They also point to the ubiquitousness of alloparenting. Whether they live in gregarious communities, or whether they live more solitary lives, primate mothers are likely to have some direct help in rearing their young.

In this chapter, I propose to examine some of the variations in parenting and alloparenting/substitute parenting which exist cross-culturally. I realize that the word 'cross-cultural' itself raises conceptual and methodological issues about the possibility of comparing very different kinds of experiences (Spiro 1990; Rosaldo 1993), but I am going to take that debate for granted. I know it is problematic to compare; to simplify and cherry-pick experiences, perceptions and habits from one group and match them with those of another different group to make a general point with little acknowledgement of the context or history of either. However, I also assume that although problematic, such comparisons may offer some salutary lessons about variation in experiences.

In the North the debate is increasingly dominated by a particular narrow model of family life, and by the increasing commercialism of any alloparenting/childcare alternatives. This dominant debate is very much contradicted by experiences of allo-parenting in the South.

Some Key Ideas and Assumptions about Parenting and Childcare in the North

Although the evolutionary evidence may caution us otherwise, the discourse of the family in the social sciences is narrowly focused on the nuclear family: the biological mother (and sometimes the father) and one or two children; sometimes, more rarely, grandparents. Conventionally, in the Euro-American literature on parenting we make all kinds of assumptions – and go through all kinds of agonies – about the obligations and responsibilities that biological parents bear towards their young children. Our conception of these obligations and responsibilities is also the yardstick by which we judge any kind of substitute parenting, and is often justified in terms of biological essentialism.

This discourse of the family pervades North American and European psychological and social welfare literature. In the social work/social welfare literature the notion of the family is frequently conflated with a particular kind of parenting instruction. With my colleague, David Gough, I carried out a small study in the U.K. on professional understanding of the term 'family support'. In almost all cases it meant professionals assisting mothers with managing the behaviour of their children, as opposed to any kind of substitute or relief care (Penn and Gough 2002). Parenting is not generally conceived of as reciprocal, that is as a communal effort in which people within a household or a small community share to a greater or lesser extent in the upbringing of the next generation. Children are commonly viewed as the responsibility and possession of their biological parents. The Australian writer Lyn Craig, in her study of the impact of children on mother's time, remarks that in contemporary society, having children is regarded 'as a private indulgence, very similar to having pets' (2007: 2). The costs of bringing up children, financially and emotionally, are regarded as a matter of individual family responsibility rather than as a public good. The result, as she points out, is that, in the absence of acceptable alloparenting arrangements, mothers who undertake paid work do so at considerable strain to themselves: they go without sleep, they have little leisure, they have no time to care for themselves, they risk 'overwork, exhaustion, stress and ill-health' (2007: 145)

Lamb has summarized, the pervading – but unjustified – assumptions about the family in the psychological literature as:

- Children need two parents, one of each sex
- Family responsibilities should be divided between the parents, with fathers as the economic providers, and mothers as home-makers and caretakers.
- Mothers are better suited for child-rearing and care-taking than fathers:

- Young children should be cared for primarily by family members; and
- White middle-class parents have superior parenting skills and have children who are more likely to excel. (1999: 4)

This discourse is explicit or implicit in much of the academic and professional literature on parenting and substitute parenting; it is also assumed to have universal relevance throughout the world. Major international agencies working in the South draw freely on these assumptions (WHO 2004). Yet this limited view of parenting is not widely shared or practiced in the South.

Attachment Theory and Infant Determinism

For some time from the 1960s to the 1980s the Euro-American literature on parenting was heavily influenced by attachment theory; that is, the notion that a young child (usually he) required a dyadic relationship with a primary caretaker (usually his mother) devoted to meeting his needs in order for him to thrive not only physically, but emotionally. Without such a relationship the child's future would be blighted. The dependency of young children is a biological fact, one rightly emphasized by Bowlby (1951). If children perceive that they are being neglected or harmed they show signs of stress, whether measured behaviourally, metabolically or hormonally.

Nevertheless, the explanations of how parents and other carers handle children's dependency, and how children in turn respond to the handling, are likely to be culturally determined – as Gottlieb's chapter (this volume) clearly demonstrates. Attachment theory has become progressively modified, not least because of anthropological and psychological evidence which suggested that the intensity of this attachment varied considerably according to the particular group of children and adults, and the time and place where they were being studied (Kagan et al. 1978).[1]

Allied to ideas of attachment is what Kagan (1998) calls 'the myth of infant determinism', the belief that parents profoundly influence their young children and shape how they develop. At the level of survival, maternal input is indispensable. But the range of gradations of behaviour is enormous and complex, and there are many arguments to be had about critical periods for development, and the lasting or powerful influence of parents and caregivers. Robert LeVine (2003), the Harvard anthropologist (who described himself as a 'gadfly' on the back of developmental psychology), pointed to the pervasive 'folklore' reinforced by psychoanalytic theorists, about the importance of early years in shaping adult life.

The beliefs about infant determinism, while pervasive in the North, are not widely shared. LeVine and New (2008) have edited an anthropological reader on child development in which they explore cultural variation in parental goals across cultures. In many groups or communities in the South, parents do not see themselves as having influence or power over their children's future. They do not provide the kind of warm, responsive, intense caregiver focus on individual infants that theorists in the North regard as indispensable to young children's development (see Belsky, this volume).

Individuality

For children in the North, a prime parental strategy is to emphasize individuality, to develop 'the individual and self-contained child' to use Kessen's famous phrase (1981: 29). Instead of a strategy of maximizing physical survival, survival is taken for granted. Parents emphasize those characteristics that will enable a child to articulate her wants and preferences, to establish her selfhood; her separateness, self-sufficiency and self-confidence – in the novelist Malcolm Bradbury's words, to become 'a push-push-pushing individual' (1998: 89). LeVine (2003) describes, from an anthropological point of view, how in the North it is commonly expected that young children will be a focal point for adult attention in most daytime situations in a way that feeds their individuality and sense of self-primacy, and heightens the emotionality of encounters between mother or father and child. The ideal care giving is inextricably linked to the ideal childhood; certain types of care produce certain types of children.

Materialism

Individuality is achieved above all through the articulation and exercise of choice over possessions. LeVine also argues that becoming an individual in the North is learning to discriminate and exercise preferences in the material world.

> From infancy onwards, the child is encouraged to characterize himself in terms of his favourite toys and foods and those he dislikes; his tastes, aversions and consumer preferences are viewed not only as legitimate but essential aspects of his growing individuality – and a prized quality of an independent person. (2003: 95)

Sutton Smith (1986) critiques how children's development (and parents' love) is given expression through the provision of toys. Tobin goes further and describes how nurseries in the U.S. epitomize consumerism. 'Consumer desire is reproduced by the material reality of our pre-schools. We create cluttered overstimulating environments modelled on the shopping mall and amusement park' (1995: 232).

'Doing without' has pejorative overtones. There is no point, except perhaps a self-flagellatory, religious one, in self-denial, and in a consumer culture, even modest consumption is an almost impossible stance. In North America, being poor is usually seen as an indication of failure and lack of initiative (Phipps 2001). In widely cited North American studies on early childhood, the description 'low-income' family is used interchangeably with 'multi-problem' family (Campbell et al. 2001). Being able to provide a cornucopia of possessions for one's child is regarded as an aspect of good parenting: poverty, by contrast, is often taken as a sign of irresponsible parenting.

I could elaborate on these discourses of parenting, but my point is essentially that, in the North, a good parent is one who provides a safe, stable, predictable and limited family environment, who focuses on the child's emotional dependence, individuality and verbal self-expression, who ensures material prosperity and surrounds the child with possessions. These broad aims may be realized through all kinds of sub-goals and strategies; they encompass considerable variation.

The State's Role in Childcare in the North

As Hrdy comments:

> [G]rouping infants together – like bats in a communal nursery – for a certain number of hours every day under the supervision of *paid* alloparents who are not kin, but who are expected to act as if they are, is an evolutionary novelty, completely experimental. (1999: 506)

Because of changing employment patterns and the increasing participation of women in the labour force, the provision of childcare is now a major issue in all industrialized countries. Yet, any kind of substitute parenting arrangements sit, sometimes uncomfortably, or improbably within the discourses of the family. Attachment – warm, responsive contingent care – which rewards individuality and self-expression, has somehow to be realized within childcare arrangements.

Yet arguments about childcare in the North are as much political and economic as psychological. There is international and national discussion about the broad childcare systems that are established within a country, and the role of the state in subsidizing and regulating those systems. The Organisation for Economic Co-operation and Development (OECD), for example, has carried out a review across twenty member countries of arrangements for early education and care (2006). In Nordic countries and Eastern Europe, the state assumes responsibility for the funding, regulation and standards of the childcare. This OECD Report suggests that, where the state assumes responsibility for funding and regulation, childcare tends to be of a uniformly good standard. The 'quality' of this childcare is not related to the ability of parents to pay for it, and the child carers must meet minimum training requirements. In some cases, staff are very highly trained, and reasonably well remunerated. In Nordic countries, for example, there is public discourse about what constitutes necessary parental commitment to infants, i.e., maternity and paternity leave, and parental leave (which can be taken by either parent), and about what constitutes good childcare.

In Nordic countries, in particular, the quality of children's collective life outside home, the values that might inform such care, and how those values can be put into practice are all matters for public discussion. It is assumed that child carers are competent and knowledgeable, as are parents and, within very broad parameters set by a statement of values, parents and carers together will discuss and arrive at appropriate local solutions. This kind of care too inevitably reflects local customs and traditions, but it does also admit the possibility of open-endedness, and the possibility of change through mutual discussion (Cohen et al. 2004). Specialist professional knowledge is assumed to be necessary to do the job of childcare or alloparenting. In the 'best' systems, this professional knowledge is a matter of open discourse and discussion.

But, as the OECD also points out, some countries are withdrawing from responsibility for funding and regulation, and provision is largely for-profit. In this scenario, childcare arrangements are essentially a private contract between parent and carer. The responsibility rests with the parent to identify, find and pay for good childcare, although the only choice the parent can make is to find and buy another type of childcare if the childcare is unsatisfactory. Increasingly, childcare has become a corporate enterprise. Stephen Timms, the Minister for State for Competitiveness in the U.K., has described how the U.K. Government sees state provision 'as a last resort', and expects the commercial sector to respond to the increased demand for childcare (Timms 2007). Various commentators have speculated how the commercialization of care, and the paramount profit motive, affect the ethics of care (Sumsion 2006; Penn 2007). For example, young, untrained staff are much cheaper to employ than older, experienced women, although the latter may offer better allocare, but a nursery business seeks to make a profit and minimize costs as its first priority.

In countries where the private market predominates, the quality of childcare in nurseries, or with childminding (family daycare), is very variable. Frequently childcarers are not reliably trained or vetted, and they come and go with alarming frequency; childcare staff turnover in the U.S. and U.K. is very high. Pay is poor and conditions of work often unattractive. In these kinds of situations it is implicitly assumed that child carers will perform poorly unless regulations and other mechanisms are put in place to encourage them or force them to do otherwise.

One widely cited attempt to offer guidance on quality of childcare in the U.S. is a document called 'Developmentally Appropriate Practice in Early Childhood Programs' (DAP), produced by the National Association for the Education of Young Children (Bredekamp and Copple 1997). This advises child carers, whether at home or institutionally based, on what is the most appropriate way to relate to and bring up young children. DAP does not attempt to discuss values or cultural perceptions as a basis for practice. Instead, it assumes a relative lack of knowledge and competence in child carers, which must be rectified. It compensates for this perceived inadequacy by giving very detailed advice about what to do at each 'age and stage' of a child's life. DAP is mirrored by the widespread use of the Early Childhood Environmental Rating Scale (ECERS) by researchers and others. It is commonly used to measure the quality of settings in which young children are being provided with care. ECERS uses a range of sub-scales to measure different aspects of provisioning and staffing in the nursery. It is also open to the same critique of postulating as 'neutral' and 'scientific' an approach which accepts for-profit care as inevitable, and presents individualism and materialism as integral to understanding of child development.

An alternative to nursery care for relatively well-to-do parents has been, and still is, to employ women to act as nannies-cum-domestic servants in the home (a function previously performed in the U.S. by black slaves or domestic workers; and increasingly by migrants from the South, irrespective of the migrant's own family obligations or circumstances). This kind of childcare involves little reciprocity, and could partly be described as a service exacted by the dominant and powerful from the subordinate and less powerful (Hochschild 2001).

Some Key Ideas and Assumptions about Parenting and Childcare in the South

In global terms, the understandings I have described of family life and childcare represent a minority perspective. In this section, I describe and discuss other patterns of parenting and childcare.

My own family has for the last ten years provided me with a golden opportunity to be an ethnographer in very different circumstances from the childrearing experiences of the North. My daughter married an African, a man from the Northern Southu group, whose family comes from a small township in Limpopo Province in South Africa. His first language is an oral language, Pedi, although he also speaks seven other languages fluently, only one of which he was formally taught. Language is the unique human marker. It enables us to shape and reshape our environment in a way that lifts us clear of any other species in terms of our flexibility and the subtleties of our behaviour. Oral languages are sometimes regarded as defective, an earlier stumbling step along the road to written language. But oralcy also confers advantages; it trains you to listen carefully, to remember, to be aware of ambiguities, and nuances of tone and pitch that may be lost in written language (Goody 1990). Bilingualism or multilingualism is also the norm in much of the South, so much so that both ambiguity and awareness of difference pervades everyday existence in the very words you speak. The importance of language communities in parenting and child-rearing is almost certainly underestimated, yet is likely to colour most interactions (Abley 2003).

Households in Africa vary constantly in their composition. As Newman (2007) has described in South Africa, children live with various adults in the course of their childhoods, depending on who is best able to offer accommodation and care at a particular time in the cycle of childhood. This also describes the household I know. My son-in-law's eighteen-year-old niece lives with his family semi-permanently, although she regularly goes back to the township to stay with her grandmother. Her mother, my son-in-law's sister, used to live nearby and often dropped in, but has now moved back to the township. My daughter temporarily had a friend living in the house. The friend has three children; two live with her. The third child, who is under two years of age, lives in a township with her grandmother. In separate quarters, also living in the house is the domestic servant, Provia, who has a nine-year-old son, who lives in another township with his grandmother. Many teenage women in this culture have children, and it is a common practice to send babies away to older relatives to be brought up. In fact, many women of all ages do this; a reflection of the hardness of servitude and city life under the apartheid regime; but also a distant reflection of older traditions about upbringing. Permutations of adults and children in such households seem to shift constantly. Daily life is conducted in at least two languages, sometimes more.

Wole Soyinka (2007), the Nobel-prize winning Nigerian writer, described his childhood in his autobiography, *Ake*. Among many other examples of communal compound life, he describes his mother's bedroom, where every night there was an assorted collection of children, in her bed and on the floor. Some were children of distant relatives temporarily living in the household, others were children of visitors staying for a couple of nights, as well as her own children. The Mauritanian film-maker, Abderrahmane Sissako, offers an extraordinary picture of compound life in his film, *Bamako* (2006), where people come and go constantly, and children mingle unconcernedly with a variety of adults doing a variety of tasks. Sissako says, of his own childhood, that there were never less than thiry-five people in his household. Some of my own students too, have similar recollections. Here is an extract from a Ghanaian student's account of her childhood:

> I was raised in a town called Abeokuta. I grew up in a big compound (with) … my grandmums, sisters, stepfather, stepmother, step-sisters, great-great-grandchildren and so on. At my grandmother's there were only 15 children living together as a family. We played together; we ate together from one bowl. We only ate separately when we wanted to eat rice. We also showered in an open bathroom. We slept together on a mat in the big front room … we respect people older than us and we found it easy to live with people. (Penn 2005a: 17)

In this communal household context, with much movement of people, care for children takes place casually, at least by the standards of the North. My granddaughter, Nobantu, aged four years, was partly brought up by Provia, the maid. Provia has a full round of household duties, and my granddaughter was expected to fit in alongside these domestic duties, which she did in a very self-contained way, happily imitating Provia's activities, dusting, cleaning and folding clothes alongside her. Provia spoke to her in Pedi, but their communications appeared to be utilitarian rather than encompassing any notion of stimulation or encouragement. Nobantu used to nap during the day tied on Provia's back, soothed by the rhythms of her work. Provia fed her with every expectation that there would be no choice and no fuss, the food was just eaten quickly and sensibly since it was too precious a commodity to play with or waste.

Children are expected to get on with things themselves. Beyond early infancy, adult attention and direction is unnecessary and even inappropriate, unless it is a direct instruction to carry out an errand, or to avoid danger (and even ideas about what constitutes danger and risk are very different).

Within these communal household structures, there are always hierarchies. Wole Soyinka's father was the supreme arbiter of his household. His mother was also powerful in the practical affairs of the compound. Similarly, my son-in-law and my daughter are the heads of their household. Their word is law, at least to everyone except my grandson (who is already aware of his status and privileges as eldest son of the head of the household and the negotiating power this gives him; my granddaughter is now following the same route, despite her early care routines). My son-in-law and daughter dispense money and justice, adjudicate and arbitrate and, if there is a breakdown, the miscreant will be banished from the house, at least temporarily.

Their household is more like a small feudal court, in the midst of a society where one echelon has embraced modernism very fast but where the majority of people are still vulnerable and dependent. The tensions in the household – and there are many – come less from the way of life per se, but from the gradual consciousness that, in the new South Africa, this way of doing things may, in the future, no longer be acceptable or desirable. Ideas about allocation of time: dependence, independence and deference, about possessions and purchasing; about personal space and privacy; about the status of languages, in many, if not most ways, are shifting rapidly. Above all, for the purposes of this chapter ideas about parenting and children are changing.

Conventional Euro-American understandings about middle-class parenthood and childhood, and the intricate relationships and responsibilities that characterize them, give us a particular point of view, which, because of its global status, is a very powerful one. We, in the North, really think the world is the way we see it through our lenses.

By contrast, in the South, in many countries, the family may be a misleading concept. It is more appropriate to talk about multi-generational households and peoples' ranking within them. This rank may be partly gender- and age-related and may depend on order of birth, on marital status, or on wealth. It may reflect consanguinity, or matrilineality, or patrilineality. It may be affected by polygamy or polyandry. Maturity may be a sign of status rather than of age. Multi-disciplinary studies could contribute to expanding the rather narrow views of child developmentalists about optimal arrangements for young children.

The Continued Colonization of the South

It is more widely understood and more commonly accepted that parenting is 'culturally embedded', that it does not make sense to describe parenting and childcare unless one also describes the broader cultural conditions under which it is being carried out (Lamb and Sternberg 1992; LeVine et al. 1994; Super and Harkness 1986; Serpell 1999; Zeitlin 1990; LeVine and New 2008). The French anthropologist, Jaqueline Rabain, puts it still more strongly:

The observation of the attitudes, the behaviour and the events taken by themselves teaches us nothing of their psychosocial significance, precisely because of the absence of the location of words and deeds in a discourse, in a code which positions conduct in collective meaning. (1979: 21)[2]

From this kind of work arise very different understandings of the themes of attachment, individuality and materialism that so dominate discourse about parenting and alloparenting in the North. Yet, paradoxically, the childcare discourses of the North continue to be pursued as if there were no alternatives, and as if the scientific findings that arise out of the study of largely private childcare in the U.S. had universal relevance. Conversely, it is assumed – not least by a variety of development agencies – that the patterns of childcare and alloparenting in the North should be unproblematically extended to the South.

Despite the unobtainability and/or the undesirability of the version of parenting and the family that holds good in the North – and this is my essential point – this view of parenthood and family is promoted relentlessly at a number of levels. It is globalized. Most conceptualization of parenthood takes the statistically extreme practices of North America as its starting point, with token asides to 'cultural diversity'; that is, the excuses that are made for those parents who do not quite fit into the dominant model.

Jay Belsky, in his chapter (this volume) focuses on a particular aspect of 'quality' in childcare in the U.S., that is, of warm, responsive, contingent care giving in infancy and its relationship to subsequent developmental outcomes for children. I would not wish to dispute either the importance of such care or the outcomes it produces (although my South African relatives might not understand the emphasis that is put on warm, responsive, and contingent, and see it instead as a continuous lesson in self-centredness). But my argument would be that this discussion on quality refers to a highly specific set of cultural priorities and practices.

Many countries in the South, faced by increasing urbanization, are now attempting to regulate their informal childcare sector. There is a strong recommendation to do so in the UNESCO (2000) Dakar 'Education for All' (EFA) agreement, which suggests that the first goal of education expansion for all children is the provision of early childhood development and care for the most vulnerable children. Most countries and international donors have signed up to this statement of intent. The latest EFA monitoring document, published in 2007, makes a particular point of emphasizing the need for early childhood services; yet nowhere in the document is there any mention of alternative anthropological views about childhood and family.

Despite the predominant and contradictory business ethos, nurseries or childcare settings in the U.S. and U.K. are expected to emulate a conventional parenthood. They are expected to assume a model of intense, mother–child relationships;[3] to surround a child with possessions and teach rules about their use, and to stimulate children to become loquacious, self-regarding, competitive individuals (developing their verbal skills). As children become older, care givers are expected to emphasize the acquisition of the skills needed for schooling – reading, writing and numeracy. These ideals are encapsulated in advice and manuals circulated in the South (Penn 2005b).

Quite apart from the impossibility of offering the same material standards, there are other issues, from my South African viewpoint, that are not addressed at all in the discourses about 'quality' childcare and their supposed long-term impact. They do not address the relationships children might have with one another, or with a range of related and non-related adults. They do not address age hierarchy (the assumption that age and family position confers particular kinds of status). Children's physical exuberance, or prowess, or risk taking are downplayed to the point of obliteration. Bilingualism and multilingualism and oral traditions exist, if at all, as a problem rather than as an asset. Children's own responsibilities and obligations to others, and their self-reliance, so much a part of African thinking, are generally ignored as an aspect of parenting and childcare in the North.

Not only are alternative conceptions of the family and childrearing overlooked, but economic pressures have grossly distorted the 'traditional' lives of millions of families in the South. For poor men and women, creating or maintaining a household will frequently involve some kind of migration. The United Nations Development Programme estimates one in thirty-seven people in the world is a migrant (UNDP 2003)! Studies of township (slum, favela) dwellers suggest that a majority are recent migrants to the city, and the households these migrants create are characterized by considerable mobility (Munyakho 1992; Bourgois 1998; Barbarin and Richter 2001).

Human history is full of accounts of wholesale movements of peoples, of warfare, slavery and displacement, and such massive disruption is, sadly, not new. Deleterious changes are happening all around us all the time. But while those in the North have secured for themselves some recent immunity from these catastrophes,[4] in the South life remains more precarious. Epidemics such as HIV/AIDS are causing further havoc as outlined by Lorraine van Blerk and Nicola Ansell (Chapter 12). In this context, the prescriptions of donor agencies about parenting and childcare imported from the North, and in particular from the U.S.,[5] are simply inappropriate.

Possibly the biggest challenge theoretically in understanding the dimensions of parenting and childcare is not to uncover universals – if indeed they exist – but to find ways of charting these transitions, from one set of understandings to another, and from one set of practices to another, and to link these changes to the pressures that produce them. As Jones and Villar, writing about the *Young Lives* longitudinal study of childhood in the South point out:

> [I]t is critical to systematically unpack culturally specific understandings of the core cultural concepts with which a research project is engaging (such as 'childhood' 'family' 'work') and how these are subject to competing interpre-

tations in societies undergoing rapid social, political and economic transitions. (2008: 49)

Wider economic changes impact profoundly on the arrangements that parents try to make for their children but, at the micro-level of child development, such changes barely seem to penetrate research. So, it is possible, as Stephens (1995) has shown, to believe in a notion of family, childhood and progress that is profoundly undermined and contradicted by the political and economic status quo.

Like other blueprints of progress used in the 'developing' world, the notions of 'parenting' and 'childcare' have been drawn from recent (very recent) Euro-American models. The rich experiences and traditions of parenting, alloparenting, childcare and childhood in the South, and the lessons that they might offer, are being obliterated. We, in the North, have an obligation to contribute to the documentation of these changes, and to reflect on their implications, not least because of the suffering that we might occasion by ignoring them.

Notes

1. Attachment studies are also queried now on ethical grounds. Any intervention that causes distress to subjects in the interests of empirical investigation is now problematic.
2. Author's translation.
3. Yet their failure rate in this respect is immense, because of staff turnover.
4. Although still prepared to inflict it on others, for example in Afghanistan and Iraq – see Glover 2003.
5. A Brazilian colleague, Fulvia Rosemberg, has provided a list of twenty *don'ts* for donor agencies from the North seeking to introduce childcare to the South. These include *not* generalizing assumptions about childcare from the U.S.; *not* transposing assumptions about childcare from one country to another; *not* ignoring local socioeconomic conditions, etc. (in Penn 2005b).

References

Abley, M., 2003. *Spoken Here: Travels Amongst Threatened Languages.* New York: Random House.

Barbarin, O., and Richter, L., 2001. *Mandela's Children: Growing Up in Post-Apartheid South Africa.* London: Routledge.

Bourgois, P., 1998. Families and children in pain in the US inner city. In N. Scheper-Hughes and C. Sargent, eds., *Small Wars.* Berkeley: University of California Press, 331–51.

Bowlby, J., 1951. *Maternal Care and Mental Health.* Geneva: World Health Organization.

Bradbury, M., 1998. *To The Hermitage.* London: Macmillan.

Bredekamp, S., and Copple, S., 1997. *Developmentally Appropriate Practice in Early Childhood Programs.* Washington: NAEYC.

Campbell, F., Pungello, E., Miller-Johnson, S., Burchinal, M., and Ramey, C., 2001. The Abecedarian project: the development of cognitive and academic abilities: growth curves from an early childhood educational experiment. *Developmental Psychology* 37, 231–42.

Clifford, J., and Marcus, G., 1984. *Writing Culture: The Poetics and Politics of Ethnography.* Berkeley: University of California Press.

Cohen, B., Moss, P., Petrie, P., and Wallace, J., 2004. *A New Deal for Children? Re-forming Education and Care in England, Scotland and Sweden.* Bristol: The Policy Press.

Craig, L., 2007. *Contemporary Motherhood: The Impact of Children on Adult Time.* Aldershot: Ashgate.

Glover, J., 2003. Can we justify the killing of children in Iraq? *The Guardian* February 2002: G2, 6.

Goody, J., 1990. *The Interface between the Written and the Oral.* Cambridge: Cambridge University Press.

Gottlieb, A., 2004. *The Afterlife is Where we Come From: The Culture of Infancy in West Africa.* Chicago: University of Chicago Press.

Harkness, S., and Super, C., 1996. *Parent's Cultural Belief Systems: Their Origin, Expressions and Consequences.* London: The Guildford Press.

Harris, J., 1995. Where is the child's environment? A group socialization theory of development. *Psychological Review* 103(3), 458–89.

Hochschild, A., 2001. Global care chains and emotional surplus value. In W. Hutton and A. Giddens, *On the Edge.* London: Vintage.

Hrdy, S.B., 1999. *Mother Nature.* New York: Random House.

Jones, N., with Villar, E. 2008. Situating children in development policy: challenges involved in successful evidence-informed policy influencing. *Evidence and Policy* 4(1), 31–51.

Kagan, J., Kearsley, R.B., and Zelazo, P., 1978. *Infancy: Its Place in Human Development.* Cambridge: Harvard University Press.

Kagan, J., 1998. *Three Seductive Ideas.* Cambridge: Harvard University Press.

Katz, C., 2004. *Growing Up Global: Economic Structuring of Children's Everyday Lives.* Minnesota: University of Minnesota Press.

Kessen, W., 1981. The child and other Cultural Inventions. In E. Kessel and S. Siegel, eds., *The Child and Other Cultural Inventions.* New York: Praeger.

Lamb, M., and Sternberg, K., 1992. Socio-cultural perspectives on non-parental care. In M. Lamb, K. Sternberg, P. Hwang, and A. Goteborg, eds., *Child-care in Context: Cross-cultural Perspectives.* New Jersey. Lawrence Erlbaum, 1–26.

Lamb, M., 1999. *Parenting and Child Development in Non-Traditional Families.* New Jersey Lawrence Erlbaum.

Levine, R., Dixon, S., LeVine, S.,Richman, A., Keefer, C., Liederman, P. and Brazelton, T. 1994. *Child Care and Culture; Lessons from Africa.* New York: Cambridge University Press.

LeVine, R., 2003. *Childhood Socialization: Comparative Studies of Parenting, Learning and Educational Change.* Hong Kong: Comparative Education Research Centre.

LeVine, R., and New, R., 2008. *Anthropology and Child Development: A Cross-Cultural Reader.* Oxford: Blackwell.

Munyakho, D., 1992. *Kenya: Child Newcomers in the Urban Jungle.* Florence: UNICEF Innocenti Centre.

Newman, M., 2007. Family involvement in early child development in South Africa. In M.Cochran and R.New, eds., *Early Childhood Education: An International Encyclopaedia.* Westport Connecticut, 1211–15.

OECD, 2000. *United States: Early Childhood Education and Care Country Note.* Paris. OECD.

——— 2006. *Starting Strong II: Thematic Review of Early Education and Care.* Paris: OECD.

Penn, H., 2005a. *Understanding Early Childhood: Issues and Controversies.* Maidenhead: Open University Press.

——— 2005b. *Unequal Childhoods: Young Children's lives in Poor Countries.* London: Routledge.

Penn, H. 2007. 'Childcare Market Management: How the UK Government has reshaped its role in developing early education and care.' *Contemporary Issues in Early Childhood.* 8 (3) 192–207.

Penn, H., and Gough, D., 2002. The price of a loaf of bread: some conceptions of family support. *Children and Society* 16, 17–32.

Penn, H., Burton, V., Lloyd, E., Mugford, M., Potter, S., and Sayeed, Z., 2006. *What is Known about the Long-term Economic Impact of Centre-based Early Childhood Interventions?* Research Evidence in Education Library. London: Social Science Research Unit, Institute of Education.

Phipps, S., 2001. Values, policies and the well-being of young children in Canada, Norway and the United States. In K.Vleminckx and T. Smeeding, eds., *Child Well-being, Child Poverty and Child Policy in Modern Nations: What Do we Know?* Bristol: The Policy Press, 79–98.

Rabain, J., 1979. *L'enfant du Lignage.* Paris: Payot.

Rosaldo, R., 1993. *Culture and Truth: The Remaking of Social Analysis.* London: Routledge.

Serpell, R., 1999. *Theoretical Conceptions of Human Development.* In: L.Eldering and P. Leseman (eds) *Effective Early Education:cross-cultural perspectives.* London. Falmer 41–66.

Soyinka, W., 2007. *Ake: The Years of Childhood.* London: Methuen.

Spiro, M., 1990. On the strange and the familiar in recent anthropological thought. In J. Stigler, R. Shweder, and G. Herdt, eds., *Essays on Comparative Human Development.* Chicago: Chicago University Press, 47–61.

Stephens, S., 1995. *Children and the Politics of Culture.* Princeton: Princeton University Press.

Sumsion, J., 2006. The corporatization of Australian childcare: towards an ethical and research agenda. *Journal of Early Childhood Research* 4(2), 99–120.

Super, C., and Harkness, S., 1986. The developmental niche: a conceptualization at the interface of society and the individual. *Journal of Behavioural Development* 9, 545–70.

Sutton-Smith, B., 1986. *Toys as Culture.* New York: Gardner Press.

Timms, S., 2007. *The Mixed Economy of Childcare.* Online document, http://www.uel.ac.uk/icmec/presentations/documents/stephen_timms.doc. Retrieved 6.10.2008.

Tobin, J., 1995. Post-structural research in early childhood education. In J. Hatch, ed., *Qualitative Research in Early Childhood Settings.* Westport, CT: Praeger, 223–43.

UNDP, 2003. *Human Development Report 2003.* New York: UNDP.

Viruru, R., 2001. *Early Childhood Education: Post-colonial Perspectives from India.* New Delhi: Sage.

WHO, 2004. *The Importance of Caregiver-Child Interactions for the Survival and Healthy Development of Young Children: A Review.* Geneva: Department of Child and Adolescent Health and Development, WHO.

Young, M.E., 1998. Policy implications of early childhood development programmes. In *Nutrition, Health and Child Development.* Washington: Pan American Health Organization/ World Bank, 209–24.

Zeitlin, M., 1990. My child is my crown: Yoruba parental theories and practices in early childhood. In S. Harkness and C. Super, eds., *Parents' Cultural Belief Systems: Their Origin, Expressions and Consequences.* London: The Guildford Press, 496–531.

• 10 •

Adoption, Adopters and Adopted Children

An Evolutionary Perspective

David Howe

Introduction

It is in our close relationships with others that our psychological selves form and we learn to become socially competent. The process begins at birth and continues throughout life. For most children in the West, first long-term relationships form within the body of small 'nuclear families' in which children are raised by one or both of their biological parents. But what of children who, for one reason or another, cannot be looked after by their mothers or fathers? Who meets their needs? Tizard (1977: 2) observes that 'couples without children, and children without parents, are likely to have unsatisfied needs for giving and receiving affection, and for maintaining enduring relationships.' Although adoption originally was seen as a way of meeting the needs of childless couples, over the century the philosophy has shifted to one of seeing adoption as a way of meeting the development needs of children in need. Adoption therefore appears to be a neat solution solving the emotional needs of child-seeking adults and parent-seeking children.

However, these particular arrangements of helping people meet their emotional needs are not universal. Some cultures, for example, have evolved more communal patterns to bring people into close, encompassing relationships. This is reflected in the way the needs of young children are met, including those who are not looked after directly by their parents. Benet (1976) discusses a variety of adoption practices that do not involve the legal placement of a child with biologically unrelated parents.

'Kinship fostering' sees children and their upbringing being the responsibility of the extended family or whole community. She cites examples from Africa, Polynesia and the Caribbean where children are raised collectively. In this way they are integrated into the life of the whole community. This theme is also covered by Helen Penn (Chapter 9). Biological, or perhaps more correctly, genetic parents can continue to have contact with their children but they are not totally or continuously responsible for their day-to-day care. Raising children is a shared activity.

All of this is in contrast to traditional twentieth-century adoption practices in Europe and America in which relationships between children and their genetic parents have to be ruptured and closed before they can 'belong' to a new set of parents. In these situations, biological or 'birth' parents of children placed for adoption are those who could not, would not or should not look after their children. They have been generally required to surrender all legal (and in effect, emotional) claims on the adopted child so that they can be transferred to a new set of parents. Modern adoption practices began to emerge towards the end of the nineteenth and the beginning of the twentieth century. The first Adoption Law in the U.K., for example, was enacted in 1926.

Adoption, it has often been remarked, is like a 'natural experiment', in which children with biological inheritances from one set of parents are raised by parents to whom they have no genetic relation. The adopted child's situation therefore presents researchers with a golden opportunity to ask a number of basic questions, the answers to which have the capacity to throw much light on the parts that biology and the environment might play in the make-up and development of human beings and their close relationships. Scientists are curious to know whether adopted children's achievements and characteristics are the result of their genes or upbringing. Children's separation from their biological parents represents a socially contrived split between nature and nurture, genes and environment.

Changes in contraceptive practices, the legal availability of abortion, a less socially hostile reaction to having children without being married, and improved financial support for lone parents meant that the number of babies available for adoption by 'strangers' (that is, unrelated) began to drop drastically from a U.K. peak of over 12,000 in 1968 to around only a few hundred a year by the beginning of the twenty-first century. It was in the early 1970s that researchers also noted that many older children appeared to be either drifting or languishing in public care (Rowe and Lambert 1973). Adoption practice up to this time believed that early deprivation or physical disabilities rendered children 'unfit for adoption.' But this long-held wisdom came under increasing pressure. Pioneering attempts to place older children for adoption were proving successful, encouraging further innovation and experimentation in placement practice. And so it was that the adoption of older children became increasingly common. In the U.K., children age one year and older at the time of placement now outnumber baby adoptions, running at several thousand annually and likely to continue increasing.

The reasons for older children being accommodated in either foster homes or residential care vary. Some have been rejected by their parents while others have been neglected, abused or abandoned. Some parents fail to cope with the behavioural problems of their sons or daughters. Many children come from homes where there is poverty, discord and upset or a parent suffers a psychiatric illness. Children with physical disabilities or learning difficulties can also find themselves in public care if their parents feel unable or unwilling to rear them. Many children in public care experience multiple changes of carer. Collectively, children with one or more of these difficult histories became known as 'special needs' children. By the mid 1970s determined efforts began to be made to place as many of these previously 'hard-to-place' children for adoption as possible. Pioneering projects in the United States, Britain and other countries showed that it was possible to locate these children with willing and able adoptive parents.

In order to facilitate the placement of 'special needs' children, new principles were developed to underpin the work. Rowe (in Fratter et al. 1991: 11) records that prospective adopters began to be seen as colleagues and that more direct work with children was necessary to prepare them for their move into a new family. Infertile couples no longer formed the only pool out of which adopters were selected. People, whether or not they already had children, who could demonstrate that they understood the needs of children, were eligible to be considered as potential adoptive parents.

By the 1980s the cry was heard that no child in need should be seen as 'unadoptable'. The aim of permanency planning, as it became known, provided children with an opportunity to form life-long relationships, whether with their biological families or new adoptive parents (Triseliotis and Russell 1984; Thoburn 1990). There was a good deal of optimism about the ability of adopters to cope with the particular needs and demands of older placed children, even those who had been badly disturbed by the emotional upsets and adversities suffered in their early months and years. Indeed, the idea quickly gained ground that given a good social environment, full developmental recovery might be expected. Thus, with the increasing number of older children being placed for adoption, we are witnessing a shift from the 'voluntary' placement of babies born to women unable to care for their infants because of social pressures (stigma, poverty) to the adoption of statutorily removed older children whose pre-placement histories are often ones of maltreatment, neglect and rejection.

Reasons Why Parents Want to Adopt

For most people, the desire to have children is powerful and deep-rooted. It is not surprising, therefore, to learn that many couples who want children but are unable to conceive turn to adoption as a possible solution. For many infertile couples, the ideal is to adopt a baby as young as possible. However, the current reality means that most in fact will adopt an older child. A few adults, including those who are fertile, decide to adopt for other reasons including a wish not to add to the world's growing population, or an unwillingness to become pregnant and bear children. Many experienced parents, same-sex partners, and single people also choose to adopt. Some simply declare that they love children and would like to offer a home to those in need. Others want to increase the size of their family, provide a brother or sister for an existing birth-child, or replace a child who has died. In some of these cases, parents either cannot have any more children of their own or have no wish to become pregnant again.

Adopted Children's Psychosocial Development

Psychologists and other social scientists have long had an interest in the behaviour and development of adopted children. Most children are raised by their biological parents. This makes it difficult to determine whether a child's characteristics have been acquired genetically (nature) or experientially (nurture). However, in the case of a child adopted at birth, it is possible to examine the separate effects of genes and environment. On the one hand, to the extent adopted children are like their biological parents, with whom they have never lived, those traits are likely to have been inherited. And on the other, characteristics that correlate with those possessed by their adoptive parents indicate the power of environmental experiences to shape development.

Current evidence based on adoption and twin studies increases the weight given to the effect of genes on children's psychosocial development, although the preferred view sees a complex interplay between heredity and environment (Plomin 1994; Rutter 2006). For example, in the case of cognitive ability, genetic inheritance appears to play the major role in children's performance, although the environment modifies actual scores, either up or down. As many baby-adopted children move from environments of poor to good quality stimulation, their IQ scores tend to be higher than those of either their birth mothers or fathers. Even so, their IQs still correlate with those of their genetic parents and not those of their adopters (Duyme et al. 2004). New adoptive environments, particularly educationally and materially advantaged ones, appear to allow children to reach their genetic potential.

However, the majority of children placed for adoption today are not babies. Prior to being adopted, older children will have spent one or more years living with their genetic parents or other carers. The early years' experiences of many of these children are often ones of abuse, neglect, deprivation, rejection, or multiple placements. These experiences adversely affect aspects of their development and behaviour. Many arrive in their adoptive homes, not only at older ages but also with one or more problem behaviours and a variety of major socio-emotional developmental needs. Older-placed children therefore provide researchers with the opportunity to examine the extent to which children are able to recover from early life adversity and impaired development when placed in more advantaged environments.

The development of children adopted as babies is seen as a product of genetic inheritance; the psychosocial environment generated by the adoptive parents; and the psychological meaning, interpretation and experience of being an adopted child or adoptive parent. In general, the developmental outcome of children adopted as babies has been found to be extremely positive (Howe 1998). There is a slightly increased risk that these children will experience difficulties or deficits in a number of psychosocial domains, including social and peer relationships, and issues around identity. However, much of this risk is accounted for by a small minority of baby-adopted children who do develop mental health and behavioural problems, leaving the majority to progress through their childhood in good psychological order. And although the origins of a particular difficulty might be understood independently of children's adoptive status, in practice, being adopted often becomes a meaningful factor in many children's minds which affects their interaction with their adoptive parents.

Older-placed children, particularly those who have suffered histories of early and prolonged maltreatment, neglect and deprivation, are at increased risk of behavioural difficulties, mental health problems, and developmental impairment. Studies generally show that children adopted after the age of six months compared to baby-placed children show higher rates of anxiety, feelings of insecurity and antisocial 'externalising' problem behaviour, particularly during adolescence (Haugaard et al. 1999, Humphrey and Ounsted 1963, Kotsopoulos et al. 1993), but that these rates are much lower than for children who remain in birth families where there is neglect, abuse or rejection. The major study by the English and Romanian Adoptees Research Team has looked specifically at the effects of early severe deprivation on children's physical, cognitive and social development. In broad terms, the earlier a child was placed in deprived institutional care and the longer they remained in that extreme neglectful environment, the more severe is the affect on their cognitive and social development. And although adoption does confer significant developmental recovery, catch-up is not complete, and in the case of children exposed to the longest period of global privation, cognitive and psychosocial impairments remain relatively significant (e.g., Rutter et al. 1998; Rutter et al. 2000).

Adoption therefore appears to provide the possibility of major developmental recovery for those placed with high levels of need as well as conferring some protection against maladjustment. Early adversity does not necessarily predict problem behaviour, although a degree of elevated risk remains, suggesting a complex interaction between older-placed children's continuing vulnerability and the protective potential provided by adoption. There is emerging evidence that adopters who are most open, reflective, empathic, 'mind-minded' and psychologically resolved in terms of their own life experiences, particularly negative experiences, generate environments which are the most enhancing for children, especially those who have suffered maltreatment and deprivation prior to being adopted (e.g., Steele et al. 2003).

Developmental Needs of Adopted Children

Adopted children's development is affected by: (i) the quality of attachment to their adoptive parents; (ii) the way they experience and deal with the fact of being adopted, including issues of loss and rejection; and (iii) the nature of, and the meaning they give to, the relationship with each set of parents, one of which (adopters) is founded on a legal event and cemented socially over time, and the other (genetic parents) based on biological and genetic ties.

As implied above, adoptive parents with psychologically 'resolved', reflective and empathic states of mind are most likely to have children, especially those adopted as babies, who are securely attached. Securely attached children generally achieve optimum levels of psychosocial development. Adoptive parents with 'unresolved' states of mind with respect to loss and other negative life experiences increase the risk of children developing more anxious and insecure attachments. Children with histories of serious maltreatment and severe deprivation, even if they receive good quality parenting, remain at risk of achieving only sub-optimum levels of psychosocial development, though there is no doubting that developmentally most of these children are less impaired than they would have been if they had remained in environments of abuse and neglect.

The fact of being adopted implies the inability, unwillingness or unsuitability of your genetic parents to care for you. This fact is often felt as a loss, a rejection, or both by many adopted children. Children and their adoptive parents have to deal with this psychological experience. If children sense that the subject of adoption makes their parents feel anxious, they may suppress any mention of matters that clearly carry a high emotional charge. Anxiety in parents causes anxiety in children who may fear a second rejection. This refusal to face up to and deal with highly pertinent information can distort relationships and interfere with the ability of adopted children to establish a strong self-identity.

A number of investigators have explored how children and their adoptive parents handle what it means to be adopted and what it means to adopt. One of the first people to study how parents and children handle adoption was Kirk. He realized that people who decide to adopt, particularly childless couples adopting babies, have to cope with a number of difficulties. They have to approach other people to acquire a child. They are not certain about the status of the parent in adoption. And they are unclear about the status of their relationship with the adopted child (Kirk 1964; 1981). To some extent, these issues may act as a handicap in people's performance of the role of parent. Kirk points out that adopters are faced with conflicting obligations. They are required to *integrate* the child fully into their family. But they are also expected to tell their child that they are adopted and that in some way they are '*different*'. There is therefore a tension between integration and differentiation that both parents and child have to try and resolve. Kirk also calls this 'the paradox of adoption.' From the children's point of view, they have to reflect on the fact that they are both chosen (by the adopters) *and* given up (by the genetic parents).

In his early formulations, Kirk (1964), in a meta-analysis of his research studies of over 2,000 adoptive families, believed that adopters resolved the tension in one or other of two ways: by rejecting 'difference' or by acknowledging 'difference' (low versus high distinguishing families according to Kaye 1990).

Rejection of difference covers adopters who *deny* that there is any difference between adopted and non-adopted children; that the fact of being adopted is not seen as a relevant difference. The parents cope with the role handicaps of adoptive parenthood by taking the 'sting' out of adoption 'by simulating nonadoptive family life as closely as possible' (Brodzinsky 1990, p 19). The argument is that denial and the rejection of difference may help assuage the pain of loss and infertility but in the long run it undermines the child's integration into the family. This strategy may be effective while children are young, but by the time they reach adolescence and begin to ponder on such matters as origins and identity, problems can arise.

Rejection of difference therefore frustrates opportunities for the adopted child to discuss a centrally important topic. In some cases, the feeling begins to emerge that to be different is somehow to be either deficient or deviant. 'Difference' receives a negative connotation. Some children handle this negativity by denying important aspects of being adopted. However, these coping strategies can affect children's self-esteem and ability to adjust to the realities of what it means to be adopted. Brinich (1990, p7), in his clinical experience, found that in such cases adopters accepted certain aspects of their child while rejecting others. The bits of the child they did not like were projected onto the child's genetic inheritance: 'she doesn't get that from us.'

Acknowledgement of difference occurs when parents recognize that there are aspects of adoptive family life which are different to family life in which children are biologically born to the parents. Kirk (1981: 46–47) believes that parents who are able to acknowledge difference can relate to and communicate more openly and accurately with their adopted children. They are also able to empathize with their children. Empathy and good communication are associated with readiness on the part of the adopters to think about and acknowledge their children's birth parents, their roots and origins (Kirk 1964: 95). What at first sight might appear paradoxical – that acknowledging difference promotes integration – makes sense in terms of allowing sensitive, responsive relationships to develop between parents and children. To acknowledge difference is not to give it a negative connotation. It is simply to accept that it is present. It gives children a stronger sense of identity and who they are.

Brodzinsky (1987) develops Kirk's classification by adding a third strategy in which some adopters not only acknowledge difference but accentuate it. He calls this adverse coping strategy *insistence of difference*. Adopted children are not seen as an integral part of family life. Children may 'see themselves as so different from their parents and siblings that they feel totally alien within the family; they may be unable· to find anything within the adoptive parents with which to identify; they may feel psychologically rejected and abandoned in the midst of their own family' (Brodzinsky 1987: 42). Further studies have suggested that the children of adoptive mothers who display an 'insistence of difference' pattern have lower levels of social competence and higher behaviour problems than children who experience either of the other two strategies (Brodzinsky and Reeves 1987, cited in Brodzinsky 1990).

In his research, Kaye (1990) also refined Kirk's original two-fold classification. Without denying that some adopters do reject difference while others acknowledge it, he found that most parents and children expressed a mixture of high and low distinguishing strategies. He felt that low distinguishing families were not necessarily 'rejection of difference' families. It seems that in some families adoption has not been a major distinguishing factor, not because denial is taking place but because 'difference' really is not looming large in the conduct of family relationships.

> So 'openness' is certainly important. But there is no evidence that asserting 'I don't feel that I myself or my relationships with my family are different in any important way because I'm (or he's or she's) adopted' has anything to do with a lack of open family communication … For at least some adolescents, and probably for their parents as well, 'denial of difference' is simply a manifestation of actually not having experienced many negative experiences, rather than of having repressed them … Perhaps the *moderately* acknowledging, are the best adapted adoptees. (Kaye 1990: 140)

Kaye's most important observation is that the ability of adopted children to develop a strong, secure sense of self is inseparable from them having a strong sense of belonging.

Reviewing the research triggered by Kirk's original classification, Brodzinsky (1990: 21) concludes that perhaps while children are young, 'rejection of difference' coping patterns 'may serve the family well by supporting the primary socialization goals of building family unity, connectedness, and interpersonal trust.' But in later stages of the family life cycle when the full meaning of adoption becomes apparent to the child, rejection of difference may be a much less successful strategy. Openness, honesty and acknowledgment of difference form a more effective basis of communication (Brodzinsky 2005).

Brodzinsky's (1987; 1990) work in this area helped him develop 'a stress and coping model of adoption adjustment'. The model adapts Erikson's (1963) work on psychosocial development. As Brodzinsky (1987: 30) explains:

> The basic thesis of the model is that the experience of adoption exposes parents and children to a unique set of psychosocial tasks that interact with and complicate the more universal developmental tasks of family life … it is assumed that the degree to which adoptive parents and their children acknowledge the unique challenges in their life, and the way in which they attempt to cope with them, largely determines their pattern of adjustment.

Thus, the adopted child has the same developmental tasks as the non-adopted child plus a few more in addition that are peculiar to being adopted. The successful negotiation of these extra tasks requires adopters to be responsive and empathic, accepting and flexible. Adopted children have to work out what adoption means to them and other people in order to work out who they are, both to themselves and others. If they are successful in this, self-esteem and self-confidence – both known to be major protection factors – increase.

However, adoption practice has not stood still. There are strong moves in the U.K., U.S. and other Western countries to develop 'adoption with contact' by which is meant that whenever appropriate, placed children might retain some form of direct or indirect contact with their biological parents. In cases in which children have suffered extreme abuse or neglect, continued contact is unlikely to be indicated. But in other cases there is a growing body of evidence that some form of ongoing contact with the genetic family (mother, siblings, father, grandparents) helps both adopted children and adopters with issues of identity, genealogical connectedness, and possibly psychosocial development and mental health (e.g., Grotevant and McRoy 1998; Neil and Howe 2004).

Genealogical Connectedness

Many, perhaps the majority of adopted people admit to being curious about their genetic parents and background. These thoughts are particularly strong during adolescence. For example, fourteen-year-old adopted Jessica reflected:

> I get on OK with my mum and dad. I kind of know it's not their fault. But I keep thinking that there's supposed to be a natural, loving bond thing between a mum and daughter. And there is. But I've got this other mum that for a few years now I've been thinking of, off and on. Why did she give me up and have me adopted? I know I've been told that she was in her late teens and her own parents were not supporting her, but it does make me feel rejected, that I was, like, not wanted. I keep thinking I mustn't have been good enough in some way, which makes me feel a bit hurt and annoyed. And I wanted to know things that my mum and dad didn't know. Like what was I like in those first few months after I was born? Who do I look like? Why did she give me away? At the moment I kind of can't get these thoughts out of my mind.

U.K. legislation allows adopted people upon reaching the age of majority to access information about their adoption and the circumstances surrounding it. Armed with this information, a significant number of adult adopted people typically, when they reach their early thirties, search for one or both of their biological parents, often with a view to making contact and having a reunion (Howe and Feast 2000). In most cases, this search and reunion process is driven by a number of needs, including the need to know about one's origins, to find the missing pieces to complete the jigsaw of one's origins, background and identity, to discover who one looks like physically, and to know why one was 'given up' for adoption. Thus, in most cases, issues of loss and identity appear to lie behind the initial search. The search and desire for a reunion is rarely driven by dissatisfaction with the adoption. On the contrary, there is evidence that more secure adoptions give adopted people the psychological strength to embark on the reunion process, often with the full support of their adoptive parents (Howe and Feast 2001).

These search and reunion journeys typically work out very well, particularly in terms of providing the adopted person with important autobiographical information and a sense of genealogical connectedness, defined by Owusa-Bempah and Howitt (1997: 201) as:

> the extent to which children identify with their natural parents' biological and social backgrounds. A basic tenet of this theory is that the degree to which children identify with their natural parents' background is dependent upon the amount and quality of information they possess about their parents ... Socio-genealogical knowledge is fundamental to our psychological integrity. It is essential to our sense of who we are, what we want to be, where we come from, and where we belong in the order of things.

However, even in cases where the adopted person has met and established a relationship with one or both biological parents, it is the relationship with the adoptive parents which tends to remain the more dominant, intense and enduring. In other words, adopted people who have met a biological parent will typically maintain some form of contact with them, but 'home' and 'family' are still primarily associated with one's adoptive parents (Howe and Feast 2001). The social and emotional ties established throughout childhood appear, in most cases, to be more robust, meaningful and enduring than the basic ties of genes and biology. Many adopted people seek a clarification and understanding of their 'genealogy' and establish some form of 'genealogical connectedness' with their genetic families, but in terms of filial bonds, relationships with birth parents tend to play a secondary role, albeit an important one (Howe and Feast 2000).

The subject of search and reunion is a complex one in which nature and nurture interact dynamically and transactionally. However, if broad generalizations might be made, secure adoptions are generated by supportive, empathic, open-minded adopters who not only understand that adopted people will be naturally curious (and anxious) about their background and origins, but they provide the adopted adult with the psychological strength and emotional 'permission' to seek out their biological parents. This need to search and have contact does not threaten or undermine the adopted parent–child relationship; indeed it appears to strengthen it. Less secure, less open, more vulnerable adoptive parents not only increase the risk of their child feeling more ambivalent about their adoption, the parents are also more likely to feel anxious and threatened by the prospect of their son or daughter searching for their genetic parents. In these cases, the search and reunion process may be conducted without adoptive parental support or in a clandestine manner, and ironically in these cases there is an increased risk that the adopted person's contact and relationship experiences with their newly found genetic parent are less satisfactory. Again, risking a further generalisation, children placed as young babies tend to experience more secure adoptions compared to those placed at older ages, further factors which play into the search and reunion experience and outcome.

Adoption and Evolutionary Theory

Research evidence is overwhelmingly supportive of adoption as a practice which provides (i) secure, successful placements for babies who cannot be reared by their biological parents, and (ii) caregiving environments which help many disturbed, disadvantaged and deprived older children achieve a worthwhile measure of developmental recovery.

To this extent, adoption and its reported outcomes appear not to fit too straightforwardly with modern evolutionary theory which emphasises reproductive fitness. As Belsky (1999: 141) writes:

> Genetic replication is the goal of (all) life, and thus the ultimate target of natural selection. That is, simple survival is not selected for. Only if survival fosters the *reproduction of the surviving individual's genes* (via his or her own survival and/or that of kin, including descendants), rather than those of the species, does natural selection operate on a behaviour or behaviour system – perhaps like attachment – that fosters survival.

Selection pressure operates on the gene and not the individual.

This is a strong reminder that evolutionary theory is not about survival of the species or survival of the fittest, rather it is about the ability of individuals 'to maximise the representation of their genes in future generations' (Simpson 1999: 116). Adaptive success ultimately reveals itself in terms of reproductive success or 'fitness'. Using a cost–benefit analysis, an individual's total or 'inclusive fitness' depends on his or her own reproductive success plus the total reproductive success of other people to whom one is genetically related, that is people who share a proportion of one's genes. The behaviour of individuals therefore facilitates their own reproductive output and/ or that of their biological relatives (Hamilton 1964). If the investment of parents in the care, protection and socialisation of their children is a valuable resource that can be expended then 'natural selection must operate continuously against its being dispensed ineffectually' (Daly and Wilson 1987: 217). Parental psychology will therefore have evolved to discriminate in favour of being more solicitous towards one's own children and children of one's close relatives.

Daly and Wilson, in a series of books and papers, have used the concept of inclusive fitness to explore the relationship between stepparents and stepchildren. Their basic thesis is that stepparents are less inclined to invest resources in their non-biological children. In more extreme forms, this manifests itself in terms of increased likelihood of stepfathers, for example, abusing, neglecting and even killing their stepchildren. Parents are more likely to discriminate in favour of their own biological children at the expense of any stepchildren they may have. Daly and Wilson (1985) have calculated that even with adjustments for a whole range of confounds, stepchildren are one hundred times more likely to suffer abuse and neglect in families where there is a stepparent. Children are also much more likely to be killed by a stepfather than a biological father (Daly and Wilson 1988).

Evolutionary theorists predict that offspring are valued more as they age. 'This,' explain Daly and Wilson (1987: 208), 'is because the offspring's expected fitness (hence contribution to parental fitness) increases as maturity approaches, primarily by simple virtue of having survived thus far.' They predict and go on to show that, indeed, rates of homicide of children by natural parents are highest for babies and decrease thereafter with age (Daly and Wilson 1987: 209). When the two risks of stepparenting and young age are combined, the authors demonstrate that the children most at risk of parental abuse, neglect and murder are babies and toddlers living with a stepparent, especially a stepfather (Daly and Wilson 1987: 227).

However, adoptive parents' apparent investment in and behaviour towards their non-genetically related children appears to fit less easily with this analysis. In the case of adoption, neither parent is genetically related to the adopted child. It might therefore be expected that adopted children face a double jeopardy, particularly those in adoptions where the adopters also have genetic children of their own, a situation met increasingly frequently with rises in the number of older children being placed for adoption. As neither parent has any genetic investment in the long-term survival of the adopted child, it might be anticipated that the risks faced by adopted children could be at least as great as those faced by stepchildren. As we have seen, although adopted children do experience a number of developmental risks associated with being adopted, they are of a different kind and order to those experienced by stepchildren. Daly and Wilson acknowledge that adoption raises some potentially awkward questions but they tend either to glide over the difficulties or to slip in explanations that seem somewhat fuzzy compared to the iron-like rigour and impersonal nature of an evolutionary cost–benefit analyses. For example:

> One relevant consideration in predicting the success of artificial parent–offspring relations must surely be the initial strength of the substitute parent's *wish* to simulate a genuine parental love. And therein lies an important reason to discriminate step from adoptive parent relationships. Adoptions by 'strangers' … are primarily the recourse of childless couples, who are strongly motivated to simulate a natural family experience, and who have been carefully screened by adoption agencies. While the adoptive couple may not be in perfect agreement about the desirability of adopting, there is at least no exploitation of one partner's efforts for the other's fitness benefit … Stepparenthood presents itself, *a priori*, as a much more dangerous circumstance. Whereas the adoptive couple specifically desires to establish a fictive parent–offspring relationship, the stepparent will usually have entered into such a

relationship incidentally to the establishment of a desired mateship. (Daly and Wilson 1987 218–19, emphases original)

More recent writings by Daly and Wilson (1998: 45) continue to recognise that 'if stepfamily conflicts and violence are indeed the byproducts of an evolutionary structured discriminative parental solicitude … then adoptive children should suffer similar or greater risks'. But again, they explain that in practice adoption turns out to be less hazardous, pointing out that adopters are 'eager' to become parents and they have 'the option of changing their minds' (ibid.: 45). These observations ignore the increasing numbers of older children being placed with couples who already have genetic children of their own. However, the authors do concede that the case of adoption 'is a complex topic in need of investigation' (ibid.). It is an ethically problematic and somewhat sensitive matter to research whether adoptive parents invest the same amount of protective and developmental energy in their adopted child as they do in their own genetic children. This is still a subject in need of further investigation.

At first sight then, it might appear that adoption outcome research is destined to remain a thorn in the side of Darwinian views of family relationships in general, and the concept of inclusive fitness in particular. But adoption has always proved fertile ground for scientists of all kinds. So, rather than see adoption and its broadly benign character as tricky to handle, there might be potential in trying to see whether it might, in some way, support rather than undermine current thinking in evolutionary biology; to see whether in fact it might be an exception that proves the rule. The task is made easier by reminding ourselves that Bowlby (1969) was heavily influenced by evolutionary perspectives and that attachment theory sits well with modern understandings of evolutionary theory. By taking a conceptually deeper view, we might look for possible links that help us connect caregiving, attachment and parentally solicitous behaviour. Should such links occur, it might be possible to explain the different degrees of risk faced by children, including step and adopted children, who are raised by parents to whom they are genetically unrelated.

Evolutionary biology suggests the caregiving system of adult females is activated by a wide range of stimuli, including the biochemical changes associated with pregnancy, the extraordinarily subtle and sophisticated array of proximity and careseeking behaviours displayed by young infants, and the carer's own experiences of being cared for and protected. Investigation of the caregiving system normally implies that the carer is the biological parent of the infant. Less attention has been paid to carers who are not biologically related to the infant, including foster carers and adoptive parents. Although the absence of a pregnancy and birthing experience mean that any physiological factors that bring on caregiving behaviour are absent, it appears that the caregiving system of the majority of substitute carers does become activated in the presence of dependent young children in need of care and protection, and most powerfully in the case of babies. This might explain the relative security and success, from the child's point of view, of baby adoptions. Thus, the compulsion to raise children shown by many women and men unable to conceive their own offspring motivates them to become adoptive parents. The desire to have children overrides the inhibitions to invest heavily in raising other people's children predicted by notions of inclusive fitness.

Of course, this does not invalidate the concept of inclusive fitness; it merely means that other powerful evolutionary forces also have to be considered, including young infants' influential social and relationship behaviour in the presence of familiar adults and the emotional and behavioural responsiveness of those adults in the presence of babies who are vulnerable, dependent and capable of some very effective behavioural signals that trigger caregiving responses in proximate adults. In the case of adoption, there is very little direct evidence of whether the investment shown by parents in their adopted children is more or less than that shown by biological parents in their children. However, we do know that in the case of children adopted as babies, their development and social success compares well with matched populations of non-adopted children. In contrast, children placed at older ages, often with histories of maltreatment, are at increased risk of exhibiting problem behaviours compared to children from socioeconomic backgrounds similar to those of the adoptive parents.

The increased likelihood of older-placed children either ceasing contact with their adoptive parents in adulthood or having levels of contact that are less than those for people placed as babies might be explained in terms of early social bonding. The initial primary selective attachment figures of children placed as babies before the age of seven months will be their adoptive parents. Most adoption agencies employ rigorous assessment procedures in their selection of would-be parents. It might be expected, therefore, that the proportion of adopted young babies classified as securely attached might be at least as high as those found in normative populations of parents of similar socioeconomic status.

As Bowlby (1979) observed, close affectional bonds formed with caregivers in early childhood are likely to endure. Although there is no genetic tie between child and parent, the powerful and early activation of the adopted infant's attachment system, itself a product of evolution, ensures strong ties of affection. In adulthood, this translates into continued and regular contact with parents. But how might we explain the finding that adults adopted as babies are also the group most likely to remain in contact with their birth mother and most likely to have the highest rates of contact with her post-reunion?

First thoughts might intuitively suggest that high levels of contact with one's adoptive mother might predict low levels of contact with one's birth mother. But close relationships are not a zero-sum game. Children and adults who have enjoyed secure attachment histories tend to develop the highest levels of social empathy, understanding, acceptance, cooperation, flexibility, fluency and overall competence. To the extent that children adopted as very young babies are most likely, given the stringent assessment criteria for choosing adoptive parents, to develop an initially secure attachment style, then it will be these children who will cope best with the emotional challenges of meeting their genetic birth mother in adulthood. The emotional demands of meeting one's birth mother can be processed and reflected upon independently of the adopted person's relationship with their adoptive mother. People who can access, fully and without defensive distortion, emotional as well as cognitive information, are most likely to handle complex relationships with skill and competence. Adopted people placed as babies achieve the most robust and successful postreunion outcomes in terms of their ability to maintain relationships with both their adoptive and birth mothers (Howe and Feast 2000, 2001).

Children placed with adopters at older ages are slightly more likely to cease contact with their adoptive mother in adulthood than those placed as babies. Older-placed children are also significantly more likely than baby-placed children to say that they felt they did not belong in their adoptive families while growing up. Older-placed children who have experienced a reunion with their genetic birth mother are more likely than those placed as babies to cease contact with their birth mother, and less likely to stay in touch with her on a high frequency basis.

Children who join adoptive families after the age of one or two will normally have developed a clear-cut attachment (albeit an insecure one in most cases) with their genetic mother prior to being placed. A small number of older-placed children will have been raised institutionally, in which case they might not have been able to develop an attachment relationship with a primary caregiver. In the majority of cases, older-placed children are likely to have experienced neglect, rejection, hostility, or abuse prior to being placed first in public care and then for adoption. It is not unusual for older-placed children to have been in one or more foster homes before joining their adoptive family. The patterns of attachment developed by these children will therefore reflect their attempts to cope with and adapt to caregiving which is either uncertain, rejecting, or helpless. Given these caregiving histories, in broad terms we might expect the majority of children to be showing insecure patterns of attachment at the point of placement. More specifically, children who have suffered rejection, maltreatment and multiple placements are more likely to develop avoidant and disorganised/controlling attachments and less emotionally engaging behaviours.

Stovall and Dozier (1998) argue that fostered and adopted children bring their attachment styles and internal working models to their new caregiving environments. 'If insecure attachment behaviours are carried into other relationships,' argue Stovall and Dozier (2000: 135), 'they are likely to alienate new caregivers.' Children with avoidant and controlling attachment styles arrive in their new families 'ill-equipped for eliciting or responding to sensitive, involved care' (Stovall and Dozier 1998: 65). This increases the risk of maltreated and rejected children replicating elements of their earlier caregiving experiences as new carers, feeling rejected, not needed and pushed away, interact with their adopted child in an increasingly disengaged manner.

Clearly many new carers overcome this challenge and respond with understanding, sensitivity, and high levels of cooperation and availability, thus helping children disconfirm their insecure working model of the self, the other and the attachment relationship. Nevertheless, a transactional model of insecure children in new care-giving environments would allow for the generation of less responsive, less confident, and more disengaged forms of caregiving by some adopters who find themselves having to parent very avoidant, disorganized or controlling children. Indeed, Stovall and Dozier (1998: 67) argue that 'some infants' histories place them at risk for failing to develop secure relationships with even the most available and responsive caregiver.'

If late-placed children are more likely to join their new families with insecure and avoidant internal working models, and if these models increase the risk of children and their new carers developing an insecure, avoidant relationship, this might explain, at least in part, why children placed after their first birthday are at increased risk of (i) feeling that they did not belong in their adoptive families when growing up, and (ii) losing contact with their adoptive mothers in adulthood. And to the extent that issues of intimacy and proximity remain problematic for avoidant personality types, it might also explain why late-placed people are less likely than people placed as babies to sustain contact with their new-found birth mother.

Although an evolutionary perspective is used to explain the present findings, the appeal is to a different set of adaptive reflex behaviours that trigger attachment and caregiving behaviour whenever *very young infants* are looked after by adults who assume a parental role. Daly and Wilson observe that as children get older they are less likely to suffer abuse and neglect because their biological parents have invested considerable resources in their development towards reproductive maturity.

The investment calculus needs some adaptation in the case of older-placed adopted children. By the time a baby-placed child and an older-placed child reach a common age, the adopters will have invested more resources in the baby-placed child than in the older. The present argument suggests that a different biological force (that of caregiving) is more likely to be strongly activated (and so amplify close bonding) in the case of babies placed with substitute carers than in the case of older-placed children. This means that adopted babies are at lower risk of experiencing 'rejecting', low-investment caregiving than those placed at older ages. A pre-placement history of adversity, a lack of early bonding, and a lack of early years investment by adopters poses a two-fold risk for older-placed children. First, they are more likely to bring an avoidant attachment strategy to their placement. Second, their adoptive parents missed the opportunity to have their caregiving and bonding instincts activated by caring for their child when he or she was a baby. George and Solomon (1999: 656) argue that 'central to the development of the caregiving system, and therefore of caregiving behaviour, is the product of a complex transaction among an array of biological and experiential factors.'

Older placed children with histories of abuse, rejection and neglect, will have developed adaptive survival strategies that do not presume adult carers to be an automatic source of care and protection. In an uncertain, hostile world, many of these children will have developed high levels of self-reliance as they defended themselves against the fear and uncertainty experienced in relationships with genetic parents who were rejecting, hostile or helpless. The combination of these two factors increases the risk of disengagement between adoptive parents and older-placed children. Although the skills, understanding and commitment of many adopters helps older-placed children disconfirm their avoidant internal working model, there remains a risk that the child's insecure internal working model will undermine the new carer's confidence in their ability to provide the child with care and protection. As adopters back off being intimate with their son or daughter, the child once more experiences carers as disengaged and somewhat 'rejecting'. This experience confirms the relative unavailability of others and the adaptive and defensive value of an avoidant, self-sufficient strategy. This increased risk manifests itself in the much higher rates of discontinued contact with both adoptive and genetic mothers by older-placed children in adulthood than that shown by adopted people placed as babies.

Although the suggestion that older-placed children who join families where there are also genetic children of the adopters are most at risk of rejection, or at least of being treated emotionally differently, is a contentious claim, it does square with evolutionary theory. Age for age, adopters inevitably will have invested less time and energy in their older-placed adopted child than in their own genetic children or children adopted as babies. Many late-placed children also bring with them challenging and difficult behaviours, adding further stresses to the task of being an adoptive parent. These factors would explain a range of established research findings concerning older-placed children which include the increased risk of insecure attachments, feeling different and not belonging in the adoptive family, and lower rates of contact with adoptive parents during adulthood compared to children placed as babies. It needs to be emphasised that although these risks are higher for older-placed children, by no means all children in this category develop problematic behaviours or experience these difficulties. The relative success of so many adoptions of older-placed children is testimony to the skill, altruism and caregiving competence of adoptive parents. However, to the extent there are differences between baby and older placed children, and the family-life experiences of adopted children and to the genetic children of adoptive parents, an evolutionary perspective offers an interesting, if somewhat provocative outline of a possible explanation.

References

Belsky, J., 1999. Modern evolutionary theory and patterns of attachment. In J. Cassidy and P.R. Shaver, eds., *Handbook of Attachment: Theory, Research and Clinical Applications*. New York: Guilford Press, 141–61.

Benet, M., 1976. *The Character of Adoption*. Jonathan Cape: London.

Bowlby, J., 1969. *Attachment: Attachment and Loss Vol. 1*. London: Hogarth Press.

——— 1979. *The Making and Breaking of Affectional Bonds*. London: Tavistock.

Brinich, P., 1990. Adoption, ambivalence and mourning: clinical and theoretical interrelationships. *Adoption and Fostering* 14, 6–15.

Brodzinsky, D., 1987. Adjustment to adoption: a psychosocial perspective. *Clinical Psychological Review* 25–47.

———— 1990. A stress and coping model of adoption adjustment. In: D. Brodzinsky and M. Schechter, eds., *The Psychology of Adoption*. Oxford: Oxford University Press, 3–24.

———— 2005. Reconceptualising openness in adoption: implications for theory, research and practise. In D. Brodzinsky and J. Palacios, eds., *Psychological Issues in Adoption Theory, Research and Application*. New York: Greenwood, 32–52.

Brodzinsky, D. and Reeves, L., 1987. *The Relationship Between Parental Coping Strategies and Children's Adjustment*, Unpublished manuscript.

Daly, M., and Wilson, M., 1985. Child abuse and other risks of not living with both parents. *Ethology and Sociobiology* 6, 197–210.

———— 1987. Risk of maltreatment of children living with stepparents. In R.J. Gelles and J.B. Lancaster, eds., *Child Abuse and Neglect: Biosocial Dimensions*. New York: Aldine de Gruyter, 215–32.

———— 1988. *Homicide*. New York: Aldine de Gruyter.

———— 1998. *The Truth About Cinderella: A Darwinian View of Parental Love*. London: Weidenfeld and Nicolson.

Duyme, M., Arseneault, L., and Dumaret, A-C., 2004. Envrionmental influences on intellectual abilities in childhood: findings from a longitudinal adoption study. In P.L. Chase-Landale, K., Kieman and R. Friedman, eds., *Human Development across Lives and Generations: The Potential for Change*. New York: Cambridge University Press, 278–92.

Erikson, E.H., 1963. *Childhood and Society*, Second Edition. New York: Norton.

Fratter, J., Rowe, J., Sapsford, D., and Thoburn, J., 1991. *Permanent Family Placement: A Decade of Experience*. London: BAAF.

George, C., and Solomon, J., 1999. Attachment and caregiving: the caregiving behavioural system. In J. Cassidy and P. Shaver, eds., *Handbook of Attachment: Theory, Research and Clinical Applications*. New York: Guilford Press, 649–70.

Grotevant, H., and McRoy, R., 1998. *Openness in Adoption: Exploring Family Connections*. Thousand Oaks, CA: Sage.

Hamilton, W.D., 1964. The genetical evolution of behaviour. *Journal of Theoretical Biology* 7, 1–52.

Haugaard, J., Wojslawowicz, J., and Palmer, M., 1999. Outcomes in adolescent and older-child adoptions. *Adoption Quarterly* 3(1), 61–70.

Howe, D., 1998. *Patterns of Adoption: Nature, Nurture and Psychosocial Development*. Oxford: Blackwell Science.

Howe, D., and Feast, J., 2000. *Adoption, Search and Reunion*. London: The Children's Society and BAAF.

———— 2001. The long-term outcome of reunions between adult adopted people and their birth mothers. *British Journal of Social Work* 31, 351–68.

Humphrey, M., and Ounsted, C., 1963. Adoptive families referred for psychiatric advice: 1. The children. *British Journal of Psychiatry* 109, 599–608.

Kaye, K., 1990. Acknowledgement or rejection of difference? In D. Brodzinsky and M. Schechter, eds., *The Psychology of Adoption*. Oxford: Oxford University Press, 121–43.

Kirk, H.D., 1964. *Shared Fate: A Theory of Adoption and Mental Health*. New York: Free Press.

——— 1981. *Adoptive Kinship*. Toronto: Butterworth.

Kotsopoulos, M.D., Walker, S.W., Copping, W., Cote, A., and Chryssoula, S., 1993. A psychiatric follow-up study of adoptees. *Canadian Journal of Psychiatry* 38(6), 391–96.

Neil, E., and Howe, D., eds., 2004. *Contact in Adoption and Permanent Foster Care: Research, Theory and Practice*. London: BAAF.

Owusu-Bempah, J., and Howitt, D., 1997. Socio-genealogical connectedness, attachment theory, and childcare practice. *Child and Family Social Work*. 2(4), 199–208.

Plomin, R., 1994. *Genetics and Experience: The Interplay between Nature and Nurture*. Newbury Park, CA: Sage.

Rowe, J., and Lambert, L., 1973. *Children Who Wait*. London: National Children's Bureau.

Rutter, M., 2006. *Genes and Behaviour: Nature-Nurture Interplay Explained*. Oxfrod: Blackwell Publishing.

Rutter, M., et al. (the English and Romanian Adoptees Study Team), 1998. Developmental catch-up, and deficits, following adoption after severe global early privation. *Journal of Child Psychology and Psychiatry* 39, 465–76.

Rutter, M., O'Connor, T., and Beckett, C., 2000. Recovery and deficit following profound early deprivation. In P. Selmann, ed., *Intercountry Adoption: Development, Trends and Perspectives*. London: BAAF, 107–25.

Simpson, J.A., 1999. Attachment theory in modern evolutionary perspective. In J. Cassidy and P.R. Shaver, eds., *Handbook of Attachment: Theory, Research and Clinical Applications*. New York: Guilford Press, 115–40.

Steele, M., Hodges, J., Kaniuk, J., Hillman, S., and Henderson, K., 2003. Attachment representations and adoption: associations between maternal states of mind and emotion narratives in previously maltreated children. *Journal of Child Psychotherapy* 29(2), 187–205.

Stovall, K.C., and Dozier, M., 1998. Infants in foster care: an attachment theory perspective. *Adoption Quarterly* 2(1), 55–88.

——— 2000. The development of attachment in new relationships: single subject analyses for 10 foster infants. *Development and Psychopathology* 12, 133–56.

Thoburn, J., 1990. *Success and Failure in Permanent Family Placement*. Aldershot: Averbury.

Tizard, B., 1997. *Adoption: A Second Chance*. London: Open Books.

Triseliotis, J., and Russell, J., 1984. *Hard to Place: The Outcome of Adoption and Residential Care*. London: Heinemann, London.

• 11 •

Surrogacy

The Experiences of Commissioning Couples and Surrogate Mothers

Emma Lycett

Introduction

Commissioning Couples

Developments in the field of assisted reproduction have resulted in the creation of new family types in which genetic parenthood is dissociated from social parenthood leading us to a discussion of the concept of alloparenting.[1] In the case of surrogacy, where one woman bears a child for another woman, the mother who gives birth to the child, and the mother who parents the child, are not the same. There are two types of surrogacy: (i) partial (genetic) surrogacy where the surrogate mother and the commissioning father are the genetic parents of the child, and (ii) full (non-genetic) surrogacy where the commissioning mother and the commissioning father are the genetic parents. With partial surrogacy, conception usually occurs through artificial insemination, and in the case of full surrogacy, conception takes place through in vitro fertilization (IVF). Of all the assisted reproduction procedures that have been practiced in recent years, surrogacy remains the most contentious. In many countries, including Germany and Sweden, surrogacy is illegal. Other countries, including France, Denmark and the Netherlands, and some American and Australian states, have introduced regulation, in some cases prohibiting payment to surrogate mothers (Lee and Morgan 2001).

The characteristics that distinguish surrogacy from other types of assisted reproduction, resulting from the dissociation of gestational from social motherhood, may produce problems for surrogacy families. In particular, commissioning parents must live throughout the pregnancy with the uncertainty of whether or not the surrogate mother will relinquish the child. In addition, commissioning parents must establish a mutually acceptable relationship with the surrogate mother during the pregnancy and ensure that this relationship does not break down. Not only is this situation likely to produce anxiety in the commissioning parents but it may also result in marital strain particularly for couples where one partner is more in favour of the surrogacy arrangement than the other. From the perspective of the commissioning mother who is unable to give birth herself, the relationship with the fertile and often younger surrogate mother, to whom she is indebted, may result in feelings of inadequacy, depression and low self-esteem. In addition, there is a great deal of prejudice against the practice of surrogacy, and commissioning couples are likely to experience disapproval from family, friends and the wider social world. Unlike other forms of assisted reproduction where the mother experiences a pregnancy and birth and there is no need to be open about the circumstances of the child's conception, couples who become parents through surrogacy must explain the arrival of their newborn child.

All of these factors have the potential to impact negatively not only on psychological well-being but also on the quality of parenting of commissioning parents. It is well established that parental anxiety and depression (Downey and Coyne 1990) and marital conflict (Cummings and Davies 1994; Grych and Fincham 1990) constitute risk factors for the child, operating both directly and indirectly by adversely affecting the parent–child relationship (Harold and Conger 1997). Parents' lack of social support from family and friends has also been shown to interfere with the quality of parent–child relationships (Crockenberg 1981). Moreover, the need to resort to surrogacy, in itself, may interfere with the quality of parenting of commissioning parents. For example, couples whose children were born through a surrogacy arrangement may view surrogacy as an inferior route to parenthood, or may feel less confident as parents.

There are also specific aspects of the surrogacy arrangement that may influence the psychological state and quality of parenting of commissioning couples. Greater difficulties may be expected in surrogacy arrangements where the surrogate mother is also the genetic mother of the child, since commissioning mothers who are neither the genetic nor the gestational mother may feel greater insecurity in their mothering role. Similarly, whether the surrogate mother was known or unknown to the commissioning parents prior to the surrogacy arrangement may impact upon parenting. Better outcomes may be predicted where the surrogate mother is a relative or a friend of the commissioning couple due to the longevity and closeness of the relationship. A further factor that may influence parenting is whether or not the surrogate mother remains in contact with the family after the birth of the child. It has been argued that contact with the surrogate mother will be of benefit to the child by providing a greater understanding of his or her genetic origins. However, the ongoing involvement of the surrogate mother with the family may have an undermining effect on the parenting of the commissioning couple.

In addition, it is well established that the security of a child's attachment to parents is associated with the quality of the relationship between the parent and the child (Bowlby 1982; Ainsworth et al. 1978), with secure attachment relationships in infancy being predictive of more positive outcomes for children in the pre-school and early school years (Youngblade and Belsky 1992). Attachment develops through interaction between the parent and the child (Bowlby 1982), and is influenced by aspects of the parent's behaviour including sensitive responding, affection and level of stimulation (De Wolff and van Ijzendoorn 1997). Not only do children develop representations of their relationships with parents, for example, as available and responsive in the case of a securely attached child, but it is increasingly being acknowledged that parents may also develop representations of their relationship with their child. These parental representations are believed to influence thoughts and feelings in relation to the child, and thus affect parenting behaviour and child outcomes (Bowlby 1982).

In families created through a surrogacy arrangement, the circumstances of the child's birth may impact negatively on parents' representations of their child. For the commissioning couple, the transition to parenthood differs in a number of ways from that of parents who conceived their child naturally. Firstly, the absence of a pregnancy may alter the experience of pre-natal bonding, a process that has been associated with more positive parent–child relationships (Grace 1989). To the extent that parents develop representations of the child as they prepare for parenthood, this process may be adversely affected by the involvement of a third party in the pregnancy and the possibility that the surrogate mother may not relinquish the child. Second, the child may lack a genetic link with the commissioning mother. Third, the surrogate mother may remain in contact with the family after the birth of the child. This may have an undermining effect on mothers' and fathers' feelings of entitlement as parents, especially if the surrogate mother is also the genetic mother of the child. Fourth, commissioning couples sometimes experience disapproval from family, friends and their wider social world. Each of these factors has the potential to interfere with the development of positive parental representations of the child.

Surrogate Mothers

Media coverage of surrogacy arrangements have tended to focus on the negative aspects of surrogacy such as the 'Baby M' case in the United States where the surrogate mother refused to relinquish the child (New Jersey Supreme Court 1987). It has been suggested that relinquishing the child may be extremely distressing and may result in psychological problems (British Medical Association 1996). It has also been feared that the surrogate mother may form a bond with the baby pre-natally that would make it particularly difficult for her to hand over the child to the commissioning parents. On the other hand, it has been proposed that surrogate mothers may tend to distance themselves from the unborn baby believing the child they carry is not theirs (Ragoné 1994). It has been argued that such a detachment may make them more likely to put themselves and the unborn child's health at risk (British Medical Association 1996). For those women who do relinquish the child, the risk of post-natal depression, as well as feelings of anger or guilt, may add further strain to the woman's psychological health. Furthermore, some have argued that surrogacy may exploit women from a more economically disadvantaged background (Blyth 1994) such that women may enter into a surrogacy arrangement because of financial hardship without being fully aware of the potential risks (Brazier et al. 1998).

The relationship between the surrogate mother and the commissioning parents, especially in cases where the surrogate mother was previously unknown, is particularly important. Where the surrogate mother is known to the couple before hand, both parties must cope with the change in role from a sister, mother or friend, to the carrier and birth mother of the commissioning couple's child. In cases where the surrogate mother was known to the commissioning couple before the surrogacy arrangement, it is generally assumed that she would remain involved in the couple's life after the child's birth. Surrogate mothers who were previously unknown to the commissioning couple may also maintain contact. In such situations the child may be told the identity of their gestational mother who, in some cases, is also their genetic mother. The consequences of this for the surrogate mother and how she copes with the decision to be involved or not with the couple following the birth is an area that lacks empirical research.

There are parallels between partial surrogacy and egg donation in that the woman is genetically related to the child. How this affects the relationship between the surrogate mother and the commissioning parents, and how the surrogate mother feels towards the child knowing that she is the genetic parent, is an issue of considerable importance from both a practical and a theoretical perspective. Other concerns relating to surrogacy include the impact on the surrogate mother's partner, her parents and any existing children. Where the surrogate mother has children of her own, the British Medical Association suggests that children should be informed about the arrangement beforehand, as the disappearance of the baby after the birth may cause them distress (British Medical Association 1996). In addition, it has been suggested that surrogate mothers will become ostracized or be shunned by disapproving neighbours and friends which may detrimentally affect the psychological well-being of some surrogate mothers and their families. Blyth (1994) found that ten of the women from his sample of nineteen surrogate mothers experienced some form of negative response from those around them.

The little research that has been carried out on the views and experiences of surrogate mothers has tended to examine small, sometimes biased, samples and has tended to be anecdotal. Systematic information from a representative sample of surrogate mothers who had given birth to a surrogate child approximately one year prior to interview is presented.

A Longintudinal Study of Surrocacy

This chapter presents the first two phases of a longitudinal study of surrogacy families, with specific focus on the quality of parenting, the parent–child relationship and the child's psychological development once an attachment relationship had been fully established. The first phase assessed families when the child was one year of age (Golombok et al. 2004; MacCallum et al. 2003) and the second phase when the child was two years of age (Golombok et al. 2004). In addition, the experiences of surrogate mothers will be presented (Jadva et al. 2003).

The surrogacy families were obtained through the General Register Office of the United Kingdom Office for National Statistics (ONS). In the U.K., a record is made of all families created through a surrogacy arrangement when the commissioning couple becomes the legal parents of the child. Legal parentage is granted to the commissioning couple by a court of law and these proceedings usually occur within the child's first year of life. All parents of children aged approximately one year old who obtained legal parenthood between March 2000 and March 2002 were asked to participate in the study. Thirty families agreed to take part, representing 60 per cent of the surrogacy families who responded to the request by ONS. As surrogacy families who had not yet become the child's legal parents would not have been identified by ONS, all thirty-four parents on the register of the United Kingdom surrogacy agency Childlessness Overcome through Surrogacy (COTS) with a child in the same age range were also asked to take part. Twenty-six of these families agreed to participate, representing a response rate of 76 per cent.

Of the forty-two surrogacy arrangements, twenty-six (62 per cent) involved partial surrogacy and sixteen (38 per cent) involved full surrogacy. Twenty-nine (69 per cent) of the surrogate mothers were unknown to the commissioning parents prior to the surrogacy arrangement. The other thirteen (31 per cent) comprised six friends and seven family members. The majority of commissioning mothers (76 per cent) had met with the surrogate mother following the birth with the child present, and almost two-thirds (64 per cent) had met with the surrogate mother with the child present at least once every three months. In ten families (24 per cent) there had been no contact between the surrogate mother and the child, either because the surrogate mother did not wish to have contact, or by mutual agreement between the surrogate mother and the commissioning parents. With respect to the quality of the relationship between the commissioning parents and the surrogate mother following the birth, thirty-eight (91 per cent) of mothers reported this to be harmonious, four (9 per cent) reported some dissatisfaction or coldness, and there were no instances of major conflict or hostility.

The surrogacy families were studied in comparison with two control groups: (i) fifty-one families with a child conceived by egg donation to control for the experience of female infertility, and (ii) eighty families with a naturally conceived child. The egg-donation families were recruited through seven fertility clinics in the U.K. In each clinic, all families with a child conceived by egg donation and aged around one year old were asked to participate in the research. Seventy-five per cent took part. Thirty-six (72 per cent) of the egg donors were anonymous and the remaining fourteen (28 per cent) were friends or relatives of the parents, a pattern that was similar to the proportion of known and previously unknown surrogate mothers. The natural-conception families were selected through maternity ward records on the basis of stratification to maximize comparability with the surrogacy and egg donation families, for example mother's age, a planned pregnancy and that the child was the first or secondborn. The cooperation rate was 73 per cent.

Thirty-seven families participated in the second phase, representing 88 per cent of the representative sample of surrogacy families who took part in the first phase, and were studied in comparison with matched samples of forty-eight families with a child conceived by egg donation and sixty-eight families with a naturally conceived child also drawn from the original sample of control groups.

Thirty-four surrogate mothers took part in the study and were recruited in two ways. Nineteen of the women were surrogate mothers for commissioning parents already participating in an ongoing study of commissioning parents and who were informed about the study by the couple. Fifteen of the women were recruited through the U.K. surrogacy organisation COTS (Childlessness Overcome through Surrogacy. All of the women had given birth to a surrogate child who at the time of interview was approximately one year old. The mean age of the women was thirty-four years. Six were single at the time of interview, twenty-three were married or cohabiting with their partner and five had a non-cohabiting partner. Thirty-two women had children of their own. The children ranged in age from two to thirty-three years old.

Fourteen of the women were not currently working, fourteen were working part time and six were working full-time. The socioeconomic status of the mothers was measured using a modified version of the Registrar Generals Classification (OPCS and the Employment Department Group 1991). Twelve per cent were in the professional/managerial bracket, 26 per cent were in the skilled non-manual category, 21 per cent were in the skilled manual category, and 41 per cent were classified as partly skilled or unskilled.

Five of the women had been a surrogate mother more than once; three had been a surrogate mother three times prior to the arrangement they were being questioned about, one had been a surrogate mother twice previously, and one had been a surrogate mother once previously. Nineteen of the women had undergone a partial-surrogacy arrangement, and fifteen had had a full-surrogacy arrangement. Seven were known surrogate mothers (i.e., sister, friend, or mother), and twenty-seven (79 per cent) were previously unknown to the commissioning couple (i.e., met though a third party).

Researchers trained in the study techniques visited the families at home. Data were obtained from the mother and the father separately by tape-recorded interview and questionnaire. Information obtained by interview was rated according to a standardized coding scheme.

Measures – Phase 1

Parents' Psychological State

Quality of Marriage

From the interview with each parent, ratings were made for mothers and fathers separately using a standardized procedure developed by Quinton and Rutter (1988):

- Mutual enjoyment was based on the enjoyment both partners experience in shared activities.
- Confiding took account of the ease of discussing important issues together.
- Arguments measured the frequency of conflicts involving shouting and/or violence, and/or denigration of each other or of each other's families, and/or not speaking after a difference for more than one hour.
  Golombok Rust Inventory of Marital State (GRIMS) (Rust et al. 1990), a questionnaire assessment of the quality of the marital relationship.

Psychological Adjustment

- The short form of the *Parenting Stress Index* (PSI/SF) (Abidin 1990) was administered to mothers and fathers separately to produce a *total* stress score for each parent, as well as sub-scale scores of *parental distress, dysfunctional interaction* and *difficult child.*
- The *Trait Anxiety Inventory* (Spielberger 1983) was completely by mothers and fathers separately to assess anxiety.
- The *Edinburgh Depression Scale* (Thorpe 1993) was completed by both mothers and fathers to assess depression.

Social Support

Ratings of social support were made from the mothers' interview data as follows:

- Partner's help in childcare was based on the extent to which the father was a help or a hindrance to her in parenting.
- Emotional support from mother's family, and emotional support from father's family, measured the extent to which the mother received a listening ear or help or advice with problems relating to the child.
- Practical help from mother's family, and practical help from father's family, assessed the extent to which the mother received help such as babysitting or money to buy the children's clothes.

Quality of Parenting

Parent Interview

Detailed accounts were obtained of the child's behaviour and the parent's response to it, with reference to the child's feeding and sleeping patterns, babysitting, daycare, the parent's feelings about the parental role, the parent's feelings about the child, and relationships within the family unit. Overall ratings of the quality of parenting were made for mothers and fathers separately as follows:

- *Expressed warmth* was based on the parent's tone of voice, facial expression and gestures when talking about the child, spontaneous expressions of warmth, sympathy and concern about any difficulties experienced by the child, and enthusiasm and interest in the child as a person.
- Emotional over-involvement measured the extent to which family life and the emotional functioning of the parent was centred on the child, the extent to which the parent was over-concerned or overprotective toward the child, and the extent to which the parent had interests apart from those relating to the child.
- Parent–child interaction measured the extent to which the child and parent spent time together, enjoyed each other's company and showed affection to one another.

1. Sensitive responding represented the mother's ability to recognize and respond appropriately to her infant's needs.

Attachment Questionnaire

The Attachment Questionnaire (Condon and Corkindale 1998), an instrument designed to measure parenting variables relevant to infant attachment was administered to both parents. The mother's questionnaire assesses tolerance, pleasure in proximity, competence as a parent and acceptance, and the father's questionnaire assesses absence of hostility, quality of attachment and pleasure in interaction.

Infant Temperament

The infant's temperament was assessed using the Infant Characteristics Questionnaire (ICQ) (Bates et al. 1979) which was completed by mothers. This instrument produces subscale scores of fussy/difficult, unadaptable, dull and unpredictable.

Measures – Phase 2

Parental Functioning

The same measures of Parenting Stress, Trait Anxiety, Depression and Marital satisfaction were used. In addition, the Vulnerable Child Scale (Perrin et al. 1989) was administered to provide an assessment of anxiety regarding the child's susceptibility to medical problems.

Parent–Child Relationships

The mothers and fathers were interviewed separately using the Experience of Parenting Interview (ExPI), an adaptation by Steele, Henderson and Hillman (2000) of the Parent Development Interview (Slade et al. 1999), an interview technique designed to assess the nature of the emotional bond between the parent and the child.

- The variables used in the present study that related to the parent's affective experience were *degree of anger, acknowledgement of support needed, satisfaction with support available, guilt, joy/pleasure, competence, level of child focus, disappointment with child, parental hostility, over-protectiveness, disciplinary over-indulgence,* and *clingy behaviour.*
- The variables that related to the child's affective experience were *child aggression/anger, child happiness/contentment, child controlling/manipulating, child affection,* and *child rejecting.*
- There were also two global variables, *reflection on relationship,* a measure of the extent to which the parent can reflect on the child and the relationship, and *coherence,* a measure of the overall coherency of ideation and feeling in the parent's representation of the child.

Children's Psychological Development

- *Brief Infant Toddler Social and Emotional Assessment* (BITSEA) (Briggs-Gowan and Carter, 2002), a questionnaire measure of social-emotional problems and competencies in 1–3 year-olds.
- The *Mental Scale* of the *Bayley Scales of Infant Development* (BSID II) (Bayley, 1993) to assess cognitive development.

Measures – Surrogate Mothers

The surrogate mothers were administered a standardized semi-structured interview in their own homes around the time of the child's first birthday. The women were asked about their motivation to become a surrogate mother; their relationship over time with the commissioning couple and the child; their experiences during and after relinquishing the child; and their openness with family and friends about the surrogacy.

Motivations for Surrogacy

The women were asked:

1. When they had first decided to become a surrogate mother.
2. What had first caused them to think about surrogacy.
3. What their reasons were for choosing to become a surrogate mother.

Relationship and Frequency of Contact with the Commissioning Couple before the Birth

The surrogate mothers were asked about:

- The quality of their relationship with the commissioning couple before treatment, during the first few months, and the last few months of the pregnancy.
- The frequency of contact between the couple and the surrogate mother at the start and at the end of the pregnancy.

- The involvement of the commissioning couple during the pregnancy.
- Satisfaction of level of involvement of each parent.

Experiences during and after Relinquishing the Child

Data were obtained about:

1. Who decided when the handing over of the child should take place.
2. Whether the surrogate mother was happy with the decision.
3. Whether the surrogate mother had any doubts about handing over the child.
4. Whether relinquishing the child affected them in weeks, months and year following the birth.
5. Whether they had seen sought medical help for psychological problems and whether they had taken any medication to treat such problems either before or after the surrogacy birth.
6. The Edinburgh Depression Scale (Thorpe 1993) was also completed by surrogate mothers.

Frequency of Contact with the Couple and the Child following the Birth

Data were obtained about:

1. The frequency of contact with the commissioning family since the birth, obtained separately for the commissioning mother, the commissioning father and the child.
2. What role the surrogate mother would play in the child's life.
3. How the surrogate mother viewed the relationship between herself and the child.

Openness about Surrogacy

Surrogate mothers were asked:

1. Whom they had told about the surrogacy arrangement, how much they had disclosed, the initial reactions of those they had told, and how those individual felt currently about the situation.
2. About their partner's and children's reactions during the pregnancy and children's reactions at the time of the handover, how supportive their partner was, and whether there were any particular difficulties for them during the surrogacy process.
3. The women were asked to complete the Golombok Rust Inventory of Marital State (GRIMS) (Rust et al. 1990).

Results – Phase 1

Multivariate analyses of covariance (MANCOVAs) were conducted for the quality of marriage variables, the parental psychological problems variables, the social support variables, the quality of parenting variables and the infant temperament variables, with separate MANCOVAs for mothers and fathers where relevant. Where a significant group difference was found, contrast analyses were carried out:(1) surrogacy versus natural conception (S vs NC) and (2) surrogacy versus egg donation (S vc ED) to establish whether the surrogacy families differed from the natural-conception families and the egg-donation families respectively.

Parents' Psychological State

For mothers' psychological problems, the parental distress, dysfunctional interaction and difficult child subscales of the Parenting Stress Index and the Trait Anxiety Inventory and Edinburgh Depression Scale scores analyses showed a non-significant trend. For the Edinburgh Depression Scale, lower scores among the surrogacy mothers than both the natural-conception and the egg-donation mothers were found. The surrogacy mothers obtained significantly lower parenting stress scores than both the natural-conception and egg-donation mothers. No significant difference was found for the social support or the marital relationship variables. There were no significant differences between the fathers in each family for any of the variables.

Quality of Parenting

A significant difference between family types for expressed warmth was found, reflecting a higher level of warmth among the surrogacy than the natural-conception mothers. There was also a significant difference for emotional over-involvement showing greater emotional over-involvement among the surrogacy than the natural-conception mothers. In addition, enjoyment of parenthood differed according to family type with greater enjoyment shown by the surrogacy than the natural conception mothers.

A significant difference between groups was found for the *pleasure in proximity* subscale of the Attachment Questionnaire with the surrogacy mothers showing greater pleasure than the natural-conception mothers. A significant group difference was also found for the *acceptance* subscale reflecting greater acceptance by the surrogacy than the natural-conception mothers.

A significant difference between groups for fathers' *expressed warmth* with higher levels of warmth were shown by the surrogacy than the natural-conception fathers. *Emotional over-involvement* differed between groups, reflecting greater emotional over-involvement by surrogacy than natural-conception fathers. For the Attachment Questionnaire, a significant difference between groups was found for the *quality of attachment* subscale, reflecting greater attachment quality among the surrogacy than the natural-conception fathers.

Infant Temperament

There was no significant difference between families on the Infant Characteristics Questionnaire.

Factors Associated with Quality of Parenting in Surrogacy Families

For the surrogacy group only, the following aspects of the surrogacy arrangement were examined in relation to the quality of parenting: (i) full vs. partial surrogacy, (ii) whether the surrogate mother was previously known or unknown to the commissioning parents, and (iii) whether or not the surrogate mother had contact with the child. Maternal and paternal expressed warmth and emotional over-involvement were chosen as measures of parenting quality. There was no difference between full and partial-surrogacy arrangements for expressed warmth or emotional over-involvement. However, commissioning mothers showed significantly higher levels of expressed warmth and a non-significant trend toward significantly higher levels of emotional over-involvement, in surrogacy arrangements where the surrogate mother was a relative or a friend. There was also a non-significant trend toward higher levels of expressed warmth, but not emotional over-involvement, among commissioning mothers whose children had contact with the surrogate mother.

Both mothers and fathers in surrogacy families reported lower levels of stress associated with parenting than their counterparts with naturally conceived children, and the mothers also showed lower levels of depression. Mothers and fathers in surrogacy families showed greater warmth and attachment-related behaviour towards their infants, and greater enjoyment of parenthood, than the natural conception parents.

There was no difference in the level of maternal or paternal expressed warmth or emotional over-involvement according to the presence or absence of a genetic link between the commissioning mother and the child. However, the nature of the relationship between the commissioning parents and the surrogate mother did appear to influence the parenting of commissioning mothers. It seems that surrogacy arrangements involving a relative or friend are associated with more positive outcomes with respect to the parenting of commissioning mothers.

Results – Phase 2

Psychological State: Mothers

A significant difference between family types for the Parenting Stress Index reflected lower levels of stress associated with parenting among the surrogacy than the natural-conception mothers.

Psychological State: Fathers

A significant difference between family types for the *Parenting Stress Index* showed lower levels of stress associated with parenting among the surrogacy than the natural-conception fathers and lower levels of stress associated with parenting among the surrogacy than the egg-donation fathers.

Parent–Child Relationships: Mothers

Parent-affective Experience

A significant difference between family types for *degree of anger* reflected lower levels of anger among surrogacy than natural-conception mothers. Surrogacy mothers also differed from natural-conception mothers with respect to *guilt* and *joy/pleasure*, reflecting lower levels of guilt and higher levels of joy/pleasure among surrogacy than natural-conception mothers. A significant difference between family types was also found for *competence*. Surrogacy mothers obtained higher ratings on competence than both the natural-conception and egg-donation mothers. There was also a significant difference for *disappointment with child* showing a lower level of disappointment with the child by surrogacy than natural-conception mothers.

Child-affective Experience

A significant difference between family types for *child aggression/anger* indicated lower levels of child aggression in surrogacy than natural-conception families. A significant difference between family types was found for *child affection* reflecting higher levels of child affection in surrogacy than natural-conception families and higher levels of child-affection in surrogacy than egg-donation families.

Parent–Child Relationships: Fathers

No significant differences were found for the father–child relationship variables.

Children's Socio-emotional and Cognitive Development

There was no difference according to family type in the proportion of children who obtained scores above cut-off for the Problem Scale, or in the proportion of children who obtained scores below cut-off for the Competence Scale. Regarding the Bayley Scale, no difference in the Mental Development Index between family types was found. In line with this finding, there was no difference between family types in the proportion of children showing developmental delay, with 6 per cent, 9 per cent and 10 per cent of children in surrogacy, egg donation and natural-conception families respectively obtaining a Mental Development Index of less than 85.

Surrogacy Families

Comparisons were conducted according to whether or not the surrogate mother was a relative or friend of the commissioning couple (known vs. unknown) and the type of surrogacy (non-genetic vs. genetic). There were no significant differences for the parent-affective experience variables or the child-affective experience variables between families with previously known and unknown surrogate mothers, or between non-genetic and genetic surrogacy. However, for the global ratings there was a significant difference between families with known and unknown surrogate mothers. A significant difference between family types for reflection on relationship showed higher levels of reflection by commissioning mothers in families where the surrogate mother was unknown prior to the surrogacy arrangement. There was also a significant difference between family types for coherence, indicating higher levels of coherence in commissioning mothers with previously unknown surrogate mothers. There was no difference in global ratings with respect to surrogacy type.

Results – Surrogate Mothers

Motivations for Surrogacy

1. On average, the women had decided to become a surrogate mother 6.21 years before the time of interview (ranging from 1 to 20 years).
2. 68 per cent (23) of the women first heard about surrogacy from the media.
3. 15 per cent (5) first heard about it from a family member or a friend.
4. 17 per cent (5) had always known about surrogacy.
5. Motivating factors (including multiple responses):
6. 91 per cent (31) reported wanting to help a childless couple.
7. 15 per cent (5) reported enjoyment of pregnancy.
8. 6 per cent (2) reported self-fulfilment.
9. 3 per cent (1) reported payment.

Relationship and Frequency of Contact with the Commissioning Couple before the Birth

Relationship with Couple

Before pregnancy, all surrogate mothers felt that they had a 'harmonious' relationship with the commissioning couple. Thereafter:

Start of the pregnancy:
- 97 per cent (33) reported 'harmonious' relationship with the commissioning mother, 3 per cent (1) reported 'major conflict or hostility' with mother.
- 94 per cent (32) reported 'harmonious' relationship with the father, 3 per cent (1) 'dissatisfaction or coldness' in relationship, 3 per cent (1) reported 'major conflict or hostility'.

End of pregnancy:
- 97 per cent (33) reported 'harmonious' relationship with the commissioning mother
- 94 per cent (32) of surrogate mothers felt that they had a 'harmonious' relationship with the commissioning father.

Frequency of Contact

Start and end of pregnancy:
- 71 per cent (24) saw the commissioning mother at least once a month
- 65 per cent (22) saw the commissioning father at least once a month.

However, the proportion who had not seen the couple had increased to 6 per cent (2) of women not having seen the commissioning mother, and 9 per cent (3) of women not having seen the commissioning father.

Involvement
- 83 per cent (28) felt that the commissioning mother was 'very involved' in the pregnancy, 17 per cent (6) felt the commissioning mother was 'quite involved'.
- 94 per cent (32) were happy with the involvement of the mother, 6 per cent (2 previously unknown surrogate mothers) reported it was not enough.
- 44 per cent (15) of women felt that the commissioning fathers were 'very involved', 47 per cent (16) felt that they were 'quite involved', 9 per cent (3) felt that they had none or little involvement.
- 94 per cent (32) were happy with the involvement of the commissioning father, 6 per cent (2) reported that it was not enough.

Experiences during and after Relinquishing the Child
- 91 per cent (31) had a mutual agreement about when to hand over the child.
- 9 per cent (3) of surrogate mothers had decided when the child was to be handed over.

All of the women were happy with the decision reached about when to hand over the baby and none of the women experienced any doubts or difficulties whilst handing over the baby.

Weeks after the handover:
- 65 per cent (22) of the women experienced no difficulties.
- 32 per cent (11) of the women experienced some difficulties.
- 3 per cent (1) experienced moderate difficulties.

Months after the handover:
- 85 per cent (29) reported no difficulties.
- 15 per cent (5) reported some difficulties

A year after handover:
- 94 per cent (32) reporting no difficulties.
- 6 per cent (2) reported some difficulties.

Psychological Problems
Both before and after the birth,
- 91 per cent (31) reported experiencing no psychological problems.
- 9 per cent (3) had reported some psychological problems having visited her GP or having had regular contact with an outpatient clinic.

The mean score Edinburgh Depression Scale score for the thirty-three women who completed the questionnaire was 4.88 (sd=3.1).

Full surrogacy: 4.37 (sd=2.9).
Partial surrogacy: 5.57 (sd=3.34).
A t-test revealed no difference between these two means.

Frequency of Contact with the Couple and the Child following the Birth

Frequency of Contact
- 32 per cent (11) of women had seen the mother at least once a month.
- 26 per cent (9) had seen the father at least once a month.
- 21 per cent (7) had not seen the mother or the father at all.
- 32 per cent (11) of the surrogate mothers had regular contact of at least once a month. with the child.
- 24 per cent (8) of surrogate mothers had not seen the child at all since the birth.

Relationship with Child
Known surrogate mothers (n=7)
- 3 expected to play a 'special role' in the child's life.
- 4 expected not to differ in their relationship with the child.

Unknown surrogate mothers (n=27)
- 67 per cent (18) reported that they expected to have contact with the child, 4 of whom reported that they would play a 'special role' in the child's life.
- 15 per cent (4) reported that they would maintain contact with the parents but not with the child.
- 19 per cent (5) reported that they would have no involvement with the family.
- 94 per cent (32) of all surrogate mothers were happy with the level of contact with the child, 6 per cent (2) reporting that the level of contact with the child was not enough.

Current Feelings
- 59 per cent (20) felt that there was no 'special bond' with the child.
- 41 per cent (14) reported feeling a 'special bond' towards the child.
- None of the women reported feeling that the child was like their own.

Known surrogate mothers were significantly more likely to feel a special bond towards the child (86 per cent, 6) compared to unknown surrogate mothers (30 per cent, 8).

Disclosure
- 77 per cent (26) of surrogate mothers felt that the child should be told.
- 23 per cent (8) felt uncertain or felt that the decision was not theirs to make.
- 90 per cent (17) of partial surrogate mothers felt that the child should be told about the surrogacy arrangement, compared to 60 per cent (9) of full surrogate mothers. Full surrogate mothers were significantly more likely to feel

uncertain, or uninvolved in the decision to tell compared to partial surrogate mothers.

Openness about Surrogacy

Openness with Family
Excluding one mother with no familial contact.
- 97 per cent (32) had discussed the arrangement with their family to some extent.
- 3 per cent (1) had not discussed the issue with family.

Initial reactions:
- 6 per cent (2) of the women reported that their family responded negatively.
- 46 per cent (15) reported that their family had neutral or mixed reactions.
- 48 per cent (16) reported that their family had responded positively.

One year later:
- 76 per cent (25) of women reported that their families felt positive.
- 21 per cent (7) had family members who felt neutral or had mixed feelings.
- 3 per cent (1) reported that her family still felt negative.

Openness with Partner
For the twenty-one women who had a partner at the time of deciding to embark on surrogacy:
- 95 per cent (20) had discussed the arrangement in full with their partners.
- 5% per cent (1) had discussed the arrangement to some extent with her partner.
- 57 per cent (12) of the partners responded positively.
- 24 per cent (5) were neutral/ambivalent.
- 19 per cent (4) responded negatively.

One year on:
- 96 per cent (22) reported that their partner felt positive towards arrangement, with 4 per cent (1) reporting that her partner felt neutral/ambivalent.
- 87 per cent (20) reported that their partner was very supportive and reliable during the surrogacy arrangement, while 13 per cent (3) stating that their partner was mostly supportive.

The GRIMS Marital Satisfaction Questionnaire
- 78 per cent (18) of women reported an average or above average marital satisfaction
- 17 per cent (4) reported a poor marital relationship
- 4 per cent (1) reported very severe problems in the marital relationship.

Openness with Own Children

(n=32)

- 90 per cent (29) explained the surrogacy arrangement fully.
- 81 per cent (26) of women reported that their children felt positive towards the surrogacy arrangement during the pregnancy.

Of children's reactions:

At pregnancy:

- 81 per cent (28) of women reported that their child reacted positively at the time of the pregnancy.
- 16 per cent (5) reported that their children's reaction was neutral or ambivalent.

At handover:

- 88 per cent (28) of surrogate mothers reported that their children felt positive about the surrogacy arrangement at the time of the handover.
- 9 per cent (3) reported that their child's reaction was neutral or ambivalent.

At interview:

- 88 per cent (28) of surrogate mothers reported that their children felt positive about the surrogacy arrangement at the time they were interviewed.
- 12 per cent (4) of surrogate mothers described their children's current reaction as neutral or ambivalent.

None reported experiencing a negative response at any time.

Conclusions

Commissioning Couples

The surrogacy mothers, but not fathers, appeared to show more positive representations of their relationship with their child than did their natural conception counterparts. The more positive representations shown by the surrogacy parents is perhaps surprising given the potential risks associated with surrogacy for parent–child relationships. The unexpected nature of this finding raises the question of whether this is a genuine effect or a result of interviewer or interviewee bias. Couples whose children have been born through a surrogacy arrangement have gone to great lengths to have a child and are thus likely to be highly motivated and committed parents. Thus a strong desire for a child among surrogacy parents may result in more positive representations of the relationship and a higher quality parenting than among parents whose children were naturally conceived. The lower levels of parenting stress reported by surrogacy mothers and fathers than by their natural conception counterparts may also stem from their difficulties in, and eventual appreciation of, becoming parents. Many of these women had known from adolescence that they would be unable to have a child themselves because they did not have a uterus, and thus were overjoyed to become mothers through surrogacy.

Alternatively, in reaction to the widespread disapproval of surrogacy, commissioning parents may tend to emphasize the positive aspects of their relationship with their child and underplay the negative, thus giving a false impression of the nature of family relationships. They may feel the need to present their family as highly functioning in order to prove themselves as suitable parents to the outside world. The interview procedures take account of the way in which parents respond in addition to the content of their responses, and is less easy to simulate than factual reporting of behavioural aspects of the parent–child relationship. In addition, defensive responding was assessed by the interviewers at the end of each interview and there was no difference in defensive responding between family types.

Although the type of surrogacy, i.e., genetic or non-genetic, did not appear to influence maternal representations of the parent–child relationship, it is interesting to note that the global ratings of reflection and coherence were higher among commissioning mothers who had not previously known the surrogate mother. The reflection variable assesses the extent to which the mother tries to understand the child's behaviour in terms of the child's circumstances, thinks about the child's needs, and evaluates her own responses and contribution to any difficulties. The coherence variable measures the extent to which the mother gives a believable, well-organized, logical and well-illustrated picture of the child and their relationship. In the present study, the higher levels of both reflection and coherence among commissioning mothers with an unknown surrogate mother may indicate a more considered decision to embark on surrogacy with a stranger than with a relative or a friend, or a greater tendency toward reflection and coherence among commissioning mothers who opt for surrogacy with an unknown surrogate mother. Those commissioning mothers who decide to enter into a surrogacy arrangement with a previously unknown surrogate mother are likely to have thought long and hard about the consequences for their relationship with their child.

The exceptions were for the variables relating to competence and child affection, with the surrogacy mothers obtaining higher ratings of competence and child affection than the egg-donation mothers. This suggests either that women who can withstand the more difficult and demanding process of surrogacy are more competent as parents and perceive their much-wanted children as more affectionate, or that they feel they must justify their more controversial route to parenthood by presenting themselves as highly competent mothers with extremely loving children. Although both processes may have been operating, the surrogacy mothers appeared to be more relaxed in their attitude to parenting; in comparison with the stresses associated with the surrogacy process, coping with a two-year-old was viewed as relatively unproblematic. In addition, it is likely that women who can endure the challenges of a surrogacy arrangement are highly tolerant of stressful situations generally.

Contrary to the concerns that have been expressed regarding the practice of surrogacy, the differences that were identified between the surrogacy families and the other family types indicated greater psychological well-being and adaptation to parenthood by mothers and fathers of children born through a surrogacy arrangement than by the comparison group of natural-conception parents.

A possible explanation is that the children born as a result of a surrogacy arrangement are extremely wanted children who are being raised by highly committed and loving parents. This explanation is compatible with the lack of difference in the quality of parent–child relationships between the surrogacy families and the egg-donation families who also went to great lengths to have a child. In order to control for the level of desire for a child in the natural-conception comparison group, a selection criterion was that the pregnancy had been planned, so that the highly motivated surrogacy parents would not be compared with natural conception parents who had become pregnant by accident. Nevertheless, it is likely that couples who pursue assisted reproduction in order to become parents have a stronger desire for children than couples who are able to give birth without medical intervention or without the involvement of a third party; those couples who discover a fertility problem and who are not highly motivated to become parents are more likely to abandon their attempts to have children. Furthermore, the process of assisted reproduction, in itself, appears to strengthen the desire to have children. In the clinical literature, reports are to be found of couples undergoing repeated attempts of risky, costly and highly stressful procedures such as IVF in spite of a low chance of achieving a successful pregnancy (Boivin et al. 1995). It is not surprising, therefore, that those who do become parents at the end of this difficult process are highly involved with their much-wanted child.

The more positive outcomes for parent–child relationships among the surrogacy families than among the natural-conception families may also be associated with the greater psychological well-being of the parents. It is not known whether the differences in parental psychological state between the surrogacy and natural-conception families preexisted the decision to embark upon surrogacy or emerged following the birth of the child. It may be expected that couples who decide to take this difficult route to parenthood, and who do not give up along the way, are less likely to have psychological problems in the first place and are less susceptible to the negative effects of stress. In addition, as no differences in infant temperament were identified according to family type, differences in parent–child relationships between the surrogacy families and the natural-conception families cannot be attributed to the behaviour of the children.

The lower levels of depression shown by the surrogacy mothers in comparison with both the egg-donation and the natural-conception mothers are of interest. As the surrogacy mothers did not experience pregnancy, it is possible that their lower scores on depression stemmed from the absence of biological factors associated with the onset of depression in women following the birth of a child (Nolen-Hoeksema 1987). They may also have been in better physical shape and thus better able to cope with the demands of a newborn baby.

An alternative explanation for the more positive findings for surrogacy families is that because of the negative attitudes, and sometimes outright hostility, toward surrogacy, parents of children born in this way make a greater attempt than parents of naturally conceived children to present their family in the best possible light. There may be a feeling that they have to prove themselves to be good parents to overcome the prejudice against them, a phenomenon that has been reported by parents in other kinds of assisted-reproduction families. Had the findings resulted purely from the desire to present a positive picture of themselves as parents, then the parents of children born through the more controversial technique of surrogacy would have been expected to obtain higher scores on the parenting variables than the parents of children born through the less controversial and more hidden technique of egg-donation. This was not the case.

Surrogate Mothers

The findings suggest that surrogacy has been a positive experience for those surrogate mothers interviewed, and fail to lend support to many of the claims commonly held about surrogacy. For example, none of the women in the present study had any doubts about their decision to hand over the child, nor did the majority of women have any major problems with the commissioning couple during the surrogacy process. Thus there was no evidence of difficulties with respect to those aspects of surrogacy that have been the greatest cause for concern.

The most common motivation for entering into a surrogacy arrangement was to help a childless couple, with only one woman reporting that payment was a motivating factor. This research lends support to the findings by Blyth (1994) in which it was also found helping a childless couple was the most frequently mentioned motivation. Blyth's (1994) study also found that financial gain was not a prime motivating factor with only three of his sample of nineteen reporting financial motives.

The other common concern regarding surrogacy is the possibility of adverse psychological consequences for the surrogate mother. Although the study showed that surrogate mothers did experience some problems initially after the handover, these were not severe, and tended to be short lived, dissipating with time. One year on, only two women reported feeling occasionally upset. Furthermore, the Edinburgh Depression Scale showed that surrogate mothers were not suffering from post-natal depression one year following the birth.

None of the women experienced any problems at the time of handover. Interestingly, one woman, in response to the question of how she felt handing over the child, replied that she never viewed it as handing over the child instead she considered it to be handing *back* the child. Similar to the findings of Ragoné (1994), where it was found that that surrogate mothers distanced themselves from the foetus, this too indicates that surrogate mothers may precondition themselves to believe that the child they are carrying is not theirs, thereby enabling them to come to terms with the handover.

Overall, surrogate mothers had a harmonious relationship with the commissioning couple during the pregnancy. Only one woman reported this relationship as having major conflict or hostility early in the pregnancy and this seemed to have been resolved by the later stage of pregnancy, and indeed she reported having a positive relationship with the commissioning mother at the time of the interview. Interestingly, no differences were observed between the known and unknown surrogate mothers in relation to the quality of relationship with the commissioning couple. Although the sample sizes were small, these results suggest that unknown surrogate mothers are just as likely as known surrogate mothers to maintain a good relationship with the commissioning couple, thus dispelling fears that such an alliance between strangers will inevitably lead to problems. In addition, known surrogate mothers were also able to maintain a harmonious relationship with the commissioning couples despite their role changing from that of relative or friend to birth mother of the commissioning couple's child. In fact, known surrogate mothers were more likely to feel a special bond towards the resultant child suggesting that their role had perhaps strengthened their bond with the child.

Commissioning mothers tended to be more involved with the pregnancy than commissioning fathers. The surrogate mothers in the present study tended to be happy with this arrangement, and only two reported that the commissioning mother and father were not sufficiently involved. It was found that many surrogate mothers who were previously unknown to the commissioning couple still maintained contact with the couple after the child's birth. Interestingly, all five of the surrogate mothers who had opted for no involvement with the commissioning couple had been involved in a partial-surrogacy arrangement. Whether or not this was a coping mechanism for them, or they felt that their biological link to the child would create tension between the commissioning mother and themselves, is not known. However, fourteen of the surrogate mothers did maintain some level of contact with the parents despite being the genetic parent of the child. Therefore, if such feelings were leading five of the surrogate mothers to distance themselves from the couple, this was not affecting all of them in the same way. Surrogate mothers were generally very open with family and friends about the surrogacy arrangement. The majority of surrogate mothers also reported a positive reaction from their own children, and none of the surrogate mothers reported any major problems experienced by their children as a result of the surrogacy.

Overall, surrogacy appears to be a positive experience for surrogate mothers. Women who decide to embark upon surrogacy often have completed a family of their own and feel they wish to help a couple who would not otherwise be able to become parents. For surrogate mothers who have partners, the partners appear to provide a source of support during the surrogacy arrangement. Surrogate mothers often feel a positive sense of self worth, reporting for example, that seeing their commissioning couples' faces once the child is born makes the whole process worthwhile.

The present study lends little support to the commonly held expectations that surrogate mothers will experience psychological problems following the birth of the child. In addition, surrogate mothers generally report positive experiences with the commissioning couple, and many maintain contact with them and the child. Surrogate mothers who were the genetic parent of the child did not differ in their feelings towards the child from those who were not. Although few differences were found between surrogate mothers who had experienced a full-surrogacy pregnancy, and those who had experienced a partial-surrogacy pregnancy, these findings cannot be regarded as conclusive because sample sizes were small. Overall, the results of the present investigation indicate that one year after the birth of the child, surrogate mothers are not experiencing psychological problems as a result of the surrogacy arrangement.

General Conclusions

Those opposed to the practice of surrogacy have argued that surrogacy is unacceptable because it represents the commodification of children and the exploitation of economically disadvantaged women. From a psychological perspective, reservations about surrogacy have focused on the potentially negative consequences for family relationships and children's psychological well-being. In the absence of systematic information, there has been much speculation, usually negatively framed, about the outcomes of surrogacy for all of those concerned. The findings of the present study do not support these negative assumptions with respect to the child's first year of life.

In spite of the concerns that have been raised regarding the increased risk of psychological problems among children born through a surrogacy arrangement, the children in the present investigation did not differ from the naturally conceived children with respect to socio-emotional or cognitive development. As demonstrated in previous studies of assisted reproduction children, elevated parenting quality does not appear to result in raised levels of psychological adjustment in the child (e.g., Colpin et al. 1995; Golombok et al. 1995; Cederblad et al. 1996; Golombok et al. 2002a, b).

The general lack of difference between the egg-donation families and the surrogacy families indicates that the key factor that distinguishes surrogacy from egg donation, i.e., the involvement of a surrogate mother to host the pregnancy, does not, in itself, appear to influence parenting or child development. Rather, it is the characteristics that surrogacy and egg donation have in common such as the experience of infertility and the use of assisted reproduction that appear to be associated with the more positive outcomes for these families.

The findings of the second phase when the children were aged two years old are in line with the findings of the first phase of the investigation when the children were aged one year. These findings suggest that a gestational or genetic bond with the child is less important for positive maternal representations of the mother–child relationship than a strong desire for parenthood. Pregnancy, it seems, is not a prerequisite. Although no studies have yet been published of adoptive parents' representations of their relationship with their child (a family situation that is similar to surrogacy to the extent that the parents lack a genetic and gestational link with their child), these findings are consistent with studies of early-adopted children's security of attachment to their parents. It has been shown, for example, that a similar proportion of infants in adoptive families and non-adoptive families are classified as securely attached (Singer et al. 1985).

Although the process of surrogacy may affect the parenting behaviour of the commissioning couple right from the start, it will be some time before the children themselves acquire any understanding of the nature of their birth. As they grow up and develop an awareness of their surrogacy origins it is conceivable that the commissioning parents may then experience difficulties. What surrogacy means for children's sense of who is their 'real' mother, and the type of relationship the child develops with each mother, remains to be seen.

Note

1. This chapter is based on work from Golombok et al (2004), Jadva et al (2004) and Maccallum et al (2003).

References

Abidin, R., 1990. *Parenting Stress Index Test Manual.* Charlottesville, VA: Pediatric Psychology Press.

Ainsworth, M., Bleher, M., Waters, E., and Wall, S., 1978. *Patterns of Attachment: A Psychological Study of the Strange Situation.* Hillsdale, NJ: Erlbaum.

Bates, J., Freeland, C., and Loundsbury, M., 1979. Measurement of infant difficulties. *Child Development* 50, 794–802.

Bayley, N., 1993. *Bayley Scales II.* London: The Psychological Corporation.

Blyth, E., 1994. 'I wanted to be interesting. I wanted to be able to say "I've done something interesting with my life"': interviews with surrogate mothers in Britain'. *J. Reprod. Infant Psychol.* 12, 189–98

Boivin, J., Takefman, J.E., Tulandi, T., and Brender, W., 1995. Reactions to infertility based on extent of treatment failure. *Fertility and Sterility* 63, 801–7.

Bowlby, J., 1982. *Attachment and Loss. Volume 1: Attachment,* Second Edition. New York: Basic Books.

Briggs-Gowen, M.J., and Carter, A.S., 2002. *Brief-Infant-Toddler Social and Emotional Assessment (BITSEA): Manual. Version 2.0.* New Haven, CT: Yale University Press.

Brazier, M., Campbell, A., and Golombok, S., 1998. *Surrogacy: Review for Health Ministers of Current Arrangements for Payments and Regulation.* No. CM 4068. London: Department of Health.

British Medical Association, 1996. *Changing Conceptions of Motherhood. The Practice of Surrogacy in Britain.* London: British Medical Association.

Cederblad, M., Friberg, B., Ploman, F., Sjoberg, N.O., Stjernqvist, K., and Zackrisson, E., 1996. Intelligence and behaviour in children born after in-vitro fertilization treatment. *Human Reproduction* 11(9), 2052–57.

Colpin, H., Demyttenaere, K., and Vandemeulebroecke, L., 1995. New reproductive technology and the family: the parent–child relationship following *in vitro* fertilization. *Journal of Child Psychology and Psychiatry* 36(8), 1429–41.

Condon, J.T., and Corkindale, C.J., 1998. The assessment of parent-to-infant attachment: development of a self-report questionnaire instrument. *Journal of Reproductive and Infant Psychology* 16, 57–76.

Crockenberg, S.B., 1981. Infant irritability, mother responsiveness, and social support influences on the security of infant-mother attachment. *Child Development* 52, 857–65.

Cummings, E.M., and Davies, P.T., 1994. Maternal depression and child development. *Journal of Child Psychology and Psychiatry* 35(1), 73–112.

De Wolff, M., and Van Ijzendoorn, M.H., 1997. Sensitivity and attachment: a meta-analysis on parental antecedents of infant attachment. *Child Development* 68(4), 571–91.

Downey, G., and Coyne, J.C., 1990. Children of depressed parents: an integrative review. *Psychological Bulletin* 108(1), 50–76.

Golombok, S., Brewaeys, A., Giavazzi, M. T., Guerra, D. MacCallum, F. & Rust, J. (2002a) The European Study of Assisted Reproduction Families: The transition to adolescence. *Human Reproduction* 17(3), 830–840.

Golombok, S., Cook, R., Bish, A., and Murray, C., 1995. Families created by the New Reproductive Technologies: quality of parenting and social and emotional development of the children. *Child Development* 66, 285–298.

Golombok, S., MacCallum, F., Goodman, E. & Rutter, M., 2002. Families with children conceived by donor insemination: A follow-up at age 12. *Child Development* 73(3), 952–968.

Golombok, S., MacCallum, F., Murray, C., Lycett, E., and Jadva V., 2006. Surrogacy families: parental functioning, parent–child relationships and children's psychological development at age 2. *Journal of Child Psychology and Psychiatry* 47(2), 213–22.

Golombok, S., Murray, C., Jadva, V., MacCallum, F., and Lycett, E., 2004. Families created through a surrogacy arrangement: parent–child relationships in the first year of life. *Developmental Psychology* 40(3), 400–11.

Grace, J.T., 1989. Development of maternal–fetal attachment during pregnancy. *Nursing Research* 38(4), 228–32.

Grych, J.H., and Fincham, F.D., 1990. Marital conflict and children's adjustment: a cognitive-contextual framework. *Psychological Bulletin* 108(2), 267–90.

Harold, G.T., and Conger, R.D., 1997. Marital conflict and adolescent distress: the role of adolescent awareness. *Child Development* 68(2), 333–50.

Jadva, V., Murray, C., Lycett, E., MacCallum, F., and Golombok, S., 2003. Surrogacy: the experiences of surrogate mothers. *Human Reproduction* 18(10), 2196–204.

Lee, R., and Morgan, D., 2001. *Human Fertilisation and Embryology: Regulating the Reproductive Revolution.* London: Blackstone Press.

MacCallum, F., Lycett, E., Murray, C., Jadva, V., and Golombok, S., 2003. Surrogacy: the experience of commissioning couples. *Human Reproduction* 18(6), 1334–42.

New Jersey Supreme Court, 1987. In the case of baby M.

Nolen-Hoeksema, S., 1987. Sex differences in unipolar depression: evidence and theory. *Psychological Bulletin* 101, 259–82.

Office Of Population And Census Statistics (OPCS) and Employment Department Group, 1991. *Standard Classification of Occupations.* London: HMSO.

Perrin, E.C., West, P.D., and Culley, B.S., 1989. Is my child normal yet? Correlates of vulnerability. *Pediatrics* 83(3), 355–63.

Quinton, D., and Rutter, M., 1988. *Parenting Breakdown: The Making and Breaking of Intergenerational Links.* Aldershot: Avebury Gower Publishing.

Ragoné, H., 1994. *Surrogate Motherhood: Conception in the Heart.* Oxford: Westview Press.

Rust, J., Bennun, I., Crowe, M., and Golombok, S., 1990. The GRIMS: a psychometric instrument for the assessment of marital discord. *Journal of Family Therapy* 12, 45–57.

Singer, L., Brodzinsky, D., Ramsay, D., Steir, M., and Waters, E., 1985. Mother–infant attachment in adoptive families. *Child Development* 56, 1543–51.

Slade, A., Belsky, J., Aber, J.L., and Phelps, J.L., 1999. Mothers' representations of their relationships with their toddlers: links to adult attachment and observed mothering. *Developmental Psychology* 35(3), 611–19.

Spielberger, C., 1983. *The Handbook of the State-Trait Anxiety Inventory.* Palo Alto, CA.: Consulting Psychologists Press.

Steele, M., Henderson, K., and Hillman, S., 2000. *Handbook of Experience of Parenting Interview (ExPI).* London: Anna Freud Centre.

Thorpe, K., 1993. A study of the use of the Edinburgh Postnatal Depression Scale with parent groups outside the postpartum period. *Journal of Reproductive and Infant Psychology* 11, 119–25.

Youngblade, L.M., and Belsky, J., 1992. Parent–child antecedents of 5-year-olds' close friendships: a longitudinal analysis. *Developmental Psychology 28,* 700–13.

PART II

● ● ●

The Effect of Alloparenting on Children

• 12 •

Alloparenting in the Context of AIDS in Southern Africa

Complex Strategies for Care

Lorraine van Blerk and Nicola Ansell

Introduction[1]

Alloparenting, referring here to the care of children by people other than their bio-logical parents, is not uncommon across sub-Saharan Africa (Foster and Williamson 2000). There are many instances of children being cared for outside the nuclear family unit, with fluid family structures and kinship relations resulting in children spending long periods of time growing up in the homes of their grandparents, aunts and uncles (see for example Urassa et al. 1997). Children may spend time living in a different household of the extended family[2] for a number of reasons: to attend school, to help in a relative's household, to receive assistance from wealthier family members or in some instances because of parental death (Bandawe and Louw 1997; Kimane and Mturi 2001; Munthali and Ali 2000).

In recent years, across southern Africa in particular, the care of children by 'other parents' has increased due to the rapid and virulent onset of the AIDS pandemic, with many countries now showing high infection rates, of over 20 per cent in some cases (UNAIDS 2004). The clustering of illness and death among families and com-munities has resulted in large numbers of orphans, coupled with an extended fam-ily support system which is already over-burdened and in some cases disintegrating (Deininger et al. 2003; Foster et al. 1995; Nko et al. 2000). The changing nature and increasing complexity of family, household and community relationships, in light of the pandemic, has resulted in increasingly diverse arrangements for the care of young people both within and outside traditional structures.

This chapter examines the various mechanisms by which alloparenting occurs in the context of the AIDS pandemic in southern Africa. The chapter begins by discussing the impacts of AIDS on children and their families and then, using the concept of the inter-generational contract, considers the effect this is having on the care arrangements of orphans. The remainder of the chapter focuses on the findings from empirical research. Drawing on a series of case studies from qualitative research carried out with young people, aged between ten and seventeen years, and their guardians in urban and rural communities in Malawi and Lesotho, the chapter examines the complexity of current caring strategies and the implications this has for the children themselves, their families and communities. In particular the chapter draws on young people's own stories and in-depth studies of institutions, which illustrate the diversity of individual experiences and reveal that care arrangements have become increasingly complex.

AIDS in Southern Africa: The Impacts on Families and Communities

In the recent 2003 epidemic update, UNAIDS (2003) highlighted southern Africa as the region worst affected by high levels of HIV infection. Adult infection rates are over 12 per cent in every country, with several that have rates over 20 per cent (UNAIDS 2004). Those infected are mostly in the child-rearing age range, which has resulted in many children losing their parents and other relatives (Grainger et al. 2001). Malawi and Lesotho, the two countries discussed here, have respective infection rates of 14.2 per cent and 28.9 per cent (UNAIDS 2004), and respective orphan[3] population rates of 17.5 per cent and 17 per cent, with AIDS accounting for approximately 50 per cent of cases (USAID/UNICEF/UNAIDS 2002). The delay between HIV infection, the onset of AIDS and subsequent death, suggests that even if prevalence rates begin to fall, levels of orphanhood will continue to rise for several years.

The implications of such high rates of infection and associated orphanhood for families and communities are well documented (Barnett and Blaikie 1992; Cliff and Smallman-Raynor 1992; Grainger et al. 2001; Lyons 1999; Webb 1997). In particular, long-term sickness and death imposes immeasurable stress on households and their extended families economically, physically, emotionally and socially (Ainsworth and Over 1997; Ankrah 1991). Prior to the death of productive adults, illness usually results in the reduction of income through inability to engage in paid employment and the diminishing of savings due to increased expenditure on medical services as saving life is regarded as more important than saving assets (Rugalema 2000; UNAIDS 1999). Such household problems are exacerbated when death occurs: household income does not recover and may be further reduced, and any children are left without parental care (Ankrah 1991).

The particular circumstances and nature of HIV spread in southern Africa, where the majority of infections occur through heterosexual unions, makes the impacts of HIV and AIDS on families and communities all the more severe, not least because the death of an adult is often followed by the death of their spouse (Nko et al. 2000). Further, similar-aged relatives and community members are also more likely to be at risk from infection, particularly where monogamous unions are not exclusive.

The indirect effects of AIDS on children are also well documented. Hunter and Williamson (2000) list several impacts including loss of family and identity; psycho-social distress; increased malnutrition; loss of health care; increased demands for labour; fewer opportunities for schooling; loss of inheritance; forced migration and homelessness. When a productive family member first falls sick through AIDS, a depletion of household resources generally occurs (Ntozi 1997). Children's nutritional status may fall as food available for consumption decreases. Children, particularly girls, may take on extra commitments including agricultural tasks, household duties and caring responsibilities involving cleaning, feeding and administering medicine to their relatives (Bourdillon 1999; Danziger 1994; Robson 2000; Robson and Ansell 2000). Caring duties can place a heavy emotional burden on children and an increase in duties may disrupt or terminate education (Grainger et al. 2001; Kamali et al. 1996). Even where AIDS has not directly affected the children's immediate household, they may also experience a reduction in their quality of life if their primary care giver has to take on extra caring duties, financial resources are removed to support a sick relative in another household, or a cousin comes to live with them following the death of a relative (Foster and Williamson 2000). Despite this comprehensive analysis of the impacts of AIDS on children, it is important to examine what strategies are available for orphan care.

Strategies for Orphan Care

The loss of a parent either through separation or death is considered to have important emotional and psychological impacts on children, illustrating the need to carefully consider alternative strategies for care. This premise is largely based on John Bowlby's (1966) influential work on attachment theory which argued the importance of young children's contact with their mother or 'permanent mother substitute' during the first three years of life. Any disruption to this was considered detrimental to children's social and cognitive development. Although Bowlby's work highlighted that children have emotional as well as physical needs, attachment theory has largely been discredited as the research failed to recognize the varied ways in which young children deal with separation from a primary care giver (Smith and Cowie 1988; Barrett 1998). Further, throughout many parts of the non-Western world, and significantly in southern Africa, the basic unit of parents and children is generally part of a wider combined family network (George et al. 2003). Here research has shown that historically young children often formed attachments with multiple adults which enabled their mothers to engage in employment and also provided children with added security in situations where adult death rates were high (Smith and Cowie 1988; Mead 1966). This meant that when parents passed away, children were taken care of by other family members, whom they already had engaged with in parent–child relations. The nature of these care strategies and the subsequent changes that have occurred in recent years in southern Africa are particularly important for understanding the nature of orphanhood in the context of the AIDS pandemic.

Historically, in both Malawi and Lesotho, orphans often moved to live in their relatives' households as extended families undertook the burden of care (Munthali and Ali 2000). In patrilineal societies, such as in Lesotho and central and northern Malawi, orphans 'belong' to their father's brother and he takes responsibility for their care. In matrilineal societies, as found in southern Malawi, children 'belong' to their mother's line, and orphan care is the maternal uncle's responsibility. Cultural practices have, however, long become fluid, with matrilineal and patrilineal societies adopting each other's practices (Chanock 1985; White 1987). This is particularly the case where marriage occurs between couples from different traditions, which has become increasingly common with internal and international migration (Ali 1998).

The AIDS pandemic has reinforced this process of children being cared for by others than those traditionally directly responsible. Nyambedha et al. (2003) found this to be the case in one patrilineal society in Kenya, where a rise in the number of orphans had overwhelmed traditional mechanisms, resulting in a large proportion of orphans being cared for by what he terms as 'culturally inappropriate' carers, such as matrilineal kin or strangers (see also George et al. 2003). Further, much work on orphans follows the UN definition, which classifies orphans as those under fifteen who have either lost their mother or both parents. However, as this chapter will demonstrate, paternal orphans are also likely to be cared for by adults other than their surviving mother, due to AIDS-induced household poverty, and this group is generally far higher in number. Bicego et al. (2002) found, in their study across several sub-Saharan countries, that paternal orphan prevalence was higher than maternal orphan prevalence in every case. This increases the burden on extended families.

When alloparenting is arranged for orphans, many of the new caretakers are elderly or ailing and do not have adequate resources to provide proper care (Nyambedha et al. 2003). Therefore, although there has been a great deal of research regarding orphanhood, the consequences of the sharp rise in orphan numbers has been highlighted as one of the under-studied aspects of the pandemic (Bicego et al. 2002) and, in particular, little research has focused specifically on the diversity of care arrangements that occur when traditional structures break down in terms of how households are reformed and reconstituted (Baylies 2001; Young and Ansell 2003).

The lack of willing and culturally connected carers has resulted in orphans, more than other children, living in households headed by grandparents (Bicego et al. 2002). The research discussed here found that maternal grandmothers were the most likely carers for orphans in both Malawi and Lesotho regardless of whether tradition followed the matrilineal or patrilineal system (Ansell and Young 2004). Maternal grandmothers in general felt that it was their duty to care for their daughters' children rather than witness them suffer alone. These grandparent–grandchildren relationships have been noted to be problematic due to a lack of resources. Research in South Africa demonstrates that grandparents regularly contribute to the financial care of grandchildren with their pensions (and, in situations where there are no pensions, food and savings) subsidising school expenses, but how far these resources can stretch when the pension is the sole source of income for a grandparent–grandchildren household is uncertain (Bray 2003). As Foster (1995) notes, children living with grandparents are especially vulnerable since the grandparents themselves have lost one of their key support mechanisms, namely their sons and daughters (Foster 1995 in Bicego 2002).

Grandparents are not the only carers for orphaned children with parent's siblings, older siblings and step-parents also playing a role. Nyambedha et al. (2003) found that even where other relatives took children to live with them, the support received was reduced, and a number of orphans in his study had to work for other people in the village to pay school fees as well as meet household financial requirements. Similarly, children living with adults with whom they had no kin relationship were living as servants, indicating that the main reason behind the adoption could be a desire for the child's labour rather than a charitable act. Although non-related foster carers are increasingly common elsewhere in sub-Saharan Africa this is still infrequent across southern Africa, despite some governments, including Malawi, trying to establish fostering systems as an alloparenting arrangement (Bandawe and Louw 1997).

Currently, when family resources reach breaking point, some children end up on the streets or in institutional care (Bourdillon 1999; Human Rights Watch 2001). This removes children from the traditional and cultural values of their family and, although they may be well cared for physically, can increase psychological distress such as isolation, loneliness and depression due to a lack of attention paid to their emotional needs (Munthali and Ali 2000; Tolfree 1995). Despite this, many children in non-Western societies are still cared for through this means, although most could be supported by their extended families at a much lower cost if preventative strategies were employed that ensured the basic needs of families were met (Tolfree 1995).

Given that alternative strategies are emerging in light of the AIDS pandemic, it is useful to consider the importance of moral obligation towards children in families and households. Orphan care cannot be disentangled from households and extended families, in particular the care of other vulnerable household members such as the elderly, and therefore we have chosen to draw on the changing nature of the intergenerational contract as a method for understanding the means by which orphans are currently looked after. This provides a platform for explaining why some strategies that are put into place may be more appropriate than others for the children involved.

Inter-Generational Contracts

The inter-generational 'contract' or 'bargain' conceptualizes the nature of family relationships as a series of implicit shared understandings regarding the role and responsibilities of family members (Malhotra and Kabeer 2002). These responsibilities are based on the moral obligation of 'families' to transfer resources between generations (McGregor et al. 2000).

Inter-generational contracts revolve around two different kinds of dependency separated in time: the dependency associated with childhood and the dependency associated with old age (Kabeer 2000). Collard (2000) explains this process using a three-generation model. He illustrates how the working generation (or parents) make transfers of goods and services to both the young and the old. In particular human capital, such as education, health care and training, is transferred to children and resources to the elderly. Within families, parents carry out their obligations in anticipation of future returns, children in recognition of past benefits. The basic premise for this transfer is not necessarily altruistic but based on the understanding that other generations will behave in a similar way, therefore securing support in old age (Collard 2000). This requires an act of faith, but many societies make sure that power lies with the elderly in material, symbolic and emotional terms. For example, in patriarchal societies responsibility for the survival of the family is held with elderly men, this often being supported with control over family resources (Malhotra and Kabeer 2002). As long as this is the case children are likely to take the terms of the contract as given rather than seeking to contest them or renege on them (Kabeer 2000).

Contracts, however, are not fixed but constantly changing as society changes, illustrating the socially constructed nature of the relationship. For example, the resources invested in children increase as infant mortality decreases given that the greater the chance of survival to adulthood the greater chance there is of reciprocity. Similarly, changes in society influence the way resources are distributed, with increasing importance now placed on educating children both in order for them to perform their immediate household tasks (they need to be able to read) and as a modernization of the contract which will increase children's sense of duty and capacity to provide for their parents in the future (Kabeer 2000). However, Kabeer (2000) also illustrates that the socially constructed nature of the contract results in some instances of unequal allocation of resources, where parents may discriminate between sons and daughters.

Inter-generational contracts are also socially constructed through extended families, rather than simply nuclear units. Collard (2000) calls this the inter-generational cluster. This is particularly advantageous when a contract breaks down, which may occur through illness, adverse production shocks and bereavement. Here other working adults in the extended family can share their resources and re-allocate them among all the households in the extended family to meet the needs of households under stress (Collard 2000). A further extension to the break down of contracts that is important here is the notion of generational fractures (Collard 2000), which is particularly instrumental in the way contracts have changed in light of the AIDS pandemic in southern Africa. This occurs when the adult working generation is missing, in this case due to high HIV-infection rates, and children are left orphaned. Where the extended family is unable to cope there is contract dissolution. This results in the older generation and the young being left to provide their own support. Although the contract may be mended with both groups undertaking work, this often results in extreme poverty, overburdening the old and reducing investment in children's futures.

The notion of the inter-generational contract is therefore significant in three ways in relation to the changing nature of orphan care in southern Africa which this chapter will explore. First, the loss of the working generation of parents reduces the resources available to be transferred to the old and the young. This may result in orphans receiving limited resources. Second, the loss of the working group in such dramatic proportions results in a generational fracture, returning the care of children to their grandparents (and grandparents to their grandchildren). Third, the inability of the remaining working generation and the elderly generation to absorb the orphan population may result in their care being transferred out of the extended family.

The Research

The research discussed in this chapter is drawn from a much larger study examining children's migration in the context of AIDS. Children-centred qualitative and quantitative methods were used, drawing on methodologies developed by others researching the impacts of migration on children in other contexts (Camacho 1999; Jones 1993). In order to explore a wide range of migration experiences, the research was also comparative, examining the experiences of young people in both urban and rural communities and comparing Malawi's relatively long-standing experience of the pandemic with the more recent, yet virulent, experience in Lesotho.

The research was carried out over a five-month period in 2001 in four communities. In Malawi, the urban community was Ndirande, a high-density transient township located on the edge of Blantyre city in the southern region. The children were accessed mainly through Ndirande Primary School. The rural community, in contrast, Mpando village area, was located 100 km away in the tea-growing area of Thyolo, where employment-related migration to work in the estate is not uncommon. The children were accessed through Nankhulumbo Model School. In Lesotho many communities are also transient particularly in relation to employment. Maseru, the capital city, is located on the border with South Africa and is a rapidly growing commercial centre. This served as the urban community with children accessed mainly through St. James Primary and High Schools, which draw young people from a range of low to middle income suburbs.[4] Ha Tlali, the rural location, is situated in the foothills of the Maluti Mountains, located approximately 60 km from Maseru, and is mainly dependent on subsistence agriculture and remittances from labour migration.

Given that school attendance is relatively high in both countries, even among orphans, it was decided that this would be the most appropriate context for accessing large numbers of children. A questionnaire was distributed to proportionate numbers attending upper primary school (and form 1 in Lesotho) in each of the four communities. The majority were aged between twelve and fifteen years. The aim here was to identify which children had moved and whether this might be related to parental sickness or death. Following this, approximately 200 children were invited to participate in focus group discussions (organized in relation to school year and gender) to ascertain more details regarding parental death and their subsequent migration. A smaller subset of 65 children then participated in in-depth qualitative work, making their own migration storyboards where they each drew a series of pictures illustrating their migration. The storyboard then acted as a prompt for further oral description (Young and Barrett 2001). Following this, interviews were also undertaken with guardians in each community who had received children into their care. This was important to gain their perspective on the impacts of AIDS-related migration and on new caregivers and receiving households.

In order to access a range of experiences of particular relevance to this chapter, focus groups and storyboards were also employed with children not attending school in each of the communities and street children in the urban centres. Focus group discussions and staff interviews were also undertaken in orphanages to determine the experiences of those who move out of the extended family into alloparenting arrangements.

This chapter draws on the more qualitative aspects of the research and in particular young people's stories and in-depth case studies of institutions. These illustrate the diversity of individual experiences and reveal the complex care arrangements that have emerged.

Given the focus on migration, the research cannot be viewed as representing all alloparenting arrangements, for example where children are cared for by relatives or older siblings in their own homes. It does, however, illustrate the diversity of care arrangements that may not have been picked up had the research focused on static communities. Such research may have missed the specific implications of migration for understanding orphan care. In the remainder of the chapter, individual cases are discussed, which illustrate the range of experiences young people affected by AIDS-related guardian deaths face.

Complex Strategies for Care

In line with previous work on the impacts of AIDS, this research illustrates that it is poverty which is the main determinant in decisions regarding who cares for children (Ansell and Young 2004). For this reason, even where only one parent dies, especially when that parent is the main income earner (usually the father), some children find themselves in alloparenting arrangements. Children participating in this research were more likely to have lost their father than their mother, a point that is supported by the work of Nyambedha et al. (2003) in Kenya. Under such circumstances, alloparenting in the context of AIDS takes place outside as well as within the extended family, unlike traditional strategies for the care of orphans throughout southern Africa.

The research also revealed that because AIDS deaths cannot sustain the inter-generational contracts of extended families, as there are fewer adults to absorb shocks, the strategies for orphan care are not uniform and may even be contrary to convention, with the majority of children being placed with maternal grandparents (usually mothers) even in virilocal traditions. Other situations result in the establishment of 'new' contracts that have more immediate returns, with children performing particular tasks or roles as conditional for their receiving investment in their futures. Where this is problematic, orphan care takes place outside the extended family, particularly self-care, or institutional care.

Alloparenting within the Extended Family

Within the extended family, children's experiences of alloparenting arrangements can be categorized in four ways, representing different strategies put in place in relation to the inter-generational contract. First, there is the absorption of children into new households, which may be located at a distance from their parental household due to the lack of relatives able and willing to support extra children. Second, there is care based on immediate reciprocal relationships rather than the long-term 'moral economy' of the inter-generational contract. Third, when generational fracture occurs, this reciprocity is based on necessity, as survival can often only be achieved if both children and the elderly work to sustain their household. Finally, the creation of new households when one parent remarries creates alloparenting arrangements. This can result in unequal investment in children related to their biological status with orphans' status in the household related more to their immediate labour than future provision for their guardians.

Reduced Care Opportunities: Children's Adaptation to New Household Situations

Ruth's[5] story

Ruth's cousin, John, lived with his parents in Salima, a lakeside town in central Malawi. He lived a very comfortable life as the only child in a fairly wealthy family who were able to provide for all his needs. Unfortunately John's parents died less than one year apart. Ruth describes the difficulties her cousin faced coming to live with her family and how his lack of familiarity with their way of life was particularly problematic.

Ruth states that her relatives *'lived in Salima in a nice house. They would buy my cousin new clothes and he didn't do much work, only played with his friends and he was the only child in his family.*

When his parents died he came to live with us and he didn't want to do any work and he just played … We didn't feel good when he came because we did most of the work and he didn't help even though he was eight when he came. He didn't feel good because he was used to living as the only child in the house and there were six youngsters of his age here … We used to tease him because he wouldn't help. We wouldn't give him food when he wouldn't work, but only when he started working.

My father makes bricks for a living and he used to teach us these skills but my cousin didn't like it and wouldn't do it like the others, but he was made to learn this to help at home, but he didn't like it as he didn't like mud and getting dirty.

In the holidays we used to go to our home village in Thyolo and in the morning we used to get up early and go to the fields to work. So my cousin would go with us but he wouldn't work. When he was given the hoe he just cried. This made me angry and I used to shout at him … He hadn't worked in a field before so he found it really hard to work.

After some time he got used to this and living with us and he used to mould bricks on his own and do the other housework. We then became friends with him, me and my sister were then closer to him than were we to our other brothers. (Ruth's storyboard, Ndriande, Malawi)

● ● ●

This story illustrates that because extended families are dispersed, children whose parents die often have to move to receive care. Where a number of deaths within a family occur it is likely that children will have to move greater distances. When this occurs, fitting into new households is far more complex (Young and Ansell 2003). Ruth's story of her cousin's situation reveals how he had difficulties adapting to a different way of life, engaging in chores he was not used to and living with a greater number of siblings. John felt that he was being harshly treated, and that he had no control over the new way resources were provided. Over time he was able to see that this was not a breakdown in the moral provision of resources to children but merely a different method by which it was achieved. The working generation were providing for his human capital by training John in agricultural subsistence and brick moulding, a wider strategy than his parent's method of investment mainly through education. John was able to be absorbed into the household and become one of its members. His part in the contract was restored and he was provided with the same resources as the other children, although in a different form than he was used to. In such cases the inter-generational contract is still intact, although it may initially be a difficult process for children to accept. This example does, however, represent the way wider extended families can provide a context for the inter-generational contract to be fulfilled.

Immediacy in Reciprocal Relationships: Children's Responsibilities within New Households

● ● ●

Relebohile's story

Relebohile lived with his family in a rural village in Lesotho. He didn't see his father often as he drove long distance vehicles and was often on the road. When Relebohile's mother fell sick his duties within the household changed and he took on a more immediate caring role, although his grandmother also moved to live with them.

My grandmother moved to our house when my mother fell sick. I'm not sure what was wrong with Mum but she lost a lot of weight and sometimes she couldn't walk. Sometimes my grandmother would care for Mother while we were at school. When my grandmother went to town to fetch medicine for my mother I used to look after her and give her food and water. After Mum died it was very bad and I missed her a lot … Now I look after donkeys for someone in the village on the weekends and during the week I fetch them from the fields where they are grazing. (Relebohile's storyboard, rural Lesotho)

● ● ●

Rachel's story

Rachel lived with her parents and siblings in a village in rural Malawi. They moved to a different village when Rachel was nine as her father's mother was very old and needed assistance. At this time her father also began suffering from recurrent illness and eventually passed away. As Rachel's father had been the sole income earner in the family, this created problems for the remaining household. Soon after, Rachel's younger sister also died, and her remaining siblings and mother fell deeper into poverty. Her maternal uncle came and offered to look after Rachel in order to reduce the burden on the family and so she went to live with him in Blantyre.

She states: *I miss my family very much and I only visit them in the long holidays in November. At first I was happy to come to Blantyre as everything is bought. But I now have to cook for my uncle, go to the maize mill and clean the place. He has five children who are all boys so they are not helping me. I have a problem with my uncle because some of the boys say bad things about me. They tell their father that I destroyed something which isn't true.* (Rachel's storyboard, Ndirande, Malawi)

● ● ●

Both stories illustrate different perspectives on the immediate reciprocity required when parents fall sick and die. For Relebohile, the moral obligation that he would provide for his mother in her older years was 'cashed in' much earlier when she became ill. Relebohile had to miss school on occasions in order to provide care, which in turn reduced his chances of reaching his full potential as an adult. Similarly, for Relebohile's grandmother, the obligation that her daughter would provide for her was also reneged upon due to illness and instead the elder had to provide the resources. Relebohile's story also illustrates how, when his mother died, his position changed again as generational fracture had occurred. Now he had to look after donkeys in the village as a means to provide resources for himself and his grandmother.

On the other hand Rachel's story is quite different. The immediate reciprocity of her new situation is related to the inability of the family to adequately absorb all orphans. Following her father's death, there were too many siblings and some were sent to live with relatives in an effort by the extended family to share the burden. In Rachel's case going to live with her uncle was based on an immediate relationship, an explicit rather than implicit inter-generational contract. In return for his investment into her future, Rachel was expected to undertake the majority of the housework, leaving the other children in the household to concentrate on their education. In this way Rachel's uncle appears to have been exploiting her situation and in particular, her need for education, for his own strategic self-interest.

The development of these immediate relationships is related to either a lack of available resources and therefore the need to employ child labour for the survival of the household, or to the choice of the working generation to require immediate reciprocity for fear that they, or the children in their care, will not survive to old age. This is instrumental in understanding how the AIDS pandemic has changed the nature of the inter-generational contract. With the current working population falling sick, and with youth at most immediate risk of infection, there may be an assumption that the young are less likely to survive to care for parents in their old age. For this reason there is less willingness to invest resources in the young as the likelihood of return is low. Where children are orphaned due to AIDS, the associated stigma is such that often children are suspected of harbouring the disease. Fear that the orphans may also die would further reduce the incentive to invest in their future. This is akin to Kabeer's (2000) assertion that parents invest more emotional and financial resources in children as they increase in age and there is greater change of their long-term survival.

Generational Fracture: Reciprocity between Children and the Elderly

Mpho's story

Mpho is ten years old. She was born and grew up in TY in Lesotho. She lived with her father and mother (her father's second wife) and her five siblings. Mpho's mother died 'of a stitch'[6] last year and not long afterwards her father was diagnosed with stomach cancer, which proved fatal. At her father's funeral, the relatives got together to decide how best to care for the children. Given the large family size and the inability of relatives to stretch their resources to care for another six children, the siblings were split between households. Mpho went to live with her father's sister, her 77-year-old aunt, in Ha Tlali.

When she came here she had no clothes, no underwear, no blanket and no shoes ... I have given her clothes and send her to school as I pay for her fees. [Mpho] helps me by fetching water. I feel I should have someone around as I am old and not very well. My children are married and in other villages and although they help me financially and with clothes, they still have families of their own ... I was happy to receive this child as I would have someone to live with me and someone to help me, so that was good ... and she is my helping hand. It is also my duty as a family member to help the others and so I happy to have her here. (Mpho's aunt)

Mpho's story represents an important aspect of the breakdown of the inter-generational contract. Due to the large number of orphans needing care, it is not so easy for the extended family to simply absorb children. Children are split between relatives and there is a more immediate reciprocal relationship established. Mpho was deliberately selected by her aunt over her younger sisters for her ability to help around the house. This aged relative clearly needed help with her housework and Mpho was old enough to perform the necessary tasks. Further, she was selected over her brothers in order to perform duties within a particular gendered role. The concept of inter-generational contracts is useful here. Not only has the contract within the extended family broken down due to the size of the burden, there are not enough of the working generation remaining to adequately transfer the necessary resources to both the young and the old. Therefore children have a more immediate responsibility to reciprocate for their care within the new household.

Kondwani's story

Kondwani grew up in Ntcheu in Malawi. He was generally happy living there. He lived with his parents, enjoyed playing football and went to school. Kondwani loved gardening and enjoyed helping out in the fields, particularly as he was able to play football there and eat the mangoes from the trees. However, Kondwani's life changed when his parents died. First his father died, from a problem with his legs, and a few years later his mother died, suffering from TB. Kondwani went to live with his grandmother, as she was the only one who would take him in.

He states: *I loved gardening but when my parents died and I had to go and live with my grandmother, I was always doing the gardening and it was tough. She was so old that I had to do it all. I also couldn't go to school because when I went to the fields I'd come back late and couldn't go to school.*

Following the hardship Kondwani faced, he ran away to the streets, and although he felt he had done 'a wrong thing' by running away he did so because of the difficulties in his home life. (Kondwani's storyboard, street kid, Blantyre)

Kondwani's story is less optimistic and clearly illustrates the further breakdown in care arrangements that can occur. Due to the lack of a resource provider in the household Kondwani had to take on the majority of that role, which in turn reduced his ability to engage in education. With limited input into his future and therefore little apparent reciprocity in the relationship between grandmother and grandson, Kondwani decided to look after his own future and leave for the streets. In this case the inter-generational contract had dissolved completely as providing resources for the elderly was to the detriment of training and education for the young.

Both stories illustrate the more explicit contracts that are entered into between the younger and older generations, where in return for a place to stay, and sometimes financial support, children are expected to engage in household work. This helps to mend the gap left by the adult working generation as children receive care in return for supporting the home of the elderly. In some instances, such as Mpho's case, there is enough external support and resources within the household of the elderly relative for this relationship to be fruitful, with each part of the contract being honoured. However, in Kondwani's case, where the elderly are impoverished, the burden falls more directly on children, creating an unsustainable home situation.

Stepparenting and the Lack of a Contract

James's story

James grew up in Mulange district in southern Malawi and lived with his mother and father. He attended school regularly and enjoyed life. However, when James's father passed away from TB James and his mother were taken to live with his maternal grandmother in Thyolo district. It was at this point that things began to change for James. His mother remarried and his stepfather was less concerned in investing in James's future.

My father used to encourage me to go to school but my stepfather doesn't encourage me or buy me exercise books for school … Instead I was sent to work in the field all the time while my friends went to school. My stepfather said I had to go to the field instead of to school but he was hurting himself by not allowing me to go to school as school was my future. My stepfather would tell me to sell fish or to bake breads instead of going to school. He also told me to sell clothes so I would meet with thieves who would beat me up and steal the clothes I had for sale. Because of my stepfather's ill-treatment and my failure to attend school, I was failing the exams because I had no time to study. (James's story, Mpando, Malawi)

Where one parent dies and the other remarries, resentment can occur towards orphan children and they are treated less well in such households (Nyambedha et al. 2003). Often this is because the new parent has his/her own children and prefers to invest in their future. James's story illustrates how his stepfather was using James's labour to provide immediate benefits to the household and how this was to the detriment of James's education and future prospects. What is particularly interesting, however, is that James himself draws attention to the breakdown of the contract, illustrating that his stepfather is harming any future input of resources that he might receive in old age by not investing in James's future. When related to Kabeer's (2000) idea of the modern inter-generational contract, where investing in education has taken precedence over other aspects of human capital for increasing the chance of returns to the working generation from their children in later life, the stepparenting strategy appears to be based on a different and less favoured arrangement than for the other children. It is likely that those more closely related to the working generation will care for them in old age. For this reason it is less important to invest in stepchildren for the future – James's contract is therefore based on immediate reciprocity.

Strategies External to the Extended Family

In some cases internal strategies break down completely, and support mechanisms are often then found in places outside the extended family. This research investigated two ways children leave the extended family following the death of a parent: either when children decided to leave themselves, usually to the streets but sometimes to seek out another relative, or when they were taken into institutional care. Both have very different implications in relation to the moral obligation of extended families to care for their members.

Street Children's Strategies for Care

Kondwani's story (continued)

After running away from his home situation, Kondwani found life on the streets hard.

When I was in town I didn't feel good. When I came to the streets I started smoking and beating others. One of the older street boys told me to go and buy some cigarettes for him. When I came back he told me I had to smoke it first, so I had the habit of smoking, but I had to smoke to be with them.

At a later stage, Kondwani came into contact with a non-governmental organisation (NGO) working with street children, who took him to their shelter, fed him and sent him to school. He is also able to wash his clothes and learn skills such as gardening. (Kondwani's storyboard, Blantyre, Malawi)

As Kondwani's story demonstrates, children usually (but not always) stated that they went to the streets because their home-life situation was inadequate and often this occurred when their carer was not able or willing to invest in their future potential. On the streets however, children found themselves entering into different kinds of contracts. Most newcomers enter into a new implicit contract with other street children, based on seniority and physical strength on the streets. This relationship was similar to the inter-generational contract but related to hierarchies among street children rather than actual generations, and based on immediate reciprocity, like many of the other alloparenting situations discussed in this chapter. In return for training on the street, in Kondwani's case learning to fight and smoke, which are behaviours that are respected among peers, and protection, Kondwani engaged in carrying out chores for his group. In some instances children are expected to engage in criminal activity in return for the protection they receive (Young 2003). In this way the immediacy of the contract carries obligation to other street children but not the moral obligation of investing in, and providing for, other generations. This may result in a breakdown of the inter-generational contract.

Street life, however, is not simply based on one contract, and often children enter into several, and sometimes conflicting contracts, to support their survival. As Kondwani's story goes on to illustrate, many street children attach themselves to NGO programmes, which invest in both their immediate survival and future potential. Food, shelter and often education are provided as well as encouraging children to give up the harmful behaviours needed on the streets, such as smoking and stealing, as a mechanism for investing in their futures. This illustrates investment, which is supportive of providing for children's human capital, but that does not entail any direct moral obligation on children to provide for their own families.

Institutions as Carers

Institutions take on parenting responsibilities in a number of ways across a range of spatial and temporal scales. The two examples here are very different in their outlook and approach. One institution seeks to 'become' children's family and take on all responsibilities for care, while the other aims to continue the relationship between children and their extended family, merely investing in the human capital that poor families cannot provide. The outcomes of such strategies are very different and have different implications for the sustenance of inter-generational contracts within families.

Institutional care has been criticized for its inability to provide for children's emotional needs as well as their physical needs. This has largely discredited institutionalization as a means for caring for children in Western contexts, with fostering and adoption considered more appropriate alternatives. However, as noted here, the burden on extended families to provide care is too great in some instances, especially in light of the AIDS pandemic, and where there is no cultural connection of care by non-kin. The state (and NGOs) have had to fill the gap through large-scale institutions. The criticisms have not gone unnoticed and strategies have been put in place to create homelike situations but with different implications for inter-generational obligations.

● ● ●

SOS Lesotho

SOS children's village in Lesotho has attempted to create 'new' home situations for children in their care. They have split the village into individual homes, each with a housemother and approximately ten children. They are expected to work and function like normal households. However, children do not retain contact with their original relatives and, as the quotes illustrate, this results in their not wishing to return.

The way the home functions:

Ntate [social worker] comes to pick you up at your house. Then you go to the chief and you sign a letter which shows that SOS will be taking care of you – they are now responsible for you.

I think my life is better here now … I didn't know things before but now I speak English … I now go to another country for school. SOS gives us a lot of opportunities to go to another country if we get good grades so I now go to school in Ghana.

[The house mothers] take good care of us. They treat us like their own children … if I make a mistake she advises me.

Why children don't wish to return to their villages:

I am happy in Maseru because I live a good life. I have left the difficult life of gathering wood and cooking outside. I hated it. Here I cook inside and I enjoy it.

I will never go back. If you go back you end up not doing anything and just sitting at home. Some of us might get sent to initiation schools or we could have been married by now.

● ● ●

Jacaranda Children's Home, Malawi

Jacaranda children's home in Blantyre Malawi works on an integrated approach whereby children maintain contact with their families and communities. The home works more like a boarding school as it sends children back to their relatives' homes every weekend (often with food if the family is impoverished). They feel maintaining contact is healthy and gives children a place to return on completion of their schooling. The quotes below, taken from a discussion with some of the children, illustrate Jacaranda's philosophy well.

Education is at the heart of Jacaranda's investment in children:

I am here [at Jacaranda] because when my parents passed away I went to stay with my grandmother but she is unable to provide for me. She was not working and could not get money to buy the things I needed for school.

I like it here because they send me to school and give me everything I need.

Contact with families: (the first quote illustrates how much the home is integrated into relatives households).

I was staying with my aunt after my parents passed away. That's where I'm staying now.

When I came here, I stayed only two weeks and then they sent me back home to visit.

Every weekend and holiday they give us transport fare so that we can see our siblings [and relatives].

I feel good at home because I get the chance to play with my friends and chat with my grandmother.

The first case study illustrates how institutional care can break down the moral obligation for children to participate in care across the generations of their extended family by removing them completely from their community. Although a new 'surrogate family' is established within the institutional centre, this is artificial in nature.

Housemothers often have their own families, and there is no expectation that institutionalized children will provide for that mother in her old age. Despite this, the institution works hard to invest in education and future provision of its charges. In this way wider society has taken over the role of providing for the younger generation and enhances their capacity to provide for themselves as adults. However, it removes their obligation to care for the elderly of their own family and, as the case study shows, the children have severed all ties with their extended families and have no desire to regain these contacts. This raises the question of whether, as adults, they will transfer the resources they gain towards the elderly and subsequent younger generation of their extended family.

The second case study is rather different in outlook, maintaining close ties with extended families. The institution takes on a partial role in the care of children through provision for human capital. The set up is less amenable to providing for emotional needs but is temporary and the nature of extended family contacts suggests that emotional needs are also catered for there. The children were happy to visit their relatives and saw their future, at least in the short-term, to be based with family in their home villages. Rather than taking over the role of investing in children's future, this approach provides a supplementary transfer of resources to the young, which enhances their capacity to provide for themselves and also their families in the future. In this way the inter-generational contract is supported and maintained.

Conclusion

Through using inter-generational contracts as a reference point, this chapter has explored the ways in which strategies for the care of orphaned children have changed in light of the AIDS pandemic in southern Africa. The case studies drawn on in the chapter represent the diversity of alloparenting arrangements and carers that has emerged. Strategies for care have become more complex, with extended families having to deal with an inflated number of orphans in conjunction with a reduced number of adults willing and able to provide care. This has meant that there has been a change in the operation of implicit inter-generational contracts and therefore the methods by which orphans receive care in their new households.

In all cases children need to adapt to the way resources are provided in new households and the methods by which they receive (or not) investment in their future. In situations where children are less familiar with the new household, particularly if they have moved between urban and rural areas or from wealthy to more impoverished situations, this may result in children feeling that they no longer receive proper care. However, as Ruth's storyboard illustrates, in many cases children do adapt and become fully integrated into the household.

There are some circumstances, however, which are more problematic and it is helpful to look at the changing nature of inter-generational contracts for explanation. There are three aspects to this in relation to orphan care that have become apparent through this chapter. First of all, the time frame within which contracts take place has been significantly reduced in some cases, with immediate reciprocity favoured over a long-term moral obligation of the working generation to care for the old and the young. This was particularly notable where children were cared for outside usual cultural arrangements and especially when the caregiver was elderly or ailing and had no other source of support.

This immediacy was based on three conditions within new households. First, that the needs of the household are immediate. For example, Mpho's aunt took her in on the basis that she was of a suitable age for helping with housework – illustrating the immediacy of the exchange. Poverty exacerbates this immediate need because children's labour is required to sustain the household. Second, contracts were more likely to be immediate when they operated outside a moral economy of trust, for example, where stepparents and distant relatives expected their own children to provide for their future needs rather than incoming orphans. Finally, immediate reciprocity was called upon in households where it was felt that the young or the elderly carers would not be alive long enough to fulfil the obligations, or that the working population would not survive to old age.

This reduction in time frame was also apparent where contracts became more explicit. The implicit nature of the inter-generational contract means it cannot be guaranteed that each generation adheres to the moral obligation to provide for the young and old but there is an expectation that this is what will happen. However, in many cases households are not taking in children based on their moral obligation but out of necessity, particularly if the relationship can be mutually beneficial. Children require investment in their education and the carer requires the children's labour. Here it was clear that children were provided for in return for doing something: housework, agricultural work or paid work. In some cases the overtly explicit nature of the contract was related to there being other children from whom moral obligation of provision was required, such as within stepparent families.

The third area where the changing nature of orphan care can be noted is the emerging inequality in the provision of resources. There were two reasons for such inequality. First, in some instances, orphans were treated less well than other children and not provided with the human capital they felt they required. For example, James was given food and shelter from his stepfather but was unable to attend school – a right he felt he deserved. Part of this unequal treatment may be related to the stigmatization of orphans which could create fear in carers that they will not survive their working life and are therefore not worth investing in, or simply because there are other children who can provide for the carers in their old age. There is therefore less incentive to invest in the future human capital of additional, more distantly related, children. In other cases investment in children was difficult for the carer because of impoverished circumstances and children felt that they were providing resources for the carer and not receiving an equal proportion of provision for human capital. This was the case for Kondwani who felt that he was supporting his grandmother, while she was unable to fulfil her surrogate role as parent in terms of her investment potential.

Exploring the inter-generational contract as part of orphan care strategies is important for finding the most appropriate solutions. In particular, this highlights the need to consider the care of children in tandem with the care of the elderly, given that the support for both vulnerable groups is diminishing in size and its ability to provide due to the loss of productivity through sickness. Grandparents are illustrated elsewhere as the best providers of emotional support for orphans (Ansell and Young 2004), but are unable to provide adequate investment in children's future potential due to poverty. A solution, which incorporates the needs of both groups together, is needed. State facilitation of the transfer of resources from the general population (i.e., through taxation) to the young and old, would alleviate some of the difficulties faced. This, however, needs to be achieved in a way that supports rather than undermines the private inter-generational contracts of families. Strategies could include the provision of free education for the young and pensions for the elderly. This would strengthen the economic resource transfer of the inter-generational contracts, particularly where the working generation is missing, without severing emotional connections.

Notes

1. This chapter is based on an article that originally appeared as van Blerk, L., and Ansell, N., 2007, Alternative care giving in the context of AIDS: complex strategies for care, *Journal for International Development* (19) 865–84. Copyright John Wiley & Sons Limited. Reproduced with permission.

2. Due to the contentious nature of the terms household and family we refer here to household as those who reside together and extended family as those bonded through kinship ties but who do not necessarily live in the same household (Young and Ansell 2003).

3. Orphans are taken to be children aged between 0 and 14 who have lost either their mother or both parents (USAID/UNICEF/UNAIDS 2002).

4. In Lesotho the residential areas are less well-defined than in Malawi and generally contain a mix of rented and owner-occupied dwellings.

5. All names used are pseudonyms.

6. People living with AIDS in Lesotho indicated that this generally refers to AIDS when relatives do not wish to say what the cause of death was for fear of associated stigma.

References

Ainsworth, M., and Over, M., 1997. *Confronting AIDS: Public Priorities in a Global Epidemic.* New York: Oxford University Press.

Ali, S., 1998. Community perceptions of orphan care in Malawi Paper presented at the Conference on *Raising the Orphan Generation,* organized by the Children in Distress Net-

work (CINDI), Pietermaritzburg, South Africa. 9–12 June 1998. http://www.cindi.org
.za/ConferencePapers1998.

Ankrah, E.M., 1991. AIDS and the social side of health. *Social Science and Medicine* 32,
967–80.

Ansell, N., and Young, L., 2004. Children's migration as a household/family strategy: coping
with AIDS in southern Africa. *Journal of Southern African Studies* 30(3), 673–90.

Bandawe, C.R., and Louw, J., 1997. The experience of family foster care in Malawi: a preliminary investigation. *Child Welfare* LXXVI(4), 535–47.

Barnett, T., and Blaikie, P., 1992. *AIDS in Africa: Its Present and Future Impact.* London:
Belhaven.

Barrett, H., 1998. Protest-despair-detachment: questioning the myth. In I. Hutchby and
J. Moran-Ellis, eds., *Children and Social Competence: Arenas of Action.* London: Falmer,
64–84.

Baylies, C., 2001. *Precarious Futures: The New Demography of AIDS in Africa: Africa's Young
Majority: Meanings, Victims, Actors.* Edinburgh: Centre of African Studies, University of
Edinburgh.

Bicego, G., Rutstein, S., and Johnson, K., 2002. Dimensions of the emerging orphan crisis in
sub-Saharan Africa. *Social Science and Medicine* 56, 1235–1247.

Bourdillon, M.F.C., 1999. The next generation. Paper presented at *AIDS, Livelihoods and Social Change in Africa,* Wageningen Agricultural University. 15–16 April 1999.

Bowlby, J., 1966 [1951]. *Maternal Care and Mental Health.* New York: Schocken.

Bray, R., 2003. Predicting the social consequences of orphanhood in South Africa. *African
Journal of AIDS Research* 2(1), 39–55.

Burman, E., 1995. The abnormal distribution of development: policies for Southern women
and children. *Gender, Place and Culture* 2(1), 21–36.

Camacho, A.Z.V., 1999. Family, child labour and migration: child domestic workers in Metro
Manila. *Childhood: A Global Journal of Child Research* 6(1), 57–73.

Chanock, M., 1985. *Law, Custom and Social Order: The Colonial Experience in Malawi and
Zambia.* Cambridge: Cambridge University Press.

Cliff, A.D., and Smallman-Raynor, M.R., 1992. The AIDS pandemic: global geographical patterns and local spatial processes. *The Geographical Journal* 158(2), 182–98.

Collard, D., 2000. Generational transfers and the generational bargain. *Journal of International
Development* 12, 443–45.

Danziger, R., 1994. The social impact of HIV/AIDS in developing countries. *Social Science
and Medicine* 39(7), 905–17.

Deininger, K., Garcia, M., and Subbarao, K., 2003. AIDS-induced orphanhood as a systemic
shock: magnitude, impact and program interventions in Africa. *World Development* 31(7),
1201–20.

Foster, G., and Williamson, J., 2000. A review of current literature of the impact of HIV/AIDS
on children in sub-Saharan Africa. *AIDS* 14(suppl. 3), S275–84.

Foster, G., Shakespeare R, Chinemana F, Jackson H, Gregson S, Marange C, Mashumba

S.,1995. Orphan prevalence and extended family care in a peri-urban community in Zimbabwe. *AIDS Care* 7(1), 3–17.

George, S., Van Oudenhoven, N., and Wazir, R., 2003. Foster care beyond the crossroads: lessons from an international comparative analysis. *Childhood: A Global Journal of Child Research* 10(3), 343–61.

Grainger, C., Webb, D., and Elliott, L., 2001. *Children Affected by HIV/AIDS: Rights and Responsibilities in the Developing World.* London: Save the Children.

Human Rights Watch, 2001. Kenya: in the shadow of death: HIV/AIDS and children's rights in Kenya. *Human Rights Watch* 13(4[A]).

Hunter, S., and Williamson, J., 2000. *Children on the Brink: Executive Summary: Updated Estimates and Recommendations for Intervention.* Washington, DC: USAID.

Jones, S., 1993. *Assaulting Childhood: Children's Experiences of Migrancy and Hostel Life in South Africa.* Johannesburg: Witwatersrand University Press.

Kabeer, N., 2000. Inter-generational contracts, demographic transitions and the 'quantity-quality' trade-off: parents, children and investing in the future. *Journal of International Development* 12, 463–82.

Kamali, A., et al., 1996. The orphan problem: experience of a sub-Saharan Africa rural population in the AIDS epidemic. *AIDS Care* 8(5), 509–15.

Kimane, I., and Mturi, A.J., 2001. *Rapidly Assessing Children at Work in Lesotho: Volume 1: Context and Overview of Findings.* Maseru: Government of Lesotho, with financial assistance from UNICEF.

Lyons, M., 1999. *The Impact of HIV and AIDS on Children, Families and Communities: Risks and Realities of Childhood during the HIV Epidemic.* New York: UNDP HIV and Development Programme.

Malhotra, R., and Kabeer, N., 2002. *Demographic Transition, Inter-Generational Contracts and Old Age Security: An Emerging Challenge for Social Policy in Developing Countries.* IDS Working Paper No. 157. Brighton: Institute of Development Studies, University of Sussex.

McGregor, J., Copestake, J., and Wood, G., 2000. The inter-generational bargain: an introduction. *Journal of International Development* 12, 447–51.

Mead, M., 1966. A cultural anthropologist's approach to maternal deprivation. In M.D. Ainsworth, ed., *Depriviation of Maternal Care: A Reassessment of its Effects.* New York: Schocken, 45–62.

Munthali, A.C., and Ali, S., 2000. *Adaptive Strategies and Coping Mechanisms: The Effect of HIV/AIDS on the Informal Social Security System in Malawi.* Lilongwe: Government of Malawi, National Economic Council.

Nko, S., Chiduo, B., Wilson, F., Msuya, W., and Mwaluko, G., 2000. Tanzania: AIDS care – learning from experience. *Review of African Political Economy* 86, 547–57.

Ntozi, J.P.M., 1997. Effect of AIDS on children: the problem of orphans in Uganda. *Health Transition Review* 7 (supplement), 23–40.

Nyambedha, E., Wandibba, S., and Aagaard-Hansen, J., 2003. Changing patterns of orphan care due to the HIV epidemic in Western Kenya. *Social Science and Medicine* 57, 301–11.

Robson, E., 2000. Invisible carers: young people in Zimbabwe's home-based healthcare. *Area* 32(1) 59–70.

Robson, E., and Ansell, N., 2000. Young carers in southern Africa: exploring stories from Zimbabwean secondary school students. In S.L. Holloway and G. Valentine, eds., *Children's Geographies: Playing, Living, Learning*. London: Routledge.

Rugalema, G., 2000. Coping or struggling? A journey into the impact of HIV/AIDS in southern Africa. *Review of African Political Economy* 86, 537–45.

Smith, P.K., and Cowie, H., 1988. *Understanding Children's Development*. Oxford: Blackwell.

Tolfree, D., 1995. *Roofs and Roots: The Care of Separated Children in the Developing World*. Aldershot: Arena (for Save the Children).

UNAIDS, 1999. *A Review of Household and Community Responses to the HIV/AIDS Epidemic in the Rural Areas of Southern Africa*. Geneva: UNAIDS.

———— 2003. *AIDS Epidemic Update: December 2003*. Geneva: UNAIDS/WHO.

———— 2004. *Report on the Global HIV/AIDS Epidemic*. Geneva: UNAIDS.

UNICEF, 2003. *Children in Institutions: The Beginning of the End?* Florence: Innocenti Research Centre.

United Nations, 1989. Convention on the Rights of the Child. Online Document, http://www.unicef.org/crc/crc.htm. Retrieved 15 June 2003.

Urassa, M., Boerma, T., Ng'weshemi, J.Z.L., et al., 1997. Orphanhood, child fostering and the AIDS epidemic in rural Tanzania. *Health Transition Review* 7(suppl. 2), 141–53.

USAID/UNICEF/UNAIDS, 2002. *Children on the Brink 2002: A Joint Report on Orphan Estimates and Program Strategies*. Washington, DC: USAID.

Webb, D., 1997. *HIV and AIDS in Africa*. London: Pluto.

White, L., 1987. *Magomero: Portrait of an African Village*. Cambridge: Cambridge University Press.

Young, L., 2003. The place of street children in Kampala, Uganda: marginalisation, resistance and acceptance in the urban environment. *Environment and Planning D: Society and Space* 21(5), 607–28.

Young, L., and Ansell, N., 2003. Fluid households, complex families: the impacts of children's migration as a response to HIV/AIDS in southern Africa. *The Professional Geographer* 55, 464–76.

Young, L., and Barrett, H., 2001. Adapting visual methods: action research with Kampala street children. *Area* 33, 141–52.

• 13 •

Alloparental Care and the Ontogeny of Glucocorticoid Stress Response among Stepchildren

Mark V. Flinn and David Leone

Introduction

The human child has evolved to be highly dependent upon care provided by others over a long developmental period (Bogin 1999; Lancaster and Lancaster 1987). The altricial (helpless) infant requires a protective environment provided by intense parental and alloparental care in the context of kin groups (Hewlett and Lamb 2005; Hrdy 2005). The extended family is of paramount importance in a child's world. Throughout human evolutionary history, parents and close relatives provided calories, protection, and information necessary for survival, growth, health, social success, and eventual reproduction. The human mind is therefore likely to have evolved special sensitivity to interactions with family caretakers, particularly during infancy and early childhood (Belsky 2005; Geary and Flinn 2001).

The family and other kin provide important cognitive 'landmarks' for a child's understanding of its social environment. A child's family environment may be an especially important source and mediator of psychosocial stress with consequent effects on health. In this chapter we investigate the effects of alloparental relationships on the development of stress response and concomitant health status among stepchildren in 'Bwa Mawego,' a rural community on the eastern coast of the Caribbean island-nation of Dominica.

Stepparent–Stepchild Relationships

Providing scarce resources to an unrelated child appears to run counter to the logic of kin selection. Step relationships were likely to have been commonplace during human evolution, providing a basis for natural selection to have designed human neurobiology to respond appropriately to available proximate cues for kin recognition (Alexander 1990; Flinn 1992; Hurtado and Hill 1992). We might expect, therefore, that stepchildren would be at high risk for neglect and abuse (Daly and Wilson, 1995).

Stepchildren, however, are not simply unrelated parasites; they are a special type of relative-by-marriage. Similar to other affines or 'in-laws', step relationships hinge on the marital/mating relationship of a genetic relative and are embedded in the context of broader social networks. Traditional human societies have extensive networks of kin reciprocity, with favours often returned indirectly. Assessment of a potential mate by a woman involves what he has to offer her relatives, especially her children from previous relationships. The availability of alternative care-giving sources, such as grandparents who are able and motivated to provide alloparental investment, may be important considerations when evaluating new mating relationships. From the perspective of the child, there may be a wide range of relatives from whom to seek investment. For the stepchild, kin outside the immediate family may be of particular importance.

The initial establishment of a new mating relationship by a parent is a period of high risk for sub-optimal caretaking and, potentially, psychosocial stress, morbidity, and growth disruptions. The power dynamic between a child's parent and the new mate seems critical. Women with more to offer relative to their mates are in a position to demand more in the way of stepparental care. Emotional mediation (Aureli and Schaffner 2002) in such relationships might be expected to result in greater feelings of tolerance or affection towards children of women with high perceived mate value. Conversely, women with less to offer may be less able to prevent neglect or abuse of their children. Indeed, if children from a previous relationship are a serious impediment to the establishment of new relationships, mothers may themselves be motivated to remove or minimise their own parental obligations. Here again, alloparents may be relied upon to take over care-giving responsibilities when parents seek to reduce investment in their offspring.

Social reputations are another important consideration. Humans observe and gossip about one another. Men and women who mistreat children may be stigmatised and considered less desirable as partners or social allies. In the case of potential stepfathers, it may be in a man's interests to convey the impression of a 'good caretaker'. Once having obtained the initial approval of a mother, however, negotiations concerning investment in her offspring are not finished. Stepchildren are active participants in the brokering of the new family deals, working hard to create the best situations for themselves. Because the presence of a stepfather may not be in their strategic interests, stepchildren may be upset by the new arrangements, and behave badly from the perspective of their stepfathers, who in turn may be frustrated by their mates' objections to steppaternal discipline. Stepchildren may be especially motivated to seek support from relatives outside the natal household, sometimes transferring residence if that is a viable option. And stepchildren are likely to leave the natal household at an earlier age to establish a new residence than are children co-resident with both genetic parents. For example, in the community of 'Grande Anse', Trinidad (all specific places and names used in this chapter are pseudonyms) young women were more likely to emigrate from their natal households if a stepparent was co-resident (Flinn 1988a). Similarly, in the community of 'Bwa Mawego,' Dominica, the rate of emigration from maternal natal households (excluding school-related residence changes) before age seventeen was higher for stepchildren (15/21; 71.4 per cent) than for non-stepchildren (5/23; 21.7 per cent) during the 1990s.

Pregnancy and birth of a child fathered by the new mate complicates the situation. Now stepchildren are competing directly with their stepfather's genetic offspring for parental care. Mothers may be less able to defend the interests of their children from previous relationships because mothers are more dependent upon their new mates to provide for the new babies and, burdened with new babies, they are less attractive to other males (e.g., Flinn 1988b). The utility of stepchildren as alloparental caregivers (e.g., 'baby-sitters') or as links to useful social connections for their maternal half-siblings, may provide a rationale for continued tolerance by stepfathers.

Some of the challenges faced by stepchildren change with age. Social and economic support of a father can be critical for young adult males to acquire the resources and social status necessary to attract mates in many societies. Sexual pressure from stepfathers and the need to obtain support from adult males may influence adolescent girls to establish mating relationships that facilitate leaving the stepfamily environment. These aspects of family environment may influence life history traits such as age at menarche (Ellis et al. 2003; Quinlan 2006).

In summary, the absence of a genetic relation between stepchildren and stepparents may affect the quality and quantity of care – including specific behaviours that affect nutrition, sleep routines, hygiene, medical attention, work loads, breast-feeding, instruction, comforting, protection, and so forth – with consequent effects on psychosocial stress and child well being (Daly and Wilson 1988a, b; Dunn 2004; Flinn 1988b; Flinn et al. 1999; Hetherington 2003a, b). Stepchildren, therefore, may be in special need of care from relatives outside their natal households, such as nearby grandparents, aunts and uncles, older siblings, and even great-grandparents.

Stress Response Mechanisms

Current psychosocial stress research suggests that the stress hormone cortisol is stimulated by uncertainty that is perceived as significant and for which behavioural responses will have unknown effects (Dickerson and Kemeny 2004; Kirschbaum and Hellhammer 1994). Cortisol release is associated with unpredictable, uncontrollable events that require full alert readiness and mental anticipation. In appropriate circumstances, temporary moderate increases in stress hormones (and associated neurotransmitters such as dopamine) may enhance mental activity for short periods in localised areas and prime memory storage, hence improving cognitive processes for responding to social challenges (Beylin and Shors 2003; LeDoux 2003). Mental processes unnecessary for appropriate response may be inhibited, perhaps to reduce external and internal 'noise' (Servan-Schreiber et al.1990; cf. Kirschbaum et al. 1996; Lupien et al. 2005; Newcomer et al. 1994).

Stress response involves an optimal allocation problem (Sapolsky 1994). Energy resources are diverted to muscular and immediate immune functions and other short-term (stress emergency) functions, at a cost to long-term functions of growth, development, and building immunity. Under normal conditions of temporary stress, there would be little effect on health. Indeed, there may be brief enhancement and directed trafficking of immune (Dhabbar and McEwen 2001) and cognitive function. Persistent stress and associated hyper- or hypo-cortisolemia, however, is posited to result in pathological immunosuppression, depletion of energy reserves, and damage to or inhibition of neurogenesis in the hippocampus and other parts of the brain (e.g., Santarelli et al. 2003; Sheline, Gado, and Kraemer 2003). This perspective highlights the problems with a stress response system that evolved to cope with short-term emergencies. The chronic stress produced by modern human social environments – or those of other primates with complex relationships – may present novel challenges that the system is not designed to handle, hence potentially resulting in maladaptive pathology (Sapolsky 1994).

The strict version of the novelty hypothesis, however, is difficult to reconcile with the long evolutionary histories of complex sociality in primates, and especially humans, accompanied by dramatic changes in the brain. Why, given all the extensive modifications of the human brain, would selection not have weeded out this apparent big mistake? Modern human environments have many novelties that elicit stress response, but social challenges in general seem to have a much more ancient evolutionary depth, and may be a key selective pressure for the large human brain (Alexander 1989; Flinn 2006a). One possibility is that the demands of preparing for potential dangers are an unavoidable costly insurance, akin to expensive febrile response to pathogens that are usually benign – the 'smoke-detector' principle (Nesse and Young 2000). The idea is that, although physiological stress response to social challenges is costly, and most often wasteful, it may have helped our ancestors cope with rare and unpredictable serious conflicts often enough to be maintained by selection. The benefit/cost ratio could be improved by fine-tuning stress mechanisms in response to environmental conditions during ontogeny. A complementary approach to the mismatch hypothesis suggests that the neuroendocrine stress response may guide adaptive neural reorganization, such as enhancing predator detection and avoidance mechanisms (Buwalda et al. 2005; Dal Zatto et al. 2003; LeDoux 2000; Meaney 2001; Wiedenmayer 2004). The neurological effects of the stress response may both underlie adaptation to short-term contingencies and guide long-term ontogenetic adjustments of behavioural strategies (Flinn 2006b).

If physiological stress response promotes adaptive modification of neural circuits in the limbic and higher associative centres that function to solve psychosocial problems (Huether et al. 1999), then the paradox of psychosocial stress would be partly resolved. Temporary elevations of cortisol in response to social challenges could have advantageous developmental effects involving synaptogenesis and neural reorganization (Buchanan and Lovallo 2001; Huether 1996, 1998) if such changes are useful and necessary for coping with the demands of an unpredictable and dynamic social environment. Elevating stress hormones in response to social challenges makes evolutionary sense if it enhances specific acute mental functions and helps guide cortical remodeling of 'developmental exuberance' (Innocenti and Price 2005; Sur and Rubenstein 2005). Alloparental care, particularly comfort and advice, may be important for this developmental process.

Ontogeny of Stress Response to Psychosocial Stimuli: The Dominica Study

Assessment of relationships among psychosocial stressors, hormonal stress response, and health is complex, requiring (a) longitudinal monitoring of social environment, emotional states, hormone levels, immune measures, and health, (b) control of extraneous effects from physical activity, circadian rhythms, and food consumption, (c) knowledge of individual differences in temperament, experience, and perception, and (d) awareness of specific social and cultural contexts. Multi-disciplinary research that integrates human biology, psychology, and ethnography is particularly well suited to these demands (Bogin 1999; Panter-Brick 1998; Werner 1985). Physiological and medical assessment in concert with ethnography and co-residence with children and their families in anthropological study populations can provide intimate, prospective, longitudinal, naturalistic information that is not feasible to collect in clinical studies. For the past twenty years (1988–present) we have conducted such research with the help of many colleagues and students and the extraordinary cooperation of a wonderful study population.

The Study Village

'Bwa Mawego' is a rural community located on the east coast of Dominica. About 500 residents live in 160 structures/households that are loosely clumped into five 'hamlets' or neighbourhoods. The population is of mixed African, Carib, and European descent. The community is isolated because it sits at the dead-end of a rough road. Part-time residence is common, with many individuals emigrating for temporary work to other parts of Dominica, other Caribbean islands, the United States, the United Kingdom, or Canada. Most residents cultivate bananas and/or bay leaves as cash crops; and plantains, dasheen, and a variety of fruits and vegetables as subsistence crops. Fish are caught by free diving with spear guns and using lines and nets from small boats (hand-built wooden 'canoes' of Carib design). Land is communally 'owned' by kin groups, but parcelled for long-term individual use.

Most village houses are strung closely together along roads and tracks. Older homes are constructed of wooden planks and shingles hewn by hand from local forest trees; concrete block and galvanised roofing are more popular today. Most houses have one or two sleeping rooms, with the kitchen and toilet as outbuildings. Children usually sleep together on foam or rag mats. Wealthier households typically have 'parlours' with sitting furniture. Electricity became available in 1988; during the summer of 1995 about 70 per cent of homes had 'current', 41 per cent had telephones, 11 per cent had refrigerators, and 7 per cent had televisions. Water is obtained from streams, spring catchments, and run-off from roofs; public piped water became available in June 1999, but few households are connected.

The community of Bwa Mawego is appropriate for the study of relations between a child's social environment and physiological stress response for the following reasons: (1) there is substantial variability among individuals in the factors under study (family environments, social challenges, and stress response), (2) the village and housing are relatively open, hence behaviour is easily observable, (3) kin tend to reside locally, (4) the number of economic variables is reduced relative to urban areas, (5) the language and culture are familiar to the investigator, (6) there are useful medical records, and (7) local residents welcome the research and are most helpful.

The study involves 282 children and their caregivers residing in 84 households. This is a nearly complete sample (> 98 per cent) of all children living in four of the five village hamlets during the period of fieldwork. Of these, 48 children in 18 families were co-resident with a stepfather during some period of the research.

Methods and Field Techniques

In this study, sequential longitudinal monitoring was used to identify associations among psycho-social stress, health, and alloparental care among stepchildren. Data analyses examined both long term (ten years) and short term (day-to-day, hour-by-hour) associations among cortisol levels, family composition, socioeconomic conditions, behavioural activities, events, temperament, growth, medical history, immune measures, and illness. Saliva is collected from children by members of the research team at least twice a day, wherever the children happen to be (usually at their household). This direct collection and observation procedure avoids errors that occur with at-home self- or parent-collection and report protocols. Access to pharmaceuticals is rare, so extraneous effects of medications (such as aspirin on cortisol levels) are very limited. The large sample size of cortisol measures for each child (>100 samples for most children) in a variety of naturalistic contexts provides a much more extensive and reliable picture of hypothalamic-pituitary-adrenal (HPA) stress response than small sample designs.

Data analyses examine both long term (10+ years) and short term (day-to-day, hour-by-hour) associations among cortisol levels, family composition, socioeconomic conditions, behavioural activities, events, temperament, growth, medical history, immune measures, and illness. *Physiological stress response* is assessed by radioimmuno-assay (RIA) of cortisol levels in saliva. Analyses include mean values, variation, and day-to-day and hour-by-hour profiles of standardized (circadian time controlled z-scores by 5-minute intervals from wake-up time) cortisol data (Flinn 1999). *Family composition* is assessed by age, sex, genealogical relationship, and number of individuals in the household. *Care giving* is assessed by (a) observed frequencies and types of behavioural interaction, (b) informant ratings of care giving that children received, and (c) informant interviews. Here we use a dichotomous (above median, below median) composite measure of alloparental care giving. *Immune response* is assessed by turbidimetric immunoassay of secretory-immunoglobulin A from saliva; however, relatively few samples have been assayed (N=212), and interpretation is uncertain, so inferences are preliminary. *Health* is assessed by (a) observed type, frequency, and severity of medical problems (diarrhea, influenza, common cold, asthma, abrasions, rashes, etc.; most of the morbidity data analysed here are from the period 1989–94), (b) informant (parents, teachers, neighbours) ratings, (c) medical records, (d) growth (standard anthropometric measures, including height, weight, and skinfolds) and fluctuating asymmetry patterns (Flinn et al. 1999) and (e) physical examination by a medical doctor. The primary measure of health used here is *percentage of days ill*, the proportion of days that a child was observed (directly by researchers) with common benign temporary infectious disease (89 per cent were common-cold upper respiratory tract infections with nasal discharge, cough, or myalgia – e.g., rhinovirus, adenovirus, parainfluenza, and influenza; 6 per cent were diarrhoeal; 5 per cent were miscellaneous indeterminate – e.g., febrile without other symptoms). *Daily activities* and *emotional states* are assessed from (a) caretaker and child self-report questionnaires, and (b) systematic behavioural observation (focal follow and instantaneous scan sampling). Multiple sources of information are cross-checked to assess reliability (Bernard et al. 1984).

In the following section I briefly review some of the results from this study that may provide useful insights into the ontogeny of stress response to psycho-social challenges.

Cortisol Response to Naturally Occurring Social Challenges

Our analyses of naturally occurring stressors in children's lives in Bwa Mawego indicate that social challenges are important stressors, with the emphasis upon the family environment as both a primary source and mediator of stressful stimuli (Flinn and England 1995, 1997, 2003; Turner et al. 1995). Temporary moderate increases in cortisol are associated with common activities such as eating meals, active play (e.g., cricket), and hard work (e.g., carrying loads of wood to bay oil stills) among healthy children. These moderate stressors – 'arousers' might be a more appropriate term – usually have rapid attenuation, with cortisol levels diminished to normal within an hour or two (some stressors have characteristic temporal 'signatures' of cortisol level and duration).

High-stress events (cortisol increases from 100 per cent to 2000 per cent), however, most commonly involved trauma from family conflict or change (Flinn and England 2003; Flinn et al. 1996). Punishment, quarrelling, and residence change substantially increased cortisol levels, whereas calm, affectionate contact was associated with diminished (–10 per cent to –50 per cent) cortisol levels. Of all the cortisol values that were more than two standard deviations above mean levels (i.e., indicative of substantial stress), 19 per cent were temporally associated with traumatic family events (residence change of child or parent/caretaker, punishment, 'shame', serious quarrelling, and/or fighting) within a twenty-four-hour period – for comparison, 12 per cent were associated with minor family conflicts, 9 per cent with peer conflicts or school problems, 8 per cent with illness, and 6 per cent with physical exertion, the next highest categories; 43 per cent had no recorded abnormal event. In addition, 42 per cent of traumatic family events were temporally associated with substantially elevated cortisol (i.e., at least one of the saliva samples collected within twenty-four hours was > 2 SD above mean levels) – other consistent predictors of elevated cortisol included illness with fever and high profile competitive sports events. Chronic elevations of cortisol levels may also occur, but are more difficult to assess quantitatively.

There was considerable variability among children in cortisol response to family disturbances. Not all individuals had detectable changes in cortisol levels associated with family trauma. Some children had significantly elevated cortisol levels during some episodes of family trauma but not during others. Cortisol response is not a simple or uniform phenomenon. Numerous factors, including preceding events, habituation, specific individual histories, context, and temperament, might affect how children respond to particular situations.

Nonetheless, traumatic family events and social self-conscious emotions such as guilt and shame (Flinn 2005) were associated with elevated cortisol levels for all ages of children more than any other factor that we examined. These results suggest that family interactions were a critical psychosocial stressor in most children's lives, although the fact that the sample was biased towards collection during periods of relatively intense family interaction (early morning and late afternoon) may have exaggerated this association.

Children residing in bi-parental, single mother with kin, and grandparental households have moderate cortisol levels (Figure 13.1), with a higher proportion of elevations occurring in the context of positive affect situations such as competitive play, physical work, and excitement regarding novel situations. Comparison of mean cortisol levels of stepchildren with those of their half-siblings living in the same household (their mutual mother's co-resident spouse is their stepfather and genetic father, respectively) indicates a similar pattern of elevated cortisol for stepchildren (Figure 13.2).

Although elevated cortisol levels are associated with traumatic events such as family conflict, long-term stress may result in diminished cortisol response. In some cases, chronically stressed children had blunted response to physical activities that

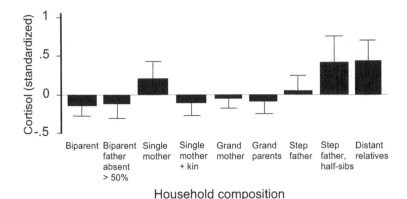

Figure 13.1. Household composition and average cortisol (time standardized) levels of children. Vertical lines represent 95% confidence intervals (±SE x 1.97). Figure adapted from Flinn 1999.

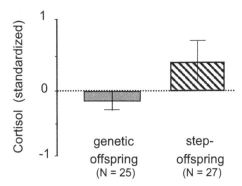

Figure 13.2. Average cortisol levels of children residing with both genetic parents compared with cortisol levels of their half-siblings in the same households who are stepchildren of one of the parents. Vertical lines represent 95% confidence intervals. Figure adapted from Flinn 2006b.

normally evoked cortisol elevation. Comparison of cortisol levels during 'non-stressful' periods (no reported or observed crying, punishment, anxiety, residence change, family conflict, or health problem during the twenty-four-hour period before saliva collection) indicates a striking reduction and, in many cases, reversal of the family environment–stress association (Flinn and England 2003). Chronically stressed children sometimes had subnormal cortisol levels when they were not in stressful situations. For example, cortisol levels immediately after school (walking home from school) and during non-competitive play were lower among some chronically stressed children (cf. Long, Ungpakorn, and Harrison 1993). Some chronically stressed children appeared socially 'tough' or withdrawn and exhibited little or no arousal to the novelty of the first few days of the saliva collection procedure. These sub-normal profiles may be similar in some respects to those of individuals with post-traumatic stress disorder (e.g., Yehuda et al. 2005).

Although elevated cortisol levels in children are usually associated with negative affect, events that involve excitement and positive affect also stimulate the stress response (Flinn 2006c). For example, cortisol levels on the day before Christmas were more than one standard deviation above normal, with some of the children from two-parent households and those having the most positive expectations exhibiting the highest cortisol. Cortisol response appears sensitive to social challenges with different affective states. Other studies further suggest that the cognitive effects of cortisol may vary with affective states, such as perceived social support (Ahnert et al. 2004; Quas et al. 2004).

There are some age and sex differences in cortisol profiles, but it is difficult to assess the extent to which this is a consequence of neurological differences (e.g., Butler et al. 2005), physical maturation processes, or the different social environments experienced, for example, during adolescence as compared with early childhood (Flinn et al 1996; Geary and Flinn 2002). For instance, young adult women have a higher incidence of depression and associated abnormal cortisol profiles than children or young men in this community.

The emerging picture of HPA stress response in naturalistic context from the Dominica study is one of sensitivity to social challenges (Flinn 2006b), consistent with clinical and experimental studies. The results further suggest that family environments are an especially important source and mediator of stressful social challenges for children. Children from difficult family environments usually have higher average cortisol levels because they have a higher frequency of stressful events, and they may ruminate trying to solve their difficult social problems. This focus of stress response on family issues unfortunately may leave fewer resources available for coping with other stressors such as school and peer relationships. In brief, elevating cortisol is not so much the problem as is what cortisol is elevated for. In the next section data on the longitudinal effects of early traumatic experiences are examined to assess the domain-specificity of changes in stress response.

Ontogeny: The Early Trauma → HPA Dysfunction Hypothesis

Early experiences can have profound and permanent effects on stress response. Exposure to pre-natal maternal stress, or prolonged separation from mothers in rodents and non-human primates, can result in life-long changes in HPA stress response (Meaney 2001; Suomi 1997, 2005; cf. Levine 2005). Research on the developmental pathways has targeted the homeostatic mechanisms of the HPA system, which appear sensitive to exposure to high levels of glucocorticoids during ontogeny. Glucocorticoid receptors in the hippocampus that are part of the negative feedback loop regulating release of corticotropin-releasing hormone (CRH) and adrenocorticotropic hormone (ACTH) can be damaged by the neurotoxic levels of cortisol associated with traumatic events (Sapolsky 1992, 2003, 2005). Hence early trauma is posited to result in permanent HPA dysregulation and hypercortisolemia, with consequent deleterious effects on the hippocampus, thymus, and other key neural, metabolic, and immune system components (Mirescu et al. 2004). These effects have additional consequences resulting from high density of glucocorticoid receptors in the pre-frontal cortex in primates (De Kloet et al. 1999; Patel et al. 2000).

Children in the Bwa Mawego study who were exposed to the stress of hurricanes and political upheavals during infancy or *in utero* do not have any apparent differences in cortisol profiles in comparison with children who were not exposed to such stressors. Children exposed to the stress of parental divorce, death, or abuse (hereafter 'early family trauma' or EFT), however, have significantly higher cortisol (Figure 13.3a) and higher morbidity (Figure 13.3b) levels at age ten than other children. Based on analogy with the non-human research, two key factors could be involved: (1) diminished hippocampal glucocorticoid receptor functioning, resulting in less effective negative feedback regulation of cortisol levels; and (2) enhanced sensitivity to perceived social threats. Children usually elevate cortisol in response to strenuous physical activity, but rapidly return to normal levels (see example in Figure 13.4). If

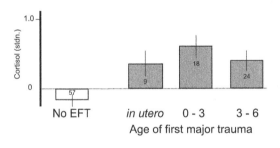

Figure 13.3a. Children exposed to early family trauma in utero or post-natal have higher average cortisol levels at age ten than children who were not exposed to early trauma.

Figure 13.3b. Children exposed to early trauma in utero or post-natal have higher average morbidity levels than children who were not exposed to early trauma (no ET). Sample sizes (# of children) are in bars. Vertical lines represent 95% confidence intervals. Figure adapted from Flinn 2006b.

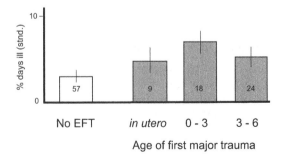

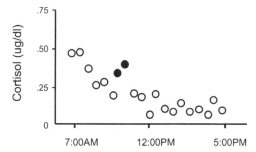

Figure 13.4. Ten-hour cortisol profile of a twelve-year-old boy. Note elevation of cortisol levels @ 10:00–10:30 AM when he was helping his father carry wood. Also note typical circadian pattern of cortisol (controlled for by standardised time since awakening Z-scores in other figures in this chapter). Figure adapted from Flinn and England 2003.

EFT has affected the negative feedback loop, then recovery to normal cortisol levels would be slower. Contrary to this damaged feedback loop hypothesis, resumption of normal cortisol levels after physical stressors is similar regardless of early experience of family trauma (Flinn 2006b). Cortisol profiles following social stressors, however, indicate that EFT children sustain elevated cortisol levels longer than non-EFT children (Flinn 2006b).

The enhanced HPA stress response of children in this community that were exposed to EFT appears primarily focused on social challenges, suggesting that the ontogenetic effects of early trauma on stress response may be domain-specific and even context-specific. These results are consistent with studies of the effects of social defeat with non-human models (e.g., Kaiser and Sachser 2005). In the following section we examine the potentially mediating effects of close alloparental relationships on the stress response of stepchildren, most of whom experienced EFT.

Alloparental Care and Stepchild Stress and Health

Comparative analysis of the patterns of stress response for stepchildren in the previous two sections indicate that early family trauma is associated with higher cortisol levels among children in this community, particularly in response to unpredictable social challenges (see also Flinn 2006b). The different cortisol response patterns to social and physical stressors suggest that domain-specific mechanisms, possibly in the limbic system, have been affected by EFT. In this section we examine whether close relationships with alloparents, such as grandmothers residing in close proximity, during early childhood are associated with individual differences among stepchildren in several outcome measures. The general hypothesis is that alloparental care reduces psychosocial stress for stepchildren. The potential negative effects of the stepfamily environment on child development are predicted to be moderated by alloparental care, as measured by cortisol levels, growth, and morbidity. This is a risky hypothesis for several reasons. Perhaps most importantly, children who have endured the most difficult family home environments may be most likely to seek outside care. Here we do not evaluate or control for such differences among stepchildren.

Analyses of data indicate that stepchildren who have close relationships with alloparents (high alloparental care) have lower cortisol (Figure 13.5a), lower morbidity (Figure 5b), and higher growth percentiles (Figure 5c) than stepchildren with low alloparental care. Stepchildren that have high alloparental care do not have lower average fluctuating asymmetry (Figure 5d) or lower gastrointestinal parasite loads (Figure 5e) than stepchildren with low alloparental care.

These results are generally consistent with the hypothesis that alloparents make important material (e.g., providing meals) and psychological contributions to stepchild well-being in this population. From these analyses it is not possible to determine the extent to which alloparents help stepchildren develop social competencies, nor the relations between social competencies and health outcome measures. It is our general impression, however, from watching interactions between children and

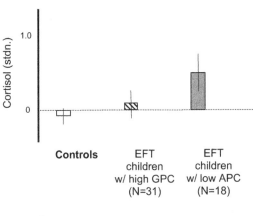

Figure 13.5a. APC and cortisol among stepchildren.

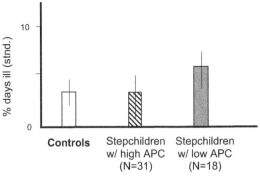

Figure 13.5b. APC and morbidity (per cent days ill) among stepchildren.

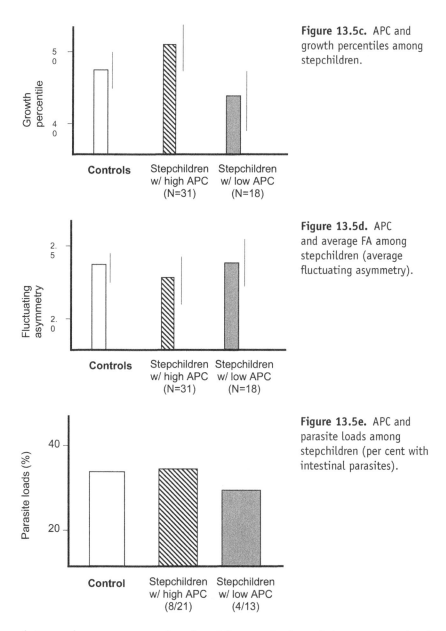

Figure 13.5c. APC and growth percentiles among stepchildren.

Figure 13.5d. APC and average FA among stepchildren (average fluctuating asymmetry).

Figure 13.5e. APC and parasite loads among stepchildren (per cent with intestinal parasites).

their grandparents, aunts and uncles, siblings, and other relatives over two decades that such relationships are of great importance for the development of emotional regulation, social skills, and self-confidence, especially for children in difficult family environments.

Conclusions

Alloparental care appears to be a significant mediator of HPA stress response and associated morbidity among stepchildren in the study community. Maternal grandmothers are especially important alloparents, although a variety of other kin (e.g., aunts, siblings, grandfathers) may also contribute, and in special cases, may be primary caregivers. These results are likely to be specific to the context of the kin networks of this community, and are likely to be contingent upon the specific patterns of kinship, although maternal grandparent–grandchild relationships appear to be broadly important cross-culturally (Lahdenperä et al. 2004; Sear et al. 2000). These results are consistent with the hypotheses that the importance of alloparents in human evolution may involve their role as providers of social information (e.g., emotional comfort, social competencies, traditions – see Coe 2003) in addition to providing calories and protection (Alexander 1974; Hawkes 2003; Hrdy 2005).

Returning to the paradox of why natural selection favoured sensitivity of stress response to social stimuli in the human child, several points emerge. Human childhood is a life-history stage that appears necessary and useful for acquiring the information and practice to build and refine mental algorithms critical for negotiating the social coalitions that are key to success in our species. Mastering the social environment presents special challenges for the human child. Results from the Dominica study indicate that family environment is a primary source and mediator of stressful events in a child's world. The sensitivity of stress physiology to the social environment may facilitate adaptive responses to this most salient and dynamic puzzle (Flinn 2006b).

Coping with social challenges, however, can have significant health consequences, ranging from dysregulation of emotional control and increased risk of psychopathology (Gilbert 2001, 2005; Nesse 1999) to broader health issues associated with social and economic disparities (Barker 1998; Dressler et al. 2005; Marmot 2004; Marmot and Wilkinson 1999). The potential for intergenerational cycles that perpetuate social relationships promoting stress and poor health are of particular concern (Belsky 2005; Belsky et al. 2005; Fleming et al. 2002; Francis et al. 1999; Maestripieri et al. 2005).

We are still far from identifying the specific connections from family environment, to stress response, to the ontogenetic plasticity of components of the limbic system and pre-frontal cortex that are involved with the acquisition of social competencies. An evolutionary developmental perspective can be useful for understanding this critical aspect of a child's world by integrating knowledge of physiological causes with the logic of adaptive design by natural selection. It reminds us that our biology and psychology have been profoundly affected by our evolutionary history as fundamentally social creatures.

References

Ahnert, L., Gunnar, M.R., Lamb, M.E., and Barthel, M., 2004. Transition to child care: associations with infant-mother attachment, negative emotion, and cortisol elevations. *Child Development* 75(3), 639–50.

Alexander, R.D., 1974. The evolution of social behavior. *Annual Review of Ecology and Systematics* 5, 325–83.

———— 1989. Evolution of the human psyche. In P. Mellars and C. Stringer, eds., *The Human Revolution: Behavioural and Biological Perspectives on the Origins of Modern Humans.* Princeton: Princeton University Press, 455–513

———— 1990. Epigenetic rules and Darwinian algorithms: the adaptive study of learning and development. *Ethology and Sociobiology* 11(3), 1–63.

Aureli, F., and Schaffner, C., 2002. Relationship assessment through emotional mediation. *Behaviour* 139, 393–420.

Barker, D.J., 1998. *In utero* programming of chronic disease. *Clinical Science* 95, 115–28.

Belsky, J., 2005. The developmental and evolutionary psychology of intergenerational transmission of attachment. In C.S. Carter, L. Ahnert, K.E. Grossmann, S.B. Hrdy, M.E. Lamb, S.W. Porges and N. Sachser, eds., *Attachment and Bonding: A New Synthesis.* Dahlem Workshop Report 92. Cambridge, MA: MIT Press.

Belsky, J., Jaffee, S.R., Sligo, J., Woodward, L., and Silva, P.A., 2005. Intergenerational transmission of warm-sensitive-stimulating parenting: a prospective study of mothers and fathers of 3-year-olds. *Child Development* 76(2), 384–96.

Bernard, H.R., Killworth, P.D., Kronenfeld, D., and Sailer, L., 1984. The problem of informant accuracy: the validity of retrospective data. *Annual Review of Anthropology* 13, 495–517.

Beylin, A.V., and Shors, T.J., 2003. Glucocorticoids are necessary for enhancing the acquisition of associative memories after acute stressful experience. *Hormones and Behavior* 43, 1124–31.

Bogin, B., 1999. *Patterns of Human Growth,* Second Edition. Cambridge: Cambridge University Press.

Buchanan, T.W., and Lovallo, W.R., 2001. Enhanced memory for emotional material following stress-level cortisol treatment in humans. *Psychoneuroendocrinology 26,* 307–17.

Butler, T., Pan, H., Epstein, J., Protopopescu, X., Tuescher, O., Goldstein, M., Cloitre, M., Yang, Y., Phelps, E., Gorman, J., Ledoux, J.E., Stern, E., and Silbersweig, D., 2005. Fear-related activity in subgenual anterior cingulate differs between men and women. *Neuroreport* 16(11), 1233–36.

Buwalda, B., Kole, M.H.P., Veenema, A.H., Huininga, M., De Boer, S.F., Korte, S.M., and Koolhas, J.M., 2005. Long term effects of social stress on brain and behavior: a focus on hippocampal functioning. *Neuroscience and Biobehavioral Reviews* 29, 83–97.

Coe, K., 2003. *The Ancestress Hypothesis: Visual Art as Adaptation.* New Brunswick: Rutgers University Press.

Daly, M., and Wilson, M., 1988a. Evolutionary social psychology and family homicide. *Science* 242, 519–24.

———— 1988b. *Homicide*. Hawthorne: Aldine de Gruyter.

———— 1995. Discriminative parental solicitude and the relevance of evolutionary models to the analysis of motivational systems. In M.S. Gazzaniga, ed., *The Cognitive Neurosciences*. Cambridge: MIT Press, 1269–86.

Dal Zatto, S., Marti, O., and Armario, A., 2003. Glucocorticoids are involved in the long-term effects of a single immobilization stress on the hypothalamic-pituitary-adrenal axis. *Psychoneuroendocrinology* 28, 992–1009.

De Kloet, E.R., Sibug, R.M., Helmerhorst, F.M., and Schmidt, M., 2005. Stress, genes, and the mechanism for programming the brain for later life. *Neuroscience and Biobehavioral Reviews* 29, 271–81.

Dhabbar, F.S. and McEwen, B.S., 2001. Bidirectional effects of stress and glucocorticoid hormones on immune function: possible explanations for paradoxical observations. In R. Ader, D.L. Felten, and N. Cohen, eds., *Psychoneuroendocrinology, Vol. 1*, Third Edition. San Diego: Academic Press, 301–38.

Dickerson, S.S., and Kemeny, M.E., 2004. Acute stressors and cortisol responses: a theoretical integration and synthesis of laboratory research. *Psychological Bulletin* 130(3), 355–91.

Dressler, W.W., Oths, K.S., and Gravely, C.C., 2005. Race and ethnicity in public health research: models to explain health disparities. *Annual Review of Anthropology* 34 (12), 231–52.

Dunn, J., 2004. Understanding children's family worlds: family transitions and children's outcome. *Merrill-Palmer Quarterly* 50(3), 224–35.

Ellis, B.J., Bates, J.E., Dodge, K.A., Fergusson, D., Horwood, J., Pettit, G.S., and Woodward, L., 2003. Does father absence place daughters at special risk for early sexual activity and teenage pregnancy? *Child Development* 74(3), 801–21.

Fleming, A., Kraemer, G.W., Gonzalez, A., Lovic, V., Rees, S., and Melo, A., 2002. Mothering begets mothering: the transmission of behavior and its neurobiology across generations. *Pharmacology, Biochemistry and Behavior* 73, 61–75.

Flinn, M.V., 1988a. Step and genetic parent/offspring relationships in a Caribbean village. *Ethology and Sociobiology, 9(3)*, 1-34.

———— 1988b. Parent-offspring interactions in a Caribbean village: daughter guarding. In L. Betzig, M. Borgerhoff Mulder, and P. Turke, eds., *Human Reproductive Behaviour*. Cambridge: Cambridge University Press, 189–200.

————1989. Household composition and female reproductive strategies. In A. Rasa, C. Vogel and E. Voland, eds., *The Sociobiology of Sexual and Reproductive Strategies*. London: Chapman and Hall, 206–33.

———— 1992. Paternal care in a Caribbean village. In B. Hewlett, ed., *Father-child Relations: Cultural and Biosocial Contexts*. Hawthorne, NY: Aldine, 57–84.

———— 1999. Family environment, stress, and health during childhood. In C. Panter-Brick and C. Worthman, eds., *Hormones, Health, and Behaviour*. Cambridge: Cambridge University Press, 105–38.

———— 2005. Temper tantrums: display or dysfunction? *American Journal of Human Biology* 16, 265.

——— 2006a. Cross-cultural universals and variations: the evolutionary paradox of informational novelty. *Psychological Inquiry* 17(2), 118–23.

——— 2006b. Ontogeny and evolution of glucocorticoid stress response in the human child. *Developmental Review* 17(2), 138–74.

——— 2006c. Evolution of stress response to social-evaluative threat. In R. Dunbar and L. Barrett, eds., *Oxford Handbook of Evolutionary Psychology.* Oxford: Oxford University Press, 272–96.

Flinn, M.V., and Alexander, R.D., 2007. Runaway social selection. In S.W. Gangestad and J.A. Simpson, eds., *The Evolution of Mind.* New York: Guilford Press, 249 –55.

Flinn, M.V., and England, B.G., 1995. Family environment and childhood stress. *Current Anthropology* 36(5), 854–66.

——— 1997. Social economics of childhood glucocorticoid stress response and health. *American Journal of Physical Anthropology* 102, 33–53.

——— 2003. Childhood stress: endocrine and immune responses to psychosocial events. In J.M. Wilce, ed., *Social and Cultural Lives of Immune Systems.* London: Routledge, 107–47.

Flinn, M.V., Leone, D.V., and Quinlan, R., 1999. Growth and fluctuating asymmetry of stepchildren. *Evolution and Human Behavior* 20(6), 465–80.

Flinn, M.V., Quinlan, R., Turner, M.T., Decker, S.D., and England, B.G., 1996. Male-female differences in effects of parental absence on glucocorticoid stress response. *Human Nature* 7(2), 125–62.

Francis, D.D., Diorio, J., Liu, D., and Meaney, M.J., 1999. Nongenomic transmission across generations of maternal behavior and stress responses in the rat. *Science* 286, 1155–58.

Geary, D.C., and Flinn, M.V., 2001. Evolution of human parental behavior and the human family. *Parenting: Science and Practice* 1(1 and 2), 5–61.

——— 2002. Sex differences in behavioral and hormonal response to social threat. *Psychological Review* 109(4), 745–50.

Gilbert, P., 2001. Evolutionary approaches to psychopathology: the role of natural defences. *Australian and New Zealand Journal of Psychiatry* 35(1), 17–27.

——— 2005. Social mentalities: a biopsychosocial and evolutionary approach to social relationships. In M.W. Baldwin, ed., *Interpersonal Cognition.* New York: Guilford Press, 299–333.

Hawkes, K., 2003. Grandmothers and the evolution of human longevity. *American Journal of Human Biology* 15, 380–400.

Heim, C., Newport, D.J., Heit, S., Graham, Y.P., Wilcox, M., Bonsall, R., Miller, A.H., and Nemeroff, C.B., 2000. Pituitary-adrenal and autonomic responses to stress in women after sexual and physical abuse in childhood. *Journal of the American Medical Association* 284(5), 592–97.

Hetherington, E.M., 2003a. Intimate pathways: changing patterns in close personal relationships across time. *Family Relations: Interdisciplinary Journal of Applied Family Studies* 52(4), 318–31.

——— 2003b. Social support and the adjustment of children in divorced and remarried families. *Childhood: A Global Journal of Child Research* 10(2), 217–36.

Hewlett, B.S., and Lamb, M.E., eds, 2005. *Hunter-gatherer Childhoods*. New Brunswick, NJ: AldineTransaction.

Hrdy, S.B., 2005. Evolutionary context of human development: the cooperative breeding model. In C.S. Carter and L. Ahnert, eds., *Attachment and Bonding: A New Synthesis*. Dahlem Workshop 92. Cambridge, MA: MIT Press.

Huether, G., 1996. The central adaptation syndrome: psychosocial stress as a trigger for adaptive modifications of brain structure and brain function. *Progress in Neurobiology* 48, 568–612.

———1998. Stress and the adaptive self organization of neuronal connectivity during early childhood. *International Journal of Developmental Neuroscience* 16 (3/4), 297–306.

Huether, G., Doering, S., Ruger, U., Ruther, E., and Schussler, G., 1999. The stress-reaction process and the adaptive modification and reorganization of neuronal networks. *Psychiatry Research,* 87(1), 83–95.

Hurtado, A.M., and Hill, K.R., 1992. Paternal effect on offspring survivorship among Ache and Hiwi hunter-gatherers: implications for modeling pair-bond stability. In B. Hewlett, ed., *Father-Child Relations: Cultural and Biosocial Contexts*. New York: Aldine De Gruyter, 31–55.

Innocenti, G.M., and Price, D.J., 2005. Exuberance in the development of cortical networks. *Nature Reviews Neuroscience* 6, 955–65.

Kaiser, S., and Sachser, N., 2005. The effects of prenatal social stress on behaviour: mechanisms and function. *Neuroscience and Biobehavioral Reviews* 29, 283–94.

Kirschbaum, C., and Hellhammer, D.H., 1994. Salivary cortisol in psychneuroendocrine research: recent developments and applications. *Psychoneuroendocrinology* 19, 313–33.

Kirschbaum, C., Wolf, O.T., May, M., Wippich, W., and Hellhammer, D.H., 1996. Stress- and treatment-induced elevations of cortisol levels associated with impaired declarative memory in healthy adults. *Life Sciences* 58(17), 1475–83.

Lahdenperä, M., Lummaa, V., Helle, S., Tremblay, M., and Russell, A.F., 2004. Fitness benefits of prolonged post-reproductive lifespan in women. *Nature* 428, 178–81.

Lamb, M.E., 2005. Attachments, social networks, and developmental contexts. *Human Development* 48, 108–12.

Lancaster, J.B., and Lancaster, C.S., 1987. The watershed: change in parental-investment and family-formation strategies in the course of human evolution. In J.B. Lancaster, J. Altmann, A.S. Rossi, and L.R. Sherrod, eds., *Parenting Across the Lifespan: Biosocial Dimensions*. New York: Aldine de Gruyter, 187–206.

Ledoux, J.E., 2000. Emotion circuits in the brain. *Annual Reviews Neuroscience* 23, 155–84.

——— 2003. The emotional brain, fear, and the amygdala. *Cellular and Molecular Neurobiology* 23(4–5), 727–38.

Levine, S., 2005. Developmental determinants of sensitivity and resistance to stress. *Psychoneuroendocrinology* 30, 939–46.

Long, B., Ungpakorn, G., and Harrison, G.A., 1993. Home-school differences in stress hormone levels in a group of Oxford primary school children. *Journal of Biosocial Sciences* 25, 73–78.

Lupien, S.J., Fiocco, A., Wan, N., Maheu, F., Lord, C., Schramek, T., and Tu, M.T., 2005. Stress hormones and human memory function across the lifespan. *Psychoneuroendocrinology* 30, 225–42.

Maestripieri, D., Lindell, S.G., Ayala, A., Gold, P.W., and Higley, J.D., 2005. Neurobiological characteristics of rhesus macaque abusive mothers and their relation to social and maternal behavior. *Neuroscience and Biobehavioral Reviews* 29, 51–57.

Marmot, M., 2004. *The Status Syndrome: How Social Standing Affects our Health and Longevity.* New York: Times Books/Henry Holt.

Marmot, M., and Wilkinson, R.G., eds., 1999. *Social Determinants of Health.* Oxford: Oxford University Press.

Meaney, M.J., 2001. Maternal care, gene expression, and the transmission of individual differences in stress reactivity across generations. *Annual Review of Neuroscience* 24, 1161–92.

Mirescu, C., Peters, J.D., and Gould, E., 2004. Early life experience alters response of adult neurogenesis to stress. *Nature Neuroscience* 7(8), 841–46.

Nesse, R., 1999. Proximate and evolutionary studies of anxiety, stress and depression: synergy at the interface. *Neuroscience and Biobehavioral Reviews* 23, 895–903.

Nesse, R.M., and Young, E.A., 2000. Evolutionary origins and functions of the stress response. *Encyclopedia of Stress, Volume 2.* New York, NY: Academic press, 79–84.

Newcomer, J.W., Craft, S., Hershey, T., Askins, K., and Bardgett, M.E., 1994. Glucocorticoid-induced impairment in declarative memory performance in adult humans. *Journal of Neuroscience* 14(4), 2047–53.

Panter-Brick, C., ed., 1998. *Biosocial Perspectives on Children.* Cambridge: Cambridge University Press.

Patel, P.D., Lopez, J.F., Lyons, D.M., Burke, S., Wallace, M., and Shatzberg, A.F., 2000. Glucocorticoid and mineralocorticoid receptor mRNA expression in squirrel monkey brain. *Journal of Psychiatric Research* 34, 383–92.

Quas, J.A., Bauer, A., and Boyce, W.T., 2004. Physiological reactivity, social support, and memory in early childhood. *Child Development* 75(3), 797–814.

Quinlan, R., 2006. Gender and risk in a Caribbean community: a view from behavioral ecology. *American Anthropologist* 108(3), 469–79.

Santarelli, L., Saxe, M., Gross, C., Surget, A., Battaglia, F., Dulawa, S., Weistaub, N., Lee, J., Duman, R., Arancio, O., Belzung, C., and Hen, R., 2003. Requirement of hippocampal neurogenesis for the behavioral effects of antidepressants. *Science* 301, 805–9.

Sapolsky, R.M., 1992. *Stress, the Aging Brain, and the Mechanisms of Neuron Death.* Cambridge, MA: MIT Press.

———— 1994. *Why Zebras Don't Get Ulcers.* New York: W.H. Freeman and Co.

———— 2003. Stress and plasticity in the limbic system. *Neurochemical Research* 28(11), 1735–42.

———— 2005. The influence of social hierarchy on primate health. *Science* 308, 648–52.

Sear, R., Mace, R., and McGregor, I.A., 2000. Maternal grandmothers improve the nutritional status and survival of children in rural Gambia. *Proceedings of the Royal Society B* 267, 1641–47.

Servan-Schreiber, D., Printz, H., and Cohen, S.D., 1990. A network model of catecholamine effects: gain, signal-to-noise ratio, and behavior. *Science* 249, 892–95.

Sheline, Y.I., Gado, M.H., and Kraemer, H.C., 2003. Untreated depression and hippocampal volume loss. *American Journal of Psychiatry* 160, 1516–18.

Suomi, S.J., 1997. Long-term effects of differential early experiences on social, emotional, and physiological development in nonhuman primates. In M.S. Keshevan and R.M. Murra, eds., *Neurodevelopmental Models of Adult Psychopathology.* Cambridge: Cambridge University Press, 104–16.

———— 2005. Mother-infant attachment, peer relationships, and the development of social networks in rhesus monkeys. *Human Development* 48, 67–79.

Sur, M., and Rubenstein, J.L.R., 2005. Patterning and plasticity of the cerebral cortex. *Science* 310, 805–10.

Turner, M.T., Flinn, M.V., and England, B.G., 1995. Mother-infant glucocorticoid stress response in a rural Caribbean village. *American Journal of Physical Anthropology,* Supplement 19, 191.

Werner, E.E., 1985. Stress and protective factors in children's lives. In A.R. Nicol, ed., *Longitudinal Studies in Child Psychology and Psychiatry.* New York: John Wiley and Sons.

Wiedenmayer, C.P., 2004. Adaptations or pathologies? Long term changes in brain and behavior after a single exposure to severe threat. *Neuroscience and Biobehavioral Reviews* 28, 1–12.

Yehuda, R., Engel, S.M., Brand, S.R., Seckl, J., Marcus, S.M., and Berkowitz, G.S., 2005. Transgenerational effects of posttraumatic stress disorder in babies of mothers exposed to the World Trade Center attacks during pregnancy. *Journal of Clinical Endocrinology and Metabolism* 90(7), 4115–18.

· 14 ·

Separation Stress in Early Childhood

Harmless Side Effect of Modern Caregiving Practices or Risk Factor for Development?

Joachim Bensel

The Biological Roots of Separation – or Why Separation Hurts

John Archer (2001) asks why grief has arisen in the course of evolution. He describes grief as a human universal which already occurs in social birds and mammals when they lose a 'significant other' through death or separation. He views it as the necessary result of the evolution of attachment, another genetically based behaviour which has brought an important fitness advantage for its bearer. The primary cause of grief for a child is separation from its attachment figure. The grief of adult humans is more complex, but is built on the basic separation reaction. Social emotions like grief appear to have arisen phylogenetically from more primitive motivation systems like those responsible for pain perception (Panksepp et al. 1997). This explains the similarity in the dynamics of opiate addiction and basal brain processes which are important for social relationships. Opiate withdrawal and social deprivation show noticeable similarities.

Grief or despair characterizes the second passive phase of the typical biphasic reaction to the separation of many young animals from their mother. It is the behavioural counterpart to an initial reaction of protest, characterized by the activation of behaviours aimed at the re-establishment of contact with the mother (screaming, searching, verbal protest, etc.) that is so necessary for survival. James Robertson and John Bowlby suggested a third phase of the reaction of human infants to maternal separation: the so-called detachment phase. However, more recent investigations have not been able to confirm this (Rennen-Allhoff 1991). The first two phases are not automatic reaction responses to maternal separation, but depend on many additional variables, and there are clear-cut differences between primate species. The typical biphasic pattern of separation is shown, for example, in rhesus monkeys, chimpanzees, orang-utans and gorillas, but not in langurs and bonnet macaques (Boccia et al. 1994). In the latter, protest is not followed by despair.

The classic studies of James and Joyce Robertson show that when children aged 1.5 to 2.5 years come into foster care they do not display disturbances if the foster parents maintain accustomed daily patterns and adjust to the individual needs of the child (Rennen-Allhoff 1991). Discrete physiological and behavioural changes may, however, also arise in these cases.

The second phase of the separation reaction may be diminished by allomaternal care. In the course of his investigations of children's separation from their mother following hospitalization, Rene Spitz described an anaclitic depression that developed only in children with a good mother–child relationship prior to separation and poor substitute care. In non-human primates, a depressive reaction following the loss of the mother can also be absent if the infant is adopted by an allomother. But allomothering only succeeds when an alternative attachment to the allomother was already present before the separation. Adoption without this attachment cannot prevent the depressive reaction (Boccia et al. 1994).

The previous relationship to the lost attachment figure is a critical point for the behaviour of the abandoned individual. The titi monkey, for example, shows signs of separation distress when removed from its father but not its mother (Hennessy 1997). In this case, both adult parents are responsible for the young, and the offspring are more attached to the father.

Age

Age is an important variable in separation behaviour. Jerome Kagan (1976) presented information from several different cultures, ranging from children of the !Kung San of Botswana to children in highly urbanized Western settings. He showed that, in each of these diverse settings, children show little separation protest before the age of eight months. The incidence and intensity of protest then increase, reaching a peak early in the second year and declining thereafter. It seems that the disruptive effect of separation is governed by a universal cognitive-developmental timetable regardless of cultural settings.

Attachment Behaviour and the Stress Reaction

For over thirty years researchers have taken advantage of a peak in the activation of attachment behaviour early in the second year of childhood to construct a research tool called the 'strange situation'. Here, under controlled laboratory conditions, children endure a short separation from their mothers. The strength of the child's protest at this separation has then been used to classify apparent attachment patterns.

Mary Ainsworth initially and erroneously rated the children who showed no protest (Type A), as securely attached to their mother until it became clear that, in fact, the absence of a strong separation reaction should be interpreted as a sign of an insecure-avoidant attachment. This interpretation remained controversial for a long time, especially in light of the fact that children with more experience with child-care in day care centres protested less in the strange situation and were thus more frequently classified as insecurely attached. Centre care, especially for small children is, in social and political terms, the most controversial form of allomaternal care. It is possible that children with more childcare experience are more accustomed to a brief separation from their mother, and do not immediately respond with a strong protest.

Indications had already been obtained that, indeed, an insecure attachment be-tween mother and child was present when the strange situation produced a lack of a protest. These indications came from observations of play involving the mother and child. Mothers of insecurely attached children were less responsive and less sensitive during these interactions and were less predictable in their reactions. Decisively con-firmed attachment classifications came, however, at the beginning of the 1990s with the aid of newer methods of stress research. It was found that the seemingly unaf-fected Type A children showed a drastic rise in the stress hormone cortisol, while Type B children with secure attachments, who exhibited external forms of protestation against separation, did not show a similar internally-manifested physiological stress reaction. Type A children therefore only seem to be unaffected *externally*. Thus, for the first time it was demonstrated using physiological measurements that separation *protest* and separation *distress* were by no means identical.

At the same time, it was clear that the open expression of affect was the more healthy style of coping from a physiological perspective. Elevated cortisol levels are, in the long term, potentially detrimental since they can lead to increased hypotha-lamic-pituitary-adrenal (HPA) activity with elevated basal plasma levels of cortisol in adulthood (Breier 1989). In separation situations, therefore (for example, the transi-tion to a new caregiver situation) one should be particularly careful with those chil-dren who seem to adapt without difficulty and show no protest.

Such physiological findings cast new light upon age-dependent changes in open protest behaviour. Could it also be that infants in the first year of life suffer from sepa-ration distress, but do not always show it openly? Evidence already suggests that new-borns cry more, the less skin contact they perceive from their mother (Christensson et al. 1995), and that premature babies develop more slowly when they are stroked less often (Field et al. 1986). The absence of tactile signals from their caregiver evi-dently triggers abandonment crying (Hassenstein 2007), which can be interpreted as the first form of separation protest. Is this a non-specific protest which can lead to pacification through any person, or is this a specific wish for the maternal presence? Can a newborn even make such a distinction?

Modern infant research has been able to reveal a number of acquired abilities of the competent infant, showing that a baby can already recognize its mother right after birth via her smell, her voice and features of her face. Even for quite young infants, the particular person offering care is very important, as shown in a Japanese study which found that, at 2–4 months, infants already notice when their mother is replaced by an unknown person (Mizukami et al. 1990). In such situations infants start to scream or their forehead temperature decreases, an invisible sign of stress measurable by means of telethermography. However, not all children exhibit such symptoms, and thus the question arises: did the infants in the study who did not cry, but nonetheless were stressed, already show precursors of an alternative coping-strategy in dealing with maternal separation (in the direction of insecure-avoidant), or is it merely that a different temperament is being displayed?

Effects of Separation Distress on the Brain: Results from Animal Models

Investigations of non-human primates have also shown that there is no systematic correlation between stress vocalisation and the hormonal response of the young animal to separation (Sanchez et al. 2001). The behavioural response and the endocrine response appear to be controlled by independent neuronal mechanisms. Not only does the endocrine system respond to maternal separation, but the central nervous system also shows visible effects. In rodents, a single twenty-four-hour separation is sufficient in newborns to alter the neuroendocrine system (Sanchez et al. 2001). Repeated separations lead to a fundamental reorganisation of the neuronal circuits which play a role in the neuroendocrine regulation of stimulation and vigilance. Using a rodent model (*Octodon degus*), Braun and colleagues (2003) were able to show that, upon separation in early infancy, the normally occurring synapse selection was absent leading to an excess proportion of excitatory spine synapses. In contrast, too few of the primarily inhibitory acting shaft synapses remain, leading among other things to a noticeable motoric restlessness when the degus get older.

Early emotional experiences thus determine the basic pattern of neuronal circuitry in these animals, which then determine which behavioural and learning potentials are possible later in life. Katharina Braun sees here analogies to the induction of hyperactivity in humans and there is a connection between mother–child relationship and later hyperactivity (Carlson et al. 1995; Keown and Woodward 2002; Gomez 2002). Whether separation experiences play a role here, however, is still unclear. Maybe in humans we have to investigate not physical separation primarily but rather psychological mother–child distance which fosters different types of attachment.

Long-term effects of earlier aversive experiences can also be found in primates in central dopaminergic function. This can influence the prefrontal cognitive functions, including working memory, as well as the inhibition of certain behaviours. Normal cognitive development is disturbed, especially the systems responsible for the cessation and inhibition of ongoing behaviour, as shown in the persistent response tendencies exhibited by deprived primates.

Other investigations have been able to demonstrate additional effects on the neurochemical system and general brain activity. PET-scans show that, when separated from their mothers, rhesus monkey babies manifest a significant activation of the right frontal cortex and a deactivation of the left frontal cortex. Human infants who are especially stressed upon separation from their mother also show these hemisphere-asymmetries in their brain activity (Davidson and Fox 1989). The question remains whether these changes in brain structure are the result of an elevated cortisol response or vice versa.

Modern brain research is always finding new stress-dependent changes in brain metabolism in animal models. Thus, a recent study from Philadelphia (Hsu et al. 2003) showed that there are changes not only in cortisol levels, but in the neurotransmitter gamma-amino butyric acid (GABA), the primary inhibitory neurotransmitter in the mammalian brain that regulates the endocrine and behavioural responses to stress. Two separation episodes during early postnatal development in rat experiments were sufficient to cause long-term changes in postsynaptic GABA function and alter the subunit expression in hippocampal (dentate granule) neurons. These neurological changes were accompanied by an increased motoric activity in distress-causing situations in the adult animals.

Maternal deprivation is known to affect a number of neurotransmitter systems, including oxytocin, dopamine and serotonin (Lovic et al. 2001; Panksepp 2002; Heinz 1999). Deficits in the production of these neurotransmitters can disturb the wiring up of the developing brain and thereby fundamentally interfere with cortical maturation (Heinz 1999).

The conclusion from the results on animal models in separation distress research (Sanchez et al. 2001) is that the early childhood period is fundamental for the modulation of further behavioural, emotional, cognitive and physiological development. The effects of aversive experiences vary in different species depending on the particular developmental stage in which the separation takes place. Some of the long-term behavioural effects of these early experiences are very similar in rodent and primate models, e.g., the increase in anxiety and the deficits in social and sexual behaviour and in cognitive ability.

Where is the Threshold of Danger in Humans?

Despite all these interesting findings from animal research it remains unclear how far and above what threshold a quantitative change becomes a disease (Coe et al. 1989). But the risks are known. Cortisol for example is known to suppress the activity of the immune system, increasing the likelihood that exposure to viruses will produce illness (Reichlin 1993). During the periods of rapid brain development in humans, contact with parents prevents an excessive rise in cortisol, in order to protect the developing brain from possible detrimental effects (de Kloet et al. 1988). This parental protective factor could be interfered with in insecure attachments (Gunnar et al. 1996). The very vulnerability of anxious, insecurely attached children towards elevated cortisol values could influence neurobiological processes, which could permit the fearful and inhibited behaviour to remain a part of these children for their whole life (Gunnar et al. 1996). But it is still unclear whether the relatively mild repeated neuroendocrine stress that could be caused by childcare – to quote the most common reason for separation experience in early childhood – is sufficient to influence brain development in humans (Watamura et al. 2003; Gunnar 1998).

Significantly elevated cortisol values, which could indicate a constantly elevated distress level, can be found in a recent example of early childhood deprivation in Romanian orphans of the now defunct Ceausescu-Regime (Carlson and Earls 1997). However, such extreme aversive experiences in early childhood cannot be effectively partitioned from actual separation from the mother, with both situations simultaneously affecting development. Ultimately the Romanian children were lacking not only their mother, but also social and other developmental stimuli and emotional embedding (Gordon 2002).

Daily Separation in Day Care

One can determine the effect of maternal separation in a more controlled fashion if one observes children in everyday separation situations. In traditional societies, allomaternal care is provided by persons already known since birth – aunts, grandmothers, siblings, fathers and other trusted persons – and in familiar surroundings. In industrial nations, however, childcare is usually performed by paid, initially unknown persons who are temporarily responsible for the child; most of the times the care takes place outside the home. Most of the time, no organic growing together of an extended circle of caring persons occurs. Instead there is an abrupt shift to a completely new caregiving situation. So it is no surprise that many children – especially the under three-year-olds – respond to such abrupt changes in caregiver with a corresponding separation protest, reduced play and even an elevated susceptibility to disease. Eating, sleeping and behavioural disturbances have been observed in the former German Democratic Republic – where children were uniformly sent to day-care centres – and have necessitated reforms in the admission process for new children. Special measures have been introduced to reduce the increased burden of coping especially for 8- to 18-month-old children (Schmidt-Kolmer 1989). Several German studies showed that the elevated rate of illness of new children after starting to attend day-care centres could be reduced if the adjustment took place more slowly and with the accompaniment of the parents (Passauer and Wiedemann 1989, 1990; Laewen 1989). This shows that the elevated susceptibility to infection in the institution has a substantial psychosomatic component.

Reactions of different children to separation can be distinctly heterogeneous. In one Berlin study (Ahnert and Rickert 2000), despite the fact that the day-care centres offered exceptionally good conditions (attractively arranged rooms, small groups, a constant caregiving person), about two-thirds of the one-year-olds showed dramatic reactions on the first separation day. They cried, screamed, fussed or reacted with anger after the mothers had left the group room. Could it be that in this real-life situation, different attachment types produced differing reactions to the separation situation, much as in the laboratory test of the strange situation? Indeed, the behaviour of the securely attached children in the day-care centre was characterized by more negative emotional expression than that of the insecurely attached children. They showed their attachment behaviour significantly more frequently and for longer. Physiological stress measurements of heart activity and the cortisol level showed however – like in the strange situation – a weaker excitement than in the insecurely attached children. The latter evidently were less able to bring out their excitement in openly manifested attachment behaviour, meaning that adaptation to childcare was more difficult for these children (Ahnert and Rickert 2000; Ahnert and Lamb 2003). The fact that openly displayed protests in children during the first weeks of childcare was accompanied by a better adaptation and a better coping style was also confirmed in the investigations of Bloom-Feshbach (1988) on three-year-olds.

After having been present for several months in the day-care centre, while the expressions of protest and the heart activity of the children were again normal (Ahnert and Rickert 2000), cortisol levels following daily separations from the mother were still elevated (Ahnert and Lamb 2003). Another research group in Berlin (Ziegenhain and Wolff 2000) found that insecure-avoidant children were increasingly withdrawn and more fatigued. They were evidently still emotionally burdened even after weeks and months of being in the day care centre.

In our own observations of one- to two-year-olds in everyday separation situations in a day-care centre we were also able to establish quite different separation behaviour at arrival and departure times, even a long time after the initial period (Bensel 1992). While among the one-year-olds the majority actively sought the caregiver or began to play, some of the two-year-olds already showed resistance to separation upon their arrival in the facility (26 per cent). These children also protested more frequently against the departure of the mother in the ensuing leaving phase. Most of the children however showed no concern externally about the departure of the mother (62 per cent).

In a follow-up study, difficulties in getting involved in daily play were above all displayed in those children who upon arrival pacified themselves with automanipulations. Even more prominently than the children with open resistance to separation these children showed an increase in their cortisol level as compared to an at-home base value (Weis et al. 1999). Instead of playing in the period after the separation, they observed the group activity more. Automanipulation and passivity characterize the behaviour of children who have difficulties with separation and this is reflected in their stress physiology.

Confronted with the unmistakeable adjustment difficulties, especially for the one- to two-year-olds, many child day-care centres and childcare homes in Germany

Figures 14.1a-e.
Resistance to separation.
(a) A two-year old boy
maintains contact to his
mother with his right
hand, while he sucks
on his left index finger
(automanipulation). The
caregiver is on the right.
(b) Then he hugs his
mother and clings to her
tightly.

are working with a new model. For an initial period of six to sixteen days, the child
is accompanied by one parent, which lets the child adjust gently to the new situation and thereby gives the new caregiving person the opportunity to prove herself as
a new secure base whom the child can trust (Laewen et al. 2000). If this succeeds,
adjustment reactions of the children are not completely eliminated, but they do not
have negative effects on the attachment quality between mother and child (Ahnert
and Lamb 2003).

Three People Take Part in the Separation Reaction

The intensity and duration of separation distress depend to a large extent upon the
three persons involved in the separation process – child, mother and caregiver – and
upon their relationships with each other.

(c) The mother tries to put down the struggling boy. (d) The caregiver has taken the boy and holds him firmly on his arm. (e) The boy has returned to his mother, who is holding his upper arms.

The Contribution of the Child

Children respond differently to separations, and some infants show minimal symptoms as a result of a separation. These resilient individuals are described as active, cuddly, good-natured and easy to deal with. Their behaviour provokes warm-hearted reactions in parents and other caretakers (Stein and Call 2001). It is quite different for emotionally vulnerable or socially shy (behaviourally inhibited) children, whose sense of security is shaken by relatively mild separation experiences (Barrett 1997).

Temperament influences the physiological reaction to separation. Here an important investigation was made by Megan Gunnar (1998). Thirteen-month-old infants were left in the laboratory for thirty minutes, alone with a babysitter. Those infants who soon became quiet, ceased playing, did not cry, and gave the impression that they were about to fall asleep showed the highest increase in cortisol. Those who gained the attention of the babysitter through positive or negative behaviour, gave her a toy, sat on her lap or cried showed no increase in cortisol. In another investigation by Gunnar a fearful temperament was found to be a significant factor in being able to predict a stress reaction to separation from the mother (Gunnar et al. 1996).

The temperament of the child plays a role which should not be underestimated in attempting to achieve a successful adaptation. First, the temperament of the child determines how easily or badly it deals with the separation situation. Secondly, the willingness of the caregiver to support the child in coping with the burden depends on the personality of the child.

It is easiest for children with a so-called 'easy' temperament. They are active, adaptable, approachable, and have an even-tempered attitude. Such children are also favoured on the part of the caregiver. The 'difficult' ones, as well as the 'active-expressive' toddlers, because of their moodiness and very intensive reaction tendencies, are unapproachable and not necessarily popular, but at least they draw to themselves the attention of the caregiver, who must attempt to maintain or restore harmony in the group.

Those with the greatest difficulty in the group are the shy children, those who are not very active and approachable and tend to withdraw in a new situation. Because they are quiet and seem to require no apparent external regulation they run the greatest risk of being overlooked and not receiving the dose of security and attention from the caregiver which they need just as urgently as the others.

Animal experiments and twin studies confirm a genetic as well as an experiential component in the individual variability of coping and of self-recovery after aversive experiences in early childhood. Sensitive, responsive and reactive parental rearing styles and sustainable designed transitions to allomaternal caregiving can reduce the genetically elevated risk of endangered development (Sanchez et al. 2001).

The Contribution of the Mother

The contribution of the mother in dealing with separation has many aspects. With her sensitivity she lays the crucial foundation for the attachment security of her child, which in turn affects its separation reactions. She is also the one who can make possible (or not) via the quality of the initial period the secure entry of the child into the new caregiving situation. Without the 'inner consent' of the mother the adaptation of the child is made more difficult or even impossible.

The morning arrival at a childcare facility can bring out the ambivalence of some mothers, who prolong the separation from their child because of their reluctance to abandon it. This ambiguous behaviour makes the child uncertain and results in delayed and reduced play after the long leave-taking (Fig. 2). The child cannot free itself from the equivocally behaving mother and accept the new situation.

In particular, mothers who are challenged by their life situations, who cannot coordinate their caregiving tasks, and who find little real support from persons in their

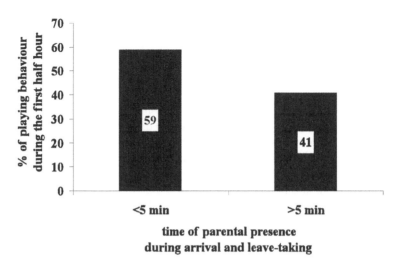

Figure 14.2. Dependence of the child's willingness to play on the time of presence during arrival and leavetaking of the accompanying parent in a day-care centre for children 15 to 35 months old (n=28). (Data from Bensel 1992.)

private environment show, according to caregivers, 'irritating behaviour' upon their arrival in the day-care centre (Andres and Laewen 1995).

The Contribution of the Caregiver

It is important for the nature of the separation not only from whom the child comes, but also to whom it goes. According to one study, at nine months old infants were already responsive to the behaviour of a babysitter who was responsible for their care for a half an hour (Gunnar 1998). If the babysitter was cold and distant, the cortisol level rose; if she was friendly, willing to play and sensitive, the level remained normal.

Only sensitive caregivers, who succeed in the course of a gentle initial period in forming a relationship to the child, can be used by the children as an alternative secure base to maintain their emotional balance. This is no easy task and is not achieved by all caregivers (Ahnert and Lamb 2003, Ahnert and Rickert 2000). Children are less frequently securely attached with their caregiver than to their mother. It can take many months for children to form a secure attachment to their caregiver. Children who already bring an insecure attachment from home are at a disadvantage here (Ziegenhain and Wolff 2000). In an American study by Raikes (1993) it took more than a year before 91 per cent of the children had succeeded in doing this, and in the first eight months it was only 50 per cent. With this as a given, clearly it is especially important that the continuity between child and responsible caregiver is maintained throughout the caregiving period (Cummings and Beagles-Ross 1984). Legendre (2003) showed in this regard that in facilities with a high caregiver fluctuation during the day the children responded with elevated cortisol values.

The Contribution of the Caregiving Environment Away from Home

Not only the caregivers themselves, but also the whole caregiving environment is decisive in determining children's stress levels. In a comparison of French and Hungarian day-care centres, Legendre (2003) was able to determine threshold values above which 1.5- to 3-year-old children responded with an increase in cortisol in the morning instead of the chronobiologically expected decrease. This was specifically when the group size was above 15, the average age difference between the children was over half a year and the area for playing was less than 5 m² per child.

Also important is a comparison of the same children at home and in day-care. Watamura (Watamura et al. 2003) found a more frequent cortisol increase over the day for 1.5- to 3-year-olds compared to infants between 2 and 16 months in the day-care centre, but not at home. It was concluded that this involved less a separation distress than stress arising through the age-dependent enhanced interaction with peers. For toddlers peer play is a more important topic than for infants. Indeed the shy and fearful toddlers, who less frequently succeeded in joining in play with other children, show the highest cortisol increase. In case the cortisol increase was to be caused by the separation distress, the infants should respond more strongly than the toddlers, since the strongest separation distress is observed at the end of the first year of life. This conclusion however does not appear necessary, since separation distress and physiological stress are not identical. The question remains as to what causes the stress reaction in the children: The separation from their parents, or the confrontation with so many children, other unknown factors, or an interplay of more than one of these causes? Crucially important are the results that show that the stress of the children can be reduced through an improvement of the caregiving quality.

Separation Experiences Suited to the Child

The human infant is, like that of the other primates, a Tragling (parent clinger), i.e., it is adapted to spending its early childhood in close contact to its caregiving persons. It needs rich tactile and vestibular stimulation, in order to be reassured of the presence of its caregiving persons. The absence of these signals represents an existential threat. With increasing age its need for the presence of signals of bodily presence decreases and instead of body contact, smell and being moved, more often the voice or simply the sight of its secure base is sufficient for it to feel secure enough even in activities at some distance from the attachment figure.

Alongside the need for contact to its caregiving persons there is also, already in the infant from the beginning, the wish for distance. Thus the infant ends eye-contact interactions with the adult also with intentional looking away, so as to be alone for a moment. These first mini-episodes of separation should also be respected by the adult social partner. Older infants coquette already with their growing autonomy. They play with separation, in that they intentionally introduce interactions during which they disappear for a while, only to reappear immediately and find the identical environment. 'Peek-a-Boo' games at the initiative of the child with hands or sheets across the eyes are an example of separation games which gain their attraction in the fact that the child keeps control of the situation and can at any time make mother or father magically reappear. It can play with any arising fears of being left in the desired dosage, and if they become too strong, make them disappear at its own initiative.

The crucial point in these enjoyable separations is that they are under the child's control. Behavioural observations of 1.5 to 2-year-olds at playgrounds have shown us that a toddler, who voluntarily separates itself from its mother and goes to the sand-box can play alone or with other children for a substantially longer time than when the mother, on her initiative, simply puts the child in the sandbox to play (Fig. 3).

A self-initiated separation takes place at exactly the optimal moment, when the child has just the minimal need for contact to the caregiving person, when its emotional batteries are fully charged, and it is completely ready to play. Then it can tolerate the separation the longest and enjoy it (Bensel and Haug-Schnabel 1993). These moments of voluntary aloneness are extended in the course of development to ever longer phases, in which a child is occupied with itself in a rewarding and enjoyable way. It learns that it can also be good to be alone, an important aspect for its personality development.

The development of this autonomy process cannot be hastened through premature separations brought about on the part of the adults when unwanted by the

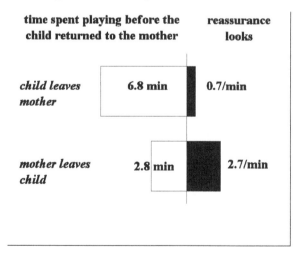

Figure 14.3. Dependence of the child's willingness to play and the frequency of reassurance on the starting conditions of a play situation. Data from Bensel and Haug-Schnabel 1993 (n=32).

infant. In the best case, the children do not protest any more during the separation, which does not by any means signify that they might not be internally very disturbed.

The optimal developmental environment to promote self-initiated autonomy is found by the children in small manageable social associations. Here there is the possibility for social contact with several allomothers and other children, but also the possibility of returning at any time to the main caregiving person in the event of being tired, excited or scared. When a small child is then left behind by the mother for a short time without direct accessibility, it remains under the protection of a familiar allomother. This socialization environment was the standard in the 'environments of evolutionary adaptedness', and still is today in many traditional societies (especially foraging societies) that have been able to maintain their original living conditions. Sarah Hrdy assumes that Pleistocene babies developed in a world surrounded by familiar allomothers, rarely encountering strangers (Hrdy 2004). Here she raises an important research question: How familiar does an allomother have to be, in order for the infant to feel comfortable with her?

Many types of non-maternal care in industrial societies confront children with a 'cage situation', in which they involuntarily land and over which they have no control. Their wish for 'return as needed' to their primary attachment figure cannot be fulfilled. The wish is intense when the adaptation fails, the quality of the care is limited, the new caregiving person is not accepted as a secure base, and the other children cannot be used by an inhibited and fearful child as a social attraction and rather are perceived as a threat. For these children in such a caretaking setting, the separation distress is high and certainly not conducive for development. On the other side are children who are securely enough attached to be cared for under conditions which let them use an alternative social platform free of fear, which makes it possible for them to gain valuable experiences which they would not be offered at home.

References

Ahnert, L., and Lamb, M., 2003. Shared care: establishing a balance between home and child care settings. *Child Development* 4, 1044–9.

Ahnert, L., and Rickert, H., 2000. Belastungsreaktionen bei beginnender Tagesbetreuung aus der Sicht früher Mutter-Kind-Bindung. *Psychologie in Erziehung und Unterricht* 3, 189–202.

Andres, B., and Laewen, H.-J., 1995. Eingewöhnung von Kleinkindern in Tageseinrichtungen und Tagespflegestellen. In D. Fuchs, ed., *Das Tor zur Welt - Krippenerziehung in der Diskussion*. Freiburg: Lambertus, 79–101.

Archer, J., 2001. Grief from an evolutionary perspective. In M.S. Stroebe and R.O. Hansson, eds., *Handbook of Bereavement Research: Consequences, Coping, and Care*. Washington: American Psychological Association, 263–83.

Barrett, H., 1997. How young children cope with separation: toward a new conceptualization. *British Journal of Medical Psychology* 4, 339–58.

Bensel, J., and Haug-Schnabel, G., 1993. The biological causes of establishing contact in human infants. Paper presented at the XXIII International Ethological Conference, Torremolinos, Spain, 1–9 September 1993.

Bensel, J., 1992. Behaviour of toddlers during daily leave-taking and separation from their parents. *Ethology and Sociobiology* 13, 229–52.

Bloom-Feshbach, S., 1988. From family to classroom: variations in adjustment to nursery school. In J. Bloom-Feshbach, S. Bloom-Feshbach et al., eds., *The Psychology of Separation and Loss – Perspectives on Development, Life Transitions, and Clinical Practice.* San Francisco: Jossey-Bass Publishers, 207–31.

Boccia, M.L., Laudenslager, M.L., and Reite, M.L., 1994. Intrinsic and extrinsic factors affect infant responses to maternal separation. *Psychiatry* 1, 43–50.

Braun, K., Kremz, P., Wetzel, W., Wagner, T., and Poeggel, G., 2003. Influence of parental deprivation on the behavioural development in Octodon degus: modulation by maternal vocalizations. *Developmental Psychobiology* 3, 237–45.

Breier, A., 1989. Experimental approaches to human stress research: assessment of neurobiological mechanisms of stress in volunteers and psychiatric patients. *Biological Psychiatry* 26, 438–62.

Carlson, E.A., Jacobvitz, D., and Sroufe, L.A., 1995. A developmental investigation of inattentiveness and hyperactivity. *Child Development* 66, 37–54.

Carlson, M., and Earls, F., 1997. Psychological and neuroendocrinological sequelae of early social deprivation in institutionalized children in Romania. *Annals of the New York Academy of Sciences* 807, 419–28.

Christensson, K., Cabrera, K., Christensson, E., Uvnas-Moberg, K., and Winberg, J., 1995. Separation distress call in the human neonate in the absence of maternal body contact. *Acta Paediatrica* 84, 468–73.

Coe, C.L., Lubach, G., and Ershler, W.B., 1989. Immunological consequences of maternal separation in infant primates. *New Directions for Child Development* 45, 65–91.

Cummings, E.M., and Beagles-Ross, J., 1984. Towards a model of infant day care: Studies of factors influencing responding to separation in day care. In R.C. Ainslie, ed., *The Child and the Day Care Setting.* New York: Praeger, 159–81.

Davidson, R., and Fox, N., 1989. Frontal brain asymmetry predicts infants' response to maternal separation. *Journal of Abnormal Psychology* 98, 127–31.

De Kloet, E.R., Rosenfeld, P., Van Eekelen, J.A., Sutanto, W., and Levine, S., 1988. Stress, glucocorticoids and development. *Progress in Brain Research* 73, 101–20.

Field, T.M., Schanberg, S.M., Scafidid, F., Bauer, C.R., Vega-Lahr, N., Garcia, R., Nystrom, J., and Kuhn, C.M., 1986. Tactile/kinesthetic stimulation effects on preterm neonates. *Pediatrics* 77, 654–58.

Gomez, R., 2002. The effects of perceived maternal parenting styles on the disruptive behaviours of children with attention deficit hyperactivity disorder/oppositional defiant disorder: mediation by hostile biased social cognitions. In S.P. Shohov, ed., *Advances in Psychology Research*. New York: Nova Science Publishers, Inc, 37–55.

Gordon, H.W., 2002. Early environmental stress and biological vulnerability to drug abuse. *Psychoneuroendocrinology* 1–2, 115–26.

Gunnar, M.R., 1998. Quality of early care and buffering of neuroendocrine stress reactions: potential effects on the developing human brain. *Preventive Medicine* 2, 208–11.

Gunnar, M.R., Brodersen, L., Nachmias, M., Buss, K., and Rigatuso, J., 1996. Stress reactivity and attachment security. *Developmental Psychobiology* 3, 191–204.

Hassenstein, B., 2007. *Verhaltensbiologie des Kindes*, Münster: Monsenstein & Vannerdat.

Heinz, A., 1999. Serotonerge Dysfunktion als Folge sozialer Isolation. Bedeutung für die Entstehung von Aggression und Alkoholabhängigkeit. *Nervenarzt* 70, 780–89.

Hennessy, M.B., 1997. Hypothalamic-pituitary-adrenal responses to brief social separation. *Neuroscience & Biobehavioural Reviews* 1, 11–29.

Hofer, M.A., 2003. The emerging neurobiology of attachment and separation: how parents shape their infant's brain and behaviour. In S.W. Coates and J.L. Rosental, eds., *Trauma and Human Bonds*. Relational Perspectives Book Series. Hillsdale, NJ: Analytic Press, 191–209.

Hrdy, S.B., 2004. Evolutionary context of human development: the cooperative breeding model. In C.S. Carter, and L. Ahnert, eds., *Attachment and Bonding: A New Synthesis*. Dahlem Workshop No. 92. Cambridge, MA: M.I.T. Press.

Hsu, F.-C., Zhang, G.-J., Raol, Y.S.H., Valentino, R.J., Coulter, D.A., and Brooks-Kayal, A.R., 2003. Repeated neonatal handling with maternal separation permanently alters hippocampal GABAA receptors and behavioural stress responses. *PNAS* 21, 12213–18.

Kagan, J., 1976. Emergent themes in human development. *American Scientist* March–April, 186–96.

Keown, L.J., and Woodward, L.J., 2002. Early parent-child relations and family functioning of preschool boys with pervasive hyperactivity. *Journal of Abnormal Child Psychology* 6, 541–53.

Laewen, H.-J., 1989. Nichtlineare Effekte einer Beteiligung von Eltern am Eingewöhnungssprozeß von Krippenkindern. *Psychologie in Erziehung und Unterricht* 36, 102–8.

Laewen, H.-J., Andres, B., and Hédervári, É., 2000. *Die ersten Tage in der Krippe*. Neuwied: Luchterhand.

Legendre, A., 2003. Environmental features influencing toddlers' bioemotional reactions in day care centers. *Environment and Behaviour* 4, 523–49.

Lovic, V., Gonzalez, A., and Fleming, A.S., 2001. Maternally separated rats show deficits in maternal care in adulthood. *Developmental Psychobiology* 1, 19–33.

Mizukami, K., Kobayashi, N., Ishii, T., and Iwata, H., 1990. First selective attachment begins in early infancy: a study using telethermography. *Infant Behaviour and Development* 3, 257–71.

Panksepp, J., 2002. Die Gehirnmechanismen der Affekte – Die Rolle von Trennungsschmerz und Spielsystemen bei sozialen Bindungen. Paper presented at a Conference, Göttingen, Germany 14 June 2002.

Panksepp, J., Nelson, E., and Bekkedal, M., 1997. Brain systems for the mediation of social separation-distress and social-reward. Evolutionary antecedents and neuropeptide intermediaries. *Annals of the New York Academy of Sciences* 807, 78–100.

Passauer, I., and Wiedemann, B., 1989. Krippentauglichkeit und Exposition. *Pädiatrie und Grenzgebiete* 4, 223–39.

———— 1990. Risikofaktoren für die Krippentauglichkeit in zwei voneinander unabhängigen Studien. *Pädiatrie und Grenzgebiete* 29, 295–303.

Raikes, H., 1993, Relationship duration in infant care: time with a high-ability teacher and infant-teacher attachment. *Early Childhood Research Quarterly* 3, 309–25.

Reichlin, S., 1993. Neuroendocrine-immune interactions. *The New England Journal of Medicine* 14, 1246–53.

Rennen-Allhoff, B., 1991. Separation in early childhood: current effects and long-term sequelae. *Acta Paedopsychiatrica* 1, 68–75.

Sánchez, M.M., Ladd, C.O., and Plotsky, P.M., 2001. Early adverse experience as a developmental risk factor for later psychopathology: evidence from rodent and primate models. *Development and Psychopathology* 13, 419–49.

Schmidt-Kolmer, E., 1989. Der Einfluß des Übergangs von der Familie in die Krippe sowie von der Krippe zum Kindergarten auf Gesundheit und Entwicklung von Vorschulkindern. *Pädiatrie und Grenzgebiete* 28, 195–203.

Stein, M.T., and Call, J.D., 2001. Extraordinary changes in behaviour in an infant after a brief separation. *Journal of Developmental and Behavioural Pediatrics* 22 (2 Suppl), 11–5.

Watamura, S.E., Donzella, B., Alwin, J., and Gunnar, M.R., 2003. Morning-to-Afternoon increases in cortisol concentrations for infant and toddlers at child care: age differences and behavioural correlates. *Child Development* 4, 1006–20.

Weis, C., Bensel, J., and Haug-Schnabel, G., 1999. Trennungsstress und Coping-Strategien. Elternabwesenheit und deren Wirkungen auf Kleinstkinder, untersucht durch Verhaltensbeobachtungen und Cortisolmessungen in der Krippe. *Mitteilungsblatt der Ethologischen Gesellschaft* 42, 23–24.

Ziegenhain, U., and Wolff, U., 2000. Der Umgang mit Unvertrautem – Bindungsbeziehung und Krippeneintritt. *Psychologie in Erziehung und Unterricht* 3, 176–88.

• 15 •

Quality, Quantity and Type of Childcare

Effects on Child Development in the U.S.

Jay Belsky

The NICHD Study of Early Child Care (SECC): A Brief History

Two major factors were responsible for the initiation of so large and ambitious an investigation of the developmental effects of early childcare experience in the U.S. One had to do with changes taking place in maternal employment and the other concerned debates within the scholarly community about the potential consequences of such changes for children's development.

Changes in Mothers' Paid Employment

Over the past thirty years, great changes have taken place in not simply the number of mothers with young children in the labour force, but most especially in the timing of mothers' return to employment following a child's birth. Consider in this regard that in 1975, 34 per cent of mothers with children under six years of age were in the workforce in the U.S., though by 1999 the corresponding figure was 61 per cent (Shonkoff and Phillips 2000). More noteworthy, however, are the changes that took place in the rates of employment of mothers with infants under a year of age. In the U.S. today, the overwhelming majority of mothers who return to employment after having a child do so before their child's first birthday. Recent figures (for 1998–1999) indicate that 58 per cent of all women with infants under a year of age are in the labour force (Bureau of Labor Statistics 2000); comparable rates in 1970 and 1985 were 27 per cent and 46 per cent, respectively (Kamerman 2000).

As it turned out, and without trying to recruit into the NICHD SECC any special kind of sample from a series of community hospitals located in the places where the ten collaborating research sites were located, the overwhelming majority of mothers enrolled in the study when their infants were one month of age ended up going back to work before the child's first birthday was celebrated and, as a result, placing their child in some kind of routine non-maternal care arrangement before the child was six months of age (NICHD Early Child Care Research Network 1997a; see also Hofferth 1996). Moreover, the amount of time that children enrolled in the NICHD study spent in non-maternal care on a weekly basis once it was initiated remained more rather than less stable. Indeed, those children who averaged thirty or more hours of care per week in some kind of routine non-maternal care arrangement in the first year of life – and these proved to be the majority of children – were likely to maintain this high level until they began school around the age of five.

What should be clear, then, is that non-maternal care initiated in infancy for an extensive period of time each week became a routine experience for many families in the U.S. in the last quarter of the twentieth century. In fact, the principle change that occurred with respect to maternal employment was not just the growing proportion of mothers of young children needing to rely upon someone others than themselves to provide regular daily care for their three-, four- and five-year-olds, but the timing of mothers' return to employment. By the late 1980s, maternal employment in the child's first year of life, indeed in the first six if not three months of the child's life, became a regular experience for millions of American children and families.

Controversy in the Scientific Community

It is hard to imagine that a study so large, so ambitious, and so expensive as the NICHD SECC would have been initiated had the only stimulus for such work been the aforementioned changes in the timing of maternal employment in the U.S. After all, major changes had occurred by 1980, but the NICHD SECC was not launched until a decade later. In retrospect, it appears that a catalyst was required to stimulate interest in – by inflaming debate about – the effects of such dramatic social change. I turned out, inadvertently, to provide the needed spark. And I did so with the publication in 1986 of an essay, followed by a series of subsequent papers, that called attention to developmental 'risks' associated with non-maternal care, of the kind routinely available in American communities, when initiated in the first year of life, especially when experienced on a full- or near-full-time basis which continued to entry into school (i.e., early, extensive and continuous care) (Belsky 1986, 1988, 1990; Belsky and Rovine 1988). I highlighted risks to the mother–child relationship, taking the form of higher rates of insecure infant–mother attachments toward the end of the first year of life, and risks to social and behavioural development, taking the form of elevated levels of aggression and disobedience when children were 3–8 years old. To be noted is that I never claimed anything about diagnosable psychiatric problems, though this has not stopped others from attributing such a view to me (e.g., Bacharach and Baumeister 2003). Indeed, one early critic who also ended up collaborating on the NICHD SECC with me (and many others) claimed, more or less, that I believed infant day care had 'malignant' effects on children, entitling her own rebuttal of my views 'Infant day care: maligned or malignant?' (Clarke-Stewart 1989).

In actuality, I presented my conclusions about risks associated with infant day care in the late 1980s in a tentative rather than authoritative manner. Indeed, in the 1986 piece which was to initiate the firestorm of controversy and, thereby, serve as catalyst for the NICHD SECC, I described the evidence leading to a conclusion of 'developmental risk' being associated with routine infant day care as 'circumstantial'. The argument I advanced for such a view was intentionally – and accurately – labelled 'inferential'. And I further noted that 'others would, could and should' read the available evidence differently than I did. Dogmatic I was not. Indeed, I titled my original essay which stimulated, as one observer called them, 'the day care wars' (Karen 1994), 'Infant day care: a cause for concern?', purposefully choosing the word 'concern' rather than 'alarm' and intentionally posing the issue as a question rather than an emphatic, 'brook-no-debate' conclusion.

The Birth of the NICHD SECC

Thus, the idea of the NICHD SECC emerged in the context of major changes occurring in maternal employment and child-care usage and heated debate about how such social change might affect children's development and, perhaps thereby, the society at large. The government agency which was to fund the NICHD SECC decided, in the face of widespread scientific and ideological controversy, to, at least initially, invest modest sums of money in six projects focused on the first three years of life. What the grant applicants could not have imagined even after having been informed of their status as 'winners' was that so much of the (fierce) grant competition would prove to be not much more than an 'essay-writing contest'. And the reason for this was because once not six but ten teams of investigators were selected on the basis of the individual research proposals each had prepared, they were brought together to design – collectively and collaboratively – a short-term longitudinal study that would be carried out in parallel in all ten sites. Each team, then, would not get to pursue the empirical agenda they individually had proposed, but instead were obliged to collaborate on a to-be-designed study which would be carried out in all the research sites! This was no tall order in light of the fact that the newly constituted 'collaborating team' were developmental psychologists who, for the preceding few years had been, more or less, at each other's intellectual throats over fundamental disagreements about research on the effects of childcare.

The NICHD Study of Early Child Care

Whether one embraced the view that developmental risks were associated with early non-maternal care of the kind typically available in the U.S. (and that not all such risk could be attributed to low quality of care) – which few in the academic community did, by the way – there was no disputing the fact that the evidentiary base for any and all conclusions was severely limited. Three of these were central to the design of the NICHD Study. Each is discussed in turn before describing the general design of this unique and massive collaborative enterprise.

Measuring the Parent–Child Relationship

Critics of my risk-factor conclusions claimed that that standard methodology for measuring children's socio-emotional development, and especially the early infant–mother relationship, was especially problematic when it came to studying the effects of early childcare. Clarke-Stewart (1989) most prominently argued that the reason that some studies, including her own meta-analysis of relevant investigations, linked infant day care with insecure infant–mother attachment, was likely due to an artefact of the Strange Situation (Ainsworth and Wittig 1969): because day-care children routinely experience separation from a parent, there were problems with assuming that this widely used and well-validated methodology, which relies upon parent–child separation to evoke attachment behaviour, equally stresses children with and without day-care experience. In consequence, she argued, children who maintain a distance from mother in the Strange Situation – rather than approaching her and seeking contact and comfort when stressed – may do so not because they are insecure-avoidant in their attachment but because they are simply less stressed and more independent than other children. When it came to designing the NICHD SECC, it was because of this widely-embraced, but empirically unsubstantiated possibility that we sought to determine (a) whether, in fact, children with varying day-care experience were differentially stressed by the Strange Situation, finding this not to be the case (NICHD Early Child Care Research Network 1997b), and (b) whether they were differentially likely to be classified as insecure (see below). The very same concern accounts for why the decision was made not to rely exclusively or even primarily upon the Strange Situation when it came to assessing the effects of day care on the parent–child relationship.

The Non-random Assignment of Children to Child Care

The available research on which I based my infant-day-care-as-risk-factor conclusion was also limited by the fact that it often, even if not always, failed to account for differences between families that covaried with their use of childcare (i.e., selection effects). Because children are not randomly assigned to varying child-care arrangements (thank goodness!), field-based research should control for pre-existing differences between families which use early childcare and those which do not, which initiate child-care usage earlier and later in the child's life, and which rely upon childcare for more and less time in a week (and across months and years). Differences in children's development attributed to early childcare could thus be an artefact of pre-existing background differences between families which had not been taken into account in much research. Thus, when it came to designing the NICHD SECC, a great deal of attention was paid to measuring (longitudinally) and controlling for background factors or 'selection effects' that could distort findings if not taken into consideration before assessing child-care effects. In fact, in all the findings presented in this chapter regarding effects of childcare on mother–child relations and child development, a myriad of statistical controls for family socioeconomic status, maternal psychological well-being, and parenting behaviour have been incorporated. It is as a result of its heavy reliance upon controls for selection effects that causal language will be employed – for heuristic purposes – in summarizing results herein.

Measuring the Quality of Child Care

The most important limitation of the then available work on which I based my risk-factor conclusion was that all too much of it did not include measurements of child-care quality. This was regarded as a fatal flaw because most developmentalists and child-care advocates believed and argued – and still believe and continue to argue – in response to my early (and more recent, post NICHD Study) observations that so long as quality of child care is high, there are no risks whatsoever to children's development, even when placed in childcare in the first months of life, on a full-time basis, which continues at that level until they begin school around the age of five (McGurk et al. 1993; Phillips et al. 1987; Scarr et al. 1989). In other words, the only reason it could be that in some studies lots of time spent in non-maternal child care beginning in the first year was found at all to be linked with lower quality parent–child interaction, increased rates of insecure attachment, and/or higher levels of aggression and disobedience was – and remains – because children experienced (unmeasured) low-quality child care.

In view of this plausible alternative explanation of the seemingly adverse effects to which I had drawn attention of early and extensive non-maternal care of the kind available in most American communities, the careful, repeated, and thus costly measurement of child-care quality figured ever so prominently in designing the NICHD SECC. Indeed, the collaborating investigators developed a brand new, two-part child-care quality measurement system – eschewing available measurements as inadequate – that could be used in whatever non-maternal child-care arrangement a child was seen. This was accomplished by focusing upon the amount and quality of attention which the study child received in child care, not on the global characteristics of the child-care setting or the general quality of care offered to however many children were in the setting. One part of this target-child focused system measured the frequency of select care-giver behaviour (e.g., talks to child, smiles at child, responds verbally to child, comforts child) and the other more global, evaluative ratings of care-giver behaviour (e.g., sensitivity, intrusiveness, positive regard).

Just as importantly, of course, measurements of the amount of child care which children experienced and the age at which they began care were obtained so that the quantity and quality of care could be examined separately, additively, and interactively. Also chronicled was the type of care that children used (see below). What this meant was that the NICHD Study was the first and largest to repeatedly/longitudinally measure multiple parameters of child care. This positioned the study to examine the effects of any feature of child care after taking into account not only family-background factors, but other important characteristics of child care as well. In other words, the NICHD SECC was not simply a study of the effects of child care, but of the effects of multiple features of child care.

General Research Design

The NICHD SECC began following some 1,364 children and their families from the time the child was one month of age, after contacting and obtaining basic identifying information from mothers in the hospital on the first day or two of the child's life. As of this writing, children participating in this prospective, longitudinal study are ten years of age, though only findings through the first five years of age (i.e., kindergarten) are reported herein. Although great efforts were made – in selecting the ten hospitals from which children were recruited and in recruiting families – to obtain an ethnically, demographically, and geographically diverse sample, it must be noted that the sample being followed, especially after (non-random) attrition, proved less diverse than would have been ideal. It must be acknowledged as well that the sample is not, nor was it ever designed to be, nationally representative.

Despite these limitations, more than 1,000 children (and their families) have been followed through school entry (around five years of age), though a sample that did not have large numbers of truly poor and/or minority children has even fewer as time goes on. All this is not to say, however, that the NICHD Study is an investigation of a 'middle-class sample'. It remains diverse. There are a sizeable number of near-poor, single-parent, and minority families, although there are very few very poor families. Details on the exact nature of the sample can be found in the many publications to be cited.

The major features of the overall study design included the *repeated* measurement of (a) the quality of the child's family-rearing environment, (b) the quality of whatever non-maternal care was provided to the child, and (c) the child's cognitive-linguistic and socio-emotional development. Multiple measurements of (a) and (b) were secured as close as possible to the time when the child was 6, 15, 24, 36 and 54 months of age, with the evaluations of children made when children were 15, 24, 36, and 54 months, typically during laboratory visits, as well as in kindergarten (parent and teacher reports only).

When it came to measuring the quality of the child's family-rearing environment, basic demographic information on the family was obtained (e.g., family composition, marital status), as was that on socio-economic status (e.g., income, benefits), family functioning (e.g., marital quality, stress), maternal well-being (e.g., depression), and the quality of mothering (e.g., cognitive stimulation, warmth, discipline). The latter was assessed using observational procedures and questionnaires completed by mothers. As already noted, to assess child-care quality, a special observational system was developed that, in addition to focusing on the experience of the child in that setting (e.g., verbally responded to), also focused on the broad setting in which the child was being cared for (e.g., classroom level). More specifically, each child was observed in their primary child-care setting, whatever it was, at each of the above-listed ages. These observations took place on two separate occasions, typically on adjacent days, for four hours on each occasion. Data-reduction-oriented statistical analysis of frequency-based behaviour codings and of global ratings yielded a general index of quality of child care at each age of measurement. These captured the degree to which the child was attended to, warmly and sensitively interacted with, and stimulated cognitively (e.g., read to, asked questions). Other important information on children's child-care experiences, including the amount of time they spent in care each week and the type(s) of care arrangements that the family used, was secured via brief maternal interviews during the course of regular phone calls, if not during face-to-face contacts. Finally, children's cognitive-linguistic and socio-emotional development was assessed using age-appropriate methods. At 15 and 24 months, the Bayley (1969, 1993) Scales of Infant Development were used and at later ages select verbal and non-verbal subscales of the Bracken (1984) School Readiness Scale (36 months) and the Woodcock–Johnson Achievement Battery (54 months) (Woodcock and Johnson 1990) were administered. In addition, standardized and widely used questionnaires were administered to mothers, care-givers or teachers (after 54 months of age) to assess children's social competence and behaviour problems, the former with appropriate versions of the Social Skills Rating Scales (Gresham and Elliott 1990) and the latter with age-appropriate versions of the Child Behavior Checklist (Achenbach 1991; Achenbach, Edelbrock and Howell 1987).

Effects of Child Care on Child Development

No simple or singular way to summarize the central findings from the NICHD Study exist, especially given the many articles and chapters which the investigatory team has produced, to say nothing of the complex nature of childcare and child development. Whereas some might be inclined to organize results in terms of the domain of development under consideration (e.g., attachment security, cognitive development, problem behaviour), or even the age of the child at the time when multiple outcomes were assessed, I have adopted a different approach in this chapter. As the chapter title implies, my reporting is framed primarily in terms of three distinctive and distinguishable, but not unrelated, features of childcare: the quality, quantity and type of care which the child experienced. The detected effects of childcare to be reviewed have emerged after controlling for an extensive set of family background factors (see above), as well as each of the other parameters of childcare under consideration. Thus, when reporting effects of time spent in childcare (i.e., quantity) effects of quality and type of care have already been discounted.

A critical take-home message of the NICHD Study is underscored in presenting the findings as I will – and that is that it no longer makes sense, if it ever did, to think in terms of the effects of childcare per se. Childcare is a multifaceted phenomenon and, indeed, one of the major goals of the NICHD SECC was always to stimulate discussion and even debate beyond the all-too-simplistic question of whether child-care is good or bad for children's development. Interestingly, although I have been repeatedly cast as someone who has been inclined to promote such simplification of a complex issue, there is virtually no evidence to substantiate it. Indeed, from the very beginning of the so-called wars, I was not writing about 'any and all' childcare, but about childcare begun in the first year of life (Belsky 1986), for more than twenty hours per week (Belsky 1988; Belsky and Rovine 1988), and which continued at such high levels until children entered school (Belsky 1994, 2001).

Quality of Child Care

It always amazed me that perhaps the foremost criticism, as indicated above, of my risk-factor conclusion focused upon child-care quality, because I never asserted that quality of care was unimportant. Rather, I contended – and still do – that it could not fully explain some of the seemingly adverse consequences of lots of time spent in routine, non-maternal care, beginning in the first year of life, that emerged repeatedly in the literature. In fact, just a few years before calling attention to risks associated with lots of time spent in care beginning in the first year of life, I reviewed evidence showing that child-care quality was systematically related to both children's cognitive-linguistic and socio-emotional development (Belsky 1984). Given these now early findings, to say nothing of a flood of subsequent evidence, I regard as some of the least surprising results to emerge from the NICHD SECC those pertaining to quality of childcare: at virtually whatever age we measured child-care quality in the NICHD SECC, the beneficial effects of more attentive, responsive and stimulating care, and, conversely, the developmental costs of poorer quality care was indisputably evident.

Consider first the result having to do with the parent–child relationship. After failing to confirm Clarke-Stewart's (1989) aforementioned, speculative, but nevertheless widely-embraced critique of the Strange Situation (see also Belsky and Braungart 1991), the NICHD Early Child Care Research Network (1997b) found that infants were more likely to develop insecure attachment to their mothers when low-quality childcare coincided with low levels of maternal sensitivity (both measured at 6 and 15 months of age). To be noted, however, and in contrast to similar findings to be reviewed below pertaining to quantity of childcare, this result implicating low child-care quality in the development of insecure attachment was not replicated when children were re-evaluated in the Strange Situation at 36 months of age (NICHD Early Child Care Research Network 2001). However, when mother–child interaction was repeatedly observed between the period 6–36 months, it was observed that more harmonious patterns of interaction were evident when children experienced higher quality of childcare during the period leading up to the time when mother–child interaction was measured (NICHD Early Child Care Research Network 1999). These findings were not as consistently evident across the 6–36 month period, though, as those to be reviewed below pertaining to quantity of childcare. This differential prediction is important in light of the repeated claims that it is quality of care that matter most – and perhaps only – to children's development when in childcare.

Results emerged, more or less, just as anticipated and as suggested by other work when attention was turned to predicting children's cognitive-linguistic functioning at ages 15, 24, and 36 months: the more attentive, responsive, and stimulating was the care which the child experienced, the better the child's cognitive-linguistic performance, measured using the Bayley Scales of Infant Development at the first two measurement occasions and the Bracken Scales of School Readiness at the third (NICHD Early Child Care Research Network 2000). Especially noteworthy was evidence that it was language stimulation in the second year in particular which was distinctively predictive of language development at two years of age. The same general – and anticipated – effect of good quality of care on intellectual development emerged when quality of care experienced through 54 months of age was used to forecast cognitive-linguistic functioning as measured at age 4.5 years using select subscales of the Woodcock-Johnson Achievement Battery (NICHD Early Child-Care Research Network 2002a, 2003a).

Efforts to determine how more 'distal' markers of child-care quality (e.g., adult–child ratio, group size, care-giver training) affected child development also revealed that two particular structural features of childcare – care-giver–child ratio and care-giver training – exerted their (indirect) influence on children's development by affecting more proximate processes of care-giver–child interaction (NICHD Early Child Care Research Network 2002b). That is, when there were fewer children per care giver and care givers had more training, care givers provided more attentive, stimulating and sensitive care and, apparently in consequence, children evidenced enhanced cognitive-linguistic development. Such findings are important from a policy perspective because ratios and training are the kinds of features of childcare that are eminently subject to government regulation and, more or less, easily monitored.

There was clear and consistent evidence of the benefits of better quality childcare when the outcome to be explained was mother- and care-giver-reported problem behaviour and social competence at ages 24 and 36 months (NICHD Early Child Care Research Network 1998): the better the quality of care, the fewer problems reported and the greater social competence (e.g., cooperation, empathy) observed by these raters with extensive knowledge of the children being studied as part of the NICHD-SECC. Interestingly and surprisingly, however, similar results were much less in evidence when the quality of childcare experienced through the first 4.5 years of life was used to predict the same developmental outcomes at 54 months of age and in the first year of school (i.e., kindergarten) (NICHD Early Child Care Research Network 2002a, 2003b). It turned out, in fact, that significant effects of child-care quality on children's social competence and/or problem behaviour at age 4.5 years could be detected only when the most liberal effect-size estimates were employed (i.e., structure coefficients which reflect the proportion of explained variance attributable to a predictor).

The NICHD SECC yielded several other empirical surprises with respect to quality-of-child-care findings. In some respects, many of these are not being fully embraced by the field of child developmentalists and child-care advocates, principally, I suspect, because they fly in the face of the standard developmental mantra of 'it's quality, stupid'. First, effect-sizes in the case of child-care quality, as with virtually all child-care effects summarized herein, were rather modest, if not small in magnitude (NICHD Early Child Care Research Network 2002a, 2003b). Second, virtually no evidence has emerged to support the proposition that the benefits of good-quality childcare, or the developmental costs of poor-quality childcare, would be greater for children growing up in the most risky contextual circumstance (i.e., poor, depressed mother) (NICHD Early Child Care Research Network 2000, 2002a,c, 2003a, b). The latter should be considered in the context, though, of the sample available for study. Recall that it did not include a large number of extremely poor families. The fact that some informal evidence suggested that child-care observers were disproportionately denied access to the poorest quality child-care settings raises the possibility – but does not confirm it – that the NICHD SECC does not afford as good an evaluation of 'the compensatory hypothesis' (i.e., that good-quality childcare could compensate for risky home environments) as would be ideal.

Another surprising finding – actually a non-finding – concerns the interaction of child-care quality and continuity, in that no evidence has emerged showing that more time spent in high-quality care carries greater developmental benefit than less time spent in high-quality care; or, conversely, that more time spent in low-quality care is related to poorer child functioning than less time spent in low-quality care (NICHD Early Child Care Research Network 2003a). And this is not because great efforts have not been expended trying to explore the proposition that quantity of care moderated the detected effects of quality of care (or vice versa). Why these non-results should characterize the developmental process remains completely unclear. They raise the possibility, however, that limited doses of good-quality care may carry the same developmental benefits of far greater doses. The lack of dose–response relations between child-care quality and children's development even raises questions about whether child-care quality is actually exerting a truly causal influence on children's development, as is so routinely supposed (NICHD Early Child Care Research Network 2003a).

Should it be the case that limited amounts of good-quality care pack the same developmental punch as more extensive doses, this could have major ramifications for thinking about child-care policy. In times of tight budgets, one can question the utility of spending money to increase child-care quality all day long or throughout a child's entire infant, toddler, and early childhood years when much less provision of high-quality care might yield the same developmental return on financial investment.

In fact, it might be possible to serve many more children with the same limited funds and not incur any developmental costs in doing so. Although such a possibility is just that and the humanitarian needs of children should not be neglected, this issue merits more attention than the silence with which the NICHD dose–response (non-) findings with respect to quality of care have received from child developmentalists, child-care advocates, and policy makers alike.

Quantity of Child Care

Whereas there are children whose regularly scheduled non-maternal care begins when they are one, two or three months of age, there are others whose enrolment does not occur until they are years older, if at all. Moreover, whether beginning early or later in life, some children are in care for thirty, forty or even more hours per week and others for much less. This means, then, that by the time the children's first, third and fifth birthday arrives, they vary hugely in terms of how much non-maternal care they have experienced across their still-young lives. In my writings about risks associated with early childcare, I first drew attention to those associated with beginning care in the first year of life (Belsky 1986). As more evidence emerged, I subsequently called attention to being in non-maternal care for more than twenty hours per week in care beginning in the first year (Belsky 1988). When even more research was reported, I hypothesized that developmental risk was associated with care initiated in the first year, for twenty or more hours per week, which continued at such high levels until the child entered school – what I referred to as early, extensive, and continuous care (Belsky 1994, 2001). Clearly, I was not making reference to any and all childcare, as many have claimed or assumed.

Moreover, as stipulated above, whenever I wrote about developmental risk I always was referring to the parent–child relationship early in life and aggression and disobedience somewhat later (but not diagnosable psychopathology). Never did I highlight risks to cognitive-linguistic development.

In light of this scholarly history, it seems noteworthy that after overcoming the core limitations of past work which provided the (not unreasonable) grounds for questioning my inferential conclusions, the NICHD SECC has found that amount of time spent in childcare across the opening years of life to be – repeatedly and systematically – related to indices of the parent–child relationship and socio-emotional adjustment. And these relations are, in the main, rather consistent with the conclusions that the evidence led me to almost twenty years ago. Thus, they are rather inconsistent with what was argued by critics who asserted – and still do – that 'it's quality, stupid' and, more or less, only quality that matters to the development of children in day care.

The first relevant findings to be considered are those pertaining to the parent–child relationship. Although more time in care in the first year did not in and of itself predict increased risk of insecure infant–mother attachment in the NICHD study, this child-care variable did operate in ways not inconsistent with my original 'risk-factor' conclusion. More specifically, it was in (statistical) interaction with other sources of risk – and specifically low levels of maternal sensitivity – that quantity of care predicted attachment security: when mothers evinced low levels of sensitivity in interacting with their infants (at 6 and 15 months) *and* averaged more than just ten hours per week of care during the period 3–15 months – that is, even less than the twenty hours per week that I speculated about – infants were more likely to develop insecure attachments to their mothers than would otherwise have been expected (NICHD Early Child Care Research Network 1997b). As noted above and in contrast to a similar child-care-X-maternal sensitivity interaction noted above with respect to quality of care, this interaction involving quantity of childcare re-emerged when the Strange Situation was readministered at 36 months of age (NICHD Early Child Care Research Network 2001). In other words, a pattern of dual risk, involving more than minimal amounts of childcare across the first 15 months of life coupled with low-sensitive mothering, was replicated at 36 months of life.

What is rather striking in light of these results is how developmentalists and child-care advocates have been inclined to conclude that the NICHD SECC did not find childcare in infancy to be related to attachment security or, if they do, only call attention to the (not replicated) interaction between quality of childcare and low levels of maternal sensitivity. Yet isn't it in interaction with other risk factors that most individual sources of risk exert their pernicious magic? After all, while smoking may contribute to heart disease, the realization of this risk is much greater if a smoker is overweight, fails to exercise and/or has a family history of heart disease. It is rather amazing how risk-factor thinking can be embraced when findings are ideologically attractive but dismissed – or distorted – when they are not. Certainly if a research project had found that exposure to poverty only predicted insecure attachment when mothers provided relatively insensitive care, few academics or policy advocates would ever conclude that poverty is unrelated to attachment insecurity. When scientific discourse is corrupted by political inclinations, great risk to both science and informed decision making by parents and policy makers alike arises.

When the NICHD study investigators turned attention to repeatedly observed (and videotaped for subsequent coding) patterns of mother–child interaction, it was discovered that the more time children spent in any kind of non-maternal care in the period 6–36 months, the less harmonious was the interaction seen (NICHD Early Child Care Research Network 1999). When these findings were examined more closely in terms of component variables of composite measures of maternal and child behaviour, evidence suggested that quantity of childcare may have first affected mothering and only thereafter child behaviour. This is because more time in care first predicted less sensitive mothering when infants were 6 months and then more negative mothering when 15 months, before predicting less positive engagement by the child of the mother when 24 and 36 months of age (NICHD Early Child Care Research Network 1997c). As it turned out, these seemingly adverse effects of amount of time spent in childcare on mother–child interaction were discerned again, though only for white children, when mother–child dyads were followed up at age 54 months and in first grade (NICHD Early Child Care Research Network 2003c).

I regard these findings concerning mother–child interaction as especially noteworthy because some collaborating investigators, worried about the validity of using the Strange Situation with children with extensive child-care experience, insisted that the most revealing way to investigate child-care effects on the parent–child relationship would be to just observe how mothers interacted with their children. Note, then, that when this was done, main effects of quantity of childcare were discerned rather than only interactive effects (i.e., maternal sensitivity X time in care), as was the case when the Strange Situation was the focus of inquiry.

More time spent in non-maternal care also proved predictive of (somewhat) elevated levels of problem behaviour involving aggression and disobedience and once again, as with all findings related to quantity of care, irrespective of quality (and even type) of care. When this possibility was first examined at ages 2 and 3, the results were decidedly mixed (NICHD Early Child Care Research Network 1998). Even though two-year-olds who spent more time in non-maternal care across their first 24 months were reported by their mothers to be less cooperative and by their care givers to exhibit more behaviour problems, these results could not be replicated when the same issue was addressed when children were three years of age. Whereas some on the investigator team felt that such findings put to rest the claim that lots of time spent in non-maternal care beginning early in life was predictive of aggression and disobedience, others like me were not so sure. 'Let us see what turns up when children are about to start school,' some of us counselled, 'development, after all, is a rather complex matter.' As it turned out, those who felt that embracing null findings might be premature were proved correct.

Even though amount of non-maternal care proved unrelated to mothers' reports of child behaviour problems at age 4.5 years, this was not the case with respect to care-giver reports. That is, more time in care across the first 4.5 years of life forecast higher levels of problem behaviour reported by care-givers. And, by the time children were in kindergarten, more time in care predicted higher levels of externalizing problems as reported by mothers and teachers alike. In other words, the relation between more time in childcare and problem behaviour emerged when ratings by three separate sets of raters, each of whom observed children in three separate settings, were examined – care givers in childcare, mothers at home, and teachers in school. Just as important as this replicated relation between quantity of childcare and problem behaviour was the fact that across all raters, more time in care predicted high externalizing scores, that is, scores one or more standard deviations above the mean (NICHD Early Child Care Research Network 2003b).

There are two features of these disconcerting and politically incorrect findings that merit especial attention: First, we proved unable to detect a threshold at which quantity of care began to exert its (pernicious?) influence; that is, no quantity threshold could be detected at which more vs. less care had a noticeably greater or lesser impact on problem behaviour. In other words, and importantly, the relation between amount of non-maternal care experienced across the first 4.5 years of life – and expressed in terms of average hours per week experienced from 3–54 months of age – and externalizing problems reflected a constant dose–response relationship: as quantity of care increased, so did problem behaviour. Importantly, subscale-level analyses revealed that it was not just the case, as Clarke-Stewart (1989) propositioned, that children with extensive child-care histories were simply more independent and assertive than other children (and thus mistakenly judged to be aggressive and disobedient). Rather, in the NICHD SECC, more time in non-maternal care across the first 4.5 years of life was found to predict, at age 54 months and later in kindergarten, higher levels of assertiveness (e.g., talks too much, bragging/boasting, argues a lot), disobedience/defiance (e.g., talks out of turn, disobedient at school, defiant - talks back to staff, disrupts school discipline), and aggression (e.g., gets into many fights, cruelty–bullying–meanness, physically attacks others, destroys own things) (NICHD Early Child Care Research Network 2003b).

It would seem, then, that results emanating from the NICHD SECC (and others) pertaining to lots of time spent in non-maternal care are not inconsistent with my original risk-factor conclusion, and especially my subsequent refinement proposing that it was lots of time spent in non-maternal care across the infancy, toddler and pre-school period which carried developmental risk (though amount of time in care in the period 3–6 months of age uniquely predicted higher levels of teacher-rated externalizing problems in kindergarten). It seems worth mentioning as well that all the findings under consideration with respect to amount of care and problem behaviour held across the sample. That is, factors like family economic status, marital status, and maternal education did not moderate the effect of quantity of childcare through kindergarten age on care-giver-reported behaviour problems. Neither, of course, did quality of care. Importantly, these failures to detect interactions were not a function of low statistical power.

What remains very much unexplained as of this writing is exactly why these, and other related findings, obtain when effects of quantity of childcare are investigated. Despite the inclusion of statistical controls for several plausible mediators (or transmitters) of the quantity-of-child-care effects – including quality of care, type of care, instability of care, and even observed parenting – more time in care still predicted higher levels of behaviour problems as reported by care-givers, mothers, and kindergarten teachers (NICHD Early Child Care Research Network 2003b). Thus, even though many investigations have now demonstrated that cumulative time spent in non-maternal childcare, seeming to reflect early, extensive, and continuous day-care experience, is predictive of indicators of poor adjustment (for review, see Belsky 2001), the reason why this is the case remains empirically uncertain. What should be incontestable, though, is that quality of childcare, as so long asserted, does not explain these potentially disconcerting effects of what has become a widespread experience for American children and that the effects detected concern truly aggressive behaviour, not just independence and assertiveness, even if not pathological levels of aggression and hostility.

Type of Care

Upon first consideration, evaluation of the effect of different types of non-maternal care seems pretty straight forward. But, as it turns out, this is simply not the case; and the reason for this is that for many, indeed the large majority of children, changes take place in the arrangements made to care for children. In terms of operationalizing the measurement of this complexity with respect to type of childcare, the NICHD SECC explored a variety of strategies. Indeed, one of its initial goals was to determine whether we could detect some consistent patterning of movement from one type of arrangement to another, say, for example, from a relative in infancy to a childminder during the toddler years, to a centre or nursery by the time the child was three or four. As it turned out, and this may say much about the nature of the child-care 'system' in the U.S., this proved impossible. There were simply too many different patterns of arrangement to make order out of the chaos of the data.

In this report, therefore, as in much of the NICHD study publications, I relied upon the number (or proportion) of measurement occasions that a child's primary child-care arrangement was a centre, a child-care home (defined as care provided by a non-relative in a home other than the study child's home, with at least one other child present), and a home-based arrangement provided by a relative (father, grand-parent, or other adult relative) in the child's or someone else's home. A measurement occasion was defined as a series of contiguous 3- or 4-month intervals between the ages of 1 and 54 months. Fortunately, these rather simple measurements predicted cognitive-linguistic and socio-emotional development (after taking into account observed quality of care, amount of time spent in all childcare arrangements and family background factors).

When children were in child-care homes on more occasions through two years of age, they scored higher on the Bayley at 24 months; and when they were in such arrangements on more occasions through 36 months, they evinced greater verbal comprehension (NICHD Early Child Care Research Network 2000). Thereafter, however, significant effects of exposure to child-care homes were no longer evident. That is, time spent in home-based care failed to predict children's development at 54 months of age; at no age did exposure to relative care prove predictive (NICHD Early Child Care Research Network, 2004). Either such types of care experience have no lasting effects in the U.S. or the NICHD SECC was simply not sufficiently well designed to detect them.

In contrast, exposure to centre-based care had seemingly farther-reaching developmental consequences. In fact, not only did evidence of the benefits of exposure to centre-based care emerge as early as 15 months of age, with more experience in centres predicting greater (mother-reported) language development (NICHD Early Child Care Research Network 2000), but it remained evident when children's cognitive and linguistic development was measured again at older ages (NICHD Early Child Care Research Network 2002a). Thus, the greater the child's time spent in centre-based care, the better the child performed on language-specific outcomes and general cognitive development and achievement on a variety of measures at 24 months (Bayley Scales), 36 months (Bracken School Readiness, Reynolds Language Assessment), and 54 months (Woodcock–Johnson Achievement) (NICHD Early Child Care Research Network 2000, 2002a, 2004).

Effects of centre-based experience were not entirely positive, however, at least in terms of the kinds of behaviour valued by parents and teachers. And this is because we also discovered that the more ages of measurement that children were in centres, the more externalizing problems and conflict with adults they manifest at 54 months in childcare, according to care-givers' reports of child behaviour, with the same being true in their first year of school, according to reports by kindergarten teachers (NICHD Early Child Care Research Network 2003b, 2004). In other words, the more time children spent in centres from 3–54 months of age, net of effects of other child-care factors and family background factors, the more cognitively and linguistically advanced they were *and* the more they manifested aggressive and disobedient behaviour.

Conclusion

The NICHD Early Child Care Network (2002a: 162I) concluded recently that early childcare across the period from birth to 4.5 years is 'associated with both developmental risks and developmental benefits for children's functioning prior to school entry, even after controlling for a host of factors including gender, ethnicity, family socioeconomic status, maternal psychological adjustment, and parenting quality.' The preceding review showed that the risks are that the more hours in (any kind of) childcare across the first 4 years of life and, independently, the more time in childcare centres, the higher the levels of problem behaviour which children manifest by the time they start school. The benefit is that higher-quality childcare and more experience in centres predict better cognitive and linguistic functioning. Furthermore, these effects emerge when other aspects of childcare are themselves taken into account (i.e., statistically controlled).

In view of the fact that these findings emanate from the study of childcare in the U.S., it is especially noteworthy that another large-scale investigation of the effects of childcare, this one of more than 3,000 children undertaken in England and known as the EPPE Study (Effective Provision of Preschool Education), has produced strikingly similar findings (Melhuish et al. 2001a; Sammons et al. 2002, 2003). In this work, children were recruited not via hospitals during the newborn period, as in the NICHD SECCC, but directly from various family- and community-based child-care arrangements when children were three years of age. Detailed child-care histories were obtained and careful observational assessments of child-care quality were con-

ducted repeatedly over time. Just as in the NICHD SECC (and so many more investigations), higher-quality childcare proved predictive of enhanced cognitive-linguistic
functioning. In addition, moderate- to high-levels of centre-based care in the first two
years of life were associated with increased anti-social behaviour. (The same was true
of very high levels of family day care provided by a non-relative, though high levels
of childcare by a relative [e.g., grandmother] were associated with lower levels of anti-
social behaviour at age three and beyond.) Similar findings also emerged in a parallel
study of over 800 children in Northern Ireland (Melhuish et al. 2001b; Melhuish et
al. 2002a, b). As in the case of the NICHD SECC, these British findings emerged
after stringent statistical control for a wide range of child, family and demographic
factors. All this is not to say that similar results would emerge if similar large-scale
studies were carried out in other Western nations, only that it would be a mistake to
conclude that the NICHD SECC findings summarized herein are narrowly restricted
to the American scene.

Whether one considers the results of the large-scale American or British investigations, it should be clear that focusing upon just a single feature of childcare or
drawing sweeping conclusions about childcare in general, be they highlighting benefits or risks, is unwarranted. It would seem, further, that the NICHD SECC and the
EPPE Study have produced a variety of interesting findings about child-care effects.
What will be most noteworthy to many given pre-existing points of view, is that as
so long asserted – and repeatedly found – the quality of childcare does seem to matter for children's development, especially their cognitive-linguistic development. Also
noteworthy, even if less welcomed, is evidence showing that children who spend
more time in non-maternal care through their infancy, toddler and pre-school years,
at least of the kind routinely available in American communities, experience somewhat less harmonious mother–child relationships through their first three years (and
beyond if Caucasian) and start school being somewhat more aggressive and disobedient than children with less non-maternal care experience; and that these disconcerting effects are simply not attributable to poor-quality childcare and seem more likely
when children experience centre-based care early in life. Particularly provocative, perhaps, is the evidence suggesting that extended exposure to centres fosters cognitive-
linguistic development, in view of its documented and seemingly negative effects on
social behavior.

Beyond these child-care effects, it is easy to overlook – as I have purposefully
done so far – perhaps even more important findings that emerged from the NICHD
SECC. And those are the ones showing that that family factors and processes employed in the data analyses as controls for selection effects were typically more predictive of child functioning than were the features of childcare around which this
summary of study findings has been organized. In other words, it appears that family
matters more to children's developmental well-being than childcare (see also Deater-
Deckard et al. 1996), though this result may be as much (if not more) a function of
shared genes as pure environmental effects.

These under-emphasized findings with respect to family influences should not be read to suggest that child care does not matter to children's psychological and be-havioural development. Even though there remains healthy debate about the size and meaningfulness of virtually all child-care effects, it must be remembered that more and more children seem to be spending more and more time at younger and younger ages in non-maternal care arrangements in the English-speaking, if not Western, world. This means that even small effects, when experienced by many children, may have broad-scale consequences. After all, many of the most important risk behaviours from a public health perspective have low or moderate relative risk but are multiplied in importance because of their wide prevalence and links to problematic outcomes (Jeffrey 1989). This may be especially so for early, extensive and continuous non-ma-ternal care and for low-quality childcare.

Ironically, this state of affairs leads to virtually the very same policy-related con-clusions which were drawn more than a decade ago (Belsky 1990), after first choosing not to draw any in order to keep separate scientific analysis and policy inference (Bel-sky 1986, 1988). First, it seems that the data considered should encourage the expan-sion of parental leave, preferably paid, ideally as lengthy as it is in some Scandinavian countries, or other strategies for reducing the time children spend in non-maternal care across the infant, toddler, and pre-school years (e.g., part-time employment). Relatedly, tax policies should support families rearing infants and young children in ways that afford parents the freedom to make child-rearing arrangements that they deem best for their child, thereby reducing the economic coercion that necessitates many, at least in the U.S. and in the U.K., to leave the care of their children to others when they would rather not. Finally, given the clear benefits of high-quality child-care, its expansion seems called for as well. Of significance is that all of these conclu-sions could be justified on humanitarian grounds alone.

References

Achenbach, T., 1991. *Manual for the Child Behavior Checklist /4–18 and 1991 Profile*. Burl-ington, VT: Author.

Achenbach, T.M., Edelbrock, C., and Howell, C.T., 1987. Empirically based assessment of behavioral/emotional problems of 2- and 3-year-old children. *Journal of Abnormal Child Psychology* 15, 629–50.

Ainsworth, M., and Wittig, B., 1969. Attachment and exploratory behavior of one-year olds in a strange situation. In B.M. Foss, ed., *Determinants of Infant Behaviour Vol. 4*. London: Methuen.

Bacharach, V., and Baumeister, A., 2003. Child care and severe externalizing behaviour in kin-dergarten children. *Applied Developmental Psychology* 23, 527–37.

Bayley, N., 1969. *Bayley Scales of Infant Development*. New York: Psychological Corporation.

——— 1993. *Bayley Scales of Infant Development*, Second Edition. San Antonio, TX: Psycho-logical Corporation.

Belsky, J., 1984. Two waves of day-care research: Developmental effects and conditions of quality. In R. Ainslie, ed., *The Child and the Day-care Setting*. New York: Prager, 1–34.

———— 1986. Infant day care: a cause for concern? *Zero to Three*, 6, 1–7.

———— 1988. The 'effects' of infant day care reconsidered. *Early Childhood Research Quarterly* 3, 235–72.

———— 1990. Developmental risks associated with infant day care: attachment insecurity, noncompliance and aggression? In S. Chehrazi, ed., *Psychosocial Issues in Day Care*. New York: American Psychiatric Press, Inc., 37–68

———— 1994. The effects of infant day care: 1986–1994. Invited plenary address to the British Psychological Association Division of Developmental Psychology, University of Portsmouth, England, 4 September 1994.

———— 2001. Developmental risks still associated with early child care. *Journal of Child Psychology and Psychiatry* 42, 845–59.

Belsky, J., and Braungart, J., 1991. Are insecure-avoidant infants with extensive day-care experience less stressed by and more independent in the Strange Situation? *Child Development* 62, 567–71.

Belsky, J., and Rovine, M., 1988. Nonmaternal care in the first year of life and the security of infant-parent attachment. *Child Development* 59, 157–67.

Belsky, J., and Steinberg, L., 1978. The effects of day care: a critical review. *Child Development* 49, 929–49.

Bracken, B.A., 1984. *Bracken Basic Concept Scales*. San Antonio, TX: Psychological Corporation.

Bronfenbrenner, U., 1974. *Is Early Intervention Effective?* Publication No. OHD76-30025. Washington, DC: Department of Health, Education, and Welfare.

Bureau of Labor Statistics, U.S. Department of Labor, 2000. Washington, D.C.: Author.

Brooks-Gunn, J., McCarton, C., Casey, P., McCormick, M., Bauer, C., Bernbaum, J., Tyson, J., Swanson, M., Bennett, F., and Scott, D., 1994. Early intervention in low birth weight premature infants. Results through 5 years from the Infant Health and Development Program. *Journal of the American Medical Association* 272, 1257–62.

Campbell, F., and Ramey, C., 1995. Cognitive and school outcomes for high risk African-American students at middle adolescence: positive effects of early intervention. *American Educational Research Journal* 32, 743–72.

Clarke-Stewart, K., 1989. Infant day care: maligned or malignant? *American Psychologist* 44, 266–73.

Deater-Deckard, K., Pinkerton, R., and Scarr, S., 1996. Child-care quality and children's behavioral adjustment: a four-year longitudinal study. *Journal of Child Psychology and Psychiatry* 37, 937–48.

Gresham, F., and Elliott, S., 1990. Social Skills Rating System: Parent Form, Elementary Level. Circle Pines, MN: American Guidance Service.

Hofferth, S., 1996. Child care in the United States today. *The Future of Children* 6, 41–61.

Jeffrey, R., 1989. Risk behaviors and health: contrasting individual and population perspectives. *American Psychologist* 44, 1194–202.

Johnson, D., and Walker, T., 1991. A follow-up evaluation of the Houston Parent-Child Development Center: school performance. *Journal of Early Intervention* 15, 226–36.

Kamerman, S., 2000. Parental leave policies: an essential ingredient in early childhood education and care policies. *Social Policy Report* 14, 3–15.

Karen, R., 1994. *Becoming Attached.* New York: Warner Books.

Love, J., Harrison, L., Sagi-Schwartz, A., Van Ijzendoorn, M., Ross, C., Ungerer, J., Raikes, H., Brady-Smith, C., Boller, K., Brooks-Gunn, J., Constantine, J., Kisker, E., Paulsell, D., and Chazan-Cohen, R., 2003. Child care quality matters: how conclusions may vary with context. *Child Development* 74, 969–1226.

McGurk, H., Caplan, M., Hennessy, E., and Moss, P., 1993. Controversy, theory and social context in contemporary day care research. *Journal of Child Psychology and Psychiatry* 34, 3–23.

Melhuish, E.C., Sylva, K., Sammons, P., Siraj-Blatchford, I., and Taggart, B., 2001a. *Social/Behavioural and Cognitive Development at 3–4 years in Relation to Family Background.* The Effective Provision of Pre-school Education Project, Technical Paper 7. London: Institute of Education/DfES.

Melhuish, E., Quinn, L., Sylva, K., Sammons, P., Siraj-Blatchford, I., Taggart, B., McSherry, K. and McCrory, M., 2001b. *Cognitive and Social/behavioural Development at 3–4 years in Relation to Family Background.* Belfast, N.I.: Stranmillis University Press.

Melhuish, E., Quinn, L., Sylva, K., Sammons, P., Siraj-Blatchford, I., Taggart, B. and Currie, G., 2002a. *Pre-school Experience and Social/Behavioural Development at the Start of Primary School.* Belfast, N.I.: Stranmillis University Press.

Melhuish, E., Quinn, L., Sylva, K., Sammons, P., Siraj-Blatchford, I., Taggart, B. and Shields, C., 2002b. *Pre-school Experience and Cognitive Development at the Start of Primary School.* Belfast, N.I.: Stranmillis University Press.

NICHD Early Child Care Research Network 1997a. Child care experiences during the first year of life. *Merrill-Palmer Quarterly* 43, 340–60.

———— 1997b. The effects of infant child care on infant-mother attachment security: Results of the NICHD Study of Early Child Care. *Child Development* 68, 860–79.

———— 1997c. Mother-child interaction and cognitive outcomes associated with early child care: results of the NICHD study. Poster symposium presented at the biennial meeting of the Society for Research in Child Development, Washington, DC, April 3-6th,1997.

———— 1998. Early child care and self-control, compliance and problem behavior at 24 and 36 months. *Child Development* 69, 1145–70.

———— 1999. Child care and mother-child interaction in the first three years of life. *Developmental Psychology* 35, 1399–413.

———— 2000. The relation of child care to cognitive and language development. *Child Development* 71, 958–78.

———— 2001. Child care and family predictors of Macarthur preschool attachment and stability from infancy. *Developmental Psychology* 37, 847–62.

———— 2002a. Child care and children's development prior to school entry. *American Education Research Journal* 39, 133–64.

————— 2002b. Structure→process→outcome: direct and indirect effects of caregiving quality on young children's development. *Psychological Science* 13, 199–206.

————— 2002c. The interaction of child care and family risk in relation to child development at 24 and 36 months. *Applied Developmental Science* 6, 144–56.

————— 2003a. Does quality of child care affect child outcomes at age 4 ? *Developmental Psychology* 39, 451–69.

————— 2003b. Does amount of time spent in child care predict socioemotional adjustment during the transition to kindergarten? *Child Development* 74, 976–1005.

————— 2003c. Early child care and mother-child interaction from 36 months through first grade. *Infant Behavior and Development* 26, 345–70.

————— 2004. Type of care and children's development at 54 months. *Early Childhood Research Quarterly,* 19, 203–230.

Olds, D., 2002. Prenatal and infancy home visiting by nurses. *Prevention Science* 3, 153–72.

Phillips, D., McCartney, K., Scarr, S. and Howes, C., 1987. Selective review of infant day care research: a cause for concern. *Zero to Three* 7, 18–21.

Sammons, P., Sylva, K., Melhuish, E.C., Siraj-Blatchford, I., Taggart, B., and Elliot, K., 2002. *Measuring the Impact on Children's Cognitive Development over the Pre-school Years.* The Effective Provision of Pre-school Education project, Technical Paper 8a. London: Institute of Education/DfES.

Sammons, P., Smees, R., Taggart, B., Sylva, K., Melhuish, E.C., Siraj-Blatchford, I., and Elliot, K., 2003. *Measuring the Impact on Children's Social Behavioural Development over the Pre-school Years.* The Effective Provision of Pre-school Education Project, Technical Paper 8b. London: Institute of Education/DfES.

Scarr, S., 1998. American child care today. *American Psychologist* 53, 95–108.

Scarr, S., Phillips, D., and McCartney, K., 1989. Facts, fantasies, and the future of child care in the United States. *Psychological Science* 1, 26–35.

Schweinhart, L., Barnes, H., and Weikart, D., 1993. *Significant Benefit: The High/Scope Perry Preschool Study through Age 27.* Ypsilanti, MI: High/Scope Press.

Shonkoff, J. and Phillips, D., eds., 2000 *From Neurons to Neighbourhoods: The Science of Early Child Development.* Washington, DC: The National Academies Press.

Thompson, R., 1988. The effects of infant day care through the prism of attachment theory. *Early Childhood Research Quarterly* 3, 273–82.

Woodcock, R.W., and Johnson, M.B., 1990. *Tests of Achievement, WJ-R. Examiner's Manual.* Allen, TX: DLM Teaching Resources.

Zoritch, B., Roberts, I., and Oakley, A., 1998. The health and welfare effects of day care: a systematic review of randomised controlled trials. *Social Science and Medicine* 47, 317–27.

• 16 •

'It feels normal that other people are split up but not *your* Mum and Dad':

Divorce through the Eyes of Children

Margaret Robinson, Lesley Scanlan and Ian Butler

Background

Over the last twenty years what constitutes normal family life has been radically redefined. With the decline in marriage as a life-long commitment and the associated increase in divorce, remarriage, stepfamilies and single parent households, many children now live in 'non-nuclear' families. Despite the number of children affected each year by such family changes it is only recently that researchers have sought to understand matters from the child's point of view (e.g., Buchanan et al. 2001; Butler et al. 2002, 2003; Smart et al. 2001; Trinder et al. 2002) rather than through secondary sources such as parents (see Rodgers and Pryor 1998 for a detailed review of earlier literature).

Study Design

This chapter draws on finding from a study conducted by the authors and colleagues (Douglas et al. 2000) and funded by the ESRC as part of the Children 5–16 Research Programme. The primary aims of our study were to explore children's views, feelings and understanding of divorce, to examine their roles as active participants during the process and to find out from children what the impact of parental separation and divorce had been on their lives. Our study has several distinctive features including:

- The 104 children who took part were recruited from a random, representative sample of families drawn from six courts located throughout South Wales and the South West of England rather than from a narrower, more self-selecting population base.
- The children (51 girls and 53 boys, aged seven to fifteen years) were interviewed relatively soon after their parents' divorce rather than some years after the event. On average interviews were conducted within fifteen months (standard deviation two months) of the divorce being obtained (i.e., *decree nisi* being granted).
- Qualitative and quantitative data were collected from children and the parent they lived with (70 parents in total) allowing direct comparisons between the child and the parent's accounts. (See Butler et al. 2003 for full details of method and design.)

The findings we report here relate to children's views and experiences of parents and parenting following separation and divorce. The children we quote are a typical cross-section of those we interviewed. We have used pseudonyms to protect identities. No two children have been given the same pseudonym.

When Parents Break Up, Family Life Breaks Down

Most of the children we talked to, including Louise (twelve years) and Ellie (ten years), suspected that their parents' relationship was not running smoothly long before matters actually came to a head.

When I was about nine, I knew something was going to go wrong. I knew that my Mum was getting angry and upset about it, so I knew that it was going to end up something like this. But divorce, I didn't think it would quite be divorce. I thought maybe my Dad would have some sense to sort out his problems.

They don't really suit. They don't really have the same things in common. When I was quite young I thought that they were okay together, but then as I got older I could see that they weren't right together. I knew what was gonna happen 'cos they argue too much.

Like Ellie, many of the children had overheard their parents arguing at some time or other and so suspected that all might not be well. In a few cases children, like eight-year-old Jenny, were left in no doubt as to the state of their parents' relationship because of the domestic violence they witnessed.

I could hear him calling her things like 'You stupid idiot', things like that. Then my father came round and told me to go in my bedroom, and he was just calling her names. In the night he pushed her down the stairs. He used to do things like that.

Regardless of the evidence or of correctly interpreting the warning signs, forewarned was seldom forearmed even for children like Jenny. So, when parents eventually did separate it still came as a great shock.

It really hit home when she left. It feels normal that other people are split up but not *your* Mum and Dad. I mean, you think your Mum and Dad are going to be together forever and you can't believe it's happened.
(Susan, aged 14)

I was in bed when he actually left. He just went in the middle of the night, and in the morning my Mum and me and everyone in my family were crying. I thought he was going to come back later, in about a month or two months, or even a week, but nothing happened.
(Sarah, aged 8)

Overnight, literally in cases as Sarah's, the normal pattern of everyday family life was knocked out of kilter, as twelve-year-old Julie observed:

You tend to take it for granted a bit. They're both there, like, 'Hi Mum', 'Hi Dad' when you come in.

On finding that their parents had separated children typically felt a range of often quite contradictory emotions, including confusion, sadness and uncertainty.

I felt pretty horrible, upset obviously. I felt a big mixture of emotions in my head. I didn't know whether I was happy that it was over because I didn't have to keep anything bottled up anymore or whether I was sad because I wanted Mum and Dad to be together – just a whole load of things.
(Sean, aged 14)

Very confused, like I didn't expect it and everyone else had their Mum and Dad together ... I got upset sometimes, wished they were together, it was very difficult to cope.
(Gareth, aged 14)

I was very upset. I tried to hold it, and I couldn't hold it, so I burst out crying.
(Joe, aged 8)

Well, I found out that they were splitting up over the telephone. Dad rang us up to say that he wasn't coming back. That's all we heard for a while.
(Rachel, aged 10)

Starting to Come to Terms

When they began to collect their thoughts, though, most of children (79 per cent) realized that practical changes, such as moving house, changing school, perhaps even losing contact with their friends, were inevitable. Few, however, realized the extent to which more emotional and psychological changes would have to be dealt with before they could once again think of family life as 'normal' or something that could be 'taken for granted'.

> I knew then that we'd probably have to move house, because Dad had left we wouldn't be able to afford to keep the house on on our own, so I knew we'd probably have to move house, which would be quite a big change. I was hoping we'd still be able to stay in the area because all my friends are here and everything. That's all I really thought about really. I didn't really think there'd be anything else.
> (Julie, aged 12)

One of the changes few children and indeed few parents, anticipated or were pre-pared for was that parents became, at least to some degree, practically and emotion-ally 'unavailable' to their children. The pattern and stability of parenting children had previously expected and relied on – whether good, bad or indifferent – changed. This 'unavailability' was compounded for non-resident parents, usually fathers[1], quite simply because they no longer lived with their children as Greg, aged ten, explained:

> I was sad 'cos I wouldn't be able to see Dad so much. I thought he was going to go a long way away and I was used to having him at home and playing with him. And 'cos Mum's a teacher she's always doing work and we just couldn't do anything I wanted to do.

Welcome Reassurances

Despite realizing their parents were less available to them nearly all of the children (99 per cent) said they were confident their parents still cared for them. Indeed, most said their parents had taken active steps to assure them of this (88 per cent reported that their resident parent, and 80 per cent their non-resident parent, had said he/she still loved them). The children welcomed these reassurances, particularly as they were often given around the time of the separation itself – typically a time of high anxiety and uncertainty for the children.

> My Mum said that 'You know we're not going to be married no more … we're not getting on very well so we've decided to divorce which means we're not going to be married anymore'. And then she told me that 'It doesn't mean you're not our children, it just means that we don't get on very well so we're not gonna be married but we're still your Mum and Dad'.
> (Sioned, aged 12)

It just happened . . . my Mum sat down and explained to us that our Dad had gone and ain't going to come back ... but he still loves us and so does my Mum.
(Becky, aged 12)

Support from Parents

Throughout the divorce process children were proactive in seeking support from a wide range of people, in part to fill the gap temporarily created by their parents' unavailability. For some children, however, parents were still the people they turned to.

Q: Who would you go to if you wanted to talk?
A: Mum, if I wanted to talk about a particular thing, would just listen. It's who I normally go to if I've a problem, I just always have more or less.
(Oliver, aged 13)

Q: Who would you go to if you wanted to talk?
A: Mummy ... first my Mum, then my Dad.
(Emy, aged 10)

Unlike Oliver and Emy some children did not have ready access to their parents, particularly their fathers, as fourteen-year-old Will explained:

Q: Was there anyone else who could have helped you cope?
A: Yea, Dad, if I sort of saw him at that time when I needed help, but he sort of wasn't always there. Well, like, if I was with Dad for the weekend and I was upset he'd be there, but then Mum wouldn't, so it was just sort of who was there at the time.

Most children however found that there were times when their parents, regardless of accessibility, were not able to provide the comfort, support and help they felt they needed. This tended to happen because parents themselves were trying to cope with the upset and imbalance in their own lives. When this happened children rarely construed it as their parents no longer caring for them. Again we quote Sioned, describing how she felt:

Just very empty and lonely ... All my Mum's family were comforting her and my Dad's family were comforting him. And I thought that me and my brother Neil had no one to go to ... I know my Mum felt sorry for us as well but it's like, I felt lonely, as though I had no one to go to and talk to ... I felt that Mum had to be comforted, and Dad had to be comforted, and I thought there's no one in between for me and Neil.

Parenting Below Par

Many of the parents we spoke to recognized that they were parenting below their own usual standards. They expressed concern that their children had 'no one to listen to them' and that they were leaving their children 'to look out for themselves'. The most common explanations parents gave for their lapses in parenting were: they were so absorbed in their own problems, including the legal side of the divorce, that they had little time and no emotional or physical energy left to help their children cope; they did not know how to explain matters to their children because they themselves were confused and unsure about what was happening – divorce was new, uncertain and uncharted territory for them just as it was for their children; they did not know how to talk to their children about the sensitive, emotive issues brought about by the divorce. Most of the children realized, at least implicitly, that their parents were parenting below par for the reasons their parents gave. Indeed the children themselves sometimes gave similar reasons for their own reticence in approaching their parents, as ten-year-old Rosie explained:

> A: Sometimes I get embarrassed to talk to my Mum and Dad 'cos it's about *them*, getting divorced, so sometimes I'm not sure. It didn't happen to them ... Sometimes if you're crying in front of them and they say 'I know what it's like' you might say 'No, you don't', because it's not happening to them and if it hasn't happened to them, then sometimes you think 'How do they know what it's like, they're not me'.
> Q: Have you spoken to Dad much about it?
> A: He just says 'Oh well, there's no need to worry', and I think 'Yes there is', it isn't just a few minutes of divorce, this is my whole life, so there *is* need to worry about it.

Like Rosie, some children felt it was either inappropriate to talk to their parents or that there was little point because parents did not understand what it was like for children. Others, like twelve-year-old Louise, were afraid of becoming upset or feared causing upset:

> My Mum, because she was upset, she didn't really talk to me much. She was always upset and I couldn't really say to her 'I'm upset, I need a really good chat with you'.

Another reason a few children gave for not approaching parents was that whilst their parents had 'moved on' they themselves had not yet had time to adjust. Cathy (thirteen years old) was one of the children who made this point:

> Well, it's sort of really weird 'cos, like, my Mum's got a new boyfriend now ... and I still haven't got over it yet ... Mum doesn't seem to want to talk about it any more, she's got a new life now.

Filling the Parenting Gap: Self-parenting by Children

Our findings are consistent with other studies that show that parents have a 'diminished capacity' to parent and feel a lack of confidence in their ability to communicate with their children at times of family crises (James and James 1999; Lyons et al.1998; Timms 1997; Walker 2001; Wallerstein and Kelly 1980). They also reflect Seltzer's (1991) proposition that there are no clear roles or norms for post-divorce parenting. Faced with a lack of status quo and parental availability, and their own reticence about approaching their parents, most of the children nonetheless proved capable of 'looking out for themselves'. Children sought out a range of people to help them cope, to listen to them and to provide comfort and support, as well as distraction. This was not an arbitrary undertaking: children were selective in the people they chose and what they chose them for.

> Q: If you wanted to talk to somebody about it who would you go to?
> A: My Mum or my Nan or my best friend, 'cos they are all really close to me. I mean, I know my best friend's not family, but she feels like family.
> (Louise, aged 12)

Like Louise and Bryon (twelve years old), many children regarded relatives, particularly grandparents, as a valuable source of reassurance, information, support and comfort.

> I think I talked to my Nan a bit … I can talk to my Nan.

Many of the children we talked to had at least one grandparent living nearby and a number reported visiting grandparents more often following their parents' separation (35 per cent saw more of maternal grandparents, 26 per cent more of paternal grandparents post-divorce). Where parents saw grandparents as convenient childminders, children, as eight-year-old Richard explained, were more likely to see grandparents as people who would give them the time and attention that they were currently unable to get from their parents:

> My aunties help me, and my Nan. They help me by taking me over their house, by giving us tea and saying 'Yes' to everything we ask.

Grandparents' homes provided 'neutral', relatively stress-free zones where children felt safe and at home. For some children, spending time with grandparents offered a welcome change from the tense atmosphere of their mother's or father's home.

> [I like to go to] my Nan … because she let me talk my mind and let me say what I'd have to say.
> (Robin, aged 11)

Grandparents themselves provided some children with the opportunity to discuss issues they could not discuss with their parents, or with information that helped them keep up to date with what was happening between their parents. Children were aware that grandparents were often providing emotional support to their mums or dads too. Some children found this helpful because they felt it took some of the pressure for supporting their parents away from them. (For a detailed, tri-generational examination of the role of grandparenting in divorce families see Ferguson et al. 2003.) A few children sought support from non-related adults including neighbours and teachers.

> I really wanted to tell my next door neighbour because if they would know, they would know to give me some advice. I wanted to tell my friends as well so they might give me advice too.
> (Lucy, aged 8)

> We had a step-in teacher and I talked to her quite a lot 'cos she was really nice. She just sort of listened.
> (Elizabeth, aged 13)

But children were somewhat ambivalent about seeking support from teachers. The majority view was that whilst it was helpful that teachers knew what was happening at home, teachers were not most children's preferred confidantes, as Michael (thirteen) and Cathy (thirteen) explained:

> I don't think that teachers should get involved too much, but they should know in case someone's upset about it.

> Well they're not counsellors and they can't do anything. All they're good at is just teaching someone really. They help in a way but not really … it's just nice they know in case something happens at home and I come to school in a state or something. They don't know why, but they know something's going wrong at home.

It might seem that siblings would be ideal people for children to turn to. This, however, proved not to be the case. Although most children (all but seven) in our study had siblings, and despite the majority reporting that they had close sibling relationships (62 per cent), less than a third (32 per cent) said they had talked to their sister or brother about the divorce. Unsurprisingly, not being close was a reason a few of the children gave for not confiding in siblings. Even where siblings thought talking to each other might help, not being close proved an insurmountable barrier for some, including Sophie, and twelve-year-old Josie and her ten-year-old brother Ted:

> Sophie: I talked to him a bit, but we get on really terribly, it's no use really.
> Interviewer: So he's not someone you would go and talk to about it?
> Sophie: Definitely not.

> Ted: It probably would have helped if I could talk to Josie, but we're always fighting, so it wouldn't work.

Other factors that mediated against siblings turning to each other for support included age difference, as Emy, aged ten, explained:

My brother [aged 6] wouldn't understand 'cos he's too young

Alternatively, children felt that their experience of the breakdown was quite different, or, conversely, too much alike.

A: I would say to my brother [Oliver, aged 12], if he had anything, a problem with anything, that he could come to speak to me, but we wouldn't speak about it together. I think it was 'cos he didn't accept it … he was very protective of Mum and he's very close to her and he didn't accept it was going on. He thought 'Oh. Mum's just gone away. She's going to come back', but now he's accepted she's gone.

Q: Have you spoken about it now?

A: No, if we sat down with Dad then maybe, but as siblings we haven't spoken about it.

(Sophie, age 15 – her brother Oliver was quoted above talking about turning to his mother for support.)

Q: Have you ever talked to your brother Gareth [aged 15] about it?

A: No … he's probably got the same feelings so he wouldn't help me.

(Callum, aged 13 – brother Gareth was quoted above talking about the confusion he felt when his parents' separated.)

As a few of the quotations have already suggested, children often preferred to turn to friends to help them cope. In marked contrast to the 32 per cent of children who said they confided in their siblings, 64 per cent said they had talked to friends. Overall, children felt friends were their best resource, not least of all because they were accessible and talked the 'same language'. Robert (twelve) is typical:

Interviewer: Did you talk to anyone about what it?

Robert: Just basically my best friends, basically the easiest people to talk to.

Although most children turned to friends and most (85 per cent) reported that they believed their peers understood how hard it was to have divorced parents, many (69 per cent), nonetheless said it would be upsetting for them if their peers asked too many personal questions. Like twelve-year-old Nicky, most children wanted to control the flow of information, partly as a form of self-protection and partly to safeguard their own and their family's privacy.

I just told my closest friends … I didn't want *everybody* to find out. I just wanted a few people to know.

To begin with, most children wanted to give themselves the time and space to come to terms with what was happening at home and to work out how to deal with the subject of their family's situation in public.

Q: Did you find that you decided not to tell people?
A: No, it was just I wanted to get to terms with it first.
(Josie, aged 13)

It was a bit strange really, 'cos I didn't know what to say really. It's not something you talk about everyday, it's a bit hard to know what to say ... I told my best friend Joe because his parents are divorced and he sort of like knew what I was talking about, he was sort of helping me a bit.
(Ted, aged 10)

When they did decide to talk to friends, children continued to exercise considerable caution, invariably selecting only friends they felt they could trust.

I told my best friend and that was about it really, 'cos I could trust her and I didn't want her to say anything.
Ellie, aged 10

I told Phil, his parents are divorced so he knew what it was going to be like. I told Pete 'cos I know him and he promised not to say anything. I just wanted people not to know 'cos they would all ask me questions.
George, aged 10

Again showing considerable resourcefulness, like George, a number of children told us how they had opted to talk to friends whose parents were also divorced. This had the benefit of providing an understanding listener combined with a source of divorce-related information, as Nicky (twelve) explained:

Q: Do most people know now?
A: Yeah, like my mate knows and John, my other mate, his Mum and Dad are divorced now so he's been through it an all.

Friends who had 'been there' provided a valuable reference point against which children, such as nine-year-old Stewart, could calculate whether or not their own situation, experience and behaviour were 'normal' for children with divorced parents.

Loads of my friends at school have had the same things happening, sort of two or three times ... They had all been through it and they were like exactly the same as I was.

Friends also provided a source of distraction, people to do 'normal things' with and with whom children could be themselves.

I'd maybe call a friend and ask them over to just *do* things to keep my mind off it. Like I'd go into town and shop with them.
(Louise, aged 12)

> I make myself happy, I go out with my friends, have a laugh, go down the park and sometimes I watch a video, a funny video, I watch that to cheer myself up.
> (Johnny, aged 10)

When Nicky (twelve) was asked whom he thought was the most helpful person during the divorce process he said:

> My friends, 'cos I wasn't really happy with talking to any of my family 'cos they were like still upset about it as well. So, if I talked with them I'd make them more upset, so I mostly talked to my friends.

Nicky's answer, like that of so many other children including Sean (fourteen) and Sioned (twelve), shows that although children were concerned about their own feelings, they were equally concerned to protect those around them from any additional hurt:

> Interviewer: Have you talked to your Mum about it?
> Sean: No, not particularly, 'cos I know that I'd get upset and I knew that Mum would get upset as well.

> I felt a bit embarrassed talking to my Mum 'cos she was very upset as well. I felt she needed a break and it's not fair on her if I keep mentioning about the divorce so I went to my friends, so they were the most helpful, I think.

Parenting Mum and Dad

Regardless of age or gender the majority of children we spoke to were keenly aware of and sympathetic to the difficulties faced by other family members. Most children (62 per cent) appreciated that divorce was difficult for their parents and said that they tried to behave well to give their parents less to worry about (84 per cent). In keeping with this caring attitude children said they had kept their own feelings of sadness and worry (61 per cent) and their own problems (76 per cent) from their parents. Typical examples of the emotional care-taking children provided come from Ceri (fifteen) who talked about her mother, her mother's new partner and the baby they were expecting together, and from Louise (twelve) who talked about her father's emotional insecurities and her mother's inability to cope:

> I don't have a choice really. It's going to be the way it is. I can only let her make her own mistakes and therefore support her. I mean, she's got another baby on the way in a couple of months, that's his [new partner]. I don't see how she's going to cope with that ... she's going to need me. She's the best Mum ever, even though she makes loads of mistakes. She does her best though.

Many other children exhibited the skill Louise showed in being able to see both her mother's side and her father's side of the story and yet take neither.

> Dad'll frequently say 'Do you love me?' 'You still love me, don't you?'. He asks me that every week ... And I'm like, 'If I didn't love you, I don't think I'd be coming here' ... I live with my Mum [and I think] he thinks that she's going to take us away from him. My Mum applies for jobs all round the world, in really foreign countries ... but I doubt my Mum will move overseas ... I gave my Mum lots of support [too] 'cos she was always upset. I'd sit with her and say 'Mum, you were happy once, you've got to make yourself happy' and I'd say 'He used to upset you, now he's gone from your life'.

Providing emotional support to parents was not the sole province of girls, boys proved adept too, though their methods were generally more practical. For example when twelve-year-old Kevin was asked if he helped his mother through the divorce he replied:

> A: A bit. She got really stressed out a couple of times ... we had to calm her down.
> Q: How did you do that then?
> A: By telling her to sit down and we'd go and get a drink or something to eat. Just sit her down to watch TV.

We have more evidence of children providing support to mothers than fathers. A number of children felt their fathers received less of their support simply because they spent less time with them than they did with their mothers. Others children however felt that their fathers preferred to deal with their problems in private. If this is the case then it may have denied boys, like fourteen-year-old Daniel, the opportunity to provide their fathers with the same emotional support they were otherwise providing their mothers.

> My father's not as much an open person. He like relieves it when you're not there and that. I *can't* really help my father as much [as my mother] as he's independent, stubborn so I can't really help my Dad.

In addition to emotional support, children provided practical support to their parents. For example, 62 per cent of children said that they helped more around the house after their parents separated. Household chores were not always carried out voluntarily, but most children accepted that with only one adult in the house parents needed extra help, as twelve-year-old Jonathan explained.

> I sometimes make my bed, tidy my room. Sometimes I take the washing in, help cook dinner, like making pasta salad which I've done at school for food technology, and I do some DIY things as well.

Some of the older boys described how helping with chores led to a change in their status within the family.

> A: Well I help my Mum in the garden, I do odd jobs and stuff. Mum says I'm a handyman. The cabinet is broken so I have to go out and fix it. I've got my new tool bag with all the stuff in.
>
> Q: Have you learned new things?
>
> A: Yeah, I used to watch people when they come over to fix the washing machine or something. I watch them, and if it breaks again I know what to do. Like, the heater up in the bedroom broke once and a man fixed it. It broke again and I fixed it and it worked again.

(Jonathan, aged 12)

> A: Now that my father has gone I'll have to do more manual jobs, like cutting the lawn, making sure the garden's kept tidy.
>
> Q: Do you feel like your role in the house has changed?
>
> A: Yeah, I've like stepped up a thing, I'm like the man of the house now, so I got to make sure everything's okay and that.
>
> Q: Is that a good thing or a bad thing?
>
> A: It's good and bad. Like, I've got to do all the jobs which is bad. But I don't mind and that's good, 'cos I've got the most control out of it.

(Daniel, aged 14)

A few children showed concern by offering financial support to parents using money they earned for themselves: eleven-year-old Martin was one of these children.

> In about two days we'll probably do [wash] ten cars, so we'll get about £30 in two days, so that'll be quite good … I usually want to give away some money if my Mum hasn't got that much. She never asks for it. I give it to her on my own decision. And, if she does take some money, she pays me back.

For some children, providing support was a purely selfless act, for others (including 'man of the house' Daniel) it was partly self-serving or even therapeutic (as it was for Oliver):

> A: I try and keep my Mum in a good mood. I get the homework done so she don't have to keep on about it, make her a cup of tea when she wants one and generally try to keep her happy – I do more now. I think if I go out up my friends, or my sister goes out down her friends and my mother's in the house on her own … like I think I have to be there more now to support her, like I help out in the garden, cut the grass and that.
>
> Q: Do you mind doing that?
>
> A: *No* I don't mind at all. If it helps my Mum then it's going to help me in the long run.

Q: And you think it does?

A: Yeah. I don't really want to stress my mother, like, 'cos she'll get worse and worse and then we'll have to do more and more!

It helped me feel better because it was doing something nice. You know, helping to get past it, so, that's another step forward isn't it? It can't be that far from the end now.

As a result of the break-up, for the first time many children saw their parents as vulnerable, fragile human beings – as people in need of help, support, comfort and guidance, indeed as child-like. Most of the children we spoke to accepted their new caring, parenting role as a normal thing for them to do given their family's 'abnormal' situation.

Maybe we've just grown up a bit. I know that my parents are both human, which means that I've had a lot of problems with them and I've seen a lot of things. Now they both cry in front of me and I've watched them both go through awful stuff and I come out of it knowing that my parents are two human beings who are capable of making mistakes and therefore I'm not inferior or/and wrong when I make mistakes.
(Ceri, aged 15)

Like Ceri, as well as Jonathan and Daniel earlier, a number of the children linked their experience of family breakdown to 'growing up'. Nicky (twelve) and Tim (ten) provide further evidence of this:

I think I've matured a lot through it. I've had to make decisions for myself and stuff, just made me more mature and more understanding of things.

I'm a bit better with my Mum now. Now I'm a lot bigger, I understand her more.

Post-divorce Child–Parent Relationships

Despite their experiences few children felt that relationships with their parents suffered because of the break up. On the contrary, 59 per cent said their relationship with their resident parent (usually their mother) had improved following the separation whilst 39 per cent noticed an improvement in the relationship they had with their non-resident parent. Fifteen-year-old Helen and ten-year-old Ralph gave typical explanations for these improvements:

I see my parents as completely different people now … I don't know how they see themselves or each other. Because I've spent time with them separately I've got to know how *they* are, sort of by themselves … Now I know them individually.

Q: How do you get on with your Dad since they split up?
A: A lot better, I suppose 'cos I didn't really know him before they got divorced.

Concluding Comments

From our study it is clear that children *are* involved in the process of their parents' divorce in that they experience the events probably in much the same terms as adults (e.g., Butler et al. 2002, 2003; Douglas et al. 2000, 2001, 2003; Robinson et al. 2002; Scanlan et al. 2000). After the initial shock and emotional upset following their parents' separation, children entered a period of adjustment as they worked to regain a sense of balance and an everyday pattern to their lives. Some children turned to their parents to help in this process, but parents were not always emotionally or physically 'available' or able to provide the support children felt they wanted or needed. Also, children did not always feel able to approach their parents for support. Given these circumstances, children selectively mobilized a wide range of strategies and people to help them cope. For most children, friends were an invaluable resource. Within the adult community, children found grandparents a considerable support, particularly if they lived nearby. By comparison, few children turned to siblings, even if they had a close relationship. Children were proactive not only in terms of their own adjustment, but also that of their parents. They showed great maturity and skill in helping parents cope, even in circumstances where parents did not seem able to contain their more negative emotions and impulses. Having witnessed their parents' vulnerability many children actively engage in 'parenting' and caring for their parents. All of this demonstrates that children do not experience their parents' divorce passively. Their involvement in the process is an active, creative and resourceful one. The contribution they make to their family's adjustment is considerable.

The children we interviewed (a typical cross-section of whom we quote here) demonstrated a resilience, coping capacity and level of maturity which might surprise some people. Some might also be surprised that they proved to be articulate individuals who were able to think reflectively and constructively about their own situations. In the light of these points, it is worth restating that the children who took part were recruited from a random, representative sample of divorced families, so are likely to have much in common with the many children whose lives are disrupted each year when their parents divorce or separate.

Overall our study provides strong evidence for recognizing children as competent, relevant witnesses to the process of family dissolution. We do not wish to privilege children's accounts nor do we say that children or parents' interests should predominate. We do however argue that children's accounts should be accorded equal weight to those of parents. We wish simply to assert that children have things to tell us which are worth listening to. On this occasion we leave the final words to Emy and to Will.

It's very hard at first because you just don't want them to split up. You'll be very sad at the beginning because of not having your Dad around, but then it'll just come automatically that your Dad lives somewhere else and life will just be normal.

It's sort of just as though it's normal now. It's like the changes that happened are normal now, so if they change back they would, you know, be abnormal … I'm pleased with the way it is at the moment, everything's fine.

Note

1. Only five fathers lived with their children and were the main carer following the divorce.

References

Buchanan, A., Hunt, J., Bretherton, H., and Bream, V., 2001. *Families in Conflict. The Family Court Welfare Service: The Perspectives of Children and Parents.* Bristol: The Policy Press.

Butler, I., Scanlan, L., Robinson, M., Douglas, G., and Murch M., 2003. *Divorcing Children.* London: Kingsley.

———— 2002. Children's involvement in their parents' divorce: implications for practice. *Children and Society* 16, 89–102.

Douglas, G., Butler, I., Murch, M., and Fincham F., 2000. Children's Perspective and Experience of the Divorce Process. ESRC End of Award Reports, Report No. L129 25 1014.

Douglas, G., Butler, I., Murch, M., Robinson, M., and Scanlan, L., 2003. Private ordering and the interests of the child. *Wales Law Journal* 3 (4), 232–43.

Douglas, G., Murch, M., Robinson, M., Scanlan, L., and Butler, I., 2001. Children's perspective and experience of the divorce process. *Family Law* 31, 373–77.

Ferguson, N., Douglas, G., Lowe, N., Murch, M., and Robinson, M., 2003. *Grandparenting in Divorced Families.* Bristol: The Policy Press.

James, A.L., and James, A., 1999. Pump up the volume: listening to children in separation and divorce. *Childhood* 6 (2), 189–206.

Lyon, C.M., Surrey, E., and Timms, J.E., 1998. *Effective Support Services for Children and Young People When Parental Relationships Breakdown: A Child-centred Approach.* Liverpool: Liverpool University Press.

Robinson, M., Scanlan, L., Butler, I., Douglas, G., and Murch, M., 2002. Listening to children talk: a methodological perspective. In A. Jensen and L. McKee, eds., *Children in Changing Families: Transformation and Negotiation.* London: Falmer Press.

Rodgers, B., and Pryor, J., 1998. *Divorce and Separation: The Outcomes for Children.* York: Joseph Rowntree Foundation.

Scanlan, L., Perry, A., and Robinson, M., 2000. Listening to children in divorce: the gap between principle and practice. *Representing Children* 131, 34–47.

Seltzer, J.A., 1991. Relationships between fathers and children who live apart: the father's role after separation. *Journal of Marriage and the Family* 53, 79–101.

Smart, C., Neale, B., and Wade, A., 2001. *The Changing Experience of Childhood: Families and Divorce.* Cambridge: Polity Press.

Timms, J., 1997. The tension between welfare and justice. *Family Law 29*, 38–47.

Trinder, L., Beek, M., And Connolly, J. 2002. *Making Contact: How Parents and Children Negotiate and Experience Contact after Divorce.* York: York Publishing Services.

Walker, J., 2001. Information Meetings and Associated Provisions within the Family Law Act 1996 – Key Findings from the Research. London: Lord Chancellor's Department.

Wallerstein, J.S., and Kelly, J.B., 1980. *Surviving the Breakup.* New York: Basic Books.

Glossary

● ● ●

Adaptive
A physical or behavioural trait belonging to an organism is considered to be adaptive in a particular environment if it enhances the expected reproductive success of that organism in its current environment and has evolved by a process of natural selection.

Allocare/alloparenting
The provision of care or parenting behaviour to an infant by any individual other than the infant's biological parents.

Allonursing
Breast-feeding by a female other than the mother.

Altriciality
Condition of underdevelopment at birth relative to condition at maturity, resulting in dependency on parents for survival.

Attachment
An emotional bond between two people. In the psychological literature this usually refers to the strong bond a child forms with his or her primary care giver.

Ecology
The environment as it relates to the organisms living in it

Endocrinology
The branch of research and medicine relating to the glands and hormones of the body, their processes and functions

Environment of Evolutionary Adaptedness
The social and ecological environment in which a species or a behavioural or physiological trait evolved. For humans the term Environment of Evolutionary Adaptedness is often used to refer to the Pleistocene.

Functionalism

A school of thought popular in the nineteenth century emphasizing conscious experiences as a precursor to behaviour. Functionalism addresses the question of how the mind affects behaviour and focuses on observable events as opposed to unobservable events

Grandmother hypothesis

The hypothesis that attempts to explain menopause in terms of investment in kin, particularly grandchildren. Reproduction is terminated significantly earlier that natural lifespan as a result of trade-offs in various life-history variables (see life-history theory and life-history variables, below).

Hamilton, Hamilton's rule

A formula relating to kin selection theory (see kin selection, below). Hamilton's rule states that individuals should behave in a way that maximizes the reproductive success of their kin, provided that the benefits to kin exceed the costs to the individual, multiplied by the degree of relatedness between the individual and the recipient(s).

Inclusive fitness

A measure of fitness which combines *direct* fitness – the individual's reproductive output – with *indirect* fitness – the contribution made by the individual to the reproductive output of its genetic relatives. An individual's inclusive fitness is equal to the individual's direct fitness plus the fitness of all the individual's relatives, weighted by their degree of relatedness.

Kin selection

The theory which states that natural selection may favour altruistic behaviour towards relatives. Whether or not such behaviour is selected for depends on whether Hamilton's rule is satisfied (see Hamilton, above).

Life-history theory

An analytical perspective which attempts to explain physiological and behavioural characteristics in terms of trade-offs in time, effort and energetic resource allocation. Individuals garner a finite amount of energy from their environment which must then be allocated to competing functions such as growth, maintenance and reproduction. Trade-offs between such functions determines factors such as number of offspring produced and investment in each one, as well as the timing of other life-history variables (see below).

Life-history variables

Developmental variables such at age at weaning, age at first reproduction, length of inter-birth intervals, lifespan etc.

Matrilineal

System in which heritable wealth is passed down the maternal line of ancestral descent.

Matrilocal
System in which males reside with their wives' family and/or place of birth after marriage.

Menarche
The first occurrence of menstruation in an individual

Nepotism (see inclusive fitness)
Behaviour that favours family/genetic relatives.

Parental investment
Any parental behaviour which increases the chances that an offspring will survive and reproduce, and which imposes costs upon the parent and hence upon their ability to invest in other offspring.

Paternity certainty
The extent to which a male can be confident that he, and not another male, sired an offspring.

Patrilineal
System in which heritable wealth is passed down the paternal line of ancestral descent.

Patrilocal
System in which females reside with their husband's family and/or place of birth after marriage.

Philopatry
Residing in adulthood with one's family or in one's place of birth.

Polygyny
A mating system in which one male mates with or marries multiple females.

Reciprocity, reciprocal altruism
The exchange of behaviours which impose costs upon the actors and benefits upon the recipients.

Socialization
The process beginning at infancy whereby an individual learns the norms, values, accumulated knowledge and social skills appropriate to his or her culture or society.

Contributors

● ● ●

Nicola Ansell is Reader in Human Geography in the Centre for Human Geography at Brunel University. Her research focuses on social and cultural change in southern Africa, and in particular the impacts of change on young people. She has numerous publications in this area, including a book, *Children, Youth and Development* (Routledge, 2005). Her current research is investigating the impacts of AIDS on young people's livelihoods and food security in Malawi and Lesotho. She also runs an MA programme in Children, Youth and International Development.

Jay Belsky is Director of the Institute for the Study of Children, Families and Social Issues and Professor of Psychology at Birkbeck, University of London. He is an internationally recognized expert in the field of child development and family studies. His areas of special expertise include the effects of day care, parent–child relations during the infancy and early childhood years, the transition to parenthood, the etiology of child maltreatment and the evolutionary basis of parent and child functioning. Professor Belsky's research is marked by a focus upon fathers as well as mothers, marriages as well as parent–child relations, and naturalistic home observations of family interaction patterns. In 1983 he won the Boyd McCandless Award for Distinguished Early Contribution from the Developmental Psychology Division of the American Psychological Association. In 2002 the Institute of Scientific Information, Philadelphia, PA, granted Professor Belsky the Highly-Cited-Researcher designation. In 2007 he was awarded the American Psychological Association Urie Bronfenbrenner Award for Lifetime Contribution to Developmental Psychology in the Service of Science and Society.

Joachim Bensel is co-owner of a private interdisciplinary research company that undertakes applied research relevant to controversial topics of child behavioural development. The knowledge gained is made available to professionals and parents in the form of evaluation reports, training courses, media information and publications. He has a PhD in Biology and has worked for over twenty years in the field of Human

Ethology. He gives lectures for students of Developmental Psychology at the University of Freiburg, Germany. His main research interests are in evolutionary infant care and behaviour of preschoolers (e.g., day care and separation stress).

Gillian R. Bentley is Professor of Anthropology at Durham University. Her work mostly focuses on reproductive ecology examining interactions between the environment and reproductive function in a variety of populations. Although most of her work has been with adults, she is currently setting up projects to compare the growth and pubertal development of migrant Bangladeshi children in the U.K., as well as a project to examine the interactions of overweight and obesity on pubertal development in school-aged children in the northeast of England. She has edited one previous book in the Biosocial Society Symposium Series (*Infertility in the Modern World*) and has published a variety of articles on reproductive ecology in anthropological and medical journals.

Ian Butler is a qualified social worker with extensive practice and managerial experience. He has published widely in the area of child care and social policy. In addition to holding a Professorship in the Department of Social and Policy Sciences at the University of Bath, he recently had a part-time secondment to the Welsh Assembly Government as Cabinet Advisor on Children and Young People's policy.

Mark V. Flinn is Professor of Anthropology at the University of Missouri and works in the area of human evolutionary biology. For the past twenty years he has studied relations among family environment, psychological development, and child health in a rural community on the island of Dominica. This project currently is examining changes in hormones – cortisol, testosterone, prolactin, DHEA/S, oxytocin, and vasopressin – that are associated with affiliative relationships and interactions among parents and offspring, grandparents and grandoffspring, siblings, mates, and coalition partners. The objective is to better understand the evolutionary functions and ontogeny of the physiological and psychological mechanisms that underpin the unusual importance in humans of extended kin networks, paternal care, grandparental care, mate bonding, and male bonding and coalitions including respect for each other's mating relationships.

Alma Gottlieb is Professor of Anthropology at the University of Illinois at Urbana-Champaign. Her research has focused on childhood and the family, gender issues, religion, fieldwork methods and ethics, and ethnographic writing. A past Guggenheim Fellow, she is the author of dozens of articles and six books, including two books on the anthropology of childhood (*A World of Babies,* ed. Judy DeLoache and Alma Gottlieb, 2000; and *The Afterlife Is Where We Come From,* 2004). Her new research focuses on Cape Verdeans (both on and off the islands) who have some Jewish ancestry.

Loren D. Hayes is an Assistant Professor in the Department of Biology at the University of Louisiana at Monroe. His research program integrates evolutionary and mechanistic questions aimed at increasing our understanding of mammalian sociality. His dissertation research with Nancy Solomon at Miami University (Ohio) focused on the reproductive benefits of alloparental care and mechanisms of parental and alloparental care of offspring by female prairie voles (Microtus ochrogaster). His research program now focuses on the causes and reproductive consequences of group-living in Octodon degus, a rodent endemic to Chile. He has published numerous scientific papers, including a review article on rodent communal rearing and allonursing, in top behavioural and taxonomic journals. His research program is funded by both state and federal (National Science Foundation) sources.

David Howe is Professor of Child and Family Social Work at the University of East Anglia, Norwich. He has research interests in emotional development, adoption, developmental attachment theory, and child abuse and neglect. He is the author of a number of books including *Patterns of Adoption: Nature, Nurture and Psychosocial Development* (Blackwell Science, 1998); *Adoption, Search and Reunion: The Long Term Experience of Adopted Adults* (with Julia Feast: BAAF, 2004); *The Adoption Reunion Handbook* (with Liz Trinder and Julia Feast: Wiley, 2004); *Contact in Adoption and Permanent Foster Care* (with Beth Neil: BAAF, 2004); *Child Abuse and Neglect: Attachment, Development and Intervention* (Palgrave/Macmillan, 2005); and *The Emotionally Intelligent Social Worker* (Palgrave/Macmillan, 2008).

Sarah B. Hrdy is Professor Emerita in the Anthropology Department of the University of California-Davis. In a 1999 book, *Mother Nature: A History of Mothers, Infants and Natural Selection,* she argued that early hominid mothers could not have successfully reared young without help from alloparents as well as fathers. In a forthcoming book, *Mothers and Others: The Emergence of Emotionally Modern Humans,* she explores the cognitive and emotional implications of this long legacy of cooperative breeding. A former Guggenheim Fellow, she has been elected to the American Academy of Arts and Sciences, the National Academy of Sciences, and the California Academy of Science. Her books include *The Langurs of Abu: Female and Male Strategies of Reproduction* and *The Woman that Never Evolved.* She is also co-editor of *Infanticide: Comparative and Evolutionary Perspectives* and of *Attachment and Bonding: A New Synthesis.*

Karen L. Kramer is an Associate Professor of Biological Anthropology at Harvard University. Her research focuses on the comparative study of life history, demography, household labour, reproductive and subsistence ecology among agriculturalists and hunter/gatherers. Her ongoing field work in a traditional Maya village in the Yucatan, Mexico has been the foundation to evaluate relationships between children's work, juvenile dependence, female energetics, and high fertility in pre-industrial populations. Her current research among the Pumé, a group of South American mobile foragers combines reproductive history and anthropometric data to address questions about variability in growth trajectories and reproductive strategies, and the effects of seasonal resource availability on child mortality. Current projects also involve collaborating with conservation biologists and primatologists to evaluate the interaction between population growth, farming practices and deforestation among horticulturalists in Madagascar.

David Leone is an Adjunct Research Scientist in the Department of Anthropology at the University of Missouri-Columbia and Lecturer in the Department of Anthropology at the University of North Carolina at Greensboro. He is conducting a long-term study of child growth and development in a rural community in Dominica. His current research focuses on psychosocial stress endocrinology during uterine and post-uterine development and associated patterns of growth in height, weight, body mass indices, and symmetry trajectories. Additional research interests include evolutionary mechanisms of chronic and infectious diseases and longitudinal changes in morbidity associated with the timing of exposure to environmental and dietary factors during development.

Emma Lycett is a Child Research Psychologist interested in the study of children conceived through assisted reproductive technologies, and in particular, examining the impact of disclosing the nature of conception to children on general well-being. She has a number of publications on topics including surrogacy, egg donation and donor insemination. Research interests also extend to the study of children's emotional and behavioural adjustment in relation to their experiences of interparental conflict, as described by the children themselves. Emma is employed as the U.K. Research & Development Manager at Pearson, one of the U.K.'s leading psychometric test publishers, directing U.K. standardization projects.

Ruth Mace is Professor of Evolutionary Anthropology at University College London. Trained originally in Zoology at Oxford, she then moved over into anthropological sciences and now works on a range of questions in human evolutionary ecology and cultural evolution, mainly but not exclusively in African populations. Her work has included the evolution of biased parental investment and kinship systems; evolutionary demography and the demographic transition to low fertility; kin effects and the evolution of the human life history; cultural phylogenetics and the cultural evolution of altruism and social heirarchy; and the cultural transmission of contraceptive uptake. Her research group at UCL, HEEG (the Human Evolutionary Ecology Group) combines human evolutionary ecology and cultural evolutionary approaches in a wide range of projects. In 2008 she was elected a Fellow of the British Academy.

Berry Mayall is Professor of Childhood Studies at the Institute of Education, University of London. She has worked for over thirty years on studies about children and their parents, their daily lives, the services they use and would like to use. In recent years she has helped to develop the sociology of childhood in the U.K., has carried out several studies with, and for, children and has many publications arising (most recent books: *Towards a Sociology for Childhood,* Open University Press, 2002, and *Childhood in Generational Perspective,* edited by B. Mayall and H. Zeiher, Institute of Education, University of London, 2003). With colleagues, she runs an MA in the Sociology of Childhood and Children's Rights, which attracts students from many countries.

Gillian Paull is a Research Associate of the Institute for Fiscal Studies. Her research interests centre on the analysis of gender inequality in the labour market, focusing on the role of motherhood and the use of non-parental childcare in explaining family labour supply patterns in the United Kingdom. Her work has specifically considered the role of government policy in the formal childcare market and policy measures to enhance employment opportunities for mothers. More recent publications have analysed the dynamic aspect of family work behaviour, focusing on how family employment choices evolve over family formation and partnership changes, while ongoing research is considering how work entry, retention and progression impacts on child poverty.

Helen Penn is Professor of Early Childhood at the University of East London, U.K., and co-director of the International Centre for the Study of the Mixed Economy of Childcare (ICMEC) at the University. She has undertaken work on policy and practice issues in early childhood in the U.K., including convening systematic reviews at the DCFS-funded Evidence for Policy and Practice Information and Co-ordinating Centre (EPPI-Centre) based at the Institute of Education, London University. Over the last ten years she has been consultant to major donor-funded education projects in Central Asia and in Southern Africa, where she has advised about early childhood projects. Her recent books include *Unequal Childhoods: Young Children's Lives in Poor Countries* (Routledge, 2005) and *Understanding Early Childhood: Issues and Controversies* (Open University Press, 2008).

Margaret Robinson is a chartered psychologist and chartered health psychologist with interests in inter-disciplinary approaches to research and methodological issues. Much of her academic research focuses on psychosocial or socio-legal issues (e.g., family decision making, divorce, legal advice giving) and was conducted whilst she was a Senior Research Associate at Cardiff University. Reflecting her involvement in inter-disciplinary research, she has published, for example, in journals including *Archives of Disease in Childhood, Children and Society, Health Education Journal* and *Family Law;* has contributed to volumes on adolescence and on family change; has co-authored a number of government reports and books on children's decision making, children's experience of divorce, and grandparenting in divorced families. Dr Robinson is now an independent research consultant.

Lesley Scanlan is a psychologist whose research interests include the impact of family breakdown on children, parents and family life. While a research associate in Cardiff Law School at Cardiff University, she was involved in studies exploring such issues from a legal perspective. Dr. Scanlan is now an independent social researcher.

Rebecca Sear is Senior Lecturer in Population Studies at the London School of Economics. Her research focuses on evolutionary demography, with a regional focus in sub-Saharan Africa. She has published on the subject in a variety of anthropology, biology and demography journals.

Nancy G. Solomon is Professor of Zoology and Director of the Animal Behavior Center at Miami University. Her research focuses primarily on social behaviour in small mammals, specifically testing hypotheses proposed to explain sociality and mating systems. She and her students have studied various aspects of cooperative breeding including delayed dispersal, reproductive suppression and alloparental behavior. More recently, she has also begun to study social and genetic aspects of mating systems in monogamous mammals. She has published numerous articles in journals focused on animal behavior and behavioral ecology and has co-edited one book on *Cooperative Breeding in Mammals*.

Claudia R. Valeggia is an Assistant Professor in the Department of Anthropology at the University of Pennsylvania, U.S. She is the director of the Chaco Area Reproductive Ecology Program and the Reproductive Ecology Laboratory. She focuses on indigenous groups in Latin America and is interested in understanding the interaction among different biocultural variables and its impact on fecundity and infant and children's growth and development.

Lorraine van Blerk is a Lecturer in the Department of Geography at the University of Reading. She has researched extensively with children and youth in East and Southern Africa ,exploring aspects of their daily lives, their interactions with family and community and their migration and mobilities. In addition her work has a strong policy focus seeking to understanding the impacts of large scale processes such as AIDS and homelessness on young people's current and future realitites. Presently Lorraine is working on two ESRC-funded research proejcts: one with street children in South Africa and the other exploring the impact of AIDS on young people's livelihood options in Malawi and Lesotho. In the last eight years she has published over thirty articles in internation peer-reviewed journals and is currently working on two books to be published later this year. From November 2009 Lorraine will take up the post of Senior Lecturer in the Department of Geography at the University of Dundee.

Index

● ● ●